CANDOR *and*
PERVERSION

Literature, Education, and the Arts

Roger Shattuck

W. W. NORTON & COMPANY

New York *London*

Copyright © 1999 by Roger Shattuck

All rights reserved
Printed in the United States of America
First published as a Norton paperback 2000

The text of this book is composed in Garamond with the display set in Centaur MT
Composition by Allentown Digital Services Center
Manufacturing by the Haddon Craftsmen, Inc.
Book design by Judith Stagnitto Abbate / Abbate Design

Library of Congress Cataloging-in-Publication Data

Shattuck, Roger.
    Candor and perversion : literature, education, and the arts /
Roger Shattuck.
        p.   cm.
    Includes bibliographical references and index.
    ISBN 0-393-04807-1
        1. Literature—History and criticism—Theory, etc.   2. American
literature—History and criticism.   3. French literature—History
and criticism.   4. Education. Higher—United States.   5. Arts—Study
and teaching.   I. Title.
    PN52.S53   1999
    809—dc21   99-27634
                                                        CIP

ISBN 0-393-32111-8 pbk.

W. W. Norton & Company, Inc., 500 Fifth Avenue, New York, N.Y. 10110

www.wwnorton.com

W. W. Norton & Company Ltd., 10 Coptic Street, London WC1A 1PU

1 2 3 4 5 6 7 8 9 0

⊡⊡⊡⊡⊡⊡⊡⊡⊡⊡⊡

To the memory of
my father and mother

HOWARD F. SHATTUCK
(1887, Clinton, Wisconsin – 1972, New York, New York)

ELIZABETH COLT SHATTUCK
(1891, Geneseo, New York – 1985, Philadelphia, Pennsylvania)

CONTENTS

FOREWORD

The calling of criticism, which includes literary journalism, requires frequent cleaning of its tools and periodic reassessment of its ground rules. These activities belong to the project for which C. Wright Mills coined the term *intellectual craftsmanship.* I use that term as the title of part 1 of this book. It includes essays, some with a polemical edge, that engage in contemporary cultural debates, and others that reach far beyond those debates.

Part 2, "A Critic's Job of Work," collects literary journalism of the past two decades that deals with works and figures of lasting appeal and significance.

I should like to think that this collection bobs brashly and loyally in the wake of the great literary journalists I admire, among them Hazlitt, Baudelaire, and Edmund Wilson.

My warm thanks go to Jennifer Lyons, Michael Prince, and Robert Weil, who helped me to choose and arrange the essays in this volume.

ROGER SHATTUCK
Lincoln, Vermont
December 1998

CANDOR *and* PERVERSION

I.

Intellectual Craftsmanship

NINETEEN THESES

ON LITERATURE

I READ *"NINETEEN THESES"* at a 1994 dinner in Boston after an all-day meeting to found the Association of Literary Scholars and Critics. The theses represent no official document, nor even any consensus established by that group. Rather, they declare my view, widely shared, I believe, of a state of affairs that calls for the existence of such an association and of such a document.

Here, in brief, is the background for posting a set of theses.

At the close of the twentieth century, we should reasonably expect a liberal education in our high schools, colleges, and universities to serve two principal goals. The first goal is to present the historic basis of our complex culture and the political and moral standards that have evolved from it. The second is to offer students the intellectual basis for an evaluation of that culture, its ideals, and its realities. The first explains and even justifies the status quo. The second questions it. In a democracy, both are necessary.

Those two opposed functions can take place together, almost simultaneously, thanks in great part to a collection of written works that both provide a basis for our Western tradition and challenge it. For instance, we find variations on the dialogue form in Plato, in Montaigne's essays, in Swift's imaginary voyages, and in Dostoevsky's fictional conversations. These supple works do not pronounce; rather, they probe and reflect. The shared reading of such foundational books gives us a basis for finding the principles and the precedents by which we can live *together as one country and one culture containing many parts and divisions, many classes and races.*

Along with political and historical writings, literature and philosophy provide two of the most important categories of such "classic" works. They form a loose core curriculum, which has changed slowly over the years. Plutarch's The Parallel Lives *and Bunyan's* Pilgrim's Progress *have faded into the background. Mary Shelley and Frederick Douglass have moved forward into a place they deserve. We also recognize non-Western works. In order to have a common frame of reference within which to reason together, I would argue that there are books everyone should read. And we should never stop discussing which ones those are.*

In recent years, however, other considerations have begun to usurp the place of literary status and quality. It is a simplification, but not a distortion, to refer to two categories of interests that tend to displace literature: politics *(including race, class, feminism, minority and cultural studies, gay and lesbian studies) and* theory *(reliance on a prior methodology or approach by which to read all works). These interests, perfectly legitimate as adjuncts to literature, have become increasingly dominant, specialized, and doctrinaire. Their cumulative effect is to eliminate the very category of literature. Current fashions favoring "interdisciplinary studies" also tend to weaken the basic disciplines of history and literature.*

"Nineteen Theses" was written as a response to the attempt to dismiss literature as a central field of study and personal reward. The note of whimsy introduced in the "Interlude" should reinforce the conviction with which I offer these theses.

THE NINETEEN THESES

Literature in General

I. A real world of material things, sometimes called *nature,* exists around us. Nature includes us, and we share it imperfectly with one another through perception, action, memory, language, love, and wonder.

II. Material nature has gradually helped shape human behavior and consciousness into patterns we recognize as cultures and as common sense. Across millions of years under a great variety of social behaviors, we have evolved a fairly stable sociogenetic compound we refer to as *human nature.* Human nature contains an elusive element of *freedom:* freedom *from* blind chance and determinism, freedom *to* choose our actions.

III. There may be more than material nature and human nature. Words like *spiritual* and *transcendent* and *ineffable* may refer to more than mere yearnings. Much around us remains unknown.

IV. Works of *literature*, through their amalgam of representation and imagination, of clarity and mystery, of the particular and the general, offer revealing evidence about material nature and human nature and whatever may lie beyond. This is why we read and study and discuss literary works.

V. Literature ranges from simple songs and sayings to elaborate and extended tales of human deeds. The most compelling literature concerns *persons* whose feelings, thoughts, and actions engage us in the lived *time* of mortality. Ideas and abstractions, which systematically separate themselves from persons and from time, do not form the essence of literature and do not surpass it.

VI. Works of literature are written by individual *authors* using an existing language with reference to material nature and human nature. The doctrine known as textuality makes a triple denial of these entities. Textuality denies the existence of the natural world, of literature, and of authors.

VII. No author has a claim to final authority. However, we do well to acknowledge, as all cultures do, sheer *seniority*. Works that have survived for centuries cannot be dismissed out of hand as stiflingly traditional, as part of the status quo, needing above all to be usurped by the modern.

VIII. In order to affirm literature in its full humanist sense, let us eschew the freestanding word *text*. Its indiscriminate use today provides evidence of deadening stylistic conformity. Rather, let us take advantage of the full range of terms like *book, work, poem, play, novel, essay, passage, chapter*, and the like. There is no need to modify serviceable expressions like "the text of" a work, and "sacred texts." But let us refrain from endorsing, indirectly and inadvertently, the doctrine of textuality by chanting "text" in every other line of what we say and write.

IX. Like our terrestrial environment, our literary, intellectual, and moral environment needs to be wisely cultivated and protected. We have as many strip miners and clear-cutters operating in the areas of literature, philosophy, and history as we have operating on the planet Earth. You know their names and their schools. Some of them believe that we who devote ourselves to literature and inquiry are an endangered species—and should fade away. We, for our part, are resolved to survive and to flourish.

Interlude—Partially Plagiarized

X. "Our lives are a fierce attempt to find an aspect of this world *not* open to interpretation" (David Mamet, *Kafka's Grave*).

XI. In the fullness of time a poet-oracle came forth upon the mountaintop, whence one could see a great distance in all directions. To the innumerable questions put to this fierce yet gentle seer, only two answers have come down to us:

1. "Everything exists in order to end up in a book."
2. "Nothing will survive unless it has been uttered."

XII. To those preparing to be shipwrecked on a desert island, I offer a miniaturized library of world literature that can be memorized in a few days. It consists of 3,001 bulls—not Papal: Irish. Bulls combine succinct style, compacted logic, and a sharp (if blunted) point; for example:

> At your age Mozart was dead.
> Reader's report to a textbook publisher: "This book does nothing for the nonreading student."
> No one goes to that restaurant anymore. It's too crowded.
> We teach what we hope to learn.
> Count no man happy till he dies.
> Freedom is the absence of choice.
> Stop it some more.
> I can never kiss her properly. Her face always gets in the way.
> He died cured.
> Don't go near the water till you've learned to swim.
> This book fills a badly needed gap.

XIII. The world scoffs at old ideas. It distrusts new ideas. It loves tricks.

XIV. Everything has been said. But nobody listens. Therefore it has to be said all over again—only better. In order to say it better, we have to know how it was said before.

XV. A friend in Missouri recently sent me a book-length manuscript. In the past, she has written intense studies of the relation between German and French philosophy as it has influenced literary theory since 1950. In her letter, my friend declared that she has undergone a profound change of heart. She now rejects the reigning schools of literary theory and attacks them in this manuscript. It is time for a more direct and less abstract approach to literature. Would I write an introduction to her book?

My friend's new book vehemently rebuts Heidegger and Adorno, Barthes and Derrida on their own ground. It reads like her earlier books— with all the signs changed. She has without question changed sides; she has not left the battlefield. As before, her discussions do not refer to any primarily literary works. The only authors she mentions from before 1950 are Plato, Aristotle, Kant, and Hegel.

I wrote my friend that I applaud her change of heart. When is she going to change her reading accordingly? I could not write an introduction to a book still transfixed by her earlier theoretical concerns, even though she has joined the other side.

I did not write to my friend that I would like to know the titles of the books she keeps within easy reach around her desk or workstation. Does she still work surrounded by Saussure and Foucault? Or does she keep beside her again now the works she loved as a graduate student: Stendhal and Balzac, George Eliot and Dickens, Hawthorne and Melville?

XVI. In literary study as in everyday life, we have entered the Age of Appliances. More and more scholars and critics write and teach by *applying* an ideology or a methodology to a cultural "text." This reliance on appliances tends to eliminate the experience and the love of literature.

Literature in Education

XVII. We have brought ourselves to great perplexity about the basic role of education. Should education socialize the young within an existing culture and offer them the basic means to succeed in that culture? Or should education give to the young the means to challenge and overthrow the existing culture, presumably in order to achieve a better life? Here I shall appeal to analogy.

Almost immediately after fertilization, the human embryo sets aside a few cells that are sheltered from the rest of the organism and from the environment. These cells retain a special ability to divide by meiosis into haploid cells needed for sexual reproduction. Our gonads represent the most stable and protected element in the body and are usually able to pass on unchanged to the next generation the genetic material we were born with. In this way, the sins of fathers and mothers during their lifetime are not visited upon their children. Except for radiation and a few diseases, the life we live does not affect our gonads.

No such biological process is built into cultures. But all cultures have discovered something similar—an activity, sometimes developed into an institution, we call *education*. By education, we pass on to the young the customs, restrictions, discoveries, and wisdom that have afforded survival so far.

There is good reason to maintain that, unlike many other institutions—political, social, and artistic—which may criticize and rebel against the status quo, education should remain primarily a conservative institution, like our gonads. We are overloading education when we ask it to reform society, to redesign culture, and to incorporate the avant-garde and bohemia into its precincts. In a free society, original and disaffected minds will always find a platform. The university need not provide the principal home for political, social, and artistic dissidents. The primary mission of a university is the transmission of a precious heritage. As the heritage is passed along, both teachers and students will test it, criticize it, and seek to improve it. That healthy modification should not supplant the essential process of transmission.

XVIII. Out of the 1960s and 1970s, one item we should not forget is the counter slogan to *relevance*. It reads: *Curriculum kills*. There was great merit in the nineteenth-century ground rule for college programs that specified: no living authors. Students can read them perfectly well on their own. Why invite stuffy old professors to paint contemporary authors over with interpretations and theories? We need scholars in the classroom to help students with the genuine otherness of the past. We need cultivated readers and discriminating critics to deal with contemporary literature. But not in the classroom. Curriculum kills.

XIX. In planning the day-to-day work of education, we shall forever be selecting curricula and programs. In so doing, let us desist from referring to *"the canon,"* or canons or—God save us—canonicity. The term *canon* was smuggled out of theology into education and literature only a few years ago by those who desperately need something to attack and subvert, something to transgress and deconstruct. Otherwise, what would they do? But they are talking about a figment of their own making. Who knows if *Pilgrim's Progress* or *The Parallel Lives* or *Twenty Thousand Leagues under the Sea* is in the canon? No one. We deal primarily with the curriculum that lies before us in the courses we teach. Here lies our path through knowledge, a path we may choose over and over again, like love in marriage. Our love of literature does not remain the same. Yet its constancy sustains us.

2

PERPLEXING
LESSONS: IS THERE
A CORE TRADITION
IN THE HUMANITIES?

THE EIGHTH CHAPTER of *Life on the Mississippi* reads like a parable on education. Mark Twain gave it a cleverly appropriate title, "Perplexing Lessons." Urged on by Mr. Bixby, an experienced river boat pilot, the narrator and cub pilot has "managed to pack my head full of islands, towns, bars, 'points,' and bends." One day when the boy has learned most of the names, Mr. Bixby turns on him.

"What is the shape of Walnut Bend?"
He might as well have asked me my grandmother's opinion of photoplasm.
By and by he said,—
"My boy, you've got to know the shape of the river perfectly. It is all there is left to steer by on a very dark night. . . . You learn it with such absolute certainty that you can always steer by the shape that's in your head, and never mind the one that's before your eyes."

With no time to adjust to his new task, the cub pilot learns a further factor: that the river's shape keeps changing.

Two things seemed pretty apparent to me. One was, that in order to be a pilot a man had got to learn more than any one man ought to be allowed to know; and the other was, that he must learn it all over again in a different way every twenty-four hours.

How much comment belongs here? The classroom teacher might have a hard time with this secular American version of *Pilgrim's Progress*. How far need a teacher go to pick out the name writ large over the whole book: The River of Life? Mark Twain is content to keep the reader laughing at Twain's bedraggled self as a boy. For us to cogitate about cores and traditions in the humanities, Mark Twain has provided a vivid metaphor for education itself. To gain initiation into the culture, you have to know the shape of things, not the names only. We shall come back to Mr. Bixby in the wheelhouse sputtering at his inept pupil.

All of us are concerned with these cultural rites of passage not only because we may be professional educators but primarily because we are citizens and parents. I envision the challenge that faces us in education as a two-headed dragon demanding daily human sacrifice to keep it placated and to prevent it from devouring the city. One awful head stands for the tens of millions of young minds all over the country waiting to receive nourishment, an almost sensible hunger for some form of knowledge that will make life possible and worth living. The second head rearing up with gaping jaws represents the other side of the same situation. It symbolizes the nearly one thousand hours each student and each teacher must spend in a classroom every year, time occupied by the long battle between boredom and alertness.

These two insatiable mouths must be fed. You know as well as I the enormous obstacles that stand in our way. For two centuries now, well-meaning and convinced educationalists have been telling us to allow children to follow their natural proclivities. The great defender of childhood as the period of natural freedom, Jean-Jacques Rousseau, proposed a notion that should have opened our eyes long ago to his program. "The first education must be purely negative" (*Emile,* Book II). He means that we should withhold any systematic or formal education, including reading, until the age of twelve. We have practiced negative education so effectively that today many students are admitted to college still unschooled and have to educate themselves six years too late, when their memories are slowing down, their doubts increasing. Rousseau devised negative education theory for a very special, highly tractable, and imaginary pupil with a full-time tutor and other privileges. Carried on by progressive schools, the misbegotten scheme of negative education intersects another present danger—not a theory but a mood. For thirty years, we have been living through a series of searing national traumas. Three major assassinations, the crises of Vietnam, Watergate, the Iran-Contra affair, and a failed impeachment may have left us disenchanted with the still-fragile progress we have made toward true democracy and equal justice. Is it worth trying to maintain a rigorous universal education in an open, pluralistic society?

I shall not answer for others. Response must come primarily as a declaration of personal faith in chosen ideals. What I can insist on is a principle that operates as inexorably in a society as it does in physics. *Nature abhors a vacuum.* If we do not provide adequate knowledge to fill those hungry minds and occupy empty schoolroom hours, something else will. That something else may well be deadening and corrupting—estrangement, anomie, idle vandalism, drugs, crime, suicide. These things cannot be said too often. In schools more than anywhere else, we can make an effort to establish the principle of equal opportunity by leveling everyone upward as far as possible. Family upbringing and college education quite properly tend to increase inequalities. Free public schools constitute our only major institution serving both all individuals and the national interest.

Yet think for a moment. No authoritative document sets out what high school students should know. Powerful legal suits challenge school boards for doing or not doing their duty. Can we blame state boards of education for wobbling? One readily available reference is the booklet *Academic Preparation for College: What Students Need to Know and Be Able to Do,* published by the College Board (1983). With regard to science and mathematics, the booklet describes fairly well-defined content requirements. In terms of the humanities (English, the arts, and foreign languages), the emphasis falls entirely on what I call "empty skills"—to read, to write, to analyze, to describe, to evaluate. To what specifics or content are these skills to be applied?

Silence. Not a single work of art or literature is mentioned. One could surmise that basic academic competencies can be acquired by working with any materials at all. Still, someone will decide on substance; too often the buck is passed down to the individual teacher, who must fill all roles—planner, helper, taskmaster, and final judge. We must reflect on the question "Is there a core tradition in the humanities?" Our answers should do something to help embattled teachers trying to maintain standards and should help put substance back into the humanities—and do so for the majority of students, not exclusively for the college-bound who read the College Board booklet.

The core of the humanities, as I envision it, is shaped less like the proverbial onion than like a simplified orange with three large sections or segments fitted closely together. My analysis leans inevitably toward a definition of culture, a term we have had in English in its general sense for barely a hundred years.

1. Official rituals and ceremonies and celebrations; monuments like the

Statue of Liberty; the flag; the national anthem; the Pledge of Allegiance. These elements are mostly associated with some form of public enactment.

2. A loose, shared store of stories (legendary and historic); folklore (including proverbs); ideas and concepts; historical and presumed facts. This common knowledge may remain unwritten and orally transmitted.

3. A collection of concrete, lasting works (images, buildings, music, writings in poetry and prose) considered significant, or revealed, or great, or beautiful.

All I ask of this schematic division is to help us deal with questions of content in education. Segment two, the common fund of lore and knowledge, corresponds to all the names cub pilot Mark Twain learned—and did well to learn—in order to begin to know the river. Segment three, the lasting works and particularly books used in schools, provide Mr. Bixby's "shape of the river"—never beheld all at once, endlessly changing, yet a shape held in the mind to refer to under the most difficult conditions. Reading is the principal activity that allows us to move between these two segments, a kind of two-way membrane or circuitry that makes the connections between an amorphous mass of materials and a collection of recognized forms. Reading gains pertinence when it mediates between our available cultural knowledge and another realm loosely called *literature.*

Schools are concerned with all three segments of the humanistic orange. Fortunately, I am not going to have to talk about the whole fruit. Recently, my colleague E. D. Hirsch, at the University of Virginia, published a book entitled *Cultural Literacy.* This intelligent synthesis of the history of education, developmental psychology, and the recent research on perception, memory, and reading eloquently reaffirms the principles of universal education in a democratic society. He diagnoses our national illness as a condition based on misguided educational theory after Rousseau and on a faulty conception of pluralism that dismisses a common culture. What Hirsch establishes persuasively is a truism we shouldn't have to be shown again.

But we do. Unless you know enough—enough facts and names and ideas—you cannot read. Decoding words and sentences will not produce meaning unless the reader knows the variety of items to which the passage refers. Then Hirsch has the imagination and the courage to go a step further. He answers the sassy question that may follow: So who's to decide what every American needs to know? He takes the dare himself. In sixty pages and about five thousand entries, he and two collaborators list the items you probably have to be able to recognize and identify in order to read and understand a newspaper. Later, he produced a dictionary and a curriculum.

Of course, such a list makes addictive reading, something between a quiz program and a collective psychoanalysis. Any citizen, reasonable or bigoted, can find fault with the entries. Most directly and importantly, the list represents a challenge to all those of us educators who have evaded the task of defining what we expect students to know. Hirsch's book is a wonderful reciprocating engine: In order to read, you have to know a lot about the world as our culture conceives it; in order to acquire that knowledge, you have to read writing that will expand your mind. Here, to help in that process, is the best existing approximation of what you have to know and what our schools should aim to teach as a minimum. A list won't do the job; a list will help set the sights. If we put our minds to it, many more citizens could really read. No utopia here; rather, a concise and exciting contribution.

Hirsch calls his list "the *extensive* curriculum," by which he means the basics of generally held information. Such basics will make available to everyone who masters them the elements of the culture through which we communicate with one another, particularly in writing. He hopes and I hope that more of these basics can be conveyed to students by revising our readers, by modifying our current approach to reading as a mere skill, and by making sure that all students, not just those from middle-class homes, learn the facts and ideas essential to understanding prose on the level of newspapers. Hirsch does not address except in passing the matter of the *intensive* curriculum—what specific books Johnny and Jenny should read in order to learn and apply these enhanced reading abilities of full literacy. Hirsch is perfectly right to proceed one step at a time. He already has an undeclared war on his hands with what I shall call—naturally—"vested educational interests." Still, someone will have to talk and finally decide about the intensive curriculum; we shall talk about it here and now.

Hirsch, then, to my great satisfaction and with my vigorous support, has demonstrated the crucial role of section two in my three-section humanities orange. He has picked up the challenge of collecting what Mark Twain refers to as the names of the places and features along the river. You have to know them in order to talk with others about the river. As the cub pilot soon learned, however, the names do not give you the river's shape. That shape, elusive, mysterious, frequently changing in detail, belongs to section three, around which I wish to build the centerpiece of my sermon.

Any discussion of a humanistic core, of how to recognize a classic or a masterpiece, of what makes up a canon, rests on three tacit presuppositions. Perhaps there are more. We assume a profound continuity in human life; to track and to measure that continuity, we turn first of all to the immense palace-archive of history, which sits at the heart of the humanities. We expect to find continuity both in the macro realm of culture—mores, institutions, artifacts—and in the micro realm of human character, of human nature.

Here, I can do no better than produce two of my favorite quotations.

Ortega y Gasset saw very deep. "Man has no nature. What he has is history." Emerson had passed that way earlier and left his unmistakable markings. "Properly speaking, there is no such thing as history. There is only biography." Whatever its precise form—history, biography, literature, the arts—a belief in the continuity of the human over many millennia lies behind any discussion of a tradition in the humanities.

Second, within that continuity of perception and imagination we have developed a limited number of versions of human greatness. These ideals— warriors, saints, martyrs, explorers, prophets, chiefs, sages, artists—provide several scales of human eminence, qualities to admire and perhaps to emulate. I cannot think of a culture or imagine a culture, without its accepted versions of greatness.

Third, human beings long ago came to believe that continuity and greatness are effectively conveyed and celebrated in lasting artifacts or classics. Greek theater, medieval stained-glass windows, modern Islamic festivals for reciting *The Qur'an* serve the purpose of broadcasting cultural traditions to a large audience. As that cultural function has become increasingly concentrated for developed societies in organized public schools, school systems have universally found that the most practical and economic instrument of acculturation is the printed book. No other teaching aid even begins to rival it. The world has three great faiths that speak of themselves as the religions of the book. In its schools at least, the United States remains, and should remain for the foreseeable future, a culture of the book.

These presuppositions—human continuity, greatness, and recognition of them in major works—often remain undiscussed. Yet they belong to my definition of the humanities—indeed, to my deepest sense of humanity. I shall proceed to how, as a teacher of a course in masterworks of Western literature since 1650, I deal with the task of selecting books from the vast number put forward by tradition and by available anthologies. A classic that stands up through years of teaching will display a series of what I used to see as polarities. I now consider them to be complementaries. A classic will make its historical moment vivid and important; it will also have other features that make it remain contemporary. In other words, it is at the same time a period piece and forever young. In my course, I would cite Molière to illustrate the point; Shakespeare does so even better.

A great work displays aspects that allow us to perceive in it a strong element of simplicity and clarity. It also awes us by the mystery and complexity it contains. We may well find it both reassuring and scary. Tolstoy's "The Death of Ivan Ilyich" will serve as an example. A classic will create the sense of confronting concrete, individual situations and characters, which at the same time reach toward the domain of the general, the universal. In her best poems, Emily Dickinson's literary persona becomes a very concrete universal.

My three presuppositions and my rules of thumb for recognizing masterworks bring me to a far more important point about a core tradition in the humanities. A meeting such as the present one would never have occurred in Europe before the eighteenth century, nor would it occur in most Islamic countries today. For those societies, the core has been revealed from on high and creates a center around which most aspects of life find an appointed place. For us, perhaps because some of us have lost our faith, certainly because of our hard-won "wall of separation" between church and state in public schools, the core cannot be presented as revealed. I would go so far as to say that in this open, pluralist society, the core is not even given. We have traditions and institutions and conventions. But they must answer to many pressures, political and commercial and religious. It seems more accurate to say that the past constantly *offers* a core tradition in the humanities, an offer each of us plays some role in refusing or accepting. Can one say that each generation comes to a decision about these traditions? But what is a generation? School principals and school boards and college professors wrestle with these decisions in terms of curriculum and requirements. As long as the people involved are acting on the basis of actual reading on their part and careful reflection about cultural literacy and the shape of the river, these debates can be exciting and fruitful. The "intensive" curriculum of books read in class should not be handed down from on high by a minister of education to all schools in the nation, as happens in most parts of the world for reasons of national unity. There are less implacable ways of establishing a core, especially for a system like ours that must incorporate into its curriculum such essentials as healthy skepticism, verification of asserted facts, scrutiny of logical argument, minority views, and "critical thinking."

Teachers and professors all over the country should be spurring one another on to select the knowledge students need most in order to face a citizen's responsibilities—not just empty skills—and the books they should not leave school without having read. Choices will vary; a few brash committees will seek consensus. The federal government may wish to favor selected programs. States may decide to establish lists of works from which school districts may choose. Publishers will play a major, yet unpredictable, role. Blue-ribbon panels may make useful recommendations.

All this swirl of seeking and dissent will contribute to the improvement of education at all levels as long as one principle stands. Even in our pluralistic society, the humanities have a core the way the river has a shape. The very process of discovering and gradually modifying that shape lends meaning and excitement to the intellectual life of a community. The most stimulating discussions I have had with my colleagues have dealt with the specific content of curriculum change and how to define the knowledge we would require of all students and why. The answers may not satisfy everyone, but without those questions seriously pressed, we resign ourselves to an invasion of empty skills and a confusing dispersion of minds. The Greeks, of course, already had a word for this state of things in which one learns primarily from the search, from the debate itself. A heuristic exchange of this kind will help us prevent education from becoming empty, the way it tends to be now, or rigid, the way some would like to see it. Established lists and recently published surveys demonstrate that a good deal of agreement already exists among educated citizens about the shape of our river. My own informal soundings on this subject over the past twenty years tell me that even a randomly picked group of intelligent and educated people will agree on a handful of books that everyone should read at some point, in some form. Then the going becomes very slow. Mark Twain seems to point at these dilemmas with his title "Perplexing Dreams."

It is time for a few specifics. If we are going to pick schoolbooks not entirely by reading level and word frequency, but by culturally useful content and effective writing, then the whole category of biography and autobiography falls beautifully into place. One of the most eloquently written and humanly valuable personal accounts available to us used to fill many classroom shelves. Helen Keller's *The Story of My Life* makes the essential revelation that what we too easily think of as a given, the very condition of being human, is not given but learned. Deprived of the two senses we rely on most, living by touch alone, this magnificent woman gave us an example that can help us learn courage and imagination and appreciation of the simplest acts of living. Every detail provokes reflection. Only late in her childhood under a teacher of genius did Keller learn not to register on her face, as though through a window or on a screen, all her inner feelings. She discovered how to write fine English without ever hearing the language.

Another modern autobiography has been almost entirely forgotten by school programs. After a colorful early life as barnstormer, army pilot, and mail carrier, Charles Lindbergh helped design the single-engine, high-wing, almost windowless monoplane in which he had to fight sleep for hours and navigate alone and without a radio from New Jersey to Paris. *We,* the book he wrote himself the same year, at age twenty-five, about his youth and that historic flight, rivals Plutarch in its depiction of small qualities of character that add up to greatness.

Allow me to pick another example perhaps too close to home. I would like to think that in a book for high schools it took me five years to write, *The Forbidden Experiment,* I learned something from Keller and Lindbergh.

For the story of the Wild Boy of Aveyron—not necessarily in my version—deserves its place, in my estimate, among these stories and in the core we are seeking and constituting.

I am not going to propose an exhaustive list for a core curriculum or even a short list. Rather, I advocate the heuristic goal of arguing over and drawing up such lists without neglecting modest candidates like Sherlock Holmes, folktales and fairy tales, the great religious works of the Greeks, the Jews, and the Christians, along with biography and autobiography.

Two prickly problems raise their heads immediately before we even begin to outline a core. First, the question of timing. Is there an optimum moment to read *Hamlet?* When should we read *Huckleberry Finn?* *The Republic? Candide?* Should there be a national agreement on which works will be kept for college students? Which could be read in primary school—perhaps in a simplified version? And there is the second problem already. Should we tolerate or even encourage the rewriting and adaptation of significant works in the humanities? *Don Quixote? War and Peace* for the schools? I once read and remembered large parts of *Moby-Dick* in such a version. There is no categorical answer to any of these questions. My own experience tells me that skillful editorial work or even a complete retelling (like the Lambs' *Tales from Shakespeare*) can serve a valuable function in schools and in homes. But edited and truncated versions must be prepared with enormous skill and devotion.

Everything I have said up to now will come to nothing unless we adopt in our schools and maintain in colleges a coherent set of examinations on the subjects taught, on the content of books read. I shall have to summarize here an argument I set out at greater length in another place ("Helping Teachers Do What They Cannot Do Alone," *The Virginia Assembly* Institute of Government, University of Virginia, 1984). Our present high school diplomas certify very little—mostly perseverance. Probably on a voluntary basis to start, our high schools should offer a state diploma based on a defined curriculum and on examinations in five basic subjects (English, history and geography, mathematics, science, foreign language). The New York State Regents examinations and the International Baccalaureate program adopted by a number of public high schools demonstrate the feasibility of such a scheme.

Objections will come tumbling out from all sides. Standardized examinations lead to teaching to the test. Some teachers will feel that their autonomy is being invaded. But the advantages outweigh the criticisms, I believe. Only outside examinations will establish anything resembling quality control. Grades given by classroom teachers make an unreliable guide to what their students have learned. State certification based on examinations will give genuine integrity to the high school diploma, help employers choose workers, and begin to break the pro–higher education prejudice, which implies that in order to be adequately educated you have to go to college. The reinstitution of meaningful, earned high school diplomas will help every aspect of our society. Furthermore, classroom teachers could benefit enormously from the coach-helper relationship that obtains in athletics and dramatics. An outside examination provides a kind of performance in preparation for which everyone can work together without the adversary relation that may set in between a student and the teacher who awards the final grade.

I began by comparing the core tradition in the humanities to the shape of Mark Twain's elusive and shifting Mississippi. I shall close by reaffirming the analogy, presented in Thesis XVII of the preceding chapter, of our biological germ line to represent the transmission of knowledge in education. A core tradition in the humanities, the three aspects of it that we expect schools to convey to all our children, operates on the essentially conservative principle of gonads. A dynamic culture needs a steady center. After we have been to school, we may decide to test the center, or challenge it, or revise it in the give-and-take of democratic process. First, we should know where the center lies. It is not idealism but, rather, deep skepticism about meliorism and about the witless inflation of our needs and desires that leads me to this analogy. Unless we teach in our schools a fairly steady sense of our humanistic traditions, of what has been called our "civil religion," I envision a runaway culture seeking all extremes at once.

3

AMERICAN EDUCATION
AGAINST ITSELF

F OR MANY YEARS now, we have heard about the decline of elementary and secondary schools. More recently, colleges and universities, once considered the pride of our educational system, have come under attack because of rising costs and falling standards. But amid all this discussion of educational reform, a key point has been ignored—that these two independent and uncoordinated levels of education are trapped in a mutually harmful alliance.

One central fact warrants honest assessment: Today, more than 50 percent of high school graduates go on to college. This fact is widely interpreted as evidence that many Americans wind up educated. I would argue, on the contrary, that it signifies the decline of a coherent twelve-year sequence of studies that leads to a diploma certifying basic readiness for the job market, along with a knowledge of history and literature adequate for citizenship in a democracy. At the college level, it signals a decline in entrance requirements and academic standards. We must face the fact that we have allowed something approaching a conspiracy between our two levels of education to pull down each other's standard of achievement.

Sixty years ago, my two brothers-in-law did not go to college. After a no-nonsense high school education, both trained on the job and worked their way up. One became the manager of a large hydroelectric plant. The other became an executive in the Magnesium Corporation of America. They were not offered four youthful years at college to mix study, play, and sport at great expense to their parents or themselves. Years later, when they became parents, they came to feel that the educational system was failing to serve their children as well as it had served them.

My brothers-in-law deplored declining standards in the schools, which did not give their children the background necessary to adapt to the work of the world. They also felt uncomfortable about spending large sums to send their children away to a college or university that they did not fully trust. But times had changed; employers wanted credentials. For their children, there seemed to be no alternative.

Many people today share the skepticism of my brothers-in-law. A bit of history may clarify the picture. The rapid growth of American colleges and universities began with the GI bill after World War II and was further spurred by economic prosperity. As campuses developed in the sixties and seventies into centers of radical political agitation, they also took on the status of a tolerated bohemia where the young went through rites of passage, coming into contact with drugs, sex, and communal living. Standards were further eroded as student and faculty agitation about the "relevance" of courses began to lead to the elimination of many academic requirements. More and more freshman courses in English and mathematics became remedial courses that should have been taken in high school at far less expense to all concerned.

Between 1956 and 1970, I watched the total enrollment at the University of Texas at Austin, where I then taught, grow from 17,000 to 35,000, with no corresponding improvement in SAT scores. No educational purpose or policy was served by that growth, nor could a few of us on the faculty convince the administration and the Board of Regents that raising admissions standards and capping enrollment would boost the scholastic level of the university and, at the same time, prevent it from becoming an impersonal leviathan. Austin landowners, real estate agencies, building contractors, and ordinary Texas boosters cheered every September when the newspapers announced a new enrollment record.

This experience occurred on campuses around the country. In essence, secondary schools increasingly allowed ill-prepared students to graduate from high school, while colleges and universities willingly admitted these students into diluted undergraduate programs. Except in the sciences, mathematics, and engineering, a college degree came to represent a collection of loosely related courses rarely certified by a comprehensive examination in the field in which a student was majoring.

What many critics cite as a failure of articulation between the two levels of education begins to look more like remarkable accommodation, a tacit arrangement—somewhat like price fixing in reverse—to produce lower standards on both levels simultaneously. The fit was and still is all too good—even though no one admits to wanting lower standards. We confer high school diplomas and bachelor's degrees that are seriously diminished.

The slackened admissions requirements at all but the most prestigious institutions deprive high schools of a major incentive to maintain rigorous standards. The responsibility for the malfunction of our elementary and secondary schools lies in great part with a bloated system of higher education—one whose immense bureaucracy now requires more than 2 million tuition-paying novitiates every fall to keep institutions in, or at least near, the black. At the same time, the decline of high school standards causes many parents and students to feel that they must assume the sometimes crushing financial burden of four years of higher education. College attendance is increasingly seen as the only road to success for young people.

Can we do anything to remedy this entrenched and faceless conspiracy against improving the quality of education? Promising solutions are available, but they are effectively blocked by widespread, tenacious, and wrongheaded beliefs about education—especially the entrenched article of faith that the content of what is taught in elementary and secondary schools must be subject to the control of local school boards. Nonetheless, let me offer four steps that could drastically improve lower and higher education.

- Each state should adopt a core curriculum for kindergarten through twelfth grade that sets the overall sequence and content of courses in English, mathematics, history, geography, and the physical and biological sciences. Such a curriculum would provide the essential framework for the voluntary national standards in core subject areas that are called for under the federal "Goals 2000" legislation. State guidelines that are currently being developed vary widely. (They are carefully surveyed and evaluated in an annual report from the American Federation of Teachers, "Making Standards Matter.")

Some independent curriculum-development projects could, if widely adopted, bring coherence to the efforts in the fifty states. For example, the "New Standards" project, supported by the independent National Center on Education and the Economy and the University of Pittsburgh's Learning Research and Development Center, has published several volumes of a highly regarded curriculum. The volumes are filled with sample lessons that follow a reasonably sequential curriculum for language arts, mathematics, science, and other areas.

The best-designed curriculum that I have seen for kindergarten through sixth grade comes from the non-profit Core Knowledge Foundation in Charlottesville, Virginia, and is available in bookstores under separate titles for each grade, such as *What Your First Grader Needs to Know.* The volumes are edited by E. D. Hirsch, Jr. More than eight hundred schools in forty states have adopted parts of the curricula set out in these volumes. Curricula for grades seven and eight are being developed.

If states will pay attention to such curricula, and if they will consult with each other, we can achieve a national understanding about what to teach in our schools—and how to raise standards in them.

• More high schools should administer standardized tests in basic subjects as a graduation requirement. Each state should set minimum scores at a reasonably demanding level, and results should be made available on request to prospective employers and to colleges and universities. Insofar as possible, all states should also have established assessments of students' knowledge in core subjects in two or three earlier grades.

• Colleges and universities should establish entrance requirements well above their present levels. The news media should pay more attention to the reasons that accrediting agencies accommodate the present lax standards. These accrediting agencies, responsible to no one outside of the profession that they are charged to regulate, are a major part of the reason why lax standards continue to exist.

Raising entrance requirements will cause enrollments at some colleges and universities to decline, and the financial stress of less tuition revenue will no doubt produce strong protest. But higher education needs such downsizing to promote quality in education at every level. Open admissions should become a thing of the past.

• Faculty members and administrators should stringently evaluate undergraduate programs and courses in new subjects such as cultural studies and gay and lesbian studies. Do they have the scholarly rigor to qualify them as alternatives to traditional disciplines in the humanities (where many of these new subjects are found)? My experience leads me to believe that most do not. Colleges and universities should also ensure that all fields in which students major require comprehensive examinations, to enhance the integrity of the undergraduate degree.

None of these four measures is new, administratively infeasible, or without strong support both inside and outside education. But each of them violates at least one of the unwritten beliefs that most Americans hold about education.

For example, we distrust uniformity, particularly when mandated by a government agency. Therefore, we resist efforts to standardize parts of schools' curricula and cling to local control of school districts as a guarantee of freedom. That freedom can become an obstacle to adopting a well-designed and comprehensive curriculum and firm standards for the schools.

We have also come to believe that a college degree is the surest path to success. That belief helps blind us to the need to demand higher standards for a high school diploma, standards that would certify the readiness of high school graduates for many jobs that do not, and should not, require a college education.

Our faith in the baccalaureate degree also has allowed many colleges and universities to avoid evaluating what their degrees actually certify.

In many fields in the humanities and social sciences, students can earn a degree without acquiring adequate knowledge of the history of our national institutions and our culture, without learning to write clearly, without studying a second language, without any rigorous comprehensive examinations, without having done anything but take a collection of one-semester courses. Not surprisingly, many parents—including many administrators and faculty members—are beginning to suspect that they are paying for an oversold boondoggle, even at the best institutions of higher education.

In sum, we need to reexamine our fundamental beliefs about educational excellence. If we do not confront these assumptions, we shall never be able to change the ways in which our two levels of education conspire today to lower standards.

EDUCATION: HIGHER

AND LOWER

DOES ANY MIDDLE ground remain in our culture wars? Or can one find only a hazardous no-man's-land between university-based radicals who denounce the Western tradition as it reaches late capitalism and conservatives who denounce the radicals and enshrine free-market forces? Some of us belong to neither warring camp and find it hard to make ourselves heard. Furthermore, how appropriate is the term *culture wars* for a struggle enacted in our educational institutions and rarely spilling over into violence or even into genuine political expression?

In August 1996 as second president of the Association of Literary Scholars and Critics, I stood up in front of its second conference and urged our members to adopt a "cautious activism" in favor of the literary imagination and a common literary culture. The crux of my message lay in a sentence I had pondered for a long time. "Some of us have come to believe that it is possible, even necessary, to be liberal in political matters and conservationist in cultural matters."

With that distinction between political and cultural, I was trying to stake out the missing middle ground between the strident extremes that provoked a group of us to found this new association. At the time, I was neither warmly cheered nor roundly challenged. But I want to elaborate on my position and why I think it can help us see things more clearly in both education and politics.

Politically, I range myself with those who believe that our tax system should not permit the gap between rich and poor in this country to widen. Capital gains and estate taxes, for example, might be indexed to that gap and raised as needed to prevent its growth. I do not believe that the working through of free-market forces is always in the long run beneficial, and I favor government regulation of certain parts of the economy in order to protect the public interest. Late capitalism needs lots of oversight precisely because it is so robust in its invasion of our lives through new technologies and multinational operations that now escape supervision by anyone. These positions represent a conventional liberal point of view.

Culturally, I believe strongly that our major cultural institution, which profoundly affects all of us both individually and as members of local and national communities, namely education, should devote itself primarily to transmitting traditional knowledge and skills and to teaching as dispassionately as possible the history of our institutions, beginning in antiquity. Education does not have a primary responsibility to change those institutions. The inequities and consequences of past events, such as slavery and the settlement of the Americas, lead to difficult questions of emphasis and interpretation. But these discussions should not transform our schools and colleges into seedbeds of revolution. For that process, we have our still-evolving political institutions. It is true that so intelligent a historian of American education as Diane Ravitch could, in *Troubled Crusade* (1983), appear to take a different view. "Americans long ago decided, without too much discussion of the matter, that education would be the best vehicle through which to change society." Ravitch is referring, however, to the central tenet in the thinking of Jefferson, Horace Mann, and John Dewey— that free public schools could serve to establish a common democratic culture in a country where customs and institutions were still forming. Today, I would argue, our schools will serve us best as a means of passing on an integrated culture, not as a means of trying to divide that culture into segregated interest groups. Such a curriculum need employ neither propaganda nor advocacy. It should present as untendentious and as factually accurate a version of history as possible, with allowance for differing interpretations and emphases. In political debates about historical and cultural issues, one may be as partisan and as programmatic as one wishes. In presenting our past history and our evolving traditions to school students, one should try to be as accurate and as evenhanded as one can. The goal remains sound even if it cannot always be attained.

Am I asking for a form of intellectual schizophrenia that cannot be sustained as a healthy condition? Is it morally contradictory to favor political and social activity directed at social change and simultaneously to favor insulating actual course content in schools and colleges from that activity? I think not. The separation resembles that of church and state established by the Constitution. And nothing prevents teachers and students from becoming politically active outside school. We tend to forget today that many of the demonstrations of the sixties and seventies took place in the political arena, away from campuses, over issues of racial integration, nuclear weapons deployment, and the conduct of the national party conventions. Campus teach-ins about Vietnam were exceptional. Today, in contrast, the engagements of the culture wars are being fought over local educational issues: the content of courses, the politicization of the curriculum, and the displacement of traditional fields like English by ideological "studies" programs representing minority groups, feminists, gays and lesbians, Marxists, and the like. These groups concentrate much of their attention on campus affairs, on the curriculum, and on the governance of higher education.

What I am asking for resembles a political lightning rod, or improved drainage, an encouragement to the politicized teachers and students to engage in genuine politics. That shift will allow the vital process of education to concern itself more with tradition than with change, more with the illuminating variety of the past than with the divisive wrenchings of the contemporary, and more with the discovery of human universals than with the interests of rival groups.

Even after this explanation, my remarks to a couple of hundred literary critics and scholars about being politically liberal and culturally conservationist need further testing and scrutiny. What I propose to do now is to find out if my original distinction between cultural and political obtains any purchase on a few very different books that have appeared recently on education.

CARY NELSON IS a chaired professor of English at the University of Illinois. One of his former students informs me that Nelson has been a patient and persuasive teacher of American poetry. *Manifesto of a Tenured Radical* registers his continuing loyalty to oral performance and to reading blind— that is, without identifying the author of a work. But Nelson underwent a conversion many years ago. He now believes it is selfevident that we live "in a fundamentally racist society" arising from "the founding acts" of genocide of Native Americans and of slavery as an institution. This version of history imposes a stark responsibility on English professors even in the teaching of literature courses.

> In this historical context, therefore, it is potentially a powerful and
> dangerous seduction to offer students literariness as something they

can identify with, as a subject position they can occupy, while constructing it as an ideology that transcends such passing material triv-
ialities as racial injustice. . . . For it is not the same to teach English
when our economy is impoverishing millions of our citizens. It is
not irrelevant to the study of literature that members of Congress
are trying to reverse the civil rights gains of the last thirty years.

The clumsy phrasing and attempted irony in the first sentence do not prevent us from grasping that Nelson opposes the reading of literature as literature in English department offerings and favors the "unashamed advocacy"
of social reform. Shouldn't he be looking for a slot in political science? Or
running for office? He has given us an answer earlier on. "Higher education
remains the only proven means of social mobility, the only antidote to
poverty, and the only large-scale corrective for the ravages of capitalism."
Nelson is not thinking of the benefits of education to an individual student,
but of the political role of higher education as an institution to effect social
change. This change, as he sees it, includes the content of literature courses
in the English department.

The revolution has been stalled in colleges and universities, we are told,
by certain kinds of theory fixated on interpreting and deconstructing cultural "texts." Nelson wants to restart the process by various forms of "cultural work." The loosely related articles that make up his book discuss aiding
the radical cause by editing anthologies, by organizing conferences, by
teaching against the canon, by unionizing part-time teachers and teaching
assistants, and by politicizing all aspects of higher education in a twelve-step
program. Above all, Nelson wishes to affirm his position as a founder and
reigning monarch in the new discipline of cultural studies. It's a whole new
career. And what does a professor of cultural studies know that the rest of us
don't? What he knows is "the history of the field," going back perhaps forty
years. I can think of no more self-absorbed and self-aggrandizing definition
of a discipline: taking itself as its principal study.

Part of Nelson's pride as a self-proclaimed tenured radical has to do with
his maneuverings to prevent cultural studies from slipping away from his
leadership and from losing its enthusiasm for revolution. But what revolution? Not one of the planks in his platform concerns off-campus civilian life.
Everything points toward a takeover of higher education. A sentence may
gesture toward a general political program, but it then collapses back onto
familiar academic ground. Nelson favors "the struggle against the global
inequities following upon the Reagan-Bush era, the struggle against the
Allan Bloom–Lynne Cheney consensus about American education and
American culture."

I read this often badly written book by a fuzzy radical without a true program as a proud betrayal of his profession as a teacher of English.

Looking out on the same academic landscape or battle scene as Cary Nelson, John Ellis has written *Literature Lost: Social Agendas and the Corruption of the Humanities.* It is a patient, carefully argued, almost avuncular book that urges not more but less political activism on campus. Ellis, the author of *Against Deconstruction,* a solid Germanist, and a founding member of the Association of Literary Scholars and Critics, expresses understandable amazement that so many English professors have turned against literature, against high culture, and against Western tradition. He also stoutly defends the Enlightenment values of rational debate founded on evidence and of common humanity given precedence over the interests of particular nations and tribes.

Ellis's method is to show that the reigning ideas, which produced the veer away from literature, have a revealing history and often fall into logical errors and contradictions. He cites Tacitus idealizing the customs of the barbaric Germanic tribes in contrast to Roman decadence, and Rousseau in the First Discourse proclaiming that the arts and sciences "cover with garlands of flowers the iron chains that bind us" in civilized life. Today, the same primitivist illusion leads some scholars to posit a higher harmony in pre-Columbian Native American societies and in precolonial Africa. Trained in formal logic, Ellis loves to ferret out paradoxes and dilemmas. If all social relations can be reduced to the single factor of power, as Foucault and his followers argue, then there remains no basis on which to found any ethical judgment of Western capitalist culture in its display of dominance and oppression. We simply play the power game better than others and deserve admiration for winning. Here is Ellis on another popular subject of debate.

> The real difference between the Western canon and the politically correct books chosen by race-gender-class critics is that the latter are ideological choices imposed by a cultural elite and only the former are backed by a long history of appreciation and interest on the part of a genuinely diverse reading public.

Ellis's combination of history of ideas and logical analysis accomplishes its goals handily in the chapters on gender and race. The chapter on class devotes fifteen hard-hitting pages to exposing the contortions of Fredric Jameson's defense of Stalinism and Maoism. But Ellis underestimates the vigor of two ideas that will support socialism as an ideal in spite of the shoddiness of some of its promoters. I mean the myth of a truly egalitarian society and the deep-seated belief in the evil of a capitalist-commodity economy that produces very unequal outcomes. These two factors show up today in many sectors of education as an almost automatic hostility toward middle-class values and toward business and commerce. We shall not finish soon or easily with these two aspects of thinking in terms of class.

In a chapter called "Knowledge Versus Activism," Ellis approaches the popular dismissal of all objective knowledge and the acceptance of bias and activism in scholarship. By assembling some dozen cases in which scholarly claims have been advanced on the basis of obviously flawed evidence and argument, Ellis makes the case for the need of a place "that cultivates—not to perfection but to the maximum possible extent—detached, rational inquiry." For him and for many of us, that place is the academy.

Ellis would agree with Cary Nelson that higher education must accept a role as a force for social change. But colleges and universities will benefit society most by staying away from political causes and from direct political advocacy in teaching and in scholarly research. Higher education should seek and defend the fragile tradition of pursuing the truth on the basis of sound evidence and rational argument, and should convey that tradition to individual students.

Now, it happens that the Modern Language Association (representing English and language professors) plus a dozen other academic associations have offered us a four-hundred-page collection of essays called *Advocacy in the Classroom: Problems and Possibilities,* (ed. Patricia Meyer Spacks, St. Martin's Press, 1996). Except for one graduate student and two high school teachers, the forty contributors are college and university professors with a doctorate or a law degree. About half the essays accept the reigning belief of our fin de siècle thinking that, in the absence of any universal truths, all communication is always already advocacy and an exercise of power. The simple transmission of knowledge must yield to the systematic criticism of received beliefs and to the reform of society. A few pedagogical conventions recommending "balance" and "full context" in presenting disputed questions remain on the books, but those conventions exert diminishing force.

Most of us who were radical young college teachers in the sixties, still abuzz with existentialist harangues in favor of engagement, confined our partisan statements to nonclassroom settings—rallies, teach-ins, debates, and SDS meetings. In formal courses, we taught the assigned subject matter as a segment of a recognizable program or field. That distinction has tended to disappear along with (at least in the humanities) the outlines of recognized fields of knowledge. Increasingly, course content is set not by departmental expectations about a body of knowledge but by the autonomous instructor resolved to practice and to instill critical thinking.

Two pithy essays by Hilde Hein and Lambert Zuidervaart reexamine the role of disinterestedness in the pursuit of knowledge and in teaching. They acknowledge it as a still-essential, if difficult, principle of scholarship. A good deal can be learned from the historical pieces on earlier cases (for example, Mark C. Smith on the 1934 American Historical Association report on teaching social sciences) and even from an essay whose conclusions are distorted (Tom Jehn on the Vietnam teach-ins as a sellout, co-opted by "the dominant ideological state apparatus").

My principal criticisms of the MLA collection concern insufficient attention in all this variety to a few basic concerns. First, in most courses and fields, one can distinguish a preliminary stage of covering technical, empirical, and factual materials (for example, in literature, dates, versification, rhetorical devices, historical background) before engaging more disputed areas of interpretation in which a balanced presentation need not preclude enthusiasm and exercise of taste. Second, the greatest danger to education today is probably not excessive advocacy in individual courses, which most students do not welcome, but the cumulative displacement of an entire curriculum, of an entire field, away from its homeland. In English departments, the proliferation of courses in cultural studies, identity politics, and theory has begun to eclipse the reading of mainline works of literature. The essay by Keith Moxie on art history takes pride in the fact that his discipline, based formerly on a Western canon of art and a universalist aesthetic, has been subverted by "advocacy of one political agenda or another" and no longer "supports the ideology of the status quo." Art history without art? English courses without literature? We might meditate a moment on the nesting habits of the European cuckoo.

Third, constant appeal in these essays to academic freedom, treated as a special privilege for professors to speak their minds, neglects the accompanying principle of academic responsibility. Quite properly, ordinary citizens do not forget it. Since one is trained and carefully selected for one's scholarly knowledge of a field, a college teacher has a higher responsibility than the ordinary citizen to speak circumspectly and with documented evidence about the subject on which he or she offers courses. The professor is professionally on trust not to pop off in the classroom and in scholarly work, particularly on political subjects. One may do so in other settings such as conversation and journalism.

Advocacy in the Classroom is worth sampling, as is another book that approaches education from a different direction. In the seven essays collected in *Channel Surfing,* Henry Giroux writes the coded "discourse" of the radical adversarial Left. Perhaps because he holds a chaired professorship in the field of secondary education, he gets one big thing right in the first two essays: All that circulates around us in the form of media, communications, art, and culture must be regarded equally as education, as pedagogy. Today, channel surfing among those tempting presences surpasses schooling as a formative influence on the young. Giroux lambasts the commercially calculated soft-porn images of Calvin Klein jeans ads and criticizes as voyeuristic and caricaturized Barry Clark's explicit film about urban teenagers, *Kids*. But Giroux's social analysis contains a trail of telltale sentences. "Klein's transgressive images fail to challenge dominant, conservative codings of youth as sexually decadent, drug-crazed, pathological, and criminal." "[*Kids*] representations resonate with specific conservative attacks on related issues of sexuality, race, and gender." Giroux's reasons for objecting to the Calvin Klein ads and to *Kids* are more ideological than pedagogical and moral. If either item had been produced not by a capitalist enterprise but by a struggling black group, Giroux would find reasons to defend their integrity.

The second set of essays in *Channel Surfing* concerns race and racism. Giroux has distinct reservations about the new field of "whiteness studies," where "being white appears by default to make one a racist." He has the courage to raise the ideal of a color-blind society as counterweight to identity politics. I applaud his criticism of the stereotypes in the film *Dangerous Minds* about a white female teacher succeeding in a troubled black school. But he wrecks his own argument by conforming his language almost comically to another set of stereotypes. He refers to the teacher's "colonizing role as a white teacher who extracts from her students love and loyalty in exchange for teaching them to be part of a system that oppresses them." A few pages later, in a section called "Toward a Pedagogy of Whiteness," Giroux states his position.

> Every student needs to feel that they have a personal stake in their racial identity (however fluid, multiple, and unstable), an identity that will allow them to assert a view of political agency in which they can join with diverse groups around a notion of democratic public life that will affirm racial differences. . . .

Where has his color-blind society disappeared to? Will we ever catch sight of common humanity again?

The following essays on black public intellectuals and on the media response to the O. J. Simpson verdict become increasingly mired in arguments about an old racism based on bigotry and a new racism based on fear. In his final sentence, Giroux blames the crisis of democracy in the United States on "intellectual storm troopers spread[ing] their message of hate, greed, and racism through the media and other public forums." Yes, we can surmise whom he's talking about on the Right. But Giroux cannot perceive how his own hackneyed and often misguided writing contributes to the crisis.

Giroux teaches secondary education at a major state university. This book demonstrates that he lacks two essential qualifications for serving that crucial vocation. He displays no awareness of a living past of people, traditions, and institutions that has shaped the present. His references to democracy, capitalism, bourgeoisie, and community are all paper-thin without their historical founding. And, partly because of this absence of the past in his thinking, he does not even suggest that the schools have an essential role to play in opposing the media culture suffocating us and that teachers can impart the excitement of other ways of life in the great treasure house of history. His strongest statement about schools asks us to recognize "the centrality of public education as a site of political struggle." I'm afraid Giroux sees himself as a storm trooper in his position as Waterbury Chair Professor of Secondary Education. He, too, has betrayed an honorable profession by trying to plunge it into a vindictive politics of race without having even a shadow of a program, educational or social, to improve anyone's lot in life.

The ordinary reader who spots *The Schools We Need: Why We Don't Have Them* in a bookstore will find a well-written book with a coherent argument based on history and analysis of ideas. That reader will probably not recognize the name of the author, E. D. Hirsch, Jr., familiar primarily to English professors and professional educators. Neither a shrill denunciation of contemporary education nor a simplistic cure, the book contains probing criticism and the outlines of a new program.

By the third chapter, Hirsch has made his first major point: the eighty-year monopoly of progressive ideas (for example, the project method: teaching the child, not the subject) has failed to improve American education compared to its own past and to other countries. Yet the National Education Association, many dedicated foundations, and education schools continue to promote progressive ideas as the only hope for the future. Based on a Romantic notion of the child learning naturally and discovering things for itself, this set of ideas has deprived American schools of a coherent and demanding curriculum and has sought to produce "independent thinkers" while opposing "rote learning." Hirsch has spent years reading the history of education, mainline twentieth-century publications in the field, and independent research, American and foreign, on the results of different pedagogical approaches. I am convinced by the evidence he marshals in chapter 5 to demonstrate that so-called higher-order thinking cannot be developed separately in students; it relies on a concurrent and constantly growing body of reliable knowledge, of facts. The contrary proposition that one can teach skills without content, though widespread today, can be disproved by its poor results. For most of us, it is counterintuitive, as well. Hirsch takes the time to point out in a separate chapter that standardized tests, though not ideal, are necessary instruments in any modern educational system and can be improved and refined more than is generally acknowledged.

Hirsch's major conclusions sound reasonable, almost pedestrian. Because successful education is cumulative and entails integration of knowledge, skills, and work habits, the curriculum needs to be planned for the entire K–12 sequence in order to make sense and to avoid gaps and repetitions. And, in a more ambitious vision of the role of education, demanding, nonprogressive schools will help most of all the economically and ethnically disadvantaged and will begin to provide an integrated culture and reduce ethnic separatism. Oddly, the weakest aspect of *The Schools We Need* concerns practical suggestions about replacing the reigning progressive doctrines with a less Romantic understanding of the child. Hirsch partially makes up for this flaw by including a "Critical Guide to Educational Terms and Phrases." These thirty pages examine about sixty slogans and weasel words, such as "Drill and kill," "Holistic learning," and "Metacognitive skills." Some of the explanations cannot avoid verging on satire.

But this book has something up its sleeve. Like a manifesto, it implies consequences in the realm of action. Here lies a singular professional story. A professor of English at the University of Virginia, E. D. Hirsch, Jr., abandoned a brilliant career in criticism and critical theory in order to devote himself to English composition and writing. That interest led him into the immense field of cultural literacy, about which he wrote two best-selling books. They explore what forms of school curriculum will favor cultural literacy for all students, especially for the culturally deprived. Because *Cultural Literacy* happened to appear in 1987, at the same time as Allan Bloom's *The Closing of the American Mind*, the two books were sometimes reviewed together. The resentful response among academics to Bloom's philosophic and political conservatism rubbed off on Hirsch and has impeded his movements ever since. But anyone who has read Hirsch attentively and followed his subsequent movements knows that he is driven by an urge to help "children from poor and illiterate homes" achieve the education they need in order to reach their full capacities. He also accepts the irony that conservative educational practices will work best to achieve that goal.

Out of his political and pedagogical convictions, Hirsch has dedicated his own intellectual energies and the proceeds from his books to founding the nonprofit Core Knowledge Foundation. Working quietly and intensely over the past decade, that organization has acted on Hirsch's rethinking of educational practices in accordance with content-based, not progressive, principles. The foundation has drawn up a comprehensive, sequential curriculum, starting at the bottom, for grades K–8. In my estimate, the widely available paperback series *What Your First/Second . . ./Grader Needs to Know* (Delta) represents a major achievement. The volumes offer a practical curriculum already adopted by some four hundred schools in fifty states, a guide to parents wanting to evaluate a school and their child's progress in it, and a demonstration of what could be done nationwide to give direction and higher expectations to primary and secondary education. Our so-called system of education is far less well planned and executed than our system of highways and of mail delivery.

The *Schools We Need* supplies the historical and intellectual foundations for a down-to-earth undertaking to refocus our schools on a demanding curriculum rather than on the idea that young minds will do best discovering knowledge on their own terms and at their own speed. Hirsch doesn't much believe in fanfares and self-promotion. He mentions his own Core Knowledge Foundation only once in the introduction, almost in an aside. But the book and the foundation form a unit in the manner of a campaign platform and a person's record in office. A double educational force is at work that asks for our support. It deserves careful scrutiny from citizens concerned with education. It has strong opponents, yet its effects are being felt. More than any other author I have discussed, Hirsch has a significant influence on the direction in which American education is moving. Many other factors, such as drastic overvaluation of computers and the fear of "cookie cutter schools," may distract us from a sound pedagogy. But *The Schools We Need* and the Core Knowledge curriculum set before us for evaluation and possible adoption a promising departure for our schools. In this domain, we are behind most of the rest of the world.

HAVE THESE FIVE books, separately or together, provided us with anything approaching a middle ground in the culture wars? *Advocacy in the Classroom* does a reasonable job of supplying essential historical background and of representing a wide range of opinion on a controversial topic. But Nelson and Ellis on higher education and Giroux and Hirsch on schools display few points of agreement or even of shared concern. Where Ellis argues for a traditional role for literature in the humanities, Nelson has simply abandoned the field in quest of the "chain reaction" of social revolution. Giroux turns his attention to the media as a proxy or prosthetic form of education and believes that racism represents the major cause of social breakdown. Hirsch says firmly that we should concentrate on the major learning institution we have: schools. Reading his book after I had given my presidential speech to the Association of Literary Scholars and Critics, I was pleased to find in the introduction the following sentence: "I would label myself a political liberal and an educational conservative, or perhaps more accurately, an educational pragmatist."

These five books do not signal any approaching peace in the humanities and literary studies in higher education. But I believe that a potential middle ground about our schools may emerge among those who understand and accept the paradox that conservative educational programs produce enhanced democratic results. And here lies a further challenge to our beliefs. Even more than highways and the postal service, schools represent a large corporate undertaking that requires an important component of central planning. Every individual classroom teacher cannot "write curriculum" according to the current catchphrase. Every local school cannot decide on all its own programs independently of district and state. On the other hand, we associate central planning with uniformity, bureaucracy, and socialism. Can we accommodate the deep-seated opposition?

In the case of our schools, we need to incorporate enough central planning at least in curriculum and assessment to establish general standards of achievement. We also need to resist passive uniformity, creeping bureaucracy, and other abuses of socialism. Recent political events have brought us to a period of constructive turmoil in education. Let us hope that we can block or shape—at least to some extent—the unraveling of disciplines in higher education by improving the curricula and the standards established in our schools.

5

HOW TO READ A BOOK

OULD YOU BUY a book called *How to Read a Book?* Only out
of annoyance, I imagine. In the company of literary scholars,
critics, and writers, we all think we know already how to read.
Otherwise, we'd be professional charlatans. Still, in 1940 tens of thousands
of people bought a book entitled *How to Read a Book,* by Mortimer J. Adler.
It stayed on the best-seller lists for several weeks. Adler wrote in an easy conversational style and promoted good books—even old ones. But he had the
essentials wrong. He believed we should read the way a tyro tours an art
museum: The tyro looks at the label before looking at the painting. Of
course our whole educational system—K plus twelve, plus four, plus even
more—inevitably follows this label-first method. I shall come back to the
basic question of the order of events in reading literature.

On the basis of my own experience and of my investigations in recent
years, I distinguish three kinds or levels of reading. We read for basic comprehension of words and sentences. We read for literary response to the parts
and the whole of a work. And we read for the relations of the work to other
works and to life itself. These tentative categories of reading do not represent
sequential stages. Our response to language may resort to one or all of these
three activities at any stage of learning.

Formal reading begins with the basic association of written word with sounded word—with a notion in the mind—with some phenomenon in the world. Since most of us have forgotten how we learned those initial associations, we understand them probably from having helped a child to read. And in that gradual process we do not usually encounter the excitement that can occur when an illiterate older child or an illiterate adult suddenly grasps the miracle of language. The exemplary case of Helen Keller concentrates into one incident at the water pump the revelation that comes to the rest of us over a period of weeks or months at a much earlier age. We should never forget one fundamental: The comprehension stage of reading is not an empty skill that can be acquired apart from meaningful content. In order to make sense of written language, we cannot just learn a mental trick of association but must also acquire much information about the world we live in.

This first category of reading for comprehension is endlessly debated by all parties, including literary scholars and critics. Almost no one speaks of the third category: how to keep track of and make use of what we read over the years, both as professionals in the field of literature and as individuals seeking to shape a life out of our experience. There exists, however, at least one striking modern essay on how to keep notes on one's reading and how to set up and constantly revise a system of files both in order to give direction to one's professional career and to constitute one's character as a person. "On Intellectual Craftsmanship" was written by C. Wright Mills as an appendix for *The Sociological Imagination* (1959). We all pick up procedures for keeping notes and files as we go along. But despite the number of methodology courses in graduate programs in literature, such basics are rarely discussed. Mills deserves much credit for raising a neglected subject essential for all writers. Intellectual craftsmanship will become even more challenging in the era of electronics and computers.

Another great scholar a century earlier saw fit to speak of these basics near the end of his autobiography.

I may mention that I keep from thirty to forty large portfolios, in cabinets with labelled shelves, into which I can at once put a detached reference or memorandum. I have bought many books and at their ends I make an index of all the facts that concern my work; or, if the book is not my own, write out a separate abstract, and of such abstracts I have a huge drawer full. Before beginning on any subject I look to all the short indexes and make a general and classified index, and by taking the one or more proper portfolios I have all the information collected during my life ready for use.

This account of intellectual craftsmanship comes from Charles Darwin. Most of us are less confident than Darwin that we have a lifetime's reading stored within reach and easily retrievable.

In my third category, then, the unit of reading is not words or sentences or whole works, but the cumulative accomplishments of an entire lifetime that result in the intellectual and moral temper of an educated individual.

After these preliminiaries, I wish to talk primarily about the second category: reading for literary response. As if this were a sermon, I have chosen a quotation from scripture to launch my argument, a quotation that will for now remain unidentified. "It appears to be quite tenable that the function of literature . . . is precisely that it does incite humanity to continue living; that it eases the mind of strain, and feeds it, I mean definitely as *nutrition of impulse.*" I applaud this declaration of literature as having a vital physical presence. The passage states affirmatively what I. A. Richards had discovered to his dismay two years earlier through his "experiment" of having students read unidentified poems and write about them. *Practical Criticism* (1929) reports that the two most serious flaws in student responses were lack of "sensuous apprehension" (12) of sounds and rhythm, and yielding to "stock responses" (14). Going beyond Richards's still-excellent book, the anonymous passage just quoted locates literature in the psychosomatic domain best described by the medical term *cœnesthesia: "cœnesthesia* (sē nis thē ′ sia) n. *med. psychol.* the aggregate of sensations, both external and internal, that gives one the organic awareness of being alive as oneself in the world. The life sense." Every literary author conveys through both style and meaning a particular form of cœnesthesia. Every literary reader registers and responds to that "nutrition of impulse." Literature is, first and foremost, visceral, not merely a matter of ideas arranged in systematic categories. How, then, shall we read if we hope to respond cœnesthetically? Before I answer, it is time to lift the veil. The quotation on living and nutrition of impulse appeared in a 1931 pamphlet entitled *How to Read,* by Ezra Pound.

An essay on reading that I often recommend to students working closely with me is Leo Spitzer's title piece in *Linguistics and Literary History* (1948). In those forty pages, the great philologist declares his love of literature and describes his "to-and-fro" reading, which alternates between noticing details of outward style and discovering "the inward form" of the work. He goes so far as to call it "the method of the 'philological circle' " (25) and then insists that it is a "negation of stages" (26).

Why do I insist that it is impossible to offer the reader a step-by-step rationale to be applied to a work of art? For one reason, that the first step, on which all may hinge, can never be planned: it must already have taken place. This first step is the awareness of having been struck by a detail, followed by a conviction that this detail is connected basically with the work of art; it means that one has made an "observation" . . . that one has been prompted to raise a question—which must find an answer. To begin by omitting this first step must doom any attempt at interpretation. (27)

Spitzer's to-and-fro movement between details noticed and larger insights arrived at amounts to a reciprocating action taking equal account of parts and wholes. Basically, he is telling us that he reads and rereads until something in the words themselves strikes him.

My "circular method" is, in fact, nothing but an expansion of the common practice of "reading books"; reading at its best requires a strange cohabitation in the human mind of two opposite capacities: contemplativity on the one hand and, on the other, a Protean mimeticism. That is to say: an undeflected patience that "stays with" a book until the forces latent in it unleash in us the recreative process. (38)

Spitzer's "method" consists in divesting himself insofar as possible of methods that interfere with direct engagement with the work. We can never read completely innocently, but we can prepare ourselves to listen attentively to a work before we "apply" to it our favorite theories and categories. Even Spitzer persists in an undeviating faith in the unity of a work of literature. But his down-to-earth remarks on how he underlines expressions that strike him "as aberrant from general usage" suggest less the application of a method than the unsystematic exploration and observation of new terrain. He looks and listens first.

Another great description of cœnesthetic reading occupies six intensely written pages near the opening of the "Combray" section in Marcel Proust's *In Search of Lost Time*. Age about twelve or thirteen, Marcel is reading in the heat of the garden. The mature narrator comments carefully on that physical and mental act and emphasizes Marcel's "belief in the philosophical richness and the beauty of the book I was reading."* Those qualities arise in great part because the characters in a book, composed of immaterial words and not of material bodies—that is, of images—can speak directly to our imagination without going through the senses. Proust describes a to-and-fro

---

*Marcel Proust, *A la recherche du temps perdue,* (Paris: Gallimard, 1954, 3 vols.), vol. 1, p. 84. My translations. Future references will be inserted parenthetically.

movement in reading not between parts and wholes but between the transparent inner world of the imagination and the opaque outer world of nature and reality. Marcel's faith in the words under his eyes makes him responsive to their author's stylistic skill: "these landscapes in the book I was reading . . . seemed to me . . . a veritable part of Nature itself, worthy of being studied and explored" (vol. 1, 86). In this inexhaustible novel, the narrator depicts Marcel suspended between the magic world of the imagination and the disappointing world of reality, and constantly moving back and forth between them in a running verification of his being alive—in both worlds.

Finally, 2,500 pages later, Proust produces an explanation for this shuttling and a term to suggest how to live with it. Late in life, after a long absence from Paris, Marcel attends a reception at the Prince de Guermantes's elegant town house. On arrival, Marcel is bowled over by a series of pleasurable involuntary memories of past sensations recurring in the present. But why the pleasure? "Time after time during the course of my life, reality had disappointed me, because at the moment I perceived it, my imagination, the only organ by which I could enjoy beauty, could not reach it, out of submission to the inevitable law that says that one can imagine only what is absent" (vol. 3, 872). The last clause is crucial. The passage goes on to propose that an involuntary memory contrives to locate a sensation between past and present, allowing it to "flicker" *(miroiter)* as if belonging to both. We can now apply that law of absence and the word *miroiter* to the magic of reading. To read a novel is not to escape from reality. The immaterial and therefore absent characters lend themselves to our imagination, which finds in them truth and beauty. At the same time our belief in their reality, reinforced by the powerful style, confers on them a reality that competes with nature itself while nourishing our impulse to continue living. Therefore, reading induces in us a condition of *miroitement* between real and imaginary—a shimmering, a glistening, an iridescence, an alternation, a reciprocation between states of mind belonging to reality and to the imagination.

In the hot Combray garden, Marcel often looks up from his unidentified novel to regard the horizon of the real world around him and to test the one against the other. He imagines a dream woman who loves him introducing him to the fascinating landscapes created in the novel. In these pages, Proust narrates the act of reading in a sensuous, complex episode that takes on the passionate tone of a love scene. Marcel holding his book through the afternoon both loses himself in it and finds himself in it. And we readers, thanks to the cœnesthetic, psychosomatic style of the scene, can also lose ourselves and find ourselves by reading Proust. To find the full effect, of course, one must read these pages—let alone the novel that embeds them—in their entirety.

After these remarks, I shall draw my conclusions in the shape of five rules of thumb addressed as much to myself as to students of literature.

1. Read blind. Ignore who wrote the book and what genre the jacket says it belongs to. Don't take Adler's advice of classifying the book even before you have read it. All books are best treated as anonymous and unclassified until read. In 1678, Madame de Lafayette published *La Princesse de Clèves* anonymously and prefaced it with a note from bookseller to reader. It states that the author will reveal "himself" only if the novel succeeds with the public. For a woman author in the seventeenth century, such a masquerade encouraged an unbiased reading. Today, literary justice at its best still benefits from remaining blind.

2. Read with both eyes open. That is, stereognostically, reciprocally. As we have two eyes in our head, we have in the mind two potential receivers: the *innocent* reader who tries to begin with the simplest, most literal, most direct form of response; and the *experienced* reader, whose alertness and sophistication allow one to read between the lines, to find the smallest hints, even to distrust the voice one hears. With time, many readers learn to perform those two readings almost simultaneously. Spitzer's to-and-fro movement points us in the right direction. There are, of course, special occasions and special works, for which it is best to close one eye and to read with the eye of faith alone or the eye of doubt alone. In general, however, it is best to keep both eyes open—even when you are reading blind.

3. Read cœnesthetically, psychosomatically, with your whole divided being. One definition of literature lies in Pound's sentence on how reading literature incites us to life and nourishes our impulses. (The question of *which* impulses belongs to another discussion.) This principle favors reading aloud whenever possible and acknowledges the physiological effects of reading (the opposite of the affective fallacy). The scene of Marcel reading in the garden opens with an image of evaporation that conveys the yawning abyss of solipsism. However, reading, as Proust presents it, does not push us into that abyss. Reading, with its reciprocating realities of nature and the imaginary, saves us from the abyss of solipsism by its incitement to live both physically and mentally, cœnesthesially.

4.   Take notes and keep files as if your life depended on it. For well it may. You will receive little help on this score. This part of our *craft* may have to remain "do it yourself."

5.   Don't take advice—particularly not about so intimate an activity as reading, and, above all, not from anyone with the presumption to choose the title "How to Read a Book."

6

THE SPIRITUAL IN ART

IN 1986, THE Los Angeles County Museum of Art opened a large
exhibit entitled "The Spiritual in Art: Abstract Painting 1898–1985."
Maurice Tuchman organized the exhibit and edited the magnificent catalog (Abbeville, 1986). Like many complacent easterners, I missed the show,
which moved from Los Angeles to the Museum of Contemporary Art in
Chicago, then to the Haags Gemeentemuseum, The Hague. The New York
art magazines sent their first-line critics and gave it good space.

I'm kicking myself for not having made the pilgrimage. The seventeen
essays and extensive illustrations in the catalog convince me of the significance of the event. It synthesized and illustrated over ten years of scholarship
on the origins of the abstract impulse in modern painting, scholarship that
had remained dispersed until Tuchman assembled its results in a new
museum and in print for all to see. The double event reemphasizes the fact
that painters continue to have insistent, extrapictorial, and sometimes very
weird notions about what they are or should be painting. Tuchman's revisionist thesis, stated in the introduction and elaborated in the other essays,
deserves consideration.

Since the thirties, critics like Alfred J. Barr, Meyer Schapiro, Clement
Greenberg, and Harold Rosenberg have persuaded us to view art since

Impressionism in essentially formalist terms. This preoccupation with design and style, line and color, surface and boundaries overlooks certain aspects of art history.

> The chief issue linking artists in the 1890s, from Paul Gauguin to Sérusier . . . was their conviction that Impressionism lacked ideas and that their role as artists was to reinvigorate painting with meaning. . . . Four leading abstract painters—Wassily Kandinsky, Frantisek Kupka, Piet Mondrian, and Kazimir Malevich—moved toward abstraction through their involvement with spiritual issues and beliefs.

Tuchman and his colleagues insist that these painters and others like Arp and Duchamp developed primarily outside the formal experiments of Cubism (a movement deeply influenced by poetic speculations about the fourth dimension) and devoted themselves intensely to content. Partly because he wrote about his convictions in *Concerning the Spiritual in Art* (1912), a slim book widely translated and read, Kandinsky had the most powerful influence. For years, art historians like Will Grohman and Werner Hofmann ignored Kandinsky's statements. "The artist must have something to say, for his task is not the mastery of form, but the suitability of that form to its content" *(Concerning the Spiritual in Art)*. "Now I knew for certain that the object harmed my paintings. . . . What should replace the missing object? . . . I felt more and more clearly that it is not a question in art of the 'formal' but of an inner wish (= content) which imperatively determines the formal. . . . Thus will mankind be enabled to experience first the spiritual in material objects and later the spiritual in abstract forms" ("Reminiscences," 1913). For Kandinsky, "content" came to mean Theosophy, the ideas of Madame Blavatsky and Rudolf Steiner, and the thought forms of Annie Besant and Charles W. Leadbetter. After a few years, his paintings sank in a pool of symbols inspired by these spiritual systems. Intelligent critics like E. H. Gombrich and Robert Hughes have long been alert to these crosscurrents; Dore Ashton pointed out their presence among American artists in her well-informed *The New York School* (1972). Tuchman and company do not permit us to nod patiently and return to our old ways of thinking.

The catalog of "The Spiritual in Art" makes exciting and tendentious reading. It even contains a measured refutation of its own thesis. Along with several other artists, Richard Diebenkorn received a prospectus of the exhibition and was asked to respond. His reply appears as a long footnote to Tuchman's introduction.

You do refer to the "formal experiments" of Cézanne, Post-Impressionists, and the Cubists as culminating in abstraction and you called it the traditional viewpoint.

But the overall impression I get from your *alternative* interpretation is that you give it all to the mystics and spiritualists in regard to the genesis and development of abstract and non-objective painting. For me, the prospectus shapes up as a kind of refutation of the traditional viewpoint rather than a much needed illumination of the total picture.

My exception is based on the fact that abstract painting was a *formal invention*. Also that major turns or changes in art historical styles are not come by easily, overnight, or by individual artists (another "traditional viewpoint" tells us that Kandinsky invented non-objective painting). What seems to get lost in your prospectus is that the formalist line from Cézanne through Cubism arrived at a point on the threshold of total abstraction wherein it was implicit, and for the most astute artists a clear option. That both Picasso and Matisse at different points in their careers rejected the crucial step is irrelevant. They had come the distance in a difficult and prolonged process of abstracting and simplifying, as did several of their "formalist" peers.

From my view, in about 1910 advanced artists were presented, so to speak, with a vehicle, which in the case of the mystics and spiritualists was made to order for their expressive needs.

This eloquent and intelligent statement calls for two responses. I would say that the exhibition and catalog, going far beyond the prospectus, do furnish what Diebenkorn asks for: an illumination of the role of the spiritual in the formation of abstract art. Furthermore, Picasso's and Matisse's rejection of total abstraction is far from irrelevant. It means that they did not choose to replace figurative images of the visible world with another content entirely—namely, the spiritual. Nor did they choose the art of pure forms and colors and lines without context—a theoretical possibility with few instances, not Mondrian, not even Islamic art. "Nature abhors a vacuum," as I have explained elsewhere at some length (see "Meyer Schapiro's Master Classes" in *The Innocent Eye,* Farrar, Straus & Giroux, 1984).

For a full-scale review of "The Spiritual in Art" catalog I would have many more observations and criticisms. One omission makes the book curiously lopsided. No contributor refers to English art criticism from Pater and Ruskin through Roger Fry and Clive Bell. Bell's *Art* appeared in 1914, two years after Kandinsky's book. " 'Significant form' is the one quality common

to all works of visual art." That sentence from Bell's opening pages, worked
out particularly on Cézanne, has associated Bell with the formalist approach
attacked by Tuchman. But Bell's emphasis falls increasingly on the word *significant.* The third chapter confronts the need, in a formal art presumably
approaching the abstract, for a subject to canalize aesthetic emotion. Bell
finds such a subject not in verisimilitude but in the thing seen in itself; it will
allow us to "become aware of its essential reality, of the God in everything,
of the universal in the particular, of the all-pervading rhythm."

Bell's "metaphysical hypothesis" affirms that significant form in art can
convey these perceptions. By the last chapter, he has surpassed Kandinsky in
proclaiming the spiritual dimensions of art. "Art is a religion. . . . It is an
expression of and a means to states of mind as holy as any men are capable of
experiencing." The added fact that both writers reproduce the Byzantine
San Vitale mosaic of the Empress Theodora to illustrate their use of "form"
suggests that Bell may have seen Kandinsky's book before he finished his
own. Two of the most widely read volumes on art during the years of teeming activity just before World War I insist on a content neither primarily figurative nor primarily formal, but ultimately spiritual.

The Spiritual in Art, the catalog of the 1986 exhibition, redresses an
imbalance in our thinking about abstract art. It also provides Diebenkorn's
dissenting view and a sly report that by 1920 the new art had already been
mocked as "cosmic wallpaper."

> The poets studied in this volume all love the physical world to such
> a degree that they sense within it some transcendent meaning, some
> hovering aura of belief. Roughly speaking, the quest each under-
> takes is to discover that hidden meaning by revealing the "hiero-
> glyphic" nature of the physical universe. (Peter Stitt, *The World's
> Hieroglyphic Beauty: Five American Poets,* 1985)

Stitt's perceptive and well written book came to my attention while I was
reading Tuchman's catalog. Stitt demonstrates the survival of spiritual motifs
and attitudes in Richard Wilbur, William Stafford, Louis Simpson, James
Wright, and Robert Penn Warren. Between them, Tuchman and Stitt deal
with what are essentially the religious beliefs of dozens of modern artists.
Many of the Europeans belonged to a cult or study group. Almost none on
either continent continued in maturity to participate actively in an organized
religion or church. Tuchman and his fellow art historians probe back to Plato
and Plotinus, Cornelius Agrippa and Jakob Böhme, Eliphas Levi and
Madame Blavatsky as sources for the nineteenth-century revival of the spiritual. Stitt's book has no historical or philosophical dimensions at all except
for brief comments on allusions in poems quoted. His five poets seem to float

on an ocean without depths, without a sense of the past. Where Stitt is content to study the poems and interview the living poets in order to find the hieroglyphic nature of their imagination, Tuchman identifies and illustrates "five underlying impulses" out of the occult traditions that recur in the "-spiritual-abstract nexus": cosmic imagery, vibration, synesthesia, duality, and sacred geometry. Are the religious lives of modern poets as limited and as naïve as Stitt paints them? Is it primarily painters who are plunged into a thick solution of spiritual motifs and imagery reaching back to hermetic traditions? Is there any way of connecting these two group portraits? I believe so.

IN THE LAST chapter of *The Great Chain of Being* (1936) A. O. Lovejoy describes how the German idealist philosopher Friedrich W. J. Schelling, pushed hard by his antagonist Jacobi, put forward a thesis on an emergent, evolutionary deity closely linked with this world and nature. This "new mood and temper of religious feeling" occurred forty years before Darwin. "The Platonistic school of the universe was turned upside down," writes Lovejoy, "and . . . the originally complete and immutable Chain of Being had been turned into a Becoming."

Schelling's role in the early nineteenth century reaches far beyond philosophical notions about Godhead. When Madame de Staël came back from her travels and wrote *De l'Allemagne* (1810; seized and banned by Napoléon), she lifted a striking passage out of Schelling without acknowledgment.

The universe is made on the model of the human soul . . . the analogy of each part of the universe to the whole is such that the same idea is reflected constantly from whole to part and part to whole.

These sentences represent one form in which a doctrine as old as Plato's *Timaeus* reenters the bloodstream of Western culture at a moment when poetry was making claims to occupy the function of religion. Spinoza's pantheism is not far away. In such a universal analogy, the spiritual starts a whole new career. Less than twenty years after Madame de Staël's borrowing, the half-cracked poet of political utopias, Charles Fourier, quoted the identical passage (fully acknowledged) in *The New Industrial and Societary Universe* (1829). A few pages later, Fourier sets himself up as the inventor of the analogical method. Hugo, Balzac, and Zola constructed elaborate literary edifices on these and similar foundations of universal correspondence.

Meanwhile, in the United States, another poet was raising his voice.

It is not words only that are emblematic; it is things which are emblematic; . . . It is easily seen that there is nothing lucky or capricious about these analogies, but that they are constant and pervade nature. . . . Because of this radical correspondence between visible things and human thoughts, savages, who have only what is necessary, converse in figures. (1836)

A man is a bundle of relations, a knot of roots, whose flower and fruit is the world. . . . I will now go behind the general statements to explore the reason of this correspondency. (1841)

Thus Emerson states the message in *Nature* and "History." Lecturing a few years later on Swedenborg, a rare hybrid of scientist and mystic, Emerson quoted from *Treatise Concerning Heaven and Hell,* a book he owned. "There is a Correspondence of all things in Heaven with all things in Man. . . . The Universe of heaven . . . resembles a man." Rather than comment I shall go on quoting.

Shortly before his suicide in 1855, Gérard de Nerval composed this credo.

How have I been able to exist for so long outside nature and without identifying with her? Everything lives, everything acts, everything corresponds with everything else; magnetic beams emanating from me or from others traverse unobstructed the infinite chain of created beings. They form a transparent network which covers the world and whose fine threads communicate directly with the planets and the stars. At this moment captive on earth, I can converse with the celestial choir, which participates in my joy and my grief. (*Aurélia,* 1855)

Two years later Baudelaire, who surely knew the Schelling passage along with a whole set of occultist and esoteric writings, published the famous sonnet-manifesto, "Correspondences." A prose version appears in his article on Victor Hugo, where he speaks of "the mystery of life" and "the morality of things."

Those who are not poets cannot understand these things. Fourier turned up one day to reveal to us, much too pompously, the mysteries of *analogy* . . . Swedenborg, who possessed a much greater soul, had already taught us that *the heavens are a vast man;* that everything, form, movement, number, color, perfume, in the *spiritual* as in the *natural* domain, is significant, reciprocal, converse, *corresponding.* . . . Now what is a poet in the largest sense but a translator, a decoder?

There is no end to the citations on the doctrine and the sense of analogy; it has vigorously survived the decline of organized religion. In the opening pages on Symbolism in *Axel's Castle* (1931), Edmund Wilson derives from the Romantic poets and Whitehead a firm personal declaration.

Human feelings and inanimate objects are interdependent and developing together in some fashion of which our traditional notions of laws, of cause and effect, of dualities of mind and matter or of body and soul, can give us no true idea.

I believe that this sweeping and all-pervasive tradition of analogy and correspondence unites and feeds the multiple strands of the spiritual discussed in Tuchman's catalog and what Stitt calls the "hieroglyphic" vision of five American poets.*

Few of us can resist the wish to put the pieces of the world together, and we give lasting recognition to some, like Jesus, Muhammad, and Gandhi, who convinced many others that they could make sense of it all. There is nothing original about saying that the widely held belief among artists and writers in a universal unity represents a survival of religion in secularized form. Few of them would reject any connection at all to spiritual experience. In an interview in Stitt's book, R. P. Warren says what most artists, let alone ordinary citizens, would agree with: "I am a man of religious temperament in the modern world who hasn't got any religion." But in fact he does. He practices religion in a diluted form, which we accept as artistic and literary, a poetic faith without worship or ethics.† It is difficult to say how long analogy alone will sustain and satisfy us.

TWO BROAD QUESTIONS now strike me as unavoidable. Does this vast sense of unity in the universe divide up into kinds or categories that will help us grasp its variety? And where do we find significant criticism of or an opposition to the belief in the connectedness of all things?

I discern three intermingling currents within the broad flow of mental

---

*A special form of analogical commentary within the Christian tradition had developed out of Aquinas and Dante, now referred to as "figurism" or "typology."

†It is worth remarking that Mme. de Staël, the enthusiast in all things, had not given up belief in a Creator and in an ethics based on analogy. The passage quoted earlier continues: "They are no purposeless play of the imagination, these continual metaphors that compare our sentiments to exterior phenomena: sadness with a cloud-covered sky. . . . It amounts to a single thought process of the Creator translating itself into two different languages. Almost all axioms of physics correspond to moral maxims."

activities I have been referring to as the spiritual in art. The first and most obvious expresses in painting and literature a sense of universal analogy and correspondence between physical, mental, and spiritual domains in an all-embracing, gently pulsating organic unity. In modern times, this mystic belief was given new impetus by Böhme in the seventeenth century, power-fully relayed in the work of Schelling and Coleridge, and by Swedenborg in the eighteenth century, whose ideas reached England through Blake and Coleridge and many religious thinkers. The relatedness of all things mani-fests itself in several strong visual images: a sacred geometry of lines travers-ing and linking the entire cosmos; the spiritual edifice or temple of nature; and the crystal. In portraiture and painting of the human figure, the scien-tific principle of physiognomy, the great buzzword of the nineteenth cen-tury, justified the discovery of the essence of things in their appearance. Such a presumed revelation of the interior by the exterior, the principle lodged at the heart of realism in the arts, runs counter to much of human experience. It soon found its ironic sequel in caricature. The new genre had scientific, aesthetic, and political roles to play in the development of both modern art and the modern novel.

Of course, the sense of unity of all things has deep scriptural sources and inspired such sturdy minds as Jonathan Edwards's. Many of his meditations sound like sustained celebrations of the principle of universal correspon-dence.

> Again it is apparent and allowed that there is a great and remarkable analogy in God's works. This is a wonderful resemblance in the effects which God produces, and consentaneity in His manner of working in one thing and another throughout all nature. . . . why is it not reasonable to suppose that He makes the whole as a shadow of the spiritual world. *(Images or Shadows of Divine Things)*

Stitt's book on American poets would benefit greatly from some consid-eration of at least this native background and other historical sources.

The second strand that forms the spiritual tradition displays a different sense of timing. Instead of feeling sure of a permanent overreaching hierar-chy in the universe, a person may experience the world as a quotidian round verging constantly on a meaningless flux. At rare intervals, one may stumble upon a fleeting surge of release and revelation. We talk almost glibly of epiphanies in Joyce and Proust and Woolf. In his 1954 Romanes Lecture, "Moments of Vision," Kenneth Clark speaks of how Millet's remarkable images of hushed communication are heightened by van Gogh's "burning-glass perception." Clark goes on to trace the sentiment of wonder into a sense of possession close to "a morsel of collective experience." Joyce's sentence in *Stephen Hero* describing an epiphany after Aquinas (". . . its soul, its whatness leaps to us from the vestment of its appearance.") sounds like a definition of physiognomy.

Carried to full intensity and conviction, the moment of vision may produce a spectral effect. I am thinking of the aura one finds in painters like Bonnard, Vuillard, Munch, and Kupka. In a long passage on "mythical thinking" in *Language and Myth* (1946), Cassirer makes a startling claim about these moments of "sheer immediacy."

> The spark jumps somehow across, the tension finds release, as the subjective excitement becomes objectified, and confronts the mind as a god or a daemon.

When Cassirer borrows from Usener the term *momentary god* for such an epiphany, he has more company than he thinks. In criticizing the propensities of modern poetry to the pathetic fallacy, Ruskin in *Modern Painters* praises Homer, who "had some feeling about the sea . . . that he calls a god." In Proust's novel, Marcel cannot decipher the signals that seem to be coming from three trees near Hudimesnil and misses a potential privileged moment. Mme. de Villeparisis in the carriage with Marcel says he looks as if he had "failed to recognize a God." Acknowledging Hegel, Barthes paints a portrait of "the ancient Greek [who] perceived in the vegetal or cosmic order a tremendous *shudder* of meaning, to which he gave the name of a god: Pan" *(The Structuralist Activity)*. In these four cases, "god" is the ultimate analogy for analogy.

The best way into the third strand of correspondence is through William James's reflections in 1909, the year before his death, about his much maligned research on psychic and spiritualist phenomena. Confessing to bafflement because of incomplete and often fraudulent evidence, he pauses for a highly personal statement.

> Out of my experience one fixed conclusion dogmatically emerges, that we with our lives are like islands in the sea, or like trees in the forest. . . . The trees also commingle their roots in the darkness underground, and the islands also hang together through the ocean's bottom. Just so there is a continuum of cosmic consciousness, against which our individuality builds but accidental fences, and into which our several minds plunge as into a mother-sea. *(Memories and Studies VIII)*

As an analogy for the yearnings of human consciousness, the ocean is probably as old as the beholding mind itself. Most graduate students today seem to think that Freud invented the "oceanic feeling" (with help from Romain Rolland) in *Civilization and Its Discontents* (1929). R. M. Bucke covered all this ground in a widely read book called *Cosmic Consciousness* (1901). Among contemporary authors, Ionesco has given in *Present Past Past Present* (1971) one of the most lyric and convincing accounts of a moment of boundlessness and euphoria.

These three categories of the spiritual in art—analogy, moments of vision, the oceanic feeling—may represent an order of increasing profundity and intensity. They are also tentative and far from exhaustive. Furthermore, though in most cases I do not question the sincerity of the individual artists or writers who had the experiences, I am aware of many physiological and psychological conditions (from stress and heart flutter to drugs and self-hypnosis) that might induce them. The two great mental poles that divide our thinking, faith and doubt, make room very reluctantly for the interloper that T. H. Huxley named only in 1869: agnosticism.

Let's look briefly at the opposition to the correspondence principle to see if the lines are clearer in that camp. But there's hardly a camp. If one looks up the subject heading "Analogy" in a library, one soon finds that most references are devoted to theology and mathematical analysis. So far as I can ascertain, the range of critical positions in philosophy from skepticism to nihilism expend little effort on attacking analogy as a mode of thought. Many of the greatest figures of the Enlightenment, who, we might expect, would reject such loose methods, attached themselves to devices that functioned as correspondences. Newton believed that space was God's sensorium. Locke had his white paper and his dark room. La Mettrie had his man-machine, Condillac his living statue. The first critical treatment of analogy is probably Kant's attack on Swedenborg in his early work, *Dreams of a Spiritseer* (1766). Then Hume tenaciously scrutinized the notion of "necessary connexion" at the heart of causality, an exercise so corrosive of our whole grasp of reality and meaning that most organized thinking, including science, has simply skirted around Hume and gone on.

Because he confined his complaints to the arts, where violent feelings, he argued, can lead to a kind of "falseness," Ruskin's coinage "pathetic fallacy" has lasted. The phrase implies censure. Though an admirer of Keats, Ruskin had grave reservations about lines like these describing a breaking wave.

> *Down whose green back the short-lived foam, all hoar*
> *Bursts gradual, with a wayward indolence.*
>
> (ENDYMION)

"Wayward indolence" attributed to a fleck of foam on tons of salt water strikes Ruskin as "a perfect example of the modern manner." Homer would have proceeded quite differently, as we have seen. Ruskin's testiness about attributing human qualities to inanimate objects anticipates a whole nihilistic strain in modernism and postmodernism that turns instead to the fragment, the junk yard, discontinuity, and isolation. In an essay called "Nature, Humanism, Tragedy" (1958), Alain Robbe-Grillet calmly carries Ruskin all the way. He takes to task the whole humanist-Christian tradition in its affirmation of a "solidarity" between human beings and the world they live in.

> In literature the experience of this solidarity appears above all as the search, constituted as a system, for analogies.
> A metaphor, for example, is never an innocent figure. To say that time is "capricious" or the mountain "majestic," speak of the "heart" of the forest, of a "pitiless" sun or of a village "snuggled into the hollow of the valley" . . . [all this] is deplorable because it leads to a notion of hidden unity.

We must banish this anthropomorphic principle and face up to "absence of meaning," the emptiness that surrounds us. Robbe-Grillet's unblinking analysis provides the essential background for the commonplaces of twenty years ago—the absurd, nausea, play, chance. They have not abandoned us.

But any vigilant observer knows that the works of Kafka and Beckett, of Arp and Barnett Newman, and of Robbe-Grillet himself are studded with analogies and symbols that shunt us back to the world of human experience, including the spiritual. We have come full circle to Kandinsky's dilemma when he prepared to eliminate objects from his painting, a dilemma raised now to the next power: Without analogies and correspondences and meanings, what can a work of art or literature be about?

HOW WE THINK AT
THE MOVIES

I. A FUNDAMENTAL
QUESTION

On Monday, September 22, 1800, Coleridge wrote William Godwin a characteristically playful and profound letter. He discussed the sentiment of being united with a greater whole, the advisability of baptism for his two infant sons, the Llama's dung pellet, the power of words, and the nature of the conscious will. He concluded the letter with a series of burning questions.

> Is *Thinking* impossible without arbitrary signs? And how far is the word "arbitrary" a misnomer? Are not words, etc., parts and germinations of the plant? And what is the law of their growth? In something of this sort I would endeavour to destroy the old antithesis of Words and Things; elevating, as it were, Words into Things and livings things too.[1]

The letter deserves its reputation. In a few sentences, Coleridge restates the fundamental themes of language theory and his own preferred hypothesis that words belong with things, not by arbitrary or conventional association, but in some organic or natural fashion. He is reviving the position Plato toyed with in the *Cratylus* on "primary names . . . which show the nature of things" by their etymology or their sound. Coleridge's metaphoric plant lies ready to overgrow everything, embracing word, idea, and thing, subject and object, consciousness and what it feeds on. But let's stay with the first barefaced question: "Is *Thinking* impossible without arbitrary signs?"

Sooner or later, we all wonder about the fundamental nature of thought. What supports it? Against what ground do we detect it? Can it ever be distinguished from the self that claims to be its subject and its agent? Since people in the same culture appear to understand one another through a set of linguistic signs that is unique, yet similar to other such sets, does thought at its deepest level observe a set of universal procedures or laws shared by all human minds? In its most mature stages, does human thought take place directly in words?

Being neither linguist nor psychologist, I shall not try to answer all these questions. Nor could I answer them if I were both linguist and psychologist. For we cannot directly observe thought at its source. Memory is no true mirror of the mind. Our verbal accounts of what we observe in other people's behavior and speech are already skewed toward existing categories of language. Introspection, potentially the most fertile source of information about the mind, tends to paralyze or to alter the very processes it would report on. Indirection appears to afford the most reliable approach.

A long history of psychobiological experiments has led lately to alleged discoveries about our two brain hemispheres and how they specialize in certain modes of thought. The investigations resemble the method of locating your opponent's fleet in the fascinating children's game of "Battleship." W.J., the epileptic "cured" by severing his *corpus sallosum,* has provided a mass of alluring revelations about right and left in the mind. But where, in all these strange cleavages and migrations of special powers to one side or the other, does humanity start and animality end? Let us go back once more to Coleridge's question about the relation of thinking to language.

There is much to suggest to us that without language there is no thought—at least no cognitive, discursive thought as it has taken shape in all developed human cultures. To begin with the most simplistic example, consider the familiar pseudojoke (E. M. Forster recorded it) about the old lady on the train. On being accused of illogicality and wandering inconsistency in her conversation, she protests: "How can I tell what I think till I see what I say?" The implication is straightforward: Vague affective rumination does not constitute thought. Verbal utterance alone can shape and certify obscure mental interchanges, which without speech remain subcognitive.

What is often referred to in anthropology and linguistics as the Sapir-

Whorf hypothesis affirms that the language the old lady speaks has shaped her thinking from the start by supplying its categories, distinctions, relations, and modalities. They have all been prepared ahead of time by the culture. We rely on the conventions and commonplaces of language more than we think for ourselves. Sometimes, through clichés and proverbs, the language appears to think for us. A skillful writer may play in and with these ready-mades of speech the way a surfer rides the waves.

Plato was exploring comparable connections between thought and language in the *Theaetetus*.

> The soul when thinking appears to me to be just talking—asking questions of herself and answering them, affirming and denying. And when she has arrived at a decision . . . this is called her opinion. I say that to form an opinion is to speak, and opinion is a word spoken,—I mean to oneself and in silence, not aloud to another.[2]

One of my most vivid childhood memories of semiforbidden experience was hiding behind a door in order to eavesdrop on an eighty-year-old neighbor lady, still spry and lucid, who began to talk aloud to herself nonstop as soon as she thought she was alone. She was a one-woman symposium. Effortlessly tapping the stream of consciousness, she uttered recognizable thoughts (even if fragmentary) about her family and friends, including, occasionally and terrifyingly, *me*. Children playing by themselves will do likewise. The rest of us middle-aged adults have simply learned how to turn down the volume.

It seems probable that the capacity to use language, the most socially useful form of behavior among us after sex, and one of the most flexible and creative, was grafted into the genetic material by natural selection. The extreme position has been taken up by the molecular biologist Jacques Monod. He does not believe that early human societies gradually developed language; on the contrary, he is convinced that the acquisition of language, at first by a few exceptional individuals, decided the future of the species and led to human society and culture as we know them. The relation of language and thought is intimate, Monod declares, because they arose together: ". . . between the cognitive functions and the symbolic language they call forth and by which they express themselves, there exists in modern man a close symbiosis which can be the result only of a long shared evolution."[3] Monod throws the full weight of his Nobel Prize behind these speculations. A few steps more and this line of argument would replace Kant's a priori categories of time, space, and causation with a single all-encompassing category: language, accompanied by its universal grammar of functions and relations. Kant called his categories "transcendental," meaning (as I understand him) that they are innate to our thought processes and mold all our experience, while themselves remaining inaccessible to investigation by those same thought processes. In the hands of thinkers like Monod, language tends to become the preeminent transcendental category of mind, an instrument remarkably well adapted for use on the scale of ordinary human perception and experience. I am compelled to add that on the scale of the infinitesimal and the astronomic, language tends to break down—as Pascal told us it would in his image of the two abysses.

The opposition to this identification of thought with language is strong and widespread. Aristotle, without whom we would probably not be talking as we are today, affirms sturdily that "the soul never thinks without an image."[4] The psychobiologists probing our left and right hemispheres emphasize the wealth of cognitive and useful processes that can take place in the brain apparently unshaped by language. However, the advanced verbal circuitry we call communication simplifies and classifies every surge and signal inside us before it emerges as speech. Can we trust any report, any authority, about the nature of thinking at its source?

Certain testimony may be privileged in the face of such circumstances. In order to explain how he made some of his most original discoveries about light and simultaneity, which led to the theory of relativity, Einstein spoke to Max Wertheimer of combining images, sometimes visual, sometimes muscular: "These thoughts did not come in any verbal formulation. I very rarely think in words at all. A thought comes, and I may try to express it in words afterward."[5]

Emerson probes down to the same level of mental activity. "A man conversing in earnest, if he watch his intellectual processes, will find that a material image more or less luminous arises in his mind, contemporaneous with every thought, which furnishes the vestment of the thought."[6]

Many anthologies of American literature have picked up Ezra Pound's description of how he composed "In a Station of the Metro." "And that evening, as I went home along the Rue Raynouard, I was still trying [to write the poem] and I found, suddenly, the expression. I do not mean that I found the words, but there came an equation . . . not in speech, but in little splotches of color."[7]

The contemporary French poet-critic Henri Meschonnic offers the most succinct formulation: "Creativity is prelinguistic."[8] His statement summarizes the important scientific work of Eric Lenneberg in *The Biological Foundations of Language*. In his superb chapter on "Language and Cognition," Lenneberg argues that conceptualization is fundamental to thought and precedes language. "Words tag the processes by which the species deals cognitively with the environment."[9]

Another persuasive modern work on the question of the fundamental nature of human thought and its relation to language is written by a scientifically trained psychologist turned art critic and historian. Rudolf Arnheim, in a book entitled *Visual Thinking*,[10] maintains that perception and thinking take place in images or articulate shapes that belong to a person's mental life from earliest childhood, long before speech and continuing after its development. Visual thinking favors a continuous field of mental events, whereas language is necessarily cast in a linear succession of preexisting categories. "Purely verbal thinking," writes Arnheim, "is the prototype of thoughtless thinking, the automatic recourse to connections retrieved from storage."[11] Such a tendentious statement underestimates the associative and poetic resources of language. And by its insistence on the visual, the book slights cœnesthesia—the aggregate of all bodily impressions, internal and external, that give us the sentiment of being alive as ourselves. Thinking may well start here. Yet Arnheim displays a steadily perceptive, widely informed mind that is never overwhelmed by the imperialist claims of contemporary linguistics. I recommend his book to anyone concerned with mental processes and with art, and with their consequences for education.

All the positions referred to in this debate, fascinating as they may be, remain speculative. To my mind, the weight of the evidence and, equally important to me, the results of my own introspection favor the second position. Except in certain routine or habitual exchanges, language comes after thought—sorting, binding, tagging, filing away, and finally providing us with miniaturized verbal tokens or claim checks to hold on to or to use. Combined in playful or artful ways, a collection of these tokens can suggest exciting new patterns of thought, quite unpredictable in range and velocity. Yet for all its remarkable achievements, language remains subordinate to the two primary elements, thought and reality, whose incorrigible elusiveness we pursue and try to connect by using language (witness this sentence).

I can do no more than affirm the last statement. I cannot prove it. Nor can the contrary be proved. We have reached the frontier of faith and belief.

If thinking *is* possible without arbitrary signs, then there is a significant conclusion to be drawn. If thinking does not consist in verbal processes, our adaptability as social creatures using a symbolic language rests upon our capacity to *translate*—to transform mental into verbal, and vice versa. I am putting forward an utterly commonplace hypothesis, which may be no more than a metaphor. In a number of languages, particularly in French, the word *translate* is often used in precisely this sense of translating nonverbal experiences into words. Proust, who spent three years wrestling with Ruskin by translating him, comes back regularly to the concept of translation lodged at the inception of thought. It is a refrain, reaffirmed at the climax of *In Search of Lost Time* when the narrator is talking about the insights into style and perception that led him to undertake a novel, this novel, in order to communicate those insights.

If I tried to describe to myself precisely what happens when something makes a strong impression on us . . . I perceived that the essential book, the only true work, is one that a great writer never need invent, as we mean that word, for it exists already in each of us, but must rather translate. The task, the duty of a great writer, is that of a translator.

Not just the writer. It is possible, in the specific domain into which we have ventured, that we could define man as the animal who translates. He translates his preverbal perceptions and impressions, not as the frog does into two alternative behaviors, attack and flight, but into the plastic medium of language, by which he retains, communicates, manipulates, and finally responds to his experience. It is more than a metaphor to say, "All language is (always, already) translation."

II. A HYPOTHESIS

If there is thought before language, we should have a look at the image as its potential medium or vehicle. I shall limit what I have to say on the subject to a modest hypothesis or historical speculation. The inventors of photography (ca. 1840) and of the moving picture (ca. 1900) have influenced our use and abuse of images in ways we are probably still unaware of. One comparison will afford us insight into how we have steered or yielded to this process. In the past hundred years, two major art forms in the West have followed what appear to be opposite courses. From Impressionism to Jackson Pollock, the still image in painting moved generally away from figuration and illustration (and from subjects adequately described by verbal titles) toward the direct rendering or exploration of inner and affective experience. In an essay in *The Innocent Eye,* I have traced the successive steps of this evolution through the extended career of Monet, who was active until 1926.[13] A number of prominent exceptions (Morandi, Magritte, Duchamp) do not invalidate the overall tendency to liberate the painted surface from the conventions of visual perception, a tendency that may well have reached its limit.

During approximately the same period, the moving image (film and television) moved away from the potential freedom of silent film (what René Clair called "pure cinema": the invention of visual and rhythmic sequences outside the narrative structures of theater and novel) toward sound film anchored in a written script usually adapted from a play or novel.[14] An unprepared audience today does not know what to make of Clair's *Entr'acte* (1924), a silent film improvised around a series of jagged images scrawled by the painter-poet Picabia. The twenty-two-minute work suggests a *danse macabre* motif soon exploded by wild juxtapositions; Clair does not follow a narrative line. He exploits a total freedom of montage to create the sensation of dilated and contracted time, multiple points of view, and childish jokes. I find the film as suggestive and as exhilarating as the best action painting and not unrelated to it. This expressionist dimension of film has now gone mostly underground into experimental cinema, except where it has resurfaced in beautiful and enigmatic sequences in films like *2001* (Kubrick) and *Last Year at Marienbad* (Resnais, script by Robbe-Grillet).

One of the consequences of this opposed evolution of painting and moving pictures in our time is that films and television programs can be seen as twice translated, twice removed from elemental and unarticulated thought processes, rather than seeking them at their source. When Gothic architecture opened huge spaces in its walls for windows, the new art of stained glass was quickly harnessed to illustrating Bible stories and the lives of saints. It developed its own imaginative nonfigurative forms only in the margins and interstices—and in a few glorious rose windows. Somewhat in the same way, film has been set to illustrating literary narratives or dramas rather than to inventing its own forms. Would we want it otherwise? A greater familiarity with the variety of the early silent film might modify some of our habits and expectations. Still, narrative plot or story remains the most universal mode of organizing human experience, and what we see on the screen is usually an illustrated story in which pictures take over from words.

Of all artists, Flaubert has expressed the strongest objections to the practice of illustrating books.

> Never, as long as I live, shall I allow anyone to illustrate me, because: the most beautiful literary description is eaten up by the most wretched drawing. As soon as a figure is fixed by the pencil, it loses that character of generality, that harmony with a thousand known objects which make the reader say: "I've seen that" or "That must be so." A woman in a drawing looks like one woman, that's all. The idea is closed, complete, and every sentence becomes useless, whereas a written woman makes one dream of a thousand women. Therefore, since this is a question of aesthetics, I absolutely refuse any kind of illustration.[15]

It was not the quality of the illustrations that enraged Flaubert. He felt in his bones the contaminating, paralyzing effect that any particularized image can have on the suggestiveness of the word. An image short-circuits the reader's imagination and prevents him from conjuring up a character or a scene out of his own associations and fantasies. Flaubert's outburst insists that the novel mirrors not nature but words—words that, in turn, evoke a special universe of virtual entities and events. He provides a needed gloss on Conrad's words in the preface to *The Nigger of the Narcissus:* "My task . . . is before all to make you see." A novel presents something deeper than visual images; it assembles laminations and overlappings and dissociations of thought that do not coincide with any simple sensation of sight or sound.

One can imagine Flaubert protesting even more vehemently against the translation or illustration of his work in *moving* pictures. Existing adaptations of *Madame Bovary,* even Renoir's, would bear him out. But I quote Flaubert's harangue because after early filmmakers like Clair, one discovers singularly few directors and critics on the cinematic side resisting the role of film as illustrating or adapting literary scripts. Almost everyone takes it for granted that a writer supplies the story for a film, even if the writer is the director's alter ego as auteur. Antonioni and Godard, though steeped in literature, have kept open only a precarious and erratic space for the nonnarrative film. The affinities of the medium with poetry and music may have to evolve in the interstices—dream sequences, flashbacks, inserts, and jokes. On the other hand, film may have reached a limit in the direction of adaptation and representation, as painting may have reached a limit in the direction of nonrepresentation.

III. MORE QUESTIONS

Beyond all fluctuations of style and fashion, I take it that sound films and TV programs based on narrative scripts are here to stay. In the course of time, we will mold them to our tastes, and the medium will mold us. At this juncture, I wish to raise a number of nagging questions that bear on how these forms affect our minds and behavior.

1. Are film and TV essentially the same medium? Most judicious critics would answer that the large size of the screen, the darkness of a movie house, the relative freedom from interruptions, and the presence of a sizable silent, and anonymous, audience give film viewing a far different texture from that of watching television in the home. These considerations have tended to make TV programs more auditory and less visual than the movies. With soap opera and the news, you can usually turn off the image with less loss than that of turning off the sound. Video remains an illustration of audio, of words.

To these not very startling observations, I would add one more. I have long been unconvinced by Bertolt Brecht's attempt to introduce into the theater a *Verfremdungseffekt,* a distancing of spectators from the stage activities by various devices in order to encourage them to reflect on the significance of what they are watching. Aristotle had a surer sense of the theater setting when he described our double fixation in terms of pity and terror. Breaking the illusion will not hold a large audience for long, and it does not explain the power of a few of Brecht's plays. On the other hand, the distancing or estranging effect is surprisingly appropriate for television, a medium that lends itself to a certain separation between spectator and screen. Watching a TV set at home among family and friends usually entails interruptions that override the program or tape, informal heckling and discussion, even turning back a tape to see what really happened. The television situation has the advantage of divesting the movie image of its opulence and its magic inviolability. Except for a few call-in shows, however, television programs have made few attempts to encourage reflective or critical reactions on the part of viewers.

2. Has sound film finally broken up the big estates handed out by Lessing to word, as the medium of narrative, and to image, as the medium of representation? Flaubert would roar back the answer that a sound film, in attempting a complete representation, constitutes a total travesty of a novel and a denial of literature. We could also reply that a sound film achieves a new synthesis of narrative and descriptive, a four-dimensional work of art that Lessing never imagined in the *Laocoön.*

Filmmakers and critics of the first rank have the strongest statements to make. In 1932, Sergei Eisenstein remarked on "the inner murmurings" in Dreiser's novels and went on: "The true material for the sound film is, of course, the monologue."[16] Few of us would swallow the "of course," and we have serious reservations about the lengthy voice-over sequences that film monologue usually employs. André Bazin, discussing Bresson's form of pure cinema, goes a step further. "The screen emptied of images and given back to literature marks the triumph of cinematographic realism."[17] Both statements imply that in sound film, word will one day subdue image and appear to welcome that development even though much of both men's work affirms the priority of image over sound.

These conclusions arise in part because the moving image, with or without sound, introduces an element absent from the still image and even from prose: strictly measured and manipulated time. As a result, film has relations to dance, music, and poetry, which are constantly luring it away from narrative prose and drama. I find myself wondering when we shall enter a new era of classical practice and find another Lessing to describe it. Not soon.

3. As an art form that to a large degree represents visible, material reality, has film developed adequate conventions of acting, cinematography, and

editing to convey abstract ideas, inner states of mind, past and future tenses, and the first person? Since we follow most films without too much difficulty, the question is not often raised. Critics speak of a narrative style of *découpage classique* developed in Hollywood during the thirties and forties, when our conventions of shooting and editing were laid down. But the conventions remain elementary and provisional.[18] What does a dissolve signify: Fantasy? Memory? Passage of time? Can one construct a negative shot like a negative sentence? Unlike language, film has no established vocabulary, syntax, or punctuation. How do you convey *yesterday* or *possibly* in images? Compared to the novelist, the director begins virtually ex nihilo.

Half a century ago, Kuleshov performed a series of experiments to demonstrate the enormous flexibility of film editing. He placed at the center of three very different sequences the identical close-up of an actor with an intense yet neutral expression. Viewers unanimously praised the convincing way in which the actor expressed the emotion appropriate to each of the three sequences: hunger, grief, joy. We may laugh at the mistake, but the suggestiveness of deadpan acting has not gone away. Every film must reinvent the conventions. You cannot be sure whether the cowboy dressed in black is the hero or the villain. There is no dictionary.

In his famous *Camera-Pen* manifesto (*L'Ecran français,* March 30, 1948), Alexandre Astruc asserts that "it will soon be possible to write ideas directly on film."[19] He refers to Eisenstein's thoughts of shooting or at least illustrating Marx's *Das Kapital.* Fortunately, we are still waiting. Film is better off without any worldwide code for concepts like *economy, justice, working class.* Because moving pictures are not the medium of ordinary communication, but potential works of art, we expect and accept in a film less cliché than we do in words. A film, no matter how closely it may record the quotidian, leans toward revelation, the marvelous, neologism. Let us hope it keeps that freedom.[20]

4. Who is more active mentally, a novel reader or a film viewer? Presumably, Flaubert would vote for the reader, who must continually transform words into images. Both Eisenstein and Bazin argue strongly for the film viewer and disagree completely about the reasons.

Eisenstein insists that "montage technique obliges spectators themselves to create."[21] He is thinking of the Kuleshov effect just described. Bazin argues that depth of focus in the extended shot *(plan séquence)* encourages "a more active mental attitude on the part of the spectator and even his positive contribution to the *mise en scène.*"[22] According to Bazin, in an uncut sequence, we can choose what to look at, whereas dynamic editing manipulates our attention and overwhelms our thought processes. Of course, all three men are right, and we will keep on going to movies and reading.[23]

The movies, which have so far remained remarkably free of settled conventions and codes, will help us reflect about Coleridge's question whether thinking is possible without language. Despite their modest appearance, speech and reading represent the primary miracles of system and economy in human communication. At their best, moving pictures offer us quite different elements: the concrete evidence of documentary, the passive incontrovertibility of dream, and the creative leaps—visual and aural—of the imagination.

NOTES

1. *Collected Letters of Samuel Taylor Coleridge,* ed. Earl Leslie Griggs (Oxford: Clarendon Press, 1956), vol. I, pp. 352–353.

2. Plato, *Theaetetus,* trans. Benjamin Jowett (New York: Random House, 1937), vol. 1, p. 193.

3. Jacques Monod, *Le Hasard et la nécessité* (Paris: Seuil, 1970), p. 150.

4. Aristotle, *On the Soul,* in *The Works of Aristotle,* ed. W. D. Ross (Oxford: Clarendon Press, 1931), vol. 3, 431a.

5. Max Wertheimer, *Productive Thinking* (New York: Harper, 1959), p. 228. See also Albert Einstein, "Letter to Jacques Hadamard," reprinted in Brewster Ghiselin, ed., *The Creative Process: A Symposium* (New York: New American Library, 1955), pp. 43–44.

6. Ralph Waldo Emerson, *Nature, IV.*

7. Ezra Pound, *Gaudier-Brzeska: A Memoir* (New York: New Directions, 1970 [1916]), p. 87. In this autobiographical discussion of the image in poetry, Pound twice refers to Kandinsky's *Concerning the Spiritual in Art* (1912) and to "the language of form and colour."

8. Henri Meschonnic, *Pour la poésie* (Paris: Gallimard, 1970), p. 115.

9. Eric Lenneberg, *The Biological Foundations of Language* (New York: Wiley, 1967), p. 334.

10. Rudolf Arnheim, *Visual Thinking* (Berkeley: University of California Press, 1969).

11. Ibid, p. 231.

12. Marcel Proust, *A la recherche du temps perdu* (Paris: Gallimard, 1954), vol. 3, p. 890.

13. "Claude Monet: Approaching the Abyss," in Roger Shattuck, *The Innocent Eye* (New York: Farrar, Straus & Giroux, 1984), pp. 269–290.

14. One of the most notable aspects of film as an art form is that we have access to its entire history, including its earliest origins. The Lascaux of the movies lies in the Lumière brothers' program of shorts projected in a Paris café in December 1895. We know with what awe the first audiences reacted to the ghostly flickerings and how insistently they peeked behind the sheet to discover the secret. The lessons of those early days about perception and vision, reality and fantasy, are too often forgotten, overlooked even in film courses. We will never know the origins of storytelling and of picture making; we should learn everything we can about the first revealing steps of the one art form that belongs to our age.

15. Gustave Flaubert to Ernest Duplan, June 12, 1862, in *Ouvres complètes: Correspondence* (Paris: Conard, 1929), vol. 5, pp. 25–26. In 1915, Franz Kafka felt an equally forceful revulsion to a proposal to illustrate the first edition of *The Metamorphosis*. "Please, not that—anything but that! The insect itself cannot be drawn. It cannot even be shown in the distance!" In a 1984 article, the painter Robert Motherwell discusses Kafka's reaction and proposes that an "identical" aversion to explicit illustration and to realist imagery contributed to the nonrepresentational art of Abstract Expressionism in the mid-forties (see Robert Motherwell, "Kafka's Visual Recoil: A Note," *Partisan Review*, no. 4, 1984). Motherwell's observations lead me to suggest that he and the other Abstract Expressionists may have been avoiding representation also in order to resist the stereotyped verbalization to which it lends itself. They favored visual thinking without words or arbitrary signs.

16. Sergei Eisenstein, *Film Form* (New York: Harcourt, Brace, 1949), p. 106.

17. André Bazin, *Qu'est-ce que le cinéma* (Paris: Cerf, 1975), p. 124.

18. The old clichés can now appear only as clichés: an ocean sunset, the wind turning the pages of a calendar. But why, at the close of every movie, do we still look, with diminishing success, for the words *The End*.

19. Alexandre Astruc, "Naissance d'une nouvelle avant-garde: la caméra-style," *L'Ecran français*, March 30, 1948.

20. I recommend three discussions of this prickly question of film and language: Christian Metz, "Le cinéma: langue ou langage?" in *Essais sur la signification au cinéma* (Paris: Klincksieck, 1971); M.-C. Ropars-Wuilleumier,

De la littérature au cinéma (Paris: Colin, 1970); and Bruce F. Kawin, *Mindscreen* (Princeton, New Jersey: Princeton University Press, 1978).

21. Sergei Eisenstein, *Film Sense* (New York: Harcourt, Brace, 1947), p. 35.

22. Bazin, "L'Evolution du langage cinématographique," in *Qu'est-ce que le cinéma,* op. cit., p. 75.

23. One must never omit from this discussion the powerful yet elusive factor represented by the habits of alertness and attention the viewer has acquired. One may sit back and expect the sound-image simply to flow through one, to take over one's mind. Or one may sit up and watch the effects and sequences carefully and critically. One may even try to do both at once. Most of us require at least two screenings to perceive the subtleties and implications of an intelligent movie.

8

LIFE BEFORE LANGUAGE:
NATHALIE SARRAUTE

MONG THE GREAT women of French letters in the twentieth century, including Simone de Beauvoir, Marguerite Duras, and Marguerite Yourcenar, Nathalie Sarraute has devoted herself the most
single-mindedly to refining and extending the novel as an instrument of
exploration. Since the appearance in 1939 of her first book of prose pieces,
Tropismes, Mme. Sarraute has published eight novels, the earliest of them
with a glowing preface by Sartre. A short book of literary essays, *The Age of
Suspicion* (1956), and a number of radio and stage plays have not distracted
her from her steady purpose to seek out the most delicate of impressions that
lie in the unnamed corners of consciousness.

Written just as Mme. Sarraute entered her eighties, *Childhood* recounts
her early years up to the eve of World War I (she was born in 1902) in a style
closely tied to that of her novels. She has constructed it more scenically than
narratively out of seventy-one short vignettes. They capture finely shaded
details of place and person as well as the feelings of a precocious child torn
between divorced parents and their two homes. In these beautifully paced
pages, the reader can watch a literary sensibility hunting persistently for that
most ridiculed of literary prizes: the truth—about what happened, particularly to ourselves. Barbara Wright's translation serves the original almost
flawlessly.

Before I examine the form in which Mme. Sarraute has cast these recol-lections, I wish to settle a score with literary journalism before it hardens into literary history. In the mid-1950s Mme. Sarraute became associated with a group of writers fifteen to twenty years her junior. Like Mme. Sar-raute, Claude Simon, Alain Robbe-Grillet, and Michel Butor had begun to abandon the traditional novel, with its well-made plot, fully rounded char-acters, and psychological analysis. Seeking a new literary school to replace existentialism, journalists pasted on the works of these writers the unimagi-native label "the New Novel." At a 1971 symposium in Cerisy on "the New Novel," Mme. Sarraute, who was unmistakably reluctant about the whole enterprise, had this to say about the effects of language on an incipient feel-ing: "Scarcely does this formless thing, all timid and trembling, try to show its face than all powerful language, always ready to intervene so as to re-establish order—its own order—jumps on it and crushes it."

In the ensuing discussion, the champions of the New Novel as a coher-ent and tendentious movement tried to close in on Mme. Sarraute. The cen-tral exchange was between Mme. Sarraute and Alain Robbe-Grillet.

NATHALIE SARRAUTE: There is always a kind of drying out pro-duced by language. . . . For me . . . there is something prior to lan-guage: a sensation, a perception, something in search of its language, which cannot exist without language.

ALAIN ROBBE-GRILLET: There are two fundamentally different positions for the writer facing the world. One kind of artist comes into a world that already exists and about which he will say some-thing; the other comes into a world that does not yet exist and which he will create through his own language. . . . I feel that what interests you in your novel is the creation of a world that doesn't yet exist.

N.S.: Yes, but that world is created out of what? Not completely out of language.

A.R.G.: In the beginning was the word.

Everything turns on the "something" that exists apart from language, which Robbe-Grillet rejects and Mme. Sarraute cherishes. In the seventies the New Novel came increasingly to represent a semidoctrinal position affirming language as supreme, autonomous, needing no referential connec-tion to a "real" (that is, bourgeois) world either outside or inside the self. Since Mme. Sarraute never subscribed to that key position, she should not be routinely associated with the New Novel any more than Beckett, the other great outrider of the contemporary French novel. In the above exchange, Mme. Sarraute's quiet affirmation of something prior to language represents an act of considerable independence and courage.

Essentially, Mme. Sarraute seeks out the first tender shoots of our mental life—more evolved than the undifferentiated static that fluctuates during every living moment, but not yet so conscious that it gets caught and stifled in the rough net of conventional language. As a result, all her novels alternate between clumsy pregnant silences and the impasse of freeze-dried clichés.

This alternation also characterizes the mood and style of *Childhood* and shapes its vignettes. Time after time, a section hinges on a commonplace expression that crashes into a young girl's consciousness and becomes the burden of her existence. "If you touch one of those poles, you'll die," her mother says as they walk along a country road strung with telegraph lines. It's an early version of fate, nearly an oracle. A man friend of her mother looks at the child's juvenile copybook novel and says, "Anyone who sets out to write a novel should first learn to spell." Her baby half sister's nurse says, "What a tragedy to have no mother"; afterward nothing will expunge the word *tragedy*. In Russian, her stepmother says, *"Tyebya podbrossili* [They have abandoned you.]."

SEVERAL SECTIONS BEGIN with such an arresting expression and patiently try to worm their way around the verbal-mental block it created in the child. Others open in an intermediate realm of the child's floating perceptions and suddenly come aground on the shoal of unfeeling words thoughtlessly uttered by adults. Sometimes these scenes carry a wistfully comic flavor, or at least a glimpse of precocious gallows humor. Mme. Sarraute's consistent and sensitive attitude toward language lends a strong unity to her work and approaches that of a troubled poet like Rilke or Mallarmé—speech as both essential and unbearable.

The comic in these unassuming memories almost disappears behind the gradual crescendo of sorrow and self-protection. Nathalie Sarraute's earliest memories of herself as Natasha Tcherniak concern her awkward, often painful shuttlings between the domiciles of her Russian parents, divorced soon after her birth and both remarried, and between Russia and Paris, where Natasha's father takes up permanent residence when Natasha is eight years old. When Natasha is eleven, her mother comes from St. Petersburg to see her in Paris after a two-year interval and cannot bear the fact that the day after her arrival Natasha chooses to visit Versailles with her stepmother rather than stay with her. Cancelling a planned month's visit, the mother leaves the next day and writes to the father: "I congratulate you, you have

managed to turn Natasha into a monster of egotism. I leave her to you."
Then, without comment, we are told the unanticipated sequel. The enraged
father shows this shattering letter to Natasha herself. During these difficult
years, Vera, Natasha's moody and well-meaning stepmother, cannot help
favoring her own daughter. The father rarely overcomes his shyness. Only a
step-grandmother on an extended visit from Russia offers Natasha the full
range of family love and care.

From an early age, Natasha has been aware of the inappropriate singu-
larity of what she calls "my ideas"—tremors that grow from a low muttering
in her mind into uncontrollable eruptions of word or deed. Disenchanted
with her mother's beauty, Natasha gets the idea that her mother's "skin is like
a monkey's" and finally blurts it out to her. Later, she tells her stepmother,
Vera, what she overheard an uncle say—that Vera is "stupid." Another time,
she asks her point-blank, "Do you hate me?" An infantile form of the
demonic seems to drive her, like a character out of Dostoevsky. But Natasha
tries hard to master her demon and sometimes believes she has succeeded.
Childhood can be read as the story of the formation of a will, though I cannot recall the word being mentioned.

Next to the sorrows of separation and the vagaries of a young will, the
third and late-arriving element in these memories is Natasha's shift from
racial innocence as a good little French child like all others in school to an
awareness of her Slavic Jewish ancestry. It comes as a quiet revelation, not as
an immediate social problem, after she goes to Mass with her governess and
then listens to her freethinking father.

The activity that sustains Natasha through these trials is her schoolwork.
For her, the highly structured system of learning and reciting and writing
brings the condition she has previously lacked: security. "Laws, which everyone has to respect, protect me." They protect her from the disappointments
of "our love," which her absent, indifferent mother insists on in her letters.
They allow her to earn the solicitude of her teachers. Her father reads her
essays attentively yet distantly; Natasha does not yearn for encouragement.
"There is never even the remotest suggestion . . . the idea never even . . . of
any 'gift for writing' . . . nothing is farther . . ." (The ellipses belong to Mme.
Sarraute and supply a major part of the book's punctuation, like Emily
Dickinson's dashes.) The topic assigned for the essay discussed in this chap-
ter is "My First Sorrow." Soon we will learn why the book stops when
Natasha is fourteen:

> It may be because I feel that this, for me, is where my childhood
> ends . . . when I look at what is facing me from now on what I see is
> something like an enormous, very congested, very well-lit space. . . .

I couldn't go on making the effort to conjure up a few moments, a few movements, that I feel are still intact, still strong enough to emerge from the protective cover they are preserved under, from those soft, whitish, cloudy layers which dissipate, which disappear with childhood.

I doubt that these last words of the book will have a sequel. The low-keyed form of *Childhood* affords it the double quality of directness and reflectiveness. Mme. Sarraute accepts without distress the fragmentary nature of her memories. She has probably made some adjustments; any probe disturbs the circumstances being probed. Events follow a loosely chronological order with enough cross-references to keep us alert. These short sections move at an almost respiratory pace that may be in part attributable to the steady weaving of the verb tenses between present and past. That oscillation springs directly from another feature of the form.

By an evidently careful decision, Mme. Sarraute has created for herself and out of herself in *Childhood* an interlocutor, an alter ego who addresses her as *tu,* questions her motives and her credibility, supplies alternative explanations, and goads her to undertake the project. The opening pages present a playful dialogue between one voice for Natasha-Nathalie, child protagonist grafted onto adult narrator, and another voice for the interlocutor-author who doubts and coaxes and also tends to push her literary effects too hard.

[Interlocutor-Author]: Is that true? Have you really not forgotten what it was like there? How everything there fluctuates, alters, escapes . . . you grope your way along, forever, never finding, ... towards what? Where? No matter where, so long as it eventually finds some fertile ground where it can develop, where it can perhaps manage to live . . . my goodness, just thinking about it . . .
[Natasha-Nathalie]: Yes, it makes you grandiloquent. I would even say presumptuous.

It sounds like a gentle mocking of her own novels. We are in good hands, a long way from the spectacular intellectual surfing of Sartre's autobiography, *Words,* traversing large expanses of time organized by *le passé simple,* and also a long way from the poised self-deprecation of *Barthes on Barthes,* another contemporary French autobiography.

I have not yet put my finger on the particular quality I find in *Childhood.* In Antonioni's film *Blow-Up,* the photographer enlarges his cryptic pictures in order to discover clues in the shrubbery. But blown up beyond a critical point of graininess, the photographs no longer yield any visual content that can be assembled and recognized as reality. This paradox of magnification relates to the writer's dilemma. The scale on which *Childhood* is written brings the reader miraculously close to the texture of life the way a child, precariously balanced between two parents, two countries, might experience it. But when you approach so close, language no longer serves adequately to record the observations; it seems to obliterate the very thing it is meant to designate. Still tiny, sitting on a park bench between her father and an alluring young woman of uncertain status, Natasha Tcherniak has just heard a tale from Hans Christian Andersen. Nathalie Sarraute, remembering the moment and operating inside the same "I" as the child Natasha, cannot accept the words *happiness* or *ecstasy* to describe Natasha's feelings, not even the simple word *joy*. Such words

> cannot gather up what fills me, brims over in me, disperses, dissolves, melts into the pink bricks, the blossom-covered espaliers, the lawn, the pink and white petals, the air vibrating with barely perceptible tremors, with waves . . . waves of life, quite simply of life, what other word? . . . I am inside them with nothing else, nothing that does not belong to them, nothing that belongs to me.

The passage, like all of *Childhood*, records a prolonged probing toward language whose full realization would bring everything to a standstill. Some say the French novel will never recover its greatness without finding great subjects. Nathalie Sarraute says in her quiet voice that a form of greatness lurks in remote twinges, in interior moments, where we rarely look for it.

9

SECOND THOUGHTS ON
A WOODEN HORSE:
MICHEL FOUCAULT

*"Let us be content with provoking second thoughts
and not worry about convincing anyone."*
—GEORGES BRAQUE, *CAHIERS*

THE CHAPTER THAT *follows was read in April 1994 to a fairly large,
mixed, and (I thought) inscrutable audience at the New School in New
York City. Five of us formed a panel to discuss James Miller's* The Passion of Michel Foucault *on the occasion of its appearance in a paperback edition.* To my amazement, the board of trustees of the New School had been
invited to attend the event. Few of the trustees—mostly New York business and
professional figures—knew anything about Foucault. Two were carrying Miller's
book under their arm and seemed all the more perplexed for having read a few
pages. I doubt that their perplexity was much dispelled by the end of the evening.
After David Halperin read a page from one of Foucault's books, two members of
the audience asked what the passage was about. The discussion following our
statements revealed that few members of the audience understood the extent of
Foucault's influence on certain segments of intellectual life, particularly in universities, and the significance of that influence.*

*Across the United States, departments of sociology, philosophy, and literature
are still offering courses on Foucault. One recent advertisement for such a course
carried a slogan that makes me wonder what goes on in some classrooms: "Take*

---

*The panel consisted of James Miller, presiding, David Halperin, Janice Sawicki, Steven Sei-
dman, and Roger Shattuck.

this course. Get a life. " *Miller's book has been attacked from all sides because it breaks the code of silence about Foucault's personal life and its close relation to his philosophy and politics. For the same reason, I welcome Miller's book—with certain reservations.*

A F T E R   Q U I T E   A few youthful years of geographic and intellectual wandering, I finally began steady work as a teacher of modern French literature. That field brought me into contact very early with the work of Michel Foucault in the original French. Before the end of the sixties, I had read both *Histoire de la folie* (1961) and *Les Mots et les choses* (1966). The strenuously paradoxical *pensée* of Pascal that opens the first and the discussion of Borges's taxonomies and Velázquez's *Las Meninas* that opens the second seemed to be intellectual siren songs directed at me personally. The social construction of madness during the Great Confinement of the insane following the decline of leprosy struck me as incontrovertible; I did not know then that Foucault's chronology and interpretation are highly speculative. He also talks intelligently about *Rameau's Nephew*. And in *The Order of Things,* he has startling things to say about Don Quijote and about Port Royal grammarians. Twice I succumbed—and twice I drew back. For, barely ten years earlier, I had gone through the same infatuation—over Sartre. *Being and Nothingness* had inoculated me. I recovered from Foucault in time to see around his brilliance and to discover his disabling weaknesses and his immense debt to Nietzsche. Many of you have done so for yourselves, I trust.

Foucault writes in cantata style. It is not necessary to understand the words and sentences in order to be swept up by the intellectual song. Dr. Johnson wrote that men are very prone to believe what they do not understand. Foucault has the knack of evasive language. I shall cite three examples. His historical argument in book after book rests on his notion of *episteme,* a Greek borrowing, meaning the network of mental and cultural conditions dominant in a period. The *episteme* supposedly produces the thought of the period. Carefully scrutinized, *episteme* reveals itself as a recostumed version of the Hegelian *Zeitgeist*—the fully discredited idea of History personified as an agent.

Foucault also increasingly exploits the ambiguity in French—lost in English—of the word *représenter.* It can mean "to represent by imitation or by signs," and it can mean "to act out or practice." "The duty to represent one's most furious desires" *(The Order of Things)* also means "The duty to act out one's most furious desires." *Discourse,* a term popularized by Foucault, among others, comes to mean not linguistic communication produced by human beings or authors but the spontaneous generation of meaning in language without attribution to an author and without distinctions of literary genre. Presumably the *episteme* itself produces all our discourse and responds to it. Writers and readers are an illusion obstructing the free proliferation of meaning. (See the essay "What Is an Author?") Do we wish to honor this legerdemain?

Finally, I began to be troubled not only by Foucault's flashy vocabulary but also by other problems, such as his contradictions. He borrows one of his principal mottoes from Pindar via Nietzsche: To Become the Thing One Is (see Miller, 68–69). Yet in the course of time, this forceful claim to personal integrity has been turned 180 degrees into a very different message. "One writes to become something other than who one is," Foucault states in a 1983 interview on Raymond Roussel. In *The Uses of Pleasure* (1985), he advocates the kind of curiosity "that permits one to get free of oneself." Consistency may be the hobgoblin of little minds, but on such a fundamental shift one expects some explanation from a professional philosopher. My own work on the case of the Wild Boy of Aveyron revealed to me how tendentious Foucault's history of psychiatry is for the early years at the opening of the nineteenth century. For he treats the institution of the asylum as a cruel technology of power and dismisses the strong philanthropic and humanitarian motives that drove Pinel and Tuke to develop a "moral treatment" of the insane that recognizes their humanity. Foucault's attempt to establish a new periodization, bringing the classical era to a close only in 1800, serves to eliminate the Enlightenment and to reinforce another maneuver I shall discuss at the end.

So in the seventies, I read no more Foucault. There were far more important writers to deal with—Proust, for example. And I believed that Foucault had yielded to the temptation of becoming a guru, a *maître à penser,* a practitioner of intellectual mystification. Before long, a friend sent me from Paris the devastating criticisms of Foucault's history and philosophy by Gladys Swain and Marcel Gauchet (*Penser la maladie mentale,* Gallimard, 1980). For this discussion, it is an essential book.

In the eighties, graduate students began showing up in my courses at the University of Virginia who made use of *discourse, desire,* and—a bit more rarely—*episteme.* They had not always read Foucault, but all had studied with a professor somewhere who had succumbed to the new gospel. I read a few more of his writings without finding reason to change my previous estimate.

In early 1992, an advance typescript of Jim Miller's book sent out by the publishers lured me back to Foucault. I knew Jim slightly as a fellow contributor to *Salmagundi* and as a friend of friends. To my amazement, I found time during a busy season to read all seven hundred pages. Each time I picked up Miller's typescript, it made me feel more vividly the wonderment of the child in the story of the emperor's new clothes. Could this adulation of a Svengali truly be taking place among people of discriminating intelligence? I woke up to the fact that the past century has produced no powerful rebuttal of Nietzsche. Partly in consequence, no one has called Foucault to task on a scale equal to his influence.* But Miller goes a long way. Let me mention a few of the episodes and arguments documented in Miller's book, many of which were little known before its publication.

1. Over the years, Foucault aimed his heaviest weapons at humanism in all forms. And he defined what he meant. "Humanism is everything in Western civilization that restricts *the desire for power"* (199).

2. In his 1971 debate with Chomsky, Foucault invoked as the ideal social model Maoist China and denied the need for law, justice, and responsibility. That same year, Foucault was welcoming from Nietzsche the acceleration of "instinctive violence" and "something of the murderous" (218). Our cruelest phantasms "should be freed from the restrictions we impose on them . . . and allowed to conduct their dance" (223–224).

3. As a prominent intellectual, Foucault was consulted in 1978 about the reform of French penal code. He argued for abolishing the age of consent for all sex acts, heterosexual and homosexual. "It could be that the child, with his own sexuality, may have desired that adult" (257). All sexual behavior, including rape, should be freed from constraints— except the physically violent element.

4. Increasingly, Foucault advocated the association of sex with cruelty (rather than with love) and with impersonality and strangers (rather than with intimacy) (259–269).

5. Foucault's celebration of "transgression" as a way of life and of psychological quest turned before long toward sadomasochistic eroticism

---

*Beginning in the seventies, Foucault was welcomed in prominent American newspapers and reviews by Richard Poirier, Leo Bersani, and Alexander Nehamas, among others, and more cautiously by Jean Starobinski, Steven Marcus, and George Steiner. Sterner criticism came a little later, from Lawrence Stone, Paul Robinson, Gordon Wright, and Erik Midelfort.

and *"la joie suppliciante"*—that is, the joy of torture (86–89). When homosexual promiscuity in San Francisco bathhouses and the reality of AIDS were added to this equation, Foucault pronounced the logical and nihilistic result: "Sex is worth dying for" (34). He did not specify whose death. Fully informed by his medical colleagues about the seriousness and the highly controllable nature of the AIDS epidemic threatening him and his friends, this prominent philosopher took the position of advocating promiscuity among male homosexuals. " 'If sex with a boy gives me pleasure'—why renounce such pleasure? *We* have the power, he said again: *we* shouldn't give it up" (353).

We readers should be grateful for the steadiness with which Miller demonstrates how Foucault spurns any middle ground of moral constraints and all political institutions that human beings may have constructed between total power and total anarchy. Foucault cannot decide which extreme to favor.

But I am deeply puzzled, sometimes appalled, by Miller's responses to what he is so conscientiously recording. On the page after reporting Foucault's recommendations about age of consent and rape, Miller writes, "Though Foucault's specific proposals are highly questionable . . . his courage is beyond dispute." Courage? Foucault was a privileged and protected insider at the summit of French and American educational establishments. Under our "bourgeois" system of justice, he did not face one shred of danger. This was no Robin Hood taking risks to help the downtrodden, no brave explorer dying on the way to the South Pole. Foucault was defending and normalizing his own homosexual, sadomasochistic tastes and pleasures. Proust, who dealt extensively with these subjects, would not have sympathized. Nor would Wilde, who wrote a sentence beyond Foucault's grasp as a thinker: "Kindliness requires imagination and intellect."

In his postscript, Miller speaks of his sympathy toward the foolhardiness of "any sexually adventurous gay man in 1983," of a "certain dignity" in Foucault's regarding AIDS as a "limit-experience," and of Miller's "conviction that what Nietzsche and Foucault have written about the genealogy of moral judgment is, in some broad sense, 'true' " (383).

The wish to stimulate the mind through the senses belongs to every era, including the most primitive and the most sophisticated. Religious sects have sought mystical experience through many forms of asceticism and also of licentiousness. It is as if the lesson of temperance can rarely be learned without the experience of excess. But certain intellectual and artistic minds have come to cultivate excess for its own sake, not as a path toward restraint or humanity. Excess itself is knowledge. The most dazzling formulation of the program came from a sixteen-year-old.

> The poet makes himself into a *seer* by a long, immense, and deliberate *debauchery of all his senses.* All forms of love, suffering, madness. He must search by himself. He runs through all the poisons in order to hold onto the most essential. . . . He becomes the great leper, the great criminal, the great outcast—and the supreme Knower.

Rimbaud's manifesto of *dérèglement* has often been used as a blanket justification for the most dissolute and self-indulgent behavior. Foucault convinced himself and his admirers that his own crapulous behavior merited some kind of perverse moral justification. But what he referred to as "the limit-experience" of sadomasochistic experimentation led—so far as we can tell—to no illumination beyond itself. It led to self-destruction; Foucault died of AIDS. In professing to find "dignity" in Foucault's life of passion, Miller makes me wonder how far he has swallowed a romantic doctrine that welcomes sheer experience for experience's sake. Or perhaps Miller is preaching a new shamanism. In either case, we are drifting very far from the shore.

To my mind, Miller's own book belies every aspect of Miller's evaluation. Could I, then, would I, write a blurb for this book, which reveals the truth and then seems not to grasp it? I'll read you my blurb in its original version, slightly longer than the one that appears on the jacket of the hardback edition.

> Miller has written truer than he knows. Foucault, the most mesmerizing of the recent French conquistadors, flirted seriously with terrorism, hoped to invent an ungovernable New Man, and tried to convert homosexual sex into an impersonal sadomasochistic experiment. Miller strips the intimidating and evasive terminology away from this intellectual horror story. Miller's scrupulousness should help bring us to our senses.

I see no reason to retract any part of that statement.

Another way of understanding Foucault's place on the scene today, as partly revealed by Miller, is to employ an ancient analogy. Publishers and admirers offer us Foucault's accumulated writings as a new departure in intellectual history, philosophy, and anthropology. I see his works as forming a remarkably successful wooden horse, like the Trojan horse Odysseus devised to introduce Greek soldiers into Troy in order to conquer the city.

On the outside, Foucault's writings make ambitious claims about periodization, *epistemes,* discourse, and institutions of repression. Anyone who reads attentively will see before long that these claims veil a doctrine of total liberation from all social and moral constraints in order to act out our most violent instincts—above all, sexual.

In *The History of Madness,* he refers to "a massive cultural fact that appeared precisely at the end of the 18th century and that constitutes one of the greatest conversions of the occidental imagination . . . madness of desire, the insane delight of love and death in the limitless presumption of appetite" (210). The corresponding passage in *The Order of Things* refers to the same "reversal" of values and the great author who produced it. "After him violence, life and death, desire, and sexuality will extend, below the level of representation, an immense expanse of darkness, which we are now attempting to recover . . . in our discourse, in our freedom, in our thought" (211).

The message recurs at the very end of *Madness:* "Through him the West has regained the possibility of surpassing reason through violence." *The Order of Things* closes with the claim that the knowledge we have gained from this author and the "mutation" he has brought down on us is the only knowledge that "has allowed the figure of man to appear" (386).

Who is the great thinker who will become the savior of humanity? It is the Marquis de Sade. He rides in the belly of this great wooden horse. A few times, he is named; more often, the reader must identify him. Sometimes Sade is misleadingly flanked by the mainline figures of Goya, Nietzsche, and van Gogh. But they have been rung in to provide camouflage. The rehabilitation and imitation of Sade represents Foucault's attempt to introduce a major revision of cultural and personal values unencumbered by moral considerations.

Foucault never quotes Sade. He never pauses to examine the nature of Sade's sustained episodes of orgasmic pleasure directly stimulated by sodomy, cruelty, torture, and murder, or to examine the philosophy used to justify them as superior to so-called virtue. Writing on what appears to be a high level of scholarly "discourse," Foucault simply invokes Sade as the heroic, model figure of the modern era. Readers who do not know Sade's work are left dangling with hortatory phrases like "the living body of desire" and "the secret nothingness of unreason." They may well be moved to seek out that vicious author as teacher and prophet. Readers familiar with Sade's work may perceive the true direction of Foucault's project: to seduce and to pervert, following the doctrine that elevates power above truth. But you would not grasp this project from an uncritical reading of Foucault's abstract, obscurantist prose.

There is a disturbing dishonesty at work here. How has it contrived to reach so high in the social and humanistic disciplines? Intellectual fashion, I believe, has become more powerful than ever. The Divine Marquis, brought secretly into the city in the wooden horse of Foucault's writings, lives again among us, not as hyena but as hero. For Miller and his readers, it is time for second thoughts. We should listen carefully for the answer to our challenge: Who goes there?

10

ART AT FIRST SIGHT

Request to the reader: Please do not look at the
illustration accompanying this essay until you come
upon the suggestion to do so.

O N THE FIRST floor of the Museum of Fine Arts in Boston, a long
corridor hung with small paintings runs east and west between a
succession of intercommunicating galleries of American art. One
winter afternoon after a couple of hours in the museum with no companion,
I had decided to leave. I was walking west along the corridor and barely
glancing at the paintings. Just before I reached the great circular stairway on
the central axis, something suddenly signaled to me from far out in my left
peripheral vision. Something had moved there that caught my attention. In
the split second before I made any overt response, I became intensely alert
and calm, as if an emergency had arisen. At the same time, a rush of images
swept through my consciousness. I can still remember two of them.

As I walk up a mountain path in my early boyhood, I notice on the for-
est floor, where everything else is still, a trillium in violent movement. It is
waving at me. Something alive there at my feet is soliciting me. While the
others go on, I stand transfixed for a long time, believing and not believing
in the eerie presence before me on the ground. Perhaps it lasts only a few seconds. . . . Another time, much later in life, after working all morning beside
an open window, I look up, to see one branch of a tall lilac gesturing at me,
dancing for me, while nothing else around it stirs. The importunate branch

will not stop moving; I cannot look away. The two incidents flash by and fuse into a single incident of unsettling communication—but with what?

In the museum corridor, I stopped without turning my head or my eyes. The corridor was empty of people ahead of me. I could hear no one behind. The signal had ceased. Then my mind replayed some words I had said in a seminar a few days earlier. "We all have the experience of privileged moments, of involuntary memories, and we make nothing of them. Too ordinary. They just slip by us. Proust was different. He decided to turn off and explore that faint path. He found a whole new world."

Trying to be deliberate, I turned to the left. At the sensitized location, I saw a smallish painting. I did not recognize it as the work of any painter I knew, or as presenting any identifiable subject or genre. Something was there and it escaped me. Across a distance of eight feet, my myopic vision is slightly blurred without glasses. I saw two contrasting horizontal bands suggesting an abstract composition—a bright turquoise strip above a luminous ruddy area. They conveyed no sense of figure and ground. Not a Mondrian, nor a Newman. Not symmetrical enough. But what? (See illustration following page 84—to begin with, at a distance if possible.)

The sequence of events from here on blurs somewhat in my memory. I recall that as I moved closer to see the painting, I decided firmly not to look right away at the identification plate attached to the frame at the bottom. Fortunately, the plate was tarnished and hard to read. Fairly quickly, I recognized the bright top strip as blue sky with a hint of wispy yellow clouds. Touching the edge on the left, the branches of a tree fanned out above the horizon. "Elm," I said to myself with satisfaction. To the right on the skyline, a small, blurred black shape, vaguely pyramidal, remained mysterious. Haystack? Hut? House? Peak of a barn hidden behind the hill? I could discern a "hill" now because the brownish green lower part of the painting had resolved itself into a rough field, probably a pasture, sloping up toward the horizon. Stalks of weed added clustered verticals, which, at the crest, blurred the horizon line. (In the photograph, the detail and perspective of the foreground seems clearer than in the painting, probably because of the rather scumbled paint surface in the lower area.) Without the familiar elm shape, the composition would remain strikingly abstract—two carefully adjusted color areas avoiding obvious symmetry, with subtle gradations and accents in the lower green segment. Even seeing the tree, one never loses the impression of an exercise in pure design. But after resisting rapid identification as any part of our visual world, the painting finally nods and smiles and subsides into delicate figuration, the simplest of landscape motifs.

Somehow I managed to hold off a little longer and looked at the adjacent paintings—for clues, for distraction, in order to savor the suspense a little longer. They, too, were small—about nine by twelve inches. To the right, I recognized a Ryder, though not typical. Under its heavy yellow film of varnish, *The Golden Hour* looked Dutch, a muted miniature nature story. To the left, a single white water lily illuminated from behind floated in a dark pool. It couldn't be a Monet. Not here with all the Americans. Not with that carefully finished brushwork. I turned back to the painting that had emitted signals to me. In spite of the rough surface, the paint in the foreground had a visual depth that suggested glazes, tinted transparent layers for the eye to penetrate before touching bottom. Glaze meant old master techniques, beaux arts training, the look of age. Yet the stark layout of the tiny composition reached out toward a later sensibility. A nearly featureless landscape, it had a distinctly modern feel. Not somber enough to be a Ryder. Too figurative for a Dove. I gave up on identifying the artist and placed it at the end of the nineteenth century.

Then, finally, I looked at the plate.

John La Farge, 1835–1910. "Hillside, Long Island," 1860–65. Oil on panel. Bequest of Mrs. Henry Lee Higginson. 35.1166

STANDING IN FRONT of *Hillside* that day, I jotted down a few notes. They provided the material for the above paragraphs. That evening, I talked to my wife about the painting that had beckoned to me in the corridor. The best I could do was to identify La Farge as part of a prominent family, a friend of writers, and an artist whose work I barely knew. Murals, I remembered.

A few months later, I returned to the museum. Even without another enchanted first encounter, *Hillside* still spoke to me with a persuasive voice. I wanted to know more about La Farge and to see more of his work. But I found nothing about him in my unsystematic collection of art books.

It turned out that in 1988 a fairly important exhibition of his works had come to Boston after opening at the Carnegie-Mellon Museum in Pittsburgh and traveling to the National Museum of American Art in Washington. The well-illustrated volume of essays that accompanied the show (*John La Farge*, Abbeville, 1987) provided all the general information I wanted. But *Hillside* is neither reproduced nor mentioned in the book. In the fall of 1989 when I returned to the site of the original revelation, I found that the paintings on both sides of the corridor had been replaced. No La Farge anywhere, and no sign to acknowledge the sweeping change of works on dis-

play. I felt like a character in a mystery story who cannot find the secret door
through which just the day before he gained access to the hidden treasure.

BY HERITAGE AND education—he was bilingual in French—La Farge
should have become a diplomat. One strong aversion blocked that career:
He hated to shake hands. To stand in a receiving line at an official reception
would have exceeded his physical capacities. Fairly early, he found that he
could resolve at the same time his handshaking problem and his choice of
profession. As a painter, he could greet his guests with both hands occupied—brush in one, palette in the other, or perhaps a rag. The need would
never arise to touch the flesh. La Farge was singularly happy as a painter. He
always spent a great deal of time in his studio and assembled a handsome
collection of brushes.

That's how Vasari or Apollinaire would have begun La Farge's story.
Royal Cortizzoz tells it almost that way in his 1911 memoir. Born in 1835
to a wealthy French émigré family in New York, La Farge began law training
and then went to Paris briefly to study painting with Couture and Millet.
While taking art classes in Newport, La Farge met Henry and William James
as fellow art students. The brothers from Boston were enormously
impressed by La Farge's powers as a conversationalist. The painter did not
produce witty quips like Whistler. He spoke in long, digressive, yet well-
formed sentences that displayed wide knowledge and an adventuresome
intelligence. Henry James called La Farge "quite the most interesting person
we knew." The painter apparently urged Henry to favor writing over painting.

Twenty years later, La Farge had married and fathered a large family and
had gained recognition as church muralist, decorator, stained-glass designer,
and expert on Japanese prints. By then, he and Henry Adams had become
close friends. Following the devastating suicide of Adams's wife, the two
men took a three-month trip together to Japan. It was not an easy voyage in
1886. Four years later, the two friends spent over a year in the South Sea
Islands, particularly on unspoiled Samoa. Most of the time, they lived
among the natives, apart from other Westerners. They left Tahiti a week
before Gauguin arrived on his first trip from Paris. La Farge had a tonic
effect on Adams's writing and steered him in the direction of Gothic architecture. Not surprisingly, La Farge discovered that he could be a successful
essayist and lecturer.

Working often on commission and in a great variety of media, La Farge
produced an uneven body of work with flashes of originality. Several of the
landscapes he painted around Newport in the 1860s and some of the

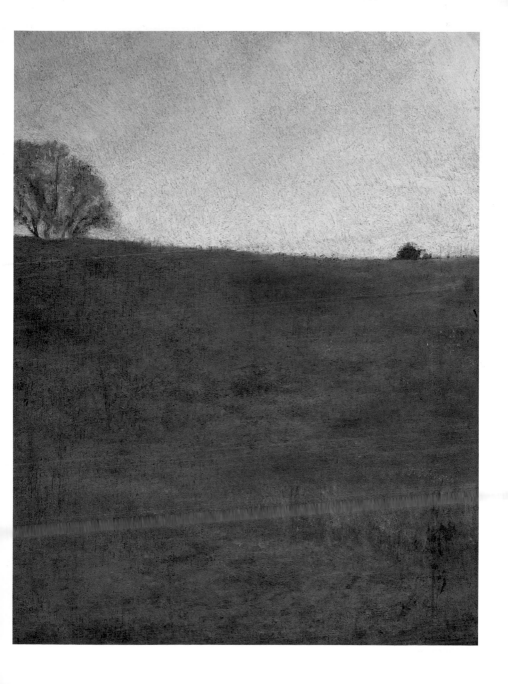

Samoan watercolors show wonderful control. Despite his closeness to French culture, he developed a strong sense of an American tradition independent of European influences. His late works register little response to Impressionism and Post-Impressionism, with which they were contemporary.

Hillside was produced during the early Newport period, when La Farge worked extensively on landscapes. Exceptionally, it represents a scene near the family estate in Glen Cove, Long Island. Few of his works are identified as Long Island subjects. Does the brevity of his stays in Glen Cove explain the small dimensions of the work? Possibly. In any case, it presents itself more as a finished painting than as a study or as a sketch for a more ambitious work.

How would I have reacted to *Hillside* if I had come upon it hanging between an Inness and a Winslow Homer (another good friend of La Farge) in an exhibit of late-nineteenth-century American landscapes? Or in a large one-man show of La Farge's work in several media? While attending a wide-ranging lecture on "American Painting at the Crossroads," would I have experienced any frisson if *Hillside* had flashed on the screen for a few seconds to establish a contrast with a group portrait by Sargent? I cannot say. What does it mean that at the time of the 1988 La Farge exhibit, this painting was shown in Boston but not at the two other locations? Is *Hillside* just a minor work by a minor American painter of the last century?

FOR THE MOST part, we come to works of art when the labels have already been pasted on. Almost before we look, we are told their value, their location in the cultural landscape, their place in the hierarchy of art. In the only two art history courses I took in college, students had to buy a box of black and white University Prints. They reproduced the works we learned to recognize and to talk about. The mass of colored images available today in books and slides has not freed us from the historical tradition, without which we would not know what art stands for and in what direction it might fruitfully develop. Only an art dealer or curator looking over portfolios by unknown artists and the really enterprising gallerygoer respond by hunch and taste to new images. Yet they are always extrapolating from the tradition. Even what I have just referred to as my frisson could not qualify as an unmediated and spontaneous response to a painting encountered on an aesthetic frontier. For the corridor of a museum constitutes a privileged place that certifies its contents as already lying within the world of art. Somebody called Higginson, a fine old Boston name I could easily look up and gossip about, acquired the painting and then left it to the MFA in 1935. Not my discovery. The machinery of cultural screening had placed the work here in an intermediate zone, neither neglected nor glorified, where I might notice it or miss it completely.

Still, one does not usually stop in one's tracks because of a mere corridor picture. Why did I turn back, look long, pursue the shiver of discovery or recognition, and go so far as to start *writing* about a modest panel by an American painter of the second rank? What's going on here? The almost full-size transparency I ordered from the MFA photographic services (and which I can only *rent* from the museum for a considerable fee) offers me a flimsy facsimile of the calm, empty landscape. I can almost recover visually the mottled turquoise strip above the slightly translucent green-tan field below. *Field,* exactly. Did La Farge ever find himself murmuring the suggestive word as he built up his paints to render them, convincingly, both flat and deep? I doubt it, yet he shows a strong sense of what we call color-field painting. I find myself speculating on how long it took him to paint this composition. For a near miniature, the panel has several rough spots. In places, the outer edges show a sketchy inner margin, especially to the left of the tree. Museum files record that in 1981 *Hillside* was cleaned of a heavy layer of varnish and grime and slightly restored. The museum examiner, F. Zuccari, commented, "Pronounced texture in sky, landscape painted thinly with transparent glazes."

A year after our first meeting and even though it has now gone into captivity, I still find this painting *handsome.* It is a word I usually associate with larger dimensions. Does the proportion of sky to ground represent a physiologically satisfying ratio, a subtle adjustment of elements? The younger semidissident Cubists found such a geometrical ideal to name one of their exhibits after: the Golden Section. But *Hillside* relies far more on vision and color than on pure geometry. Around Newport, La Farge often painted downhill vistas opening out into pastoral scenes. Several are called after a local area known as "Paradise." The uphill slope of the Long Island landscape cuts off the view and seems to impede forward movement. Yet the composition and color of the painting convey two primary feelings: mystery and hope. The alluring skyline, the amorphous house or shack, the half-invisible elm—all call one forward and upward into a space of unbounded promise. No people, no paths, no fences, yet the landscape carries a pervasive human quality.

Once again, what's going on? What gives me the wish or the right to insist on the qualities of a half-forgotten American landscape? Some might suspect that I'm intent on seeing if I can impose my taste, assert a tiny shift of judgment, create a masterpiece. A power play.

And the frisson? It could have been a random twinge at that moment. I could be inventing it for effect. But I certify that it happened. That fluttering clue provoked my hunch and my wager. The tiny message from nowhere did not betray me. It led me to an object worth contemplating. In a gallery or a shop, such a premonition would make me try to purchase the work. Possession might satisfy my curiosity about it and diminish my admiration. But I cannot ever own *Hillside*. Deprived of the painting, reduced to holding a transparency of it up to the light, I find myself driven to reflect on the whole sequence of events and on the allure of so simple a picture.

I suppose I have also described love at first sight for a painting. I wish it struck more often.

RADICAL SKEPTICISM AND

HOW WE GOT HERE

I.

I have always been both wary and fond of the expression "to bring something home." My parents expected me to bring my girlfriends home, and my girlfriends' parents had reciprocal expectations. That was before the revolution. I find a satisfying comic flat-footedness in the phrase "to bring home the bacon." Another common usage carries distinctly intellectual, even didactic overtones: "The lawsuit brought home to Scott the need for a code of business ethics."

On November 20, 1990, I received together two pieces of mail that brought home to me one of the philosophical and moral quandaries into which we have herded ourselves at the close of the twentieth century. From the Trial Court of Norfolk County of the Commonwealth of Massachusetts, I was sent *Trial Jurors Handbook* in connection with a summons for jury duty the following week. The thirty-page booklet contained a variety of information, from practicalities like parking and meals to technicalities like peremptory challenges and sequestering. I found myself marking two passages.

> The jury finds the truth. It decides the facts. This is the major function of the jury—to find the truth. The jury does not decide the rules of law to be applied to the facts in the case.

The most important qualifications of a juror are fairness and impartiality. The juror must be led by intelligence, not by emotions . . . must put aside all bias and prejudice . . . must decide the facts and apply the law impartially. The juror must treat with equal fairness the rich and the poor, the old and the young, men and women, corporations and individuals, governments and citizens, and must render justice without any regard for race, color, or creed.

The other piece of mail that arrived simultaneously was an invitation from the Association of American Colleges to participate in their seventy-seventh annual meeting in Washington in January 1991 on the general subject "Knowledge Claims and Circular Choices." The program was to open with a panel of speakers on "Contested Understandings of Knowing and Knowledge," and the brochure included the following quotation and description of the program.

From the 1960s onward the objectivist assumptions and foundations of many academic disciplines have been undermined . . . in one field after another. . . . For many, postures of disinterestedness and neutrality increasingly appeared as outmoded and illusory . . . most crucially—the notion of a determinate and unitary truth about the physical or social world, approachable if not ultimately reachable, came to be seen by a growing number of scholars as a chimera. . . .
—Peter Novick, *That Noble Dream,* 1988

In this part of the annual meeting, we review fundamental questions that scholars are raising about knowing and knowledge: in gender, ethnic, and multicultural studies; in the growing resistance to positivist science as a model for knowledge; and in the growing attention to the social negotiation of warrants for knowledge claims.
We also look at the implications of these disputed views of knowing and knowledge for our basic concepts of liberal learning and for essential goals of liberal education.

The four speakers had chosen, or had been assigned, the following topics:

Thinking Through Cultures: Objectivity, Rationality and Multiple Worlds
Contested Understandings of Inquiry and Knowledge; Implications for Undergraduate Curriculum

Recognizing Our Multiplicities: Plural Voices Within and Without
Rediscovering the New Liberal Education: Curricular Implications of
the Recent Knowledge Revolution

2.

In a classroom, one could open the discussion at this point. That's why some
of us keep the faith with teaching. In a column, convention suggests that I
now enter the fray about knowledge claims and negotiating warrants. But I
shall proceed somewhat differently. Do these two documents diverge or
converge? Which words should be examined most carefully: *Truth?*
Chimera? Revolution? Bias? Can we survive as a society if we are teaching "a
new liberal education" and welcoming a "knowledge revolution" that contradict the notions of truth and fact on which our system of justice is based?
The Association of American Colleges would probably protest that I am
leaping to the unjustified conclusion that it endorses these contestings of
knowledge and truth, whereas it is merely offering a forum for the claims
described by Novick because such current ideas deserve scrutiny. Well, yes.
But the program looks more celebratory than critical. I did not attend the
event to find out its purport.

Others would say that my questions try to associate two unrelated
domains: the operation of a jury system on the basis of evidence in specific
cases in law, and the role of education to teach students to think critically
about the general state of society and about the kinds of knowledge claims it
has institutionalized. Precisely. How wide a split between the two should we
be happy with? The vital functions of criticism and dissent exist in that gap.
But insofar as principles of establishing evidence and fact in our courts are
categorically opposed by theories of knowledge and truth advanced in our
undergraduate curricula, we approach a serious parting of the ways, a form
of social schizophrenia. The developments that have led up to the AAC program bear a limited resemblance to the situation created by Russian nihilists
at the end of the nineteenth century and described from different perspectives by Chernyshevsky, Turgenev, Dostoevsky, and many others. Chernyshevsky didn't live to see the new Soviet society inspired in part by his book
What Is to Be Done? (1863). In their strictures about his ideas, his two literary contemporaries revealed their understanding that the system of justice
would be among the first casualties of such a society.

I shall avoid the vast metaphysical debate I have half-opened about
knowledge and justice by first addressing a side issue raised by Novick—
whether we should trace the present situation to the sixties—and then by

quoting two authors whose trenchant comments demonstrate better than a long philosophical argument the vital connection between a juror's search for truth and the epistemology we preach.

Our memory of the sixties tends to be selective. We should try to remember the variety of developments that contributed to the impact of that decade: student activism from the Free Speech Movement to the direct challenge to authority and civility by sit-ins and campus takeovers; the Cuban revolution and the hero status accorded to Castro and Che Guevara; the Soviet invasion of Czechoslovakia; the war in Vietnam in all its dimensions; the assassination of the Kennedys and Martin Luther King, Jr.; the student-worker riots in Paris; the sexual revolution; and the drug revolution. Without question, these events liberated and radicalized many people then in their teens and twenties, just as the same events sobered many of us then in our thirties and forties who helped to precipitate them. But I find it very hard to connect these events directly with the growing skepticism in philosophy concerning theory of knowledge and truth claims. Political and social events affected us both superficially by claiming our attention and profoundly by alerting us to serious abuses in our society. But as I recall the sixties now, their intellectual direction was influenced more deeply by the appearance of three books in three very different domains than by what we read every day in the newspapers. The three books reinforced one another more than we realized at the time, and their authority has by no means disappeared. I do not recall that anyone then or recently has associated them.*

The first to appear, Thomas Kuhn's *The Structure of Scientific Revolutions* (1962), abandoned the concept of science as a step-by-step progress toward truth and proposed a periodic succession of quantum leaps from one overall structure of thought to the next. Kuhn characterized these "paradigms" more by their dominance over the thinking of scientists than by their increasing proximity to truth. The rapid success and wide-ranging influence of Kuhn's book attested to its timeliness. Nonscientific responses to it welcomed an interpretation of science as a substantially social and cultural product not exclusively driven by the goal of truth and knowledge to which it pays lip service. As a result, Kuhn felt impelled to add a cautionary epilogue to the second edition. Nevertheless, the book seemed to undermine the last bastion of objective truth and to reduce science to the history of its own development in the general struggle for dominance. *The Structure of Scientific Revolutions* has little affected the actual practice of scientific

*Working against a deadline in an isolated rural cabin without books, notes, and easy access to a library, I must write these pages out of my head. I have not been able to consult the three books again. That handicap may carry certain advantages.

research, but it has led to a prolonged debate about the nature of scientific truth and to a period of prosperous activity for the history, philosophy, and sociology of science. Kuhn unwittingly answered a need for uncertainty where we thought certainty had established its headquarters. The rise of relativity and quantum theory seems to have prepared the ground for this sociology of science.

In the spring of 1967, literally in the shadow of the tower at the University of Texas, I remember a young activist colleague in sociology haranguing me about a new book that would provide the solution to our most urgent political and philosophical problems and the basis for a critique of all our institutions, beginning with the university. The book he kept waving at me and which I soon had to read was *The Social Construction of Reality* (1966) by Peter Berger and Thomas Luckmann. Unaware of Kuhn's book and deriving from a tradition of German philosophy, sociology, and Marxism, Berger and Luckmann produced an apparently neutral theory that reduces everything to a relation between an infrastructure (not so exclusively economic as Marx's) and a superstructure of culture and institutions. Above all, they resist the "reification" of beliefs and values and all humanly constructed phenomena into suprahuman entities—such as human nature, universal laws, and manifestations of a divine will. Nothing is given. Everything has been created by us and can be reconstituted by us. Only by recognizing this freedom and duty to construct our world can we begin to deal with our problems. In effect, Berger and Luckmann grafted a strong dose of Sartre's reigning existentialism, which insisted on our fate of being "condemned to be free," onto the socioeconomic orientation of Marx. I believe that the striking title, more than the dry and often technical argument, left its mark on more than one generation of social thinkers and humanists. It encapsulated a manifesto and a call to action. Without endorsing the notion of revolution, *The Social Construction of Reality* implied that a unique opportunity to remake society and even human nature lay at our feet if only we could get a proper grasp of reality and how we ourselves have constructed it.

The third influential book of the sixties had been published half a century earlier and arrived on the scene gradually and indirectly through the increasingly dominant writings of French structuralists and of Russian and Czech linguists. When I offered a seminar entitled "Literature and Linguistics" in the mid-1960s, I soon found that the key to intellectual fashion was not the New Novel, was not Barthes's *Zero Degree of Writing*, but was Saussure's *Course of General Linguistics* (1915). As I have already described in *The Innocent Eye*, Saussure, with his rigidly binary mind and for purely analytic reasons, simply eliminated the referent, the thing or entity referred to, from his definition of language. In other words, he eliminated the real world out there. Linguistic signs can be adequately described as a relation between two terms: the spoken or written word (signifier) and the thought in the mind (signified) to which a word is arbitrarily and conventionally connected. Language makes sense and communicates thought because of the way we collectively place words "differentially" along a mental spectrum of meaning *(valeur)*, not because of any correspondence between language and reality. This liberation from the reality principle was seized upon by Lévi-Strauss, Jakobson, Barthes, and later by Lacan and Foucault. They had found the unimpeachable authority of a linguist to banish reality and affirm the social construction of everything.

In their different ways and reaching different yet overlapping constituencies, these three books had a profound effect on the direction of thinking in the sixties and after. Each seemed to come out of a fairly specialized discipline and to make no claims beyond that restricted field. Yet in all three cases, the substance of the argument could be generalized to apply to all forms of intellectual endeavor. These works can be seen as converging on a position of radical skepticism not only about traditional values and institutions but also about seemingly impervious entities like truth, nature and human nature, reality, scientific inquiry, and religion. The siege continues.

Scientists and philosophers of science have treated Kuhn very roughly, but *The Structure of Scientific Revolutions* continues to influence people in the social sciences and humanities. Berger and Luckmann have gone their respective ways, but the term *social construction* is still with us and has entered the language as implying the cultural relativism of everything and the absence of stable or general principles. Saussure remains the prophet of modern linguistics, and linguistics remains the ultimate authority for the central strand of poststructuralist thought, which asserts that the only world we need take account of is text and textuality. In this usage, which has insinuated itself very widely even among those who reject its tenets, the "text" refers to nothing outside itself. Language makes life; *reality, fact,* and *truth* are just words in the text. In our day, poets and intellectuals don't live in so substantial a place as an ivory tower. We all exist in a figment of words.

3 .

Now this skepticism, which in its extreme form can turn out to be more political *(1984)* than playful *(Alice)*, has led to the kind of program organized last January by the Association of American Colleges. Such skepticism will not help the prospective juror face his responsibilities. New Legal Studies derives from the same source and constitutes a short circuit in our cultural life that I shall not address here.

Hume was one of the greatest of modern skeptics. Science had to march around his scrutiny of causality the way science today is marching around Kuhn's strictures about how it does what it does. But Hume at least let the cat out of the bag and faced up to the discrepancy between the speculations of higher learning and the demands of everyday life. He could write very clearly. "Skepticism can be thought but not lived." Nothing can be so sobering and tonic as a maxim.

At the beginning of this century, an American philosopher and linguist came to a similar conclusion while discussing the perils of Descartes's doubting the evidence of the senses. Charles Sanders Peirce also phrased his response like a maxim. "Let us not doubt in philosophy what we cannot doubt in our hearts."

I hope that all intellectuals pull jury duty when they begin to abandon all hope for fact and truth and to embrace a socially constructed textuality.

12

FROM *THE SWISS FAMILY*

ROBINSON TO *NARRATUS*

INTERRUPTUS

F *EW OF US* remember learning to read. Most minds bury those early, faltering steps under recollections of later rewards—the fairy tales or comic books on which we perfected our new skill. My most vivid and complete recollection of reading, and evidently not the earliest, goes back to an illness that confined me to my bedroom on the third floor of a Manhattan brownstone just off Third Avenue. I may have been ten or twelve. All day and part of the night, I listened to the elevated trains toil slowly up the long grade from midtown and to their companions coasting joyfully down like sleighs from the higher blocks of the Nineties. With a broken chair rung, I propped up the bed covers to make a spacious tent, my home and headquarters for the span of the sickness. I crawled in with a flashlight and a fat hardcover book and found complete privacy. Curled into my hideaway, I continued my nth rereading of Wyss's *The Swiss Family Robinson*. The book had everything: a sense of excitement, practical information about survival on a jungle island, and a set of characters both idealized and familiar.

This was the first full book I remember living with and making my own. It served me both as a magic carpet to other modes of experience and as a source of reality, like the how-to articles and the ads in *Popular Mechanics*. *The Swiss Family Robinson* was my personal book, like a piece of cake I could eat over and over again with undiminished pleasure and without consuming it. I can see the exact shade of purple on the cover and the frontispiece illustrating the shipwreck.

I wonder if anyone can become a devoted reader without some such magical experience from childhood to steer by. Twenty or so years later, I found a remarkable description of that magic in another book, which has replaced Wyss's tale in my firmament. Early in the "Combray" section of *Swann's Way,* Proust inserts seven self-contained pages on Marcel reading in the garden. He is almost hidden inside a huge wicker chair. Believing that a book can unveil the unknown for us, Marcel encounters the two secret powers of the novel: the transparence of characters made of words rather than of opaque flesh and blood, and the telescopings of pace and timing that permit a lengthy period to flash by in a single sentence or a momentary impression to occupy a dozen pages. Fifty pages after the taste of a madeleine dipped in linden tea triggers in the narrator near total recall of his childhood in Combray, the privileged and half-forbidden activity of reading provokes in his earlier self, Marcel, images and experiences "more vividly represented in my imagination than those Combray offered." In this rhapsodic passage, Proust's narrator does not undercut Marcel's conviction that he has discovered in reading a higher level of being.

Both these episodes, mine and Marcel's, testifying to the spellbinding effect of reading, antedate the "electronic revolution." Since about 1945, a transformation is said to have descended upon us, a transformation propelled by television and computers. In education, where I have worked for close to forty years, I have weathered two "revolutions" that never materialized. When I moved to the University of Texas in 1956, every classroom in Batts Hall, the new building housing the modern language department, contained a built-in television set and speaker connections to a central control room in the basement. After a few months of experimentation, television and speakers lay virtually unused. The predicted replacement of living teachers by televised lessons from master teachers did not take place. Some years later, in the mid-sixties, the language laboratory with its banks of tape recorders came into fashion. Language labs spurred further investment of money, time, and personnel by colleges and schools. It took twenty years for that novelty to find the appropriate level of use as a modest supplement to classroom teaching.

Now a whole new set of claims is being made about computer instruction at all levels of education. One of the most sympathetic yet dispassionate studies of computers in schools, a book that relies more on thorough case histories than on statistics, convinces me that we are witnessing a widespread manifestation of the Hawthorne principle. Sherry Turkel's *The Second Self* tends to demonstrate that even in elementary grades *any* change of routine will *temporarily* induce improved performance, as on a factory production line. But will the effect last? Outside of education, of course, LPs and CDs, MTV and the Walkman provide both sensory stimulation and a sensory caul to retreat into. Can we measure the impact of these new factors?

The language itself can give helpful cues. Writing in *The Gutenberg Elegies* on the subject of how new technology affects reading, Sven Birkerts deploys with considerable sympathy a set of optative terms: "a new sensorium," "a new dispensation," "electronic order" as opposed to the linear order of print, and "changes in subjective space." Birkerts suggests that in this closing decade of the second millennium, we are crossing the threshold of a new electronic literacy. My comments about these claims spring from my earliest personal and professional experiences in flying, film, and journalism.

If we have developed anything approaching a new sensorium or more complex ways of thinking, the change goes back not twenty or thirty years but two centuries at least. Telegraphy and photography were invented and exploited early in the nineteenth century. The former led to telephone and wireless telegraphy, then to radio and television. The latter led in parallel evolution to silent cinema, sound cinema, and compatibility with television. Earlier, the ancient technology of writing and of fifteenth-century movable type had produced the printed book, and the daily newspaper, and, in our time, the electronic storage and retrieval of print. The three strands of print, photography, and telegraphy converge today in the computer with screen display.

Where in this history of communication and technology covering several centuries do forms appear that modified individual sensibilities and cultural behavior? After the printed book, whose truly democratizing force has not left us, I discuss two more. By the middle of the nineteenth century, improved presses (often using lithograph illustrations) could run a daily newspaper for hundreds of thousands of readers. Such newspapers, complete with telegraph bulletins, made it possible to conceive of a new state of things: "the world today." As late as 1913, the avant-garde writer Apollinaire was producing poems and manifestos to celebrate the daily newspaper as the most modern of inventions. It juxtaposes almost at random every conceivable aspect of the universe with no evident unity except the slender claim of a date. More than books and travel, the newspaper opened up people's minds to the enormous and exciting spectacle of the world beyond locality.

The second communications development struck early viewers as far more revolutionary than the newspaper—often as truly miraculous.

Descriptions of audiences at the earliest projections of the Lumière brothers' silent films amuse us with their accounts of fits and faintings, of marvelings at "people returned from the dead," of accusations of black magic and witchcraft, and of peerings behind the screen to find the actors. Pictures in motion carried the strong illusion of life. They still do so today. Has the genuine magic of film now yielded to the mainframe engineering feats of artificial intelligence?

The forecaster or hydrologist or sales manager modeling a project on a computer can instantaneously call up and correlate a vast range of information. Library computers procure in a twinkling subject references that it will take us months to consult. I am not convinced that the demands and enhancements of the electronic revolution taking place around us represent more of a reorientation to the experience of life than did the daily newspaper and the moving picture. And both are still very much with us.

Those two historical developments also leave us contemplating a deep-seated contrast between word and image—a contrast largely masked by computer displays on a screen. In which case is the mind more active: in constructing, following, and visualizing the meaning of words or in watching and assembling images on a screen? In a fascinating debate I have analyzed elsewhere (*New York Review of Books,* August 16, 1984), enthusiasts like Sergei Eisenstein maintain that montage demands great imaginative feats in order to assemble the shots into a narrative or expository order. André Bazin, on the contrary, argues for shots of long duration and deep focus, in which our imagination has to discover the center of interest within a semblance of full-bodied reality. Flaubert resisted any attempt to add illustrations to *Madame Bovery* because they would interfere with the workings of the reader's own imagination to transform printed words into visible scenes. Similarly, Bruno Bettelheim points out the confining effect of illustrations in children's editions of fairy tales. Despite my early allegiance to magical powers of the moving image, I continue to believe that the most fundamental human accomplishment after oral language is written language. Modern technology has miniaturized, accelerated, and extended these skills without modifying their basic operation. Reading remains the most miraculous widely practiced achievement of mind and body in all developed cultures.

The novel I am reading at the moment plays directly into this discussion by insisting on making a joke of novel reading and novel writing and by addressing that subject at the beginning of each chapter. Martin Amis's *London Fields* (1989) radiates self-consciousness and vanity about occupying literary terrain adjacent to *Tristam Shandy* and *The Counterfeiters.* The (fictional) narrator is an American novelist trying to produce or stage the action he is writing about among a motley set of London types. They resist and accede in various ways to the narrator's enticements. The result falls into a category I have called "the metaphysical picaresque" and am now impelled to name *narratus interruptus*. We have become highly familiar with it in what is lamely referred to as "postmodern fiction." Asides and interruptions that seem daring and funny in Sterne and Gide, because written in the teeth of a strong narrative tradition, come off as cute or perfunctory in Amis. He irritates me constantly because he feels obligated to chop up and hold out for our inspection his enormous power as an inventor of characters and situations. He will not suspend our disbelief for more than a few pages at a time, following a current literary fashion as arbitrary as hoopskirts or ruff collars. I fear that the regular practice of *narratus interruptus* will not favor the development of Amis's evident gifts as a writer of fiction.

Amis's central character, a low-life cheat, con man, and dart player, Keith Talent, represents a keen portrait of the new dispensation of electronic prowess. Keith occasionally reads from a manual on darts. But his ultimate communication skill consists not in watching TV but in playing, mixing, and fixing the tapes recorded automatically while he is out stealing car radios or cheating various clients.

> Every evening he taped six hours of TV and then screened them on his return . . . he could no longer bear to watch television at the normal speed, unmediated by the remote and by the tyranny of his own fag-browned thumb. Pause. SloMo. Picture search. What he was after were images of sex, violence, and sometimes money. Keith watched his six hours' worth at high speed. Often it was all over in twenty minutes. Had to keep your wits about you. He could spot a pin-up on a garage wall in Super fast-forward. Then Rewind, SloMo, Freeze Frame. A young dancer slowly disrobing before a mirror; an old cop getting it in the chest with both barrels; an American house. Best were the scenes that combined all three motifs. (*London Fields*, pp. 164–65)

Now here's the new sensorium in its rawest form. Some people, seeking smut, can read that way. Amis asks his readers to assimilate a 460-page novel of interruptions and restarts, of SloMo and Super-fast-forward. In spite of, or because of, these obstacles, he has many readers.

Yes, we live surrounded by new electronic devices. I cannot become accustomed to the omnipresent Walkman, like a mental intravenous feeder worn shamelessly out in the street. Many of these devices compete with the complex and demanding act of reading. But two characteristics of the human race that protect us from entropy are our capacity for boredom and our impatience with it. Reading remains the principle habit-forming drug that is not dangerous to the health and that, instead of vampirizing the mind, supplies it with nourishment. I am still prepared to put my faith in Wyss and Proust and in the vast domain that lies between.

13

TEACHING THE
UNTEACHABLE: KIPLING,
PROUST, NIETZSCHE & CO.

*I dedicate this essay to the memory of two devoted
teachers, William Arrowsmith (1924–1992) and
Tari Elizabeth Shattuck (1951–1993).*

I.

My title does not refer to the caliber of students I find in my classes at Boston University. It refers, as the subtitle certifies, to the challenging materials we find ourselves dealing with in courses in every field. My subject is a doubt or scruple about education, about the very possibility of teaching and learning anything of significance, a doubt that may come to haunt the process at any stage. In order to get a direct purchase on that subject and in order to deal first with cases rather than with generalities and theories, I shall examine a specific passage by each of the three authors in my subtitle—though in a different order.

In 1902, Rudyard Kipling, not yet forty, published *Just So Stories for Little Children* soon after the loss of a six-year-old daughter. Many of us heard "How the Leopard Got His Spots" and "The Cat That Walked Alone" in our earliest childhood. Many of us know sections virtually by heart. Our daughter Tari kept a copy in her fourth-grade classroom (as she kept a copy by her bed in the hospital) because she found it the most appealing and effective of books to read aloud to her students. Kipling's prose here engages delightfully in sound play as a fundamental element in literature, and it conveys a strong sense of the story as initiation into the mysteries of life and nature. Every good story has the power of a fable or a parable to educate.

"In the High and Faroff Times the Elephant, O Dearly Beloved, had no trunk." I am sorely tempted just to go on quoting. But we have moved beyond the fourth grade, alas, and I am expected to do more than recite a story. Let me recall some parts you may have forgotten. One young elephant, named the Elephant's Child, is filled with " 'satiable curtiosity"—a childhood malaprop for insatiable curiosity—and receives spankings from all other animals, especially his own family, for his constant questions about everything he sees or hears or feels or smells or touches. Then comes this no-nonsense episode.

One fine morning in the middle of the Precession of the Equinoxes this 'satiable Elephant's Child asked a new fine question that he had never asked before. He asked, "What does the Crocodile have for dinner?" Then everybody said, "Hush!" in a loud and dretful tone, and they spanked him immediately and directly, without stopping, for a long time.

By and by, when that was finished, he came upon Kolokolo Bird sitting in the middle of a wait-a-bit thorn bush, and he said, "My father has spanked me, and my mother has spanked me; all my aunts and uncles have spanked me for my 'satiable curiosity; and still I want to know what the Crocodile has for dinner!"

Then Kolokolo Bird said, with a mournful cry, "Go to the banks of the great grey-green, greasy Limpopo River, all set about with fever-trees, and find out."

That very next morning, when there was nothing left of the Equinoxes, because the Precession had preceded according to precedent, this 'satiable Elephant's Child took a hundred pounds of bananas (the little short red kind), and a hundred pounds of sugar-cane (the long purple kind), and seventeen melons (the greeny-crackly kind), and said to all his dear families, "Goodbye. I am going to the great grey-green, greasy Limpopo River, all set about with fever-trees, to find out what the Crocodile has for dinner." And they all spanked him once more for luck, though he asked them most politely to stop.

Then he went away, a little warm, but not at all astonished, eating melons, and throwing the rind about, because he could not pick it up.

Part of the effectiveness of this kind of writing, for little children as well as for adults, lies in the alternation and intermingling of the casual and the concise. In arranging these events, time can be both open-ended ("for a long time" and "by and by") and exact ("That very next morning"). The self-generated sound patterns can distract from the action, as in the Precession preceding according to precedent, or they come to incorporate the elusive essence of the story. "The great grey-green, greasy Limpopo River all set-about with fever-trees" contains gradations of vowels and consonants as carefully wrought as Gerard Manley Hopkins's sequence, "daylight's dauphin, dapple-dawn-drawn falcon." A "fever-tree" collapses the disease (malaria) and the cure (quinine) into one fairy-tale plant. And this exotic place is proposed to the Elephant's Child by "Kolokolo Bird sitting in the midst of a wait-a-bit thorn-bush." Garrison Keillor has surely passed this way. These succulent sounds never quite arrest the forward movement of the story, based as it is on the 'satiable curiosity of the Elephant's Child, who has no idea what a Crocodile is. But when he reaches the bank of the Limpopo River, he happens to step on one and then is deceived by the Croc-odile's tears to lean close to its "musky tusky mouth." When those jaws snap shut on the Elephant's Child's modest snout, they do not release until after the dramatic rescue by the Bi-Colored-Python-Rock-Snake. The Elephant's Child has now acquired a trunk, for which he discovers several valuable uses. Above all, when he returns home to his dear families, he uses the trunk to spank them all "till they were very warm and greatly astonished." But he never lets anyone touch the Kolokolo Bird, who sent him on his liberating quest. Then all his dear families go off to the Limpopo one by one to receive their own nose job. When they come back, no one spanks anyone anymore. The Elephant's Child's 'satiable curiosity has introduced the usefully elon-gated proboscis into the community and has apparently reduced Elephant violence to a minimum—considerable accomplishments for a mere child.

Read as a parable, Kipling's story seems to say that you'll never learn anything by staying around home and putting up with the old fogys. All you pick up that way is a succession of spankings. The aloof Kolokolo Bird has the only worthwhile advice. Go out on your own. As Kant and many others have said, *Sapere Aude!* Dare to know. Ask your questions of life itself, not of received knowledge in the culture around you.

I believe that our daughter put great faith in Kipling's *Just So Stories for Little Children* not only because of the sparkling prose style but also because of the subtlety of its message about traditional education and breaking out on one's own. I shall return to Kipling when we are ready.

FOR BILL ARROWSMITH, also an impassioned teacher, the correspond-ing writer of choice would have been not a classical author but another mav-erick classical scholar like himself. From an early age, Bill read and emulated

Nietzsche and cited him frequently in his education essays. One of Bill's early translation projects after Petronius's *Satyricon* was Nietzsche's *Wir Philologen—We Classicists.* The last book Bill published before he died was his edition of Nietzsche's *Unzeitgemässe Betrachtungen* (1874)—or *Unmodern Observations.*

In it, Bill chose to translate the third of four essays, the one called "Schopenhauer as Educator." Just thirty and already professor of classical philology at the University of Basel, Nietzsche admired Schopenhauer almost as much as he did Wagner. The sixty-page essay begins and ends with an Emerson quotation and barely mentions Schopenhauer's life or philosophy. One feels the pressure of the preceding essay, "History in the Service and Disservice of Life," which argues—or rather, asserts—that historical consciousness prevents us from living the present moment and from touching reality. (Increasingly in this essay, "history" comes to mean self-knowledge, thinking of any kind.) Nietzsche had already examined this paradox of knowledge in *The Birth of Tragedy* by writing apropos of Hamlet: "Knowledge kills action."

In "Schopenhauer as Educator," Nietzsche has not yet become the systematic revisionist of Western culture he becomes in his later writings. Here he affirms the romantic belief that the aim of all culture is to generate geniuses, and he looks for the life of genius in the philosopher—in this case, Schopenhauer. Near the end of the essay, Nietzsche sets down a passage that draws on the distinction among *ein Gelehrten* (or scholar), *ein Erzieher* (or educator), and *ein Philosoph* (or philosopher-genius), an early version of the *Übermensch,* or Superman. The passage carries strong personal meaning for its author, a philosopher-scholar who wanted to be a philosopher-poet; for its translator, a classicist-scholar who wanted to be a poet-dramatist; and for the present speaker, who wants to make a point.

Schopenhauer was also extremely fortunate in not being destined and educated for scholarship. For some time, although reluctantly, he actually worked in a commercial office, and throughout his youth he breathed the freer air of a large trading house. A scholar can never become a philosopher. Even Kant could not manage it and, despite the innate power of his genius, remained to the very end in chrysalis state. Those who think these words are unfair to Kant do not know what a philosopher is—not only a great thinker but a genuine human being [*ein wirklicher Mensch*]. And when has a scholar ever turned into a genuine human being? Anyone who lets concepts, opinions, past events, and books come between himself and things, who in the broadest sense is born to history, will never see things for the first time and will never himself be one of those prodigies that have never been seen before. But both these traits must be present in the philosopher, since most of what he teaches has to be drawn from himself and because he himself is his own image and compendium of the whole world. If a man sees himself through the opinions of others, it is no surprise if he sees in himself nothing but other people's opinions! And this is how scholars live, see, and are.

The heresy of denying that Kant was a philosopher opens the way for the first of two key sentences: "And when has a scholar ever turned into a genuine human being?" That question should make anyone familiar with German literature sit up and take notice. Was it a deliberate omission or an oversight that Nietzsche does not inform us here that his question represents the shortest paraphrase ever written of Goethe's *Faust*? Faust cut a deal with the devil and became a full-blooded man. When Napoleon met Goethe, the general is reported to have declared, "At last, a man!" Kant could not escape from his dusty study. Are we scholars condemned to live incomplete lives unless we conjure up evil spirits and fly away to greater glory? Is the whole enterprise of learning to be dismissed as misdirected? Is it possible that this challenge to culture represents the side of Nietzsche that today makes him the most popular and fashionable modern philosopher, especially in universities? To the last question only, I would answer: In great part, yes. Nietzsche is our Rousseau.

The following and second key sentence explains what is wrong with scholarship. "Anyone who lets concepts, opinions, past events, and books come between oneself and things, who in the broadest sense is born to history   " will fail to become a genuine human being. That clause contains a rough listing of the elements of a liberal education—except that Nietzsche sees in them only the dead letter of learning that does not lead to independent thinking. Learning only separates us from reality and from life. Culture and history keep us from living, in the sense of experiencing the world innocently, pristinely, for ourselves. Above all, let us not be bookish. Nietzsche is recapitulating Rousseau's influential doctrine that culture kills true humanity in us and that the best formal education is *negative*—little and late. Nietzsche is also recapitulating his own essay "History in the Service and Disservice of Life." The disgruntled scholar like Faust wants to abandon learning and to soar up to a higher level of intensity in experience, even to divinity. Nothing that counts can be taught. Shake the very dust of libraries from off your feet.

It is true that in the opening pages of "History," Nietzsche states in italics, *"The unhistorical and the historical are equally necessary to the good health of a man, a people, a culture."* But fifty pages later, he is compelled to "protest against the historical education imposed on the young" and to insist on an "inspiring power" in the service of life. Elsewhere, Nietzsche acknowledges his immense debt to Greek tragedy and our duty to read the ancient Greeks with care. But in the paragraph I have quoted from "Schopenhauer" Nietzsche is by no means evenhanded. More insistently than Kipling in his story, Nietzsche here declares that teaching, whether by the conventions of spanking or of scholarship, will not benefit the young. Traditional training will hobble them. Life cannot be approached vicariously through books.

I should now like to accompany you one stage further along this seemingly perverse path. Many years ago, I discovered a similar motif in the work of Marcel Proust. The most arresting passage occurs about a third of the way through Proust's three-thousand-page novel, *In Search of Lost Time,* a title usually mistranslated as *Remembrance of Things Past.* In the line of what I have been saying, it would be hard to find a more forthright statement. Proust wrote it during World War I.

> We do not receive wisdom; we must discover it for ourselves, after a journey through the wilderness which no one else can make for us, an effort which no one can spare us, for our wisdom is the point of view from which we come at last to view the world. The lives that you admire, the attitudes that seem noble to you have not been shaped by a paterfamilias or by a schoolmaster; those admirable lives have sprung from beginnings of a very different order, by reaction from the influence of everything evil or commonplace that prevailed round about them. Those lives represent a struggle and a victory. (trans. Moncrieff-Kilmartin, 1923–1924; altered)

Proust has aligned himself with the Kolokolo Bird and with Nietzsche. Don't expect teachers or books to convey to you any true form of wisdom; you must discover it for yourself. It would appear that these three profoundly different modern authors can speak with one voice to issue a stern antipedagogical declaration.

What, then, are we teachers doing in the academy? If we take seriously the lesson against lessons offered to us by these three authors, we should simply abandon our post, whatever it is, in the house of higher education. We should venture forth in order to find our own great grey-green, greasy Limpopo River and to distill our own experience into wisdom. Or, if we decide to remain at our post, we should have an adequate response to these three voices in their profound skepticism about culture and history, about tradition and the past.

II.

I shall begin my response to what has preceded (in the precession of antipedagogical propositions) with the case of Proust. Some of you are, I hope, ready to protest vehemently that what I cited from Proust was a quotation taken out of context.

At this juncture in the story, the mid-teenage Marcel, the novel's protagonist and narrator, is a precocious yet insecure aesthete. He has just attached himself to the famous Impressionist painter, Elstir. Marcel discovers from one of the paintings in Elstir's studio that this great sage of an artist had, many years earlier, been "a foolish, corrupt little painter" trying to make his way among the high-society patrons he now scorns. Instead of being annoyed with Marcel for learning about his past, Elstir, *"comme le maître qu'il était"*—that is, as both exemplar and teacher—decides "to say what he thought would prove instructive to me."

The passage quoted gives us not Proust's voice but Elstir the master speaking to the neophyte Marcel as he is leaving the studio. Wishing to say something "instructive," Elstir states that a person attains to wisdom neither through special election nor by education but "after a long journey through the wilderness that no one else can take for us." A few lines later, that journey is called "a struggle and a victory." Now "journey" and "struggle" do not appear here as abstract concepts. They refer concretely to developments in the characters' lives as they are taking shape in narrative time. We have seen Elstir much earlier as a vulgar opportunistic young artist in Madame Verdurin's snobbish coterie. Now, some thirty years later, he has become a true master of his own solvent style of landscape painting and also master of his personal and social life. In his case, we see two contrasting stages in the journey of his life, not the crucial episodes of how he matured, of how he got his trunk.

On the other hand, we shall follow the whole of Marcel's career before and after this passage as he first aspires to become a writer and then fails and finally succeeds. The hortatory words spoken to Marcel by an older master warn him that he must make his own journey, that no one can show him the way. Marcel does now set out resolutely to explore the alluring domains of aristocratic society, erotic love, and art. But he does not leave behind the sense of honor and of naturalness he has absorbed from his mother and grandmother, qualities he also sees expressed in the beautiful architectural lines of the Combray church of his childhood. These precious scruples and principles guide him past the homosexual blandishments of the Baron de Charlus and even past the temptations of idolatry in art. What he has learned early on serves him well. In other words, Elstir's advice, delivered on a particular occasion, is only partly true in the long haul.

The title Proust gave to his novel, *In Search of Lost Time,* emphasizes the active pursuit of knowledge and identity through time by a principal character surrounded by supporting characters. Proust seeks to encompass the past, to link it to the present as an active element. He wrote a story three thousand pages long not because he never learned verbal continence but because he understood at the start that he wanted to portray a succession of false scents and blind alleys as they gradually agglomerate into a lifetime of learning. That learning begins intensely during Marcel's childhood in the countryside of Combray. He will never forget the elements he learned there of justice and selfless love and self-reliance. Little is told us about his formal schooling, but he does not feel the need to scorn the remarkable culture he has picked up.

I hope to have shown, therefore, that Elstir's set speech to Marcel cannot be considered Proust's final word on education, or even Elstir's. The wisdom of a novel resides not in isolated passages but in the full sinuous growth of its narrative action. Proust's *Search* carries Marcel, and carries us as readers, toward a gradual encompassing of the past into an expanded present through memory and recognition. Proust leads us through several stages toward understanding that culture and a sense of the past and learning do not "stand between us and things" but, rather, grant us the possibility of reaching things in their fullest meanings.

Now we must face the possibility that we have given the Kipling story too hasty a reading. The Elephant's Child's 'satiable curiosity frees him from conformity and convention at home and finally gains him his all-purpose trunk. But let us not forget that along the way his curiosity betrays him into the jaws of Crocodile as he is being pulled into the water. The jig is up for our fruit-eating hero. What saves him? Not liberation theology. It was his scrupulous politeness and decency in an earlier encounter toward the Bi-Colored-Python-Rock-Snake that won him a friend who comes to his rescue in his hour of need. The great Snake saves his life and in the process pulls out his trunk like a piece of toffee. If the Elephant's Child had not heeded his upbringing to be considerate to others, Crocodile would have drowned and devoured him.

At first glance, the Elephant's Child's expedition to the Limpopo River seems to teach that we will do well to turn our backs on education based on conformity and enforced by spankings. You must liberate yourself from tradition to find true wisdom. But the Elephant's Child also carries with him lessons learned before he became a dissident. When he sets out to discover in the neighborhood of the great gray-green, greasy Limpopo River what the Crocodile has for dinner, the Elephant's Child does not abandon the considerate behavior he has been taught toward all other creatures. That decency saves him and equips him with a serviceable trunk and even makes a major contribution to Elephant civilization. Some childish things we should not put away.

A second observation about my three passages should be nagging some of you who have a knack for logic. Each author offers a warning against instruction, against teachers, against traditional knowledge. The three could be brought together under this injunction: *Do not take advice.* And straightway we are confounded. For that injunction becomes self-refuting by advising us not to take even this particular advice against advice. Consequently, one *should* take advice . . . and thus we are projected vigorously into the infinite regress of logical contradiction. This way lies Epimenides' paradox. It takes various forms: *This sentence is false.* Or the Cretan who says, "All Cretans are liars." This form of self-refutation or logical impasse can be used against the truth claims of a deterministic system like Islam and rubs our noses in the fact that we live at very close quarters all our lives with contradiction and paradox. In some fashion, we usually come to live at peace with both sides of the contradiction in question here—that is, to take advice and not to take advice. A large majority of people in the world believe in some form of predestination or determinism, yet they go about their lives as if they are free to choose their actions. We do not just tolerate contradiction. We thrive on it. The self-refutation argument leads to a logical impasse that appears to trouble almost no one.

My third observation about the antipedagogical prejudice addresses itself to the difference I have several times suggested between how we read Kipling and Proust and how we read Nietzsche. The passage from "The Elephant's Child" and the one from Proust's *Search* belong to a larger unit of meaning—a story that incorporates character developing in time. We cannot extract one passage to represent the whole without taking account of the entire action—beginning, middle, and end. The Elephant's Child's journey to the Limpopo River should not be read in isolation as a rejection of traditional education. It represents a stage preceded by his early upbringing in considerateness for others and followed by his homecoming with improvements in Elephant anatomy and distributive justice for the community. Elstir's strong lesson against lessons finds its place in a vast bildungsroman. At this stage of the story, Marcel needs encouragement to develop some independence of mind. At other stages, he does well to listen to his elders—particularly to his mother and grandmother and to Françoise, the proverbial serving woman of sturdy peasant stock. At the end, Marcel has himself become an elder who sets down an account of his life in a narrative intended to illuminate us about our own lives. In the long view of a person's life, learning and rejection of learning both have their place according to the timing of events in a complex process that weaves together living and education.

In his early essay on Schopenhauer as educator, from which I have quoted, Nietzsche was dealing with, among other things, the contradiction between education as discipline and education as liberation. The first section closes with this statement: "Education is rather liberation"; the second section soon affirms irritably, ". . . speaking and writing are arts that cannot be acquired without the most rigorous discipline." At the end, Nietzsche asks confidently, "What in the world does the history of philosophy matter to our young people?" Two pages earlier, he has assured us that "experience . . . teaches us better." But both Nietzsche and Schopenhauer appealed constantly to the history of philosophy to reinforce their points. Anyone who has read Nietzsche knows how often one encounters such inconsistencies within any one essay and, even more, among his different works. Increasingly broken up into short nonsequential sections, the writings become more kaleidoscopic than cumulative.

These contradictions are real and belong to the experience of life as we live it. Kipling and Proust deal with such conflicting attitudes toward learning and knowledge by placing them within the story of a developing life in its succeeding stages. In both the eighteen-page story and the multivolume *roman fleuve,* narrative allows us to see how, for the Elephant's Child, discipline and learning precede liberation and individual talent, and then alternate and intertwine in unexpected ways. Without a temporal framework to lend some shape to the education and development of a specific philosopher, his own or Schopenhauer's, Nietzsche's statements in the essay come out as peremptory and hard to reconcile. The passage I have quoted, which vehemently condemns the scholar as sterile and bookish, is not embraced by an expository or narrative line that sets it in perspective. Consequently, it sticks out like an outburst of antiintellectual zealotry. In spite of the strong current of Nietzsche's prose, "Schopenhauer as Educator" seems awkward and arbitrary compared with Kipling and Proust in dealing with the complex experience of education.

Nietzsche did try his hand twice at narrative, with unhappy results. The allegorical and possibly self-satirical *Thus Spake Zarathustra* comes frequently to a halt in order to issue pronouncements. In *Ecce Homo,* Nietzsche's incipient mental condition distorts the autobiographical story line beyond all credibility and converts it into propaganda. There is something very forlorn about what Nietzsche wrote to Lou Salomé in 1882 about case histories of philosophers. He welcomes "the reduction of philosophical systems to personal documents about their originators. . . . The system is dead and debunked—but the *person* behind it is incontrovertible; the person simply cannot be killed." Section six of *Beyond Good and Evil* affirms that every great philosophy consists in "the personal confession of its author and a kind of involuntary and unconscious memoir." Nietzsche yearns for autobiography. Alexander Nehamas has written a full book to argue that Nietzsche "created a character out of himself" (233) and "became the Plato of his own Socrates" (234). I find both claims dubious. Nietzsche has little force as a storyteller or writer of trenchant dialogue. He remains a discursive philosopher who works most effectively in projecting a voice—searching, commanding, often lapidary, rising to a sibylline style of grand proclamations and exhortations. Concrete lived situations and individual character maturing in time do not play a central role in his work.

It is probably because of the prejudices of a literary critic in favor of stories and against abstract ideas that I find Kipling's and Proust's narratives offer us more wisdom on the subject of education and teaching than do the heady pronouncements of Nietzsche.

III.

In order to make my last point about teaching the unteachable, let me ask you to bring back to mind once again the three passages I have quoted: Kipling on the Elephant's Child's 'satiable curtiosity, Nietzsche's rejection of scholarship in favor of direct pristine experience, and Proust's having Elstir counsel the boy Marcel that wisdom cannot be taught, only gleaned from the journey of life. On the surface, they represent three expressions of sweeping skepticism about books, learning, and teaching—about a whole set of cultural items I shall telescope now for convenience into one term, *literature.* But notice that these three skeptics about literature were all industrious authors who produced a corpus of writings intended for attentive readers. Once again, these passages represent a troubling contradiction. If literature is no substitute for the experience of life truly lived, why write, read, talk, study, or listen to lectures?

I have suggested already that, particularly in the cases of Kipling and Proust, the narrative form of their work modifies the separate passages and requires a more comprehensive interpretation of the words. But I want to propose another response to the dilemma of unteachability that deals with the nature of experience itself. On any topic so vast and so personal, I shall have to work in broad strokes and rely on argument by analogy.

The phrase "Once upon a time" points to our modern understanding of the events of life as happening on one unique occasion in space and time. No matter what I am taught in school, no matter what I read, no matter how much I have learned about the past, my encounters with love and suffering and pleasure will be my personal experiences. And those occasions will be confined to a single point in space and time, only faintly extended in consciousness by anticipation and memory.

Now I want to make a case for saying that experience is not so limited, and that any worthwhile Once Upon a Time may metamorphose by the nature of things and of mind into a Twice-Told Tale. No significant occasion need happen only once. Inexplicably, German appears to be the only language with a proverb to match: *Einmal ist keinmal* (Once is not enough). For example, our relation to space and time multiplies our perception of events in remarkable ways. In space, we are perfectly familiar with the phenomenon because, as higher animals, we have not one but two eyes. Binocular vision gives us stereoscopic perception of depth and relief. Such parallax vision, which takes account of the discrepancy between two or more different images of one object or occasion, allows us to calculate the distances of objects around us as well as of the closer stars. One-eyed Cyclops has a curiously powerful monstrosity to him: He cannot see properly. Beyond visual perception, parallax—or the stereologic principle—enhances our binaural hearing, as well. Each ear hears a slightly different sound, and by taking account of the difference, our incredible neurons locate and recognize the source.

In contrast to these familiar words relating to seeing and hearing double in space through two sense organs, we have only a rudimentary vocabulary to deal with a comparable set of phenomena affecting our experiences in time. In this case, we do not have exterior sense organs in pairs to reinforce our awareness of the stereologic or parallax principle in taking account of events in time. But a few existing words help show the way. The most common is *déjà vu,* meaning in its original usage "the illusory, incomprehensible, yet powerful feeling of having lived the present moment before." *Anamnesis,* a Platonic term meaning "recollection or reminiscence from an earlier life," occurs today in neurological writings with the sense of a seizure of memory, a breaking open of the door to the past. Some of you have come upon the clinical treatments of these occurrences by Dr. Oliver Sacks writing about his institutionalized patients. Sacks's general term for such complex temporal experiences is *transports.* He responds as sensitively as a novelist to our need for a linear pattern of experience—music or narrative—

to give us a feeling of wholeness in living our own identity. But even Sacks has no word for the converse of *déjà vu*—that is, the not-yet-seen, the presentiment that an event will recur in some form, that we have foreknowledge of a future moment.

Yet that feeling can be very strong. At times, we cannot confine experience to a single point. Let me cite a beautifully portentous conversation from *Absalom, Absalom!* between Quentin and Shreve about Sutpen. Faulkner gives these italicized thoughts to Quentin.

Maybe nothing ever happens once and is finished. Maybe happen is never one but like ripples maybe on water after the pebble sinks, the ripples moving on, spreading, the pool attached by a narrow umbilical water-cord to the next pool which the first pool feeds, has fed, did feed.

Such a sense of events propagating like light in time exists not only in Faulkner but also, almost obsessively, in Rousseau's *Confessions* and in the novels of Virginia Woolf. (Nietzsche's "eternal return" does not provide an instance of the doubling in time I am describing. Nietzsche refers to a moment either abiding or repeating itself over time. But, as in stereoscopic vision, it is the *difference,* not the identity, between similar perceptions that gives enhanced feeling for the experience of time.)

The most arresting quotation comes from the mathematician-philosopher, Alfred North Whitehead. In chapter 5 of *Science and the Modern World,* Whitehead traces the romantic reaction of organism against all forms of mechanism and against what he calls "the fallacy of simple location." He finds this reaction particularly in literature and in the immediate sensations registered by poetry. The logician Whitehead sounds like Swedenborg or Novalis as he makes his point. Notice his use of the verb *involve.*

. . . my theory involves the entire abandonment of the notion that simple location is the primary way in which things are involved in space-time. In a certain sense, everything is everywhere at all times. For every location involves an aspect of itself in every other location. Thus every spatio-temporal standpoint mirrors the world.

Whitehead, like Faulkner, resists any tendency to break down experience into unique isolated moments. For them, the phrase "Once upon a time" reports less accurately on life than the phrase "twice-told tale," or the *"Einmal ist keinmal."* What happens to us is not confined to a succession of unique moments; experience unfolds (or, according to Bergson, rolls up) as double and multiple along a pathway with many involvements and crossings-over and interlockings—like DNA. Of all proverbs, we should place least faith in the one that states: You live only once.

The consequences of these observations for my argument take this form. It is correct to say with Kipling, Nietzsche, and Proust that literature and education cannot replace the direct experience of life and offer no substitute for it. But the earliest *Homo sapiens* child learning from his father how to wield a club or from her mother how to build a fire was discovering the elementary economy of life—namely, that we do not have to find out everything for ourselves *from scratch*. One can draw on a fund of learned skills and arts and lessons. Literature will never replace life; yet it can shape and direct our experience of life. We read novels and stories in great part because they instruct us in how to respond to the circumstances of existence. Stories may occupy *one* of the positions in the Twice-Told Tale we call our life, not both of them.

Literature, as one among the arts, acquaints us with a special and intensified repertory of feelings and events and possibilities. Later, when we come upon an event or a significant impression, we may have a counterpart ready to hand, half-forgotten yet available. And our mind may respond with a cry: Aha! Here it is. For we have known it once already by proxy. Literature can foreshorten the complex two-part process of full living; what we participate in through reading becomes the first half of that double process. Our own life, our personal experience, can then move directly into the second beat: recognition.

This apparently simplistic explanation of the contribution of literature holds up also in reverse. The person who has lived a full, varied life frequently fails to recognize its meaning or even to appreciate its richness until encountering it anew in a work of literature. Whereas the young—in an almost optical sense—look forward to life through literature, the old look back at life through it. Proust spoke revealingly of the novel reader not as escaping oneself but as seeing into oneself, discovering oneself. Literature at its best directs more than it diverts. And life, too, early and late, may direct us toward literature.

We have some basis now for looking one final time at the three passages before us. Nietzsche's rejection of scholarship and his insistence on the uniqueness and thus the unhistorical nature of genuine experience diminishes an essential feature of human perception, which is to embody both continuity—in the form of habit and recognition—and originality. Books and past events need not come between us and things; they prepare us for the world in ways that allow us to recognize and judge things on a sound basis. Nietzsche's antipedagogical bias in the "Schopenhauer" passage underplays the temporal dynamics of life and the reciprocal relations between learning and living.

Elstir's arresting sermon to Marcel in Proust's passage errs in much the same way. However, this passage belongs to an extended story about how a person comes to discern the vital importance of the past and of early lessons about life. The novel as a whole redresses the imbalance that belongs to a single moment within the action. The experience of the book is long and multiple and reciprocal, like life itself.

Kipling's little tale presents a frisky young animal who goes off to discover his own way in the world rather than stay to face more spankings—circumstances that echo parts of Kipling's own childhood. But the Elephant's Child both retains essential lessons from his upbringing and returns to instruct his own people. The continual delicate balance between tradition and innovation, between learning and living cannot finally be taught. But every sequence of history thoroughly explored, every work of genuine literature intelligently read, carries us a partial distance toward life, experience, and wisdom. So let us keep on reading—in spite of Nietzsche and including Nietzsche. And let us pay close attention to writers like Kipling and Proust, who had a profound sense that to gain true experiences of one's own does not require that one discard the wisdom of others.

Yes, some things are unteachable, but never absolutely so. Teachers like Bill Arrowsmith and Tari Shattuck found ways of approaching those subjects obliquely, through stories and translations, and through their own devotion to the cause of living fully and wisely. It is essential that the rest of us keep on teaching and learning with every iota of patience and daring we have about us.

14

THE ALIBI OF ART

T WO CONTRASTING REVOLUTIONS jarred France in 1830. In the preceding forty years, the country had lived through the Great Revolution, the First Republic, the Terror, the emperor Napoléon and his wars, humiliating defeats, and the restoration of the Bourbon monarchy in 1815. Then, fifteen years later, France was bubbling again, culturally and politically. In February 1830, at the first night of Victor Hugo's Spanish melodrama *Hernani* at the Comédie Française, the troops of the young liberal faction outshouted the conservatives. Romanticism won its first major battle in France, thanks in part to the dedicated antics of a nineteen-year-old painter-poet with long hair and wearing a flamboyantly red vest. Théophile Gautier soon published his first collection of poems and a volume of stories about the new generation. *Les Jeune-France,* as he titled the volume—something like *France's New Generation*—both celebrated and satirized romantic excesses in a style more impudent than that of Murger's *Scènes de la vie de Bohème,* which appeared almost twenty years later. In the 1830s, there was no Puccini to immortalize Gautier's tales of artists in their garrets. *Les Jeune-France* left little mark. But Gautier was on his way.

The second 1830 revolution came in July—violent, political, and very brief. It established Louis Philippe as king of the French with a liberal constitution in writing and with a furled umbrella in his bourgeois hand.

Among other changes, censorship was lifted. But when the Citizen King began to betray his liberal principles, and when the great cartoonists Philipon and Daumier filled the popular press with devastating lithographic caricatures of a pear-headed monarch devouring and then evacuating his own people, the royal victim could not take the heat. And the conservative press was crying out for the disciplining of the young Romantics; their manners, their morals, and their dreadful versification could not be tolerated. By 1834, censorship loomed again. Gautier, not yet twenty-three, found himself under bitter attack for having written a sympathetic essay on the late-medieval poet and thief François Villon. One critic called Villon "depraved and lubricious." Gautier replied with spirit, calling his own essay "a work of art" and proclaiming that whatever is adopted by art and science "becomes chaste" (Jasinski, 193).

But Gautier had greater reason to worry. The novel he was writing in 1834, entitled *Mademoiselle de Maupin,* contained antireligious declarations, perverted and transvestite behavior, and graphic sex scenes exceeding anything else then sold on the open market. Both the aristocratic aesthete hero and his mistress fall in love with an ardent young woman, like Shakespeare's Rosalind masquerading as a man; both enjoy her favors in passages Shakespeare would never have written. A pretty page boy adds the theme of pedophilia to that of androgyny.

A little-known scholar, Eric Deudon, has demonstrated how far the religious and sexual content of *Mademoiselle de Maupin* ventured beyond any so-called immoral works of the era. The very month the novel appeared in 1835, Louis Philippe's government reestablished censorship of the theater and the press. Daumier and Philipon were muzzled. Books by Béranger, Bordeaux, Gercourt, Parny, and others, were suppressed, usually for *"outrage à la morale publique."* But none of their works held a candle to *Mademoiselle de Maupin* in respect to that offense. During the same period, works by Stendhal, Hugo, Lamartine, and Balzac were put on the Catholic Index of Forbidden Books.

Mademoiselle de Maupin escaped scot-free in France from any form of suppression. The 1835 crackdown somehow left it unscathed, and the immunity continued under the Second Empire, which took to court both Flaubert's *Madame Bovary* (unsuccessfully) and Baudelaire's *Les Fleurs du mal* (successfully). But in other countries, *Mademoiselle de Maupin* was either refused publication or stripped of offending chapters. What, then, protected Gautier's novel from prosecution in France at the exact moment when every circumstance marked it for censorship?

The answer must be partly conjectural. It appears that Gautier had the astuteness to grasp the danger his novel faced and to deploy his defense in advance. A year earlier, he had heatedly written a fifty-page polemic on the journalists who criticized the Romantic group for immorality and for breaking all traditional literary rules and decorums. Gautier's tract berates conservative critics as prudes and envious hypocrites and summons Molière, La Fontaine, and Rabelais as witnesses for the defense. Gautier proceeded to excoriate the critics who expected a novel to serve a useful social purpose. He was thinking mostly of the followers of Saint-Simon's and Fourier's versions of socialism, who wanted art to serve their cause. In reply, Gautier mounted a powerful barrage against utility of any kind in art and drew up a complementary defense of beauty. The central passage ends with a famous substantive that is usually mistranslated.

Nothing is truly beautiful except that which serves no purpose. Anything useful is ugly, for it is the expression of some need, and human needs are ignoble and disgusting, like his pitiful and feeble nature.—The most useful place in a house is the latrine. [*Lavatory* and even *toilet* provide lame euphemisms for the explicit French term *les latrines.*]

This tract never mentions government censorship, only the baying conservative critics. And it never mentions by name the nascent doctrine of "art for art's sake" even while making a vehement and striking case for it. Toward the end, in a maneuver that resembles pure effrontery, Gautier urged Louis Philippe to muzzle the prudish and conservative critics as a menace to the true beauties of Romantic art.

Mademoiselle de Maupin and the tract were written separately. But when the time came, Gautier saw that, with a few small changes, they were made for each other. The latter would provide the preface for the former. After this joint publication, the preface was soon accepted as the manifesto of art for art's sake and a milestone in the history of French literature. Ironically, Gautier, the converted painter, yearned before all to gain his reputation as a poet. After this explosive novel, he was obliged to devote most of the rest of his long career to journalism. Meanwhile, his preface served as the magic garment, the censor-proof protection for what looked and still looks like the generic filthy French novel.

IN 1954, A European writer living in the United States finished his third novel in English, and his first with an American setting. Four publishers rejected it as lewd, if not frankly pornographic, even though the action was veiled in euphemisms and the prose was free of four-letter words and of the clichés of low-grade pornography. Finally, an English-language publisher in Paris issued the novel with a three-page foreword, numbered as part of the novel and signed by a fictional doctor of psychology. The foreword presents the allegedly posthumous novel as a scientific case history, a transcendent work of art, and a moral tale. The controversy provoked by the book moved its true author to write a six-page afterword for the many later editions and translations. We have not left Théophile Gautier behind.

> I am neither a reader nor a writer of didactic fiction, and [despite the assertion to the contrary by the psychologist in the foreword,] this novel has no moral in tow. For me a work of fiction exists only insofar as it affords me what I shall bluntly call aesthetic bliss, that is a sense of being somehow, somewhere, connected with other states of being where art (curiosity, tenderness, kindness, ecstasy) is the norm. There are not many such books. (314)

No moral . . . aesthetic bliss . . . art as the norm. These are unexpected yet tactically astute claims to make about a book called *Lolita*. The debate whether *Lolita* is a dirty book or a classic continues to rage after forty years. Before his death in 1977, Vladimir Nabokov went on to publish five less controversial novels in English.

Lolita offers us the memoir, or, alternatively, the testimony to a jury, of an idle cultivated Frenchman turning forty, obsessed by prepubescent girls, and having several times been institutionalized for mental instability. Humbert Humbert comes to the United States and marries a widow in order to gain access to her twelve-year-old daughter, whom he names Lolita. When the mother is killed in an accident, Humbert can carry off his ward, the not entirely innocent Lolita, on a great journey into the hinterlands. He has in reality terrorized her into becoming his sex slave until she escapes into the clutches of another pedophile, whom Humbert tracks down and elaborately murders. Humbert's telling of his own tale rides on irresistibly satirical descriptions of small-town life and of the world of motels and inns, mixed with Humbert's pleas of self-exoneration and self-inculpation. He employs a versatile literary style that blends the uproarious, the terrifying, and the moving. Certain readers are carried so completely into Humbert's mind and mood that they come to sympathize with this criminal rapist and murderer. Only a decade earlier, Camus's *The Stranger*, using a hypnotic first-person narrative, had convinced many readers of the sincerity and fundamental innocence of Meursault, who drifted like a zombie into murder. I believe that *Lolita*, a dazzling literary exercise not unrelated to *The Stranger*, was written as a four-fold wager.

First, Nabokov wagered he could surpass James Joyce (the *Ulysses* trial is referred to in the foreword) in composing a work whose literary qualities justify the incorporation of strong pornographic content as essential to the story. Second, Nabokov ventured he could write graphically "aphrodisiac" (4) passages without using the conventions and obscene terms of commercial pornography. Third, Nabokov, the Russo-French European, wagered he could succeed in finding a literary style in English for depicting American characters and settings both convincingly and satirically. Fourth, Nabokov gambled that he could, by taking on the three previous wagers, produce a best-seller, earn financial independence from teaching, and return to Europe.

Nabokov won all four bets handily, but at a steep price. In order to get *Lolita* past the gates of taste and the law, Nabokov, like Gautier and like Judge Woolsey in the *Ulysses* case, invoked the aesthetic alibi. But he didn't mean it. First of all, Humbert himself constantly lays claim to the sanctuary of art for his memoir and even for his behavior. "You have to be an artist and a madman" (17) to discern the true nymphet. Later: "The artist has been given the upper hand over the gentleman" (71). "The gentle and dreamy regions through which I crept were the patrimonies of poets—*not* crime's prowling-ground" (131). And in the closing words of the novel, Humbert claims that "the refuge of art . . . is the only immortality you and I share, my Lolita" (309). Refuge *from* immorality and psychopathology. And refuge, he hopes, *into* the immortality of art. We call this topos "perpetuation by poetry." Sleep with me and I'll make you famous forever. In other words, Humbert's superior account of these events represents the work not of a madman but of an artist, not of a criminal but of a poet.

By now, however, Humbert's status as unreliable narrator with a mad imagination has been, or should have been, fully established. Therefore, his bogus claim to artistic status as a privilege for his lies discredits both the status and the privilege. Nabokov's own parallel claims in the afterword to "aesthetic bliss" and "art as the norm" are undermined by Humbert's preening as an artist in the novel we are reading. Later in the afterword, Nabokov makes a concession to potential reservations about the moral effects of his book. "That my novel does contain various allusions to the physiological urges of a pervert is quite true. But after all we are not children" (316). Nabokov grants, therefore, that this book should not fall into the hands of children. Furthermore, we have evidence to contradict the declaration that *Lolita* "has no moral in tow." To an interviewer, who found Humbert "touching," Nabokov replied, "I would put it differently: Humbert Humbert is a vain and cruel wretch who manages to *appear* 'touching.' " To his friend and rival, Edmund Wilson, Nabokov wrote in 1956, "When you do read *Lolita,* please mark that it is a highly moral affair" (Levine, 37). Nabokov wrote these words ten months before he composed the afterword claiming the alibi of art and the refuge of aesthetic bliss. A change of mind? I doubt it. Literary tactics? Probably, yes. Like Gautier in the preface to *Mademoiselle de Maupin*, Nabokov found it wise in his afterword to construct a defense for his novel.

Humbert, the character, makes a few unconvincing gestures toward undermining civilization and its constraints (17–18, 96). But grasped as a complete work, which gradually reveals Humbert's true character, *Lolita* comes down on the side of civilized constraints and not in favor of cruel exploitation and perversion masquerading as art. Therefore, it is appalling to find on the book's front cover as a laudatory blurb (from *Vanity Fair*) a sentence expressing an obtuse and perverse misunderstanding of the novel: "The only convincing love story of our century." Humbert loves no human person and only lusts after total possession of the unformed demonic nymphet imagined by his insane mind. Lolita, not daisy-fresh but not depraved when Humbert finds her, despises her stepfather and lives in terror of him. For she knows "she has absolutely nowhere else to go" (142).

Unlike *Mademoiselle de Maupin*, *Lolita* can stand on its own feet as a literary and moral creation. It does not need the alibi of art to protect it. Nabokov was nourished on a highly developed European tradition that values art as a special category, and he was impelled by what I am calling "a wager" to test that tradition by injecting into it a strong dose of elegant pornography. Accordingly, he costumed *Lolita* carefully and, I think, mistakenly in the doctrine of pure art, of aesthetic detachment. The book does not need that protection. In referring to "a general lesson" that lurks in the story (5), the fictional author of the foreword, John Ray, Jr., Ph D , speaks truer than the real author of the novel when he claims in the afterword that "*Lolita* has no moral in tow" (314).

A FEW PAGES of literary history will enlighten us now on why, a century after the 1830 revolutions, Nabokov behaved like Gautier, and why the alibi of art looked so appealing to both of them. I shall cover the ground in two rash simplifications—first the ancients and then the moderns.

The ancients agreed generally that the arts, particularly music and poetry, have real and lasting effects on our behavior. These works do not remain in an autonomous realm, to be contemplated at a distance. In the Tenth Book of *The Republic*, Plato settles the ancient quarrel between philosophy based on reason and poetry based on imagination and inspiration in favor of philosophy. Poetry exists at two removes from reality and, by watering the passions, it leads us into trouble. Except for hymns to the gods and a few restful modes in music, the arts for Plato have the effect of dangerous infection. Better do without and rely on philosophy and physical exercise.

For Aristotle, on the other hand, the effects of true art, particularly great tragedy, are quite different. In the *Poetics* and the *Politics,* Aristotle suggests that art may have healthy consequences, comparable to a medical purge (catharsis) or to religious purification. But the most important outcome of ancient approaches to poetry and drama was the emergence of a satisfactory and durable synthesis. Horace's brief and celebrated lines in *The Art of Poetry* are ordered in such a way as to suggest that painting and poetry at their best fulfill a double purpose: to instruct and to delight. This affirmation of the didactic principle along with the hedonistic principle was accepted by the Christian tradition as a defense against the iconoclastic impulse that dominated in Judaism and in Islam. The eighth-century Christian Council of Nicea decided in favor of images in spite of the Second Commandment, which prohibits idolatry. When the English Puritans revived the spirit of image smashing and iconoclasm in the sixteenth and seventeenth centuries, Sir Philip Sidney's influential *An Apology for Poetry* cited the Horatian double formula of delight and instruction as an important argument in favor of the poet's work.

The modern period, roughly since the seventeenth century, offers far less opportunity to simplify the picture. As the middle class emerged in England and Scotland, seventeenth- and eighteenth-century authors like Hobbes and Mandeville selected human motives of self-interest and personal advantage as primary. Through the desire to possess pleasing objects and through the vanity of fashion and conspicuous consumption, these motives of selfishness threatened to discredit the cultivation of taste and the pursuit of the arts. Shaftesbury and Hutcheson defended the arts by associating them with a nobler self and a higher sense of beauty linked not only to selfish pleasure but also to morality and truth. And each of them twice puts forward very tentatively the word *disinterestedness:* It excludes personal advantage and appeals to the public good. Thus the arts and taste were rescued from ordinary self-interest.

At the opening of part I of the *Critique of Judgment,* Immanuel Kant picks up the tune from Shaftesbury and Hutcheson and proposes a form of "mere contemplation" apart from self-interest. Kant's state of "pure disinterested and free delight" appears at first to exist independently of all other values and interests. But further reading reveals that Kant tied the aesthetic imagination of beauty to morality, human knowledge, and the general happiness of mankind.

And now the swift action and the confusion begin. Taking the new name of aesthetics from Baumgarten, Kant and Schiller developed the discipline of aesthetics as implying a certain independence and superiority for art, yet tying it still to the paired hedonistic and didactic functions of Horace's formula, *dulce et utile,* to entertain and to instruct. Then, these ideas about the status of art traveled rapidly across the Western world in an extended diaspora whose history remains to be told in full. Gene Bell-Villada's recent book, *Art for Art's Sake and Literary Life* (1996), though incomplete and pulled off course by political tendencies, gives the fullest account. Kant and Schiller inspired Coleridge traveling in Germany, and Mme. de Stael living in exile, and also Victor Cousin teaching philosophy in Paris. The French Romantics and particularly Gautier adopted and adapted German aesthetic ideas very freely. They modified abstract "disinterestedness" into a flashy slogan, *l'art pour l'art,* meaning "art for art's sake." This form of pure art went beyond Shaftesbury and Kant to demand full autonomy from morality and the public good. Bell-Villada calls this further stage "aesthetic separatism."

There is also a less recognized itinerary to take account of in this dispersion and regrouping of ideas. Coleridge's works reached across the Atlantic and struck deep into the mind of a brilliant and lonely American writer. In an essay called "The Poetic Principle" (1850), Edgar Allan Poe carried Kant's ideas to their logical extreme. Poetry at its noblest dissociates itself from truth and from the good—from what Poe calls "the heresy of The Didactic." The supreme work is "the poem per se . . . this poem written solely for the poem's sake." Poe's bold thoughts were not by any means the end of the line.

In the mid-1850s, Charles Baudelaire, in Paris, discovered Poe and recognized his literary and moral alter ego. While translating Poe's stories, Baudelaire plagiarized whole paragraphs of "The Poetic Principle" for his own literary criticism. And it was in great part Poe who turned Baudelaire from his early scorn of art for art's sake as a "puerile" (281) attitude leading to "unknown and monstrous disorders" (304) to a second stage, where Baudelaire accepted the independence of art from "teaching" and from "great ideas." But Baudelaire continued the debate with himself and his contemporaries in his powerful "New Notes on Edgar Poe" (1859). He grants that poetry has the power to ennoble humankind and to raise us above the level of vulgar interests. But a *result* does not prove a corresponding *purpose* on the part of the poet. Here, Baudelaire is categorical. "I say that if the poet has pursued a moral goal, he has diminished his poetic power. It is not imprudent to wager that his work will be bad" (352). Baudelaire never stopped meditating about the correlation between poetry and morality.

The flow of ideas continued with the transfer of Gautier's and Baudelaire's thinking on art for art's sake back across the English Channel into the works of Ruskin, Pater, Wilde, Swinburne, Yeats, Joyce, and Eliot. These exchanges have been treated by a number of scholars, including Richard Ellman, Bell-Villada, and the historians of Decadence as a movement. The best generalization one might venture about this remarkable two-century migration of ideas from Shaftesbury back and forth across Europe and the Atlantic is that we must now add a third term to the two that Horace successfully linked and even fused for over fifteen centuries. Today, I would propose, we have to deal with three positions. First, through both its infectious and its cathartic powers, art can be didactic, not only in the domains of knowledge and morality but also politically, through engagement, social reform, and bearing witness. Second, through its treatment of beauty in a very broad sense, now encompassing the grotesque, the comic, the unexpected, and even the ugly, art can please and entertain us. And third, through its capacity to lift us out of ordinary selfish interests and to refocus our attention on the purely sensuous and formal qualities of a poem or a painting or a piece of music, art can assume value for its own sake alone, in an autonomous aesthetic condition independent of all other considerations.

Horace's two factors, delight and instruction, lived and worked together for centuries. We respond to that harmony in the works of Molière and of George Eliot. When a third factor, art for art's sake, the autonomy of art, entered the picture, it demanded superior rank, as expressed in the high polemics of Gautier's preface to *Mademoiselle de Maupin* and in Oscar Wilde's haughtiest pronouncements (for example, "aesthetics is higher than ethics"). The conflict among the three elements continues unabated, in Baudelaire's writings, in Nabokov's contradictory statements about *Lolita,* and in our stumbling debates about violence and obscenity in the media. We shall not rest, I believe, until we find a new balance among these three elements. For, in some areas, the aesthetic has usurped the kingdom of art.

IN HIS "PREFACE to Shakespeare" (1765), Dr. Johnson did not shrink from keeping Horace's double formula at the center. "The end of writing is to instruct; the end of poetry is to instruct by pleasing." A modern author of novels known in part for their licentiousness, D. H. Lawrence, wrote very plainly about an American poet who celebrated the flesh, Walt Whitman. "The essential function of art," states Lawrence in that essay, "is moral." But some nineteenth-century artists had already begun to reach for art as an alibi for certain kinds of conduct. When Edouard Manet's huge painting and small lithograph of Emperor Maximilian's execution in Mexico were suppressed by the censor in 1869, Manet protested in vain that he had treated the subject "from a purely artistic point of view." Under Napoléon III, however, the aesthetic plea could not yet protect or exculpate a work that had strong political content.

In the past half a century, we have given almost limitless authority to the aesthetic alibi. The new dispensation has properly rescued Joyce's *Ulysses* and Nabokov's *Lolita* from repression, even though the *Lolita* case has ragged edges not adequately acknowledged in the adulatory paperback edition, *The Annotated Lolita*. But the gates have now opened so wide that pornography has begun to claim vanguard or fine-art status. One example, which I have addressed in a long chapter in my book *Forbidden Knowledge*, is the rehabilitation of the Marquis de Sade as a great literary artist and thinker.

A different example turns up in an eloquent defense of the category of aesthetic experience in a book entitled *The Scandal of Pleasure* (1995) by Wendy Steiner. In a lengthy account of the case of Robert Mapplethorpe's photography exhibit, "The Perfect Moment," Steiner documents how Mapplethorpe's defenders published in the *New York Times* Hitler's statement "It is not the function of art to wallow in dirt for dirt's sake" and how Senator Jesse Helms and his allies aimed to redefine American culture along such lines and to eliminate art "experts" as the final authority.

Then Steiner opens a new section. "This was the conflict that was to be enacted in the Cincinnati courts—some version of 'Hitler Meets the Marquis de Sade.' As so often happens in fairy tales, the fascist bully was defeated by the refined aristocrat" (31). In other words, prosecutor Frank Prouty was a fascist bully to find obscenity in this work, and the expert witnesses who defended the photographs as works of art and as therefore by definition exempt from the charge of obscenity were refined aristocrats defending civilization and freedom—presumably like the Marquis de Sade. I find it hard to say whether it is ignorance, naïveté, or bad faith on Wendy Steiner's part when she sets up Sade as the representative of freedom and civilization opposing Hitler. Sade was on the same side as Hitler. The only freedom and the only culture Sade could care about was his own, systematically arrayed against everyone else's, even his best friends'. Sade wanted his own fascist state. In attempting to defend art against some of its benighted enemies, Wendy Steiner has overlooked others, like herself, who take the position that anything can call itself art, and that art can do no wrong because it has only "virtual," not real-life, effects. I would respond that art is too powerful to be confined to the realm of the virtual. By definition, art touches us and leaves its mark.

In the face of these confusions, we should not be surprised that a few authors have expressed irreverence and distrust toward the category of the aesthetic. During his brief editorship of the *Westminster Gazette* in 1818, Thomas De Quincey displayed keen journalistic concern with German metaphysics, including Kant's category of the aesthetic, as well as with lurid crime stories, particularly those victimizing beautiful young girls. A decade later, he combined these two interests in an essay called "Murder Considered as One of the Fine Arts" (1827). With deadpan humor not unrelated to that of Swift's "Modest Proposal," De Quincey writes about various London clubs and associations that discuss the purpose, grouping, lighting, and timing of certain famous crimes. For even murder has "two handles": a moral handle and an aesthetic handle. One takes care of moral concerns by paying one's taxes to have the murderers apprehended. One can then proceed to the second concern, aesthetics. Accordingly, De Quincey reports that Mr. Williams, a notorious multiple murderer of 1811, "has carried his art to a point of colossal sublimity, and as Mr. Wordsworth observes, has in a manner created the taste by which he is to be enjoyed" (86). According to this logic, "Cain must have been a man of first-rate genius" (89). A series of preposterous examples leads De Quincey to his final sweeping claim. "For the final purpose of murder, considered as a fine art, is precisely the same as that of tragedy in Aristotle's account of it: viz. 'To cleanse the heart by means of pity and terror' " (100–101).

A follow-up essay of 1839 carries almost the same title, "On Murder Considered as One of the Fine Arts." Here, De Quincey stages the nineteenth-century equivalent of a well-funded, widely publicized academic conference in our day on "The Aesthetics of Crime and Violence." He describes a dinner at a gentlemen's club for the communication of new ideas, a dinner at which the narrator is principal speaker. He favors the discussion and careful study of the general principles of "our art" (342)—namely, the art of murder. But any lapse into *practice* of that art is counseled against. Such conduct would fatally decline into inferior crimes, such as robbery, drinking, breaking the Sabbath, and procrastination. De Quincey sustains his irony without a misstep. A series of increasingly frenzied toasts to great and beautiful murders leads to a final tribute: "To Thugdom in all its branches" (355). The evening ends in drunkenness and song.

This second version of De Quincey's prank has more punch than the first. He shows the aesthetes and dilettantes at work transforming crime into art. Their elevation of actual behavior into the virtual realm of art diddles with the firm line of demarcation stoutly defended by Gautier and sometimes by Nabokov and unreservedly by Wendy Steiner. De Quincey's sendup of the aesthetic alibi relies on reductio ad absurdum, which he attributes, tongue in cheek, to "the logic of a sensible man" (1827:89). De Quincey's subject (the philosophical squishiness and moral risk entailed in carrying the aesthetic category too far), his mock pompous tone, and his satirical clubdinner setting are still pertinent and tonic today.

De Quincey's manipulation of the essay form into satire displays a number of similarities with a much-discussed 1994 movie that manipulates the genre of the violent crime thriller. A loose set of narrative strands in this movie picks out a pair of killers, one black and the other white. The black killer believes a divine miracle has saved his life; he wants to abandon crime for holy vagabondage. The white killer tags along, blows a man's head off in a car by mistake, and loses his life because he goes to the toilet without his gun. Vapid small talk and running cinematic allusions frame scenes of hideous violence—or rather, they defang and routinize that violence to the level of small talk and jokes. *Pulp Fiction*, as the film is called, asks for total suspension of disbelief, attempts no psychological exploration of character, and turns its back on law and justice. No moral sense or center emerges anywhere in the story. The much-repeated magic word that explains and endorses the characters' behavior is *cool*. Cool means seeing outrageous actions as routine and inconsequential. The most enthusiastic reviewers tended to present the film as a brilliant and original satire of our tired media culture.

Pulp Fiction does not satirize our media culture. It succumbs willingly to that culture, celebrates it, exploits it, and successfully spreads its meaningless violence and jokiness across all human lives shown. Even the black killer's incipient religious conversion is assimilated to the general affectlessness, best expressed by the prolonged comedy of cleaning up the blood and brains scattered everywhere by the white killer's inadvertent mayhem in a car. In my estimation, *Pulp Fiction* succeeds in doing what Alfred Appel mistakenly believes Nabokov was doing in *Lolita,* and it succeeds in performing the operation De Quincey was caricaturing. It aestheticizes crime. *Pulp Fiction*'s sustained portrayal of an amusingly violent world leads the spectator particularly the cool, detached spectator—to a loss of the sense of reality. The cinematic attitude that everything is a spectacle, a camera shot, or a dream sequence now applies to all life, even our own. No clue in the movie sends any different message. Look, it says, you could live this way.

In De Quincey's deadpan, even cool, essays, we can soon detect the butt of the joke. He mocks the aesthetes who would brush aside the responsibilities of reality by affirming the sublime value of "beautiful" murders and by frenziedly toasting heroic crimes. In *Lolita,* Humbert's evident insanity, his own claims to have "solipsised" the nymphet Lolita, and his final uncompromising verdict against himself (thirty-five years for rape) give us an unambiguous fix on where reality lies. Appel, the postmodern annotator, would have us believe that because Nabokov sometimes puts the word *reality* between quotation marks, his book implies the "collapse . . . of the authenticity of the larger world" outside the book. Appel does a disservice to his friend in making this false claim. *Lolita* gradually wins its way back to reality.

Pulp Fiction, on the other hand, does set out to eliminate the reference point of reality. In that affectless world, coolness reveals itself as a form of autism. Members of the audience not repelled by this emptiness respond with compulsive laughter. Everyone comes through desensitized to violence and a little more detached from one's own encounters with real life. *Pulp Fiction* has a message: What a lark crime can be! Inadvertently blowing someone's head off is not murder in this icy universe. It's merely a movie sequence and a mess to be cleaned up. The message that "all is film" provides an extreme twist to Gautier's plea that "art is harmless." And De Quincey's elaborate joke, that murder can be considered a fine art, turns into a cool conspiracy in *Pulp Fiction.*

Horace counseled us that poetry should both delight and instruct. We stayed fairly close to this principle for many centuries, even after the invention of a new category of experience: the disinterested, autonomous contemplation of a work of pure art. As my examples may have shown, I believe that this allegedly new form of experience, when isolated from the demands of "real life," can lead us to a new idolatry—the idolatry of art. We are tempted, not religiously but commercially, to accept the alluring category of the aesthetic whose cool detachment is made to look as if it will wash away everyone's sins and excesses. The consequences of that illusion will be very destructive.

On the other hand, art as a category of responsible experience that sustains us by a reciprocating relation to life belongs to the metabolism of our culture and possibly of all culture. It deserves to be protected with all our powers from those who would borrow its mantle to protect and ennoble displays of unredeemed depravity and violence.

REFERENCES

Baudelaire, Charles. *Œuvres complètes.* Edited by Marcel Ruff. "L'Intégrale." Paris: Seuil, 1968.

De Quincey, Thomas. "Murder Considered as One of the Fine Arts" (1827). In *Thomas De Quincey.* Edited by Bonamy Dobrée. New York: Schocken Books, 1995.

———. "On Murder Considered as One of the Fine Arts" (1839). In *Selections from De Quincey.* Edited by Melton Haight Turk. New York: Ginn, 1902.

Deudon, Eric. "Mademoiselle de Maupin, rescapé de la censure orléaniste." *Les Amis de Flaubert* no. 66 (May 1985).

Jasinski, René. *Les Années romantiques de Théophile Gautier.* Paris: Vuibert, 1921.

Levine, Peter. "Lolita and Aristotle's Ethics." *Philosophy and Literature,* April 1991.

Nobokov, Vladimir. *The Annotated Lolita.* Edited by Alfred Appel, Jr. New York: Vintage, 1991.

Steiner, Wendy. *The Scandal of Pleasure: Art in an Age of Fundamentalism.* Chicago: University of Chicago Press, 1995.

II.

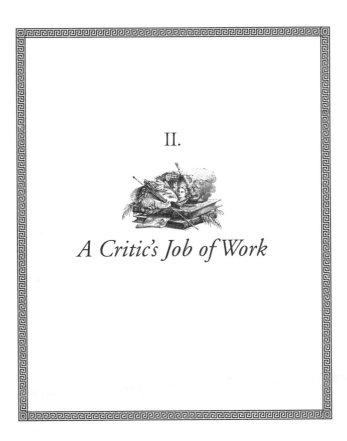

A Critic's Job of Work

TRACKING THE
AVANT-GARDE IN
FRANCE

THE SOCIAL
INSTITUTIONS OF
MODERN ART

W*E ARE ALL* numerologists and hypostatizers under the skin. The most common classification in English for our recent past, modernism, implies the existence of a period and a style. Yet there is as much disagreement about the dating and the essential features of modernism as about the existence and nature of a fundamental particle in physics. Richard Ellmann's and Charles Feidelson's widely used anthology, *The Modern Tradition* (1965), carries it back to Kant and the eighteenth century. *The Idea of the Modern* (1967), edited by Irving Howe, allows ten contributors to pick their dates. The collection of essays edited by Bradbury and McFarlane, *Modernism* (1976), proposes the dates 1890–1930. Sanford Schwartz and Ricardo Quinones have published more recent assessments, before debates about postmodernism occupied the terrain. The debate about the meanings of *modern* and its derivatives has been going on at least since Matthew Arnold and Baudelaire, or, more accurately, since the Battle of the Ancients and the Moderns.

When made to stand for virtually all developments in the arts during a certain period, *modernism* becomes no more than an umbrella or bucket word. To a Spaniard, furthermore, *modernismo* has a very specific meaning. German critics are not comfortable with the term and apply it mostly to other cultures. The French prefer *modernité,* an intense and widespread attention to the conditions of modern life since the early nineteenth century rather than to a particular set of writers and artists. I find that in speaking of the major works of the nineteenth and twentieth centuries, I avoid the word *modernism.* It has become a universal category with little explanatory power, creates the illusion of coherence, and serves as an intellectual red herring.[1]

Drastically restricted, the term still may serve a purpose. The vagaries of cultural exchange at the turn of the century led to an accelerated assimilation of continental currents in English-speaking countries. "Younger generations can hardly realize the intellectual desert of England and America during the first decade and more of this century. The predominance of Paris was incontestable." What Eliot wrote in the *Criterion* in 1934 was echoed by Pound. Arthur Symons's *The Symbolist Movement in Literature* (1899), Cubism and Futurism, the London Post-Impressionist exhibit of 1910 (it provoked Virginia Woolf's notorious comment that "human character changed"), Diaghilev's tours, and the New York Armory Show (1913)— these events produced a mighty response in English, Irish, and American literature and art, to which, I believe, the term *modernism* might usefully be applied for the period 1900–1930.[2]

In this limited definition, modernism displays as one of its distinguishing characteristics a feature that usually escapes observation. Spiritual experience survives in Virginia Woolf, in early Eliot, and in Joyce as a momentary vision or extratemporal insight, a privileged moment, an epiphany. With the addition of Proust's privileged moments and the Surrealists' revelations, the theme became so powerful that Sartre felt compelled to mock it in *Nausea* (1938) and succeeded in doing exactly the opposite. As time drains into an expanded present, spiritual life shrinks into momentary illuminations.

The other two academic terms available for dealing with the recent past, *bohemia* and the *avant-garde,* are French in origin. They raise the question why so much writing on cultural history centers around nineteenth- and twentieth-century France. In 1850, reporting on "the class struggles in France" as they unfolded, Marx still believed that England was "the demiurge of the bourgeois cosmos." Thirty-five years later, Engels modified that view in his preface to Marx's *The Eighteenth Brumaire of Louis Napoleon.*

France is the land where, more than anywhere else, the historical class struggles were each time fought out to a decision, and where, consequently, the changing political forms within which they move and in which their results are summarized have been stamped in the sharpest outline.

A wrenching series of revolutions and regimes; intense conflict among a still-powerful nobility, the ascendant bourgeoisie, and a downtrodden people; the dominance of Paris; the survival of institutions like the Napoleonic Code, the Academy, and the Salon; the political theater of the Dreyfus case—innumerable factors lend urgency to the history of postrevolutionary France and contribute to the high relief of developments in the arts. Everything, including *bohemia* and *avant-garde,* seemed to take the form of a response to, and a revulsion from, the all-pervasive bourgeoisie, great and small.

The idle, fun-loving waiting room of fame and power that Balzac depicts in *A Prince of Bohemia* (1845) contrasts markedly with the villainous street people that appear in an 1843 play, *The Bohemians of Paris,* by Adolphe d'Ennery and Eugène Grangé. In a review of that play, Théophile Gautier tried to set things straight by distinguishing genuine vagabond gypsies (bohemians, or *gitans*) from Paris ruffians improperly called "bohemians," and from a "charming and poetic" bohemia of laziness and freedom "of which we have all been more or less members."[3] He prefers to overlook hardworking groups dedicated to literature and poverty, such as the Water-Drinkers of the forties. Like the poor, the bohemians we shall always have with us in some form.

THE HISTORIAN DONALD D. Egbert has traced the term *avant-garde* back to an 1825 dialogue written by Saint-Simon in which an artist claims his rightful place beside industrialists and scientists "in exercising a positive power over society." Saint-Simon sounds like Trotsky in *Literature and Revolution,* calling on artists "to direct events" and to find the poetry of revolution in action. More than the nebulous, heterogenous country of bohemia, the avant-garde stood for innovation in the arts and in society. Though artists like Baudelaire rejected the military metaphor as connoting conformity and progress, the concept of an artistic avant-garde flourished well into the middle of the twentieth century and has not entirely lost its force.

France gave birth not only to the terms *bohemia, avant-garde,* and *art for art's sake,* it also produced a series of increasingly self-conscious and organized movements or schools, from Impressionism and Symbolism to Dada and Surrealism.[4] To some critics, one or the other of these named movements captures the essential spirit and formal qualities of all art in our time. Lukács picked Realism; Arnold Hauser picked Impressionism; Edmund Wilson chose Symbolism; John Berger favors Cubism. They are by no means foolish choices.

All these terms and isms can have the effect of carrying us away from what was set down by writers and artists and leading us toward abstract categories. In compensation, I should like to mention an opposed tendency. Nineteenth-century French artists had a knack, closely connected to the remarkable development of caricature, of creating a prototype and stereotype for some of these groups. When Murger and a collaborator produced a stage version in 1849 of his earlier sketches, *Scènes de la vie de Bohème,* Rodolphe, Mimi, and the others rapidly assumed a mythological existence certified by a popular opera and scores of imitations. Three years later, under a different regime, the caricaturist-actor-writer Henri Monnier staged his *Grandeur et décadence de M. Joseph Prudhomme.* That pompous, benevolent dupe stands for the perfect bourgeois in all his foolish aspirations to honor and power. Monnier's later writings fill in the portrait of Monsieur Prudhomme by giving him a past in bohemia as an aspiring poet and by particularizing his habits and dress.[5] In a little-known preface, Gide refers to the impression made on Gautier and Baudelaire by Monsieur Prudhomme and to his continuing importance. Verlaine wrote a deadpan sonnet about him that begins, *"Il est grave. Il est maire et père de famille."* In the drawn, acted, and written versions of Monsieur Prudhomme, Monnier prepared the royal road for Père Ubu.

The vivid caricature figures created by Murger and Monnier offer us a backdoor entry into a period we usually approach through its movements and isms, and through broader concepts like "bohemia" and "avant-garde."

IT MAY BE a long time before we grasp how wide and deep was the break that occurred in the arts between 1880 and 1930. I believe that after long gestation, a set of antinomies converge on this period to produce a radical testing of traditions and practices. The hiatus—which was also some kind of turning point—reached its moment of highest stress and activity in France between 1905 and 1914, a few years before comparable crises in Russia, Germany, England, Ireland, and (in somewhat muted and displaced form) the United States. The four antinomies I shall mention are composed of what, at the end of the nineteenth century, appeared to be paired opposites and of what we would do better to see now as complementaries.

First, the embracing of primitive art by Picasso, Matisse, Derain, Apollinaire, Stravinsky, and many others coincided with a widespread affirmative response by artists and writers to science and technology. Futurism in Italy and Russia gave that response a name and a doctrine. The same artists and writers who welcomed the unfamiliar forms and magical content of African sculpture also reveled in powerful automobiles; they went to movies, speculated about airplane flight and the fourth dimension.[6] In works like Apollinaire's "Zone" (1913) and Picasso's Cubist heads of 1909, primitivist elements are inseparable, almost indistinguishable, from a deep-seated futurism. yet primitivism and Futurism are usually treated separately.

At the same time, the widespread loss of religion, institutionalized in France by the separation of church and state, was accompanied by an equally widespread continuation of religion in other forms. The woods were full of new spiritualist and occultist sects. Proust and Yeats explored the spiritual in art as persistently as Kandinsky. The writers who championed Cubism spoke fervently of its spiritual aspirations.

In another domain, ever since Courbet, a defiant attempt to depict appearances directly and faithfully had been paralleled—often in the same artists—by the deformation and exaggeration of appearances in the wonderfully inventive development of caricature. With all their excesses and violations of convention, Impressionist and Cubist paintings could and did claim to be more "realistic" than traditional figurative painting.

Finally, art for art's sake and social radicalism in the arts appeared to pull in diametrically opposed directions. Yet the pages we read today as the manifesto of art for art's sake, the 1835 preface ("everything useful is ugly") to the sulfurous *Mademoiselle de Maupin,* represent Gautier's protest against the strict censorship reimposed just two months earlier by Louis Philippe. The poet most clearly associated with art for art's sake did not refer to residence in an ivory tower; he described the appropriate attitude of the poet as that of being "on strike against society" and "an outlaw." The gentle Mallarmé was capable of a certain vehemence. Even in the Romantic era one does not find so strong an ambition in artists and writers to embrace explosive new forces, to change people's sensibilities, and to modify society rather than represent the status quo in works of art.

By affirming both terms of these antinomies, in reaching for a synthesis that would require profound modification of all aspects of life and society, Western art between 1880 and 1930 attempted to jump out of its own skin. I believe the jump succeeded only in part and for a limited time. Yet the attempt has wide significance. Where did these artists land, if at all? I see two distinct places.

The desire to found a new society, especially when channeled through loyalties to a dominant political party, ran the risk of changing art and literature into agents of social engineering. In Germany, in the Soviet Union, and in Cuba, we know the story now. We are never so alert as we think to the co-optation of art by politics.

The other direction in which the arts moved is less evident. It goes back to the figure of the dandy, to Proudhon's statements on the role of art, to the writings and posturings of decadents and aesthetes, and it emerges in a tendency to channel the energies of artistic creation away from artworks into the living of life itself as an adventure. The biting ironies of Huysmans's *Against Nature* (1884) are usually forgotten in favor of the elaborate project of the main character, Des Esseintes, to transform his environment, his very material and moral ecology, into a work of art—total interior decoration. It is in part through Huysmans that Valéry imagined his own artistic alter ego, Monsieur Teste, who lives a life not of exquisite enjoyment but of refined intellectual meditation and produces no works. Both Des Esseintes and Teste are portrayed as embodying the ideal that Murger imagined in 1850 for his bohemians. "Their existence each day is a work of genius."

THE STORY DOES not end there. One of the sturdiest antiart strains in Paris, Dada derived from Breton's fascination, when he was barely twenty, with Valéry's abandonment of poetry, with his silence echoing Rimbaud's. Breton's Barcelona speech mentioned in note 4 begins its argument with a deliberately ominous sentence. "There are abroad today in the world a few individuals for whom art . . . is no longer a goal." Breton was alluding to the secret pact sworn by Aragon and himself three years earlier, in 1919, not to be taken in by the blandishments of art and fame, to practice poetry in their lives, and to write only as a form of *réclame*—the signaling necessary to find other kindred spirits.

When the Surrealists launched their manifesto and their review, they attacked the novel, published dream accounts and "surrealist texts" in preference to poetry, favored a scientific attitude, and presented the group as a cross between a sociopolitical conspiracy and a medical emergency team trying to save Western civilization from itself. Literature and the arts were spat upon as "alibis" and as "lamentable expedients." Because we have now classified the "surrealist revolution" under literature and painting, we fail to realize how resolutely and systematically Breton and Aragon and Soupault set out to flout the traditions and rewards of art as an autonomous activity. They advocated the withering away of art not into social engineering but into the discovery and cultivating of the marvelous, the lyric in everyday life. The antinomies that had long beset the arts could now be subsumed and surpassed by declaring that the only true art is life itself.

Literature and the arts have not withered away; they have flourished. Still, the Surrealist campaign to direct the artistic impulse back toward everyday life, toward love, dreams, language, found objects, chance encounters, and magic, has a long history and has left its mark on the way we see and enjoy life.

There is another respect in which Surrealism represents a culmination of the histories of bohemia and the avant-garde. Breton sternly censured his comrades if they engaged in any form of conventional work—salaried jobs, journalism, even collaboration with Diaghilev. The vows of nonparticipation in order to serve a higher goal revive the vows of the original Water-Drinkers in the 1840s, whom Murger refers to as "the disciples of art for art's sake" and "obstinate dreamers" whose only activity was art. Dedication of this kind is predicated upon the rare state of affairs we refer to as leisure. The entire history of bohemia from Mimi to Saint-Germain-des-Prés presents the quest for an ideal leisure within changing cultural circumstances. The best commentary still comes from the third chapter of the eighth book of Aristotle's *Politics*. "Nature herself requires that we should be able, not only to work, but to use leisure as well; for . . . the first principle of all action is leisure. Both are required, but leisure is better than occupation and its end."

From Aristotle's time until well after the French Revolution, leisure and pleasure belonged almost exclusively to a ruling class; the rest of humanity existed in order to supply them. After that, it is hard to know what thread to follow. Is there a continuity of endeavor to establish a new aristocracy, a new leisure class, that links dandy, bohemian, aesthete, Surrealist, Beat, and hippie? Perhaps, but the perspective is too limited. I have already referred to Saint-Simon's aborted attempt to launch a new ruling class composed of scientists, industrialists, and artists—a group to be known as the avant-garde, devoted not to leisure but to leadership and service. When the bourgeoisie became the new class of the nineteenth century under capitalism, the search for different social arrangements and descriptions did not, therefore, cease.

THE DEBATES BETWEEN Marx and Bakunin, and later between Lenin and Kautsky, over the existence of an intellectual class in addition to peasant and proletarian were played out in France at the time of the Dreyfus Affair. The much-needed substantive *"un intellectuel"* was coined in 1898 by Clemenceau for the resounding "Manifesto of the Intellectuals." Immediately picked up as a term of abuse, the word suggests the existence of an intermediate class apart from bourgeois and workers.[7] A parallel discussion peaked around 1940 when, probably influenced by Trotsky, Bruno Rizzi and James Burnham called attention to the emergence of a new class, which they called, respectively, "bureaucratic" and "managerial." Neither capitalists nor workers were really running things. On the basis of expertise, a new group had insinuated itself into power everywhere. (Rizzi called his pamphlet *The Bureaucratization of the World.*)

On the question of a new class, history never stops providing revealing precedents. In March 1847 in the Chamber of Deputies, Prime Minister Guizot spoke on an amendment to the electoral law that would grant the vote to persons of intellectual distinction, apart from property and income. Himself far more an intellectual than a philistine, Guizot nevertheless valued the social order.

> Excessive confidence in human intelligence, human pride, intellectual pride . . . these things are the disease. . . . Intelligence . . . must at all times be guarded, restrained, guided by social conditions. The proponents of the amendment treat modern intelligence as in former days one treated the aristocracy.[8]

This significant debate in the last year of the reign of Louis Philippe, the Bourgeois King, raises the central issues. One can hear echoes of Rousseau a century earlier trumpeting the uniqueness of his sensibility and at the same time proposing a social contract into which that precious individuality could be merged. One can hear Flaubert inveighing against the tide of nineteenth-century philistinism rising around him and his desperate oath of allegiance to bohemia as his "fatherland." And one can foresee the situation, now stood on its head, discussed in the last part of Richard Hofstadter's *Anti-Intellectualism in American Life.* There he examines the debate among certain American intellectuals in the fifties about the extent to which their approach to prestige and power had made them surrender to the status quo. Only a few clung to alienation as a "moral imperative." One case is particularly revealing for us. "[Irving] Howe's counterideal to this complacent adaptation was an old one: the community of Bohemia."

In Russia, a comparable appeal to the past would cite not bohemia but the intelligentsia, often defined as that part of the population that thinks critically. For at least a century, it constituted a way of life in Russia, virtually a social class, recognized by the publication of D. N. Ovsyaniko Kulikovsky's three-volume *History of the Russian Intelligentsia* (1909–1911). The Soviet system either took over or stifled the intelligentsia. In the United States, bohemia has suffered a different fate. As two other recent books have suggested, commercialism has appropriated its most popular and pleasurable elements and injected them into the daily expectations of everyone.[9] The counterculture of the sixties surrendered a large part of its impetus to universally marketed products like rock music. To a great extent, the intel-

lectual side of the counterculture has been incorporated into higher education. In what direction are intellectuals and artists to turn if they see as available to them neither a genuinely dissident intelligentsia nor a livable
bohemia?

HAVE WE, THEN, no native or imported institutions that would foster our
hard-earned individualism without overrestricting or overindulging it?
Think tanks, research centers, and artists' colonies provide an eerily artificial
environment. Where have all the "freelancers" gone? There seem to be no
powerful imaginations at work on the institutions that serve, particularly,
the life of the mind. Trenchant thinking on the subject may still be found in
Max Weber's paired reflections on "Scholarship as a Vocation" and "Politics
as a Vocation" (1919). He clarifies the responsibilities imposed by our present system yet imagines no improved arrangement of things. Do we need a
religion—a religion even of science or politics or art—to inspire the leap of
imagination that would see beyond the present impasse?

Perhaps I don't read the right books. A pamphlet by Charles Newman,
The Post-Modern Aura (1985), starts out as if it is going to grapple with some
of these questions under the category of the cultural and intellectual inflation of everything. But its style and argument soon yield to the very over-
stimulation it sets out to attack. Almost on the last page, one finds this
lonely, unsupported sentence: "The crisis is largely institutional."

We are not making life any easier for ourselves today by eliminating
constraints on individual behavior and by inflating our desires into a reigning hedonism. In 1819, the liberal political thinker Benjamin Constant
foresaw the social conflicts that would preoccupy Murger and Mimica, that
would create a role for bohemia and art for art's sake and the avant-garde,
and that would continue to trouble observers like Hofstadter and Newman
down to our own time. Speaking before the Royal Atheneum, Constant distinguished between the liberty of the ancients, "active and sustained participation in collective power," and modern liberty, "tranquil enjoyment of
private independence." Then he cautioned: "The danger of modern liberty
is that, absorbed in our private independence and in the pursuit of personal
pleasures and interests, we may give up too easily our right of participation
in the political process." To what Constant observed about the need for both
politics and pleasure, I shall add that, in spite of alluring doctrines to the
contrary, it would be unwise to envision a future based on the withering
away of both art and labor. Not a small subject.

NOTES

1. I develop other aspects of this position in "The Poverty of Modernism," in *The Innocent Eye* (New York: Farrar, Straus, & Giroux, 1984).

2. See Cyrena N. Pondrom, *The Road from Paris: French Influence on English Poetry 1900–1920* (New York: Cambridge University Press, 1974).

3. Cited in the very informative, profusely illustrated study by Marilyn R. Brown, *Gypsies and Other Bohemians: The Myth of the Artist in Nineteenth-Century France* (Ann Arbor: University of Michigan Press, 1985), p.1.

4. In a talk to the Barcelona Ateneo in 1922, André Breton made the intelligent suggestion that they all belong to one larger movement "of which we do not yet know precisely the direction of the extent." Do we know even now?

5. Extravagance of dress belongs to an earlier Romantic period. Poverty among bohemian artists dictated their wardrobe more than anything else. One curious motif keeps recurring. In the famous passage from "The Heroism of Modern Life," Baudelaire half-mockingly eulogizes *l'habit noir,* the black tailcoat that clothes the modern hero and expresses both a political and a poetic beauty. "We are all celebrating some kind of burial." The high symbolism Baudelaire attaches to this article of bourgeois attire turns into low comedy in Murger's bohemia, where the artist Schaunard tricks the *habit noir* off a rich sitter's back for a friend who needs it to go out to dinner in society.

True to status, Monsieur Prudhomme wears his overblown comic version of *l'habit noir* at all times. In an 1850 review of a book about what he describes as the bohemia of political conspirators who fill Paris wine shops, Marx uses *l'habit noir* as a kind of shorthand term for educated nonproletarian conspirators. A chapter of the Goncourt brothers' novel about artists, *Manette Salomon* (1867), echoes Murger in detailing the operations performed to obtain the needed garment. At some point, the motif of *l'habit noir* was displaced by the stereotype of the bohemian artist with long hair, in loose shirt and artist's beret. He survives in the character of the mute orator in Ionesco's *The Chairs.*

6. Polemics over the " 'Primitivism' in Modern 20th-Century Art" exhibit at the Museum of Modern Art in New York and its huge catalog have helped expose the ambiguity of our tastes and our thinking on that subject. The debate between curators William Rubin and Kirk Varnedoe and critic Thomas McEvilley merits careful reading (*Artforum,* November 1984; February 1985; May 1985). I also recommend Katia Samaltano's, *Apollinaire;*

Catalyst for Primitivism, Picabia, and Duchamp (Ann Arbor: University of Michigan Press, 1984) for its contribution to the debate on artists' responses to tribal objects before World War I. Published in Dakar by the Nouvelles Editions Africaines, another invaluable book has been almost wholly ignored by scholars: Jean-Claude Blachère, *Le Modèle Nègre: Aspects littéraires du mythe primitiviste au XXe siècle chez Apollinaire, Cendrars, Tzara* (1981).

7. See Victor Brombert, "Toward a Portrait of the French Intellectual," in Victor Brombert, ed., *The Intellectual Hero* (Chicago: University of Chicago Press, 1961); and Lewis S. Feuer, "The Political Linguistics of 'Intellectual' 1898–1918," *Survey,* Winter 1971.

8. A more complete account can be found in César Graña, *Modernity and Its Discontents* (originally published in 1964 as *Bohemian versus Bourgeois*). In addition to Graña's excellent study, two very different books with a strong historical perspective explore the social status of the arts and intellectuals: Edgar Wind, *Art and Anarchy* (New York: Knopf, 1963); and Richard Hofstadter, *Anti-Intellectualism in American Life* (New York: Knopf, 1963).

9. Jerrold Seigel, *Bohemian Paris: Culture, Politics, and the Boundaries of Bourgeois Life, 1830–1930* (New York: Viking Press, 1986); and Charles Rearick, *Pleasures of the Belle Epoque: Entertainment and Festivity in Turn-of-the-Century Paris* (New Haven: Yale University Press, 1985).

16

MANET, THE
MISSING LINK

W *E KNOW THAT* art changed profoundly in the last two centuries or so, and we are still arguing about how and when. We
seek a precise moment of transition from traditional academic
painting to the modern revolution, almost as we seek the missing link in
human evolution. The logic of traditional art history and the pedagogical
needs of art historians clamor for the identification of a school or a painter
to represent the end of the old and the beginning of the new.

History, of course, never happens so neatly, and many contenders have
presented themselves. Goya and Turner and Courbet produced works that
gained official recognition and also broke the mold of traditional practice. A
little later, unleashed by the Salon des Refusés in 1863 and by their own first
exhibition in 1874, the painters who became known as Impressionists
revised the motifs and the techniques of easel painting to produce a plein-air
style whose popularity has grown steadily for more than a century. Our
identification of the missing link for modern painting may never become so
uncontroversial as, say, our identification of Giotto as the master of the transition to Renaissance painting. But gradually we seem to be settling on one
figure, and he is Edouard Manet.

It is hard to say whether Manet's contradictions make him our hero or
the supreme misfit of nineteenth-century art. He devoted so much effort to

acknowledging his predecessors that historians such as Julius Meier-Graefe considered him a museum painter. And yet, at the time of the Centennial Orangerie Show in 1932, Paul Colin wrote that "he painted the way a child plays. Nothing premeditated. Nothing willed." So was he academic or avant-garde? His reliance throughout his career on studio models during long sittings as well as his omnipresent sketch books qualified him as a scrupulous realist. Yet his friend Zola contended that Manet's was a pure artistic temperament driven "to achieve beautiful patches, beautiful contrasts."

For some, Manet was a delightful boulevardier with little depth of mind; for others, his intelligence outclassed that of most artists of his day and was equal to Baudelaire's. Manet was chosen as spokesman for the disgruntled painters who agitated for the Salon des Refusés, and he later served as a model of integrity and modernity for the Impressionists. But he never exhibited a single work at the Impressionist shows and continued to submit his work to the official Salon, with mixed results. He lived and painted with the ironic detachment of a dandy, but many would claim that his great unironic passions about life and art show themselves to anyone who can meet the gaze of his paintings.

Such contradictions are not superficial. By producing enigmatic figure paintings that refuse to tell a story or to surrender to their surfaces, Manet provoked in his day something of the puzzlement that we glimpse today in the work of Magritte, an artist of much lesser stature. We welcome Magritte's anomalies with indulgent laughter, but Manet is harder, and he suffered sustained and withering mockery. It is as if Manet, reversing Magritte's famous "This is not a pipe," set out before his contemporaries a succession of works bearing the defiant message "This is a painting." Manet's paintings embody a challenge that goes far beyond the production of an ocular image.

Manet poses genuine difficulties for the museumgoer hoping to discern the origins of modern art. His subjects vary widely, from figures of Jesus to dark Spanish portraits to brightly colored café scenes. His works do not seem to form a coherent oeuvre. Moreover, many of his paintings display an aspect widely noticed by critics during his lifetime but so difficult to discuss today that it is often dismissed as a false lead: This thoroughly schooled master of his craft produced paintings that frequently look unfinished. Women's complexions appear pasty. The perspective does not hold up. He did not hide the fact that his subjects were models in costume posing in the studio. And often there is a figure in the painting who is staring back at the viewer, knowingly or laughingly or connivingly or absently, thus breaking the theatrical illusion of the fourth wall. Painting within a tradition of illusionism,

Manet refused to complete the illusion or to observe all its conventions. He reduced halftone to a tentative buffer of shade separating starkly contrasting fields of light and dark. In *A Bar at the Folies-Bergère* (1881–1882), the optical displacements in the mirror behind the barmaid risk transforming the composition into a formal enigma and overshadowing the subtle ironies in its depiction of contemporary life.

Beth Archer Brombert's biography, *Edouard Manet: Rebel in a Frock Coat,* deeply sympathetic to Manet's character and accomplishments, uncovers a set of personal and professional dissimulations in his life, and the effect that these elaborate dissimulations had on his works. The lack of finish in Manet's art, she believes, corresponds to partially hidden anxieties in his life. Michael Fried, by contrast, in *Manet's Modernism: or, the Face of Painting in the 1860s,* pays little attention to biography and examines instead Manet's painterly ambition, specifically his divided ambition to ground painting in its past and to overcome that past by painting something new. For Fried, the unfinishedness in Manet's work has much to do with his ambivalent contribution to the adversarial stance of art represented by the Salon des Refusés and the Impressionist shows; there was nothing hypocritical or inconsistent about the fact that the greatest professional satisfaction for this modernist came from his induction into the Legion of Honor. In their very different ways, both of these books have the merit of recognizing that a part of Manet's importance lies in the fact that he does not fit.

MANET WAS BORN in 1832. The son of a wealthy Parisian magistrate and an artistically inclined mother, he overcame his father's objections and trained to be a painter in Thomas Couture's studio. Couture was the great academic painter of the day, and his monumentally academic *Romans of the Decadence* (1847) barely veiled its republican condemnation of the July Monarchy's vices, soon to be overthrown by the revolution of 1848. Manet learned from Couture's traditionalism and reacted against it. Unlike Cézanne, who became a mulish bohemian out of similar bourgeois circumstances, Manet remained close to his family and became a dandified figure during his apprenticeship and his travels. His untraditional technique and subject matter won him more opprobrium in the press than success in the Salon. After Courbet's defiant declaration of "realism," Manet appeared to seek official recognition by inappropriate means. A close friend of Baudelaire, who was eleven years his senior and published bold theories on art and the heroism of modern life, Manet became the leader of a loose circle of younger painters. They met in Right Bank cafés, denounced the Salon, and soon launched "the New Painting," or Impressionism. Manet went his own way, arranged his own shows with irregular success, weathered the assaults on his widely publicized works, and counted Mallarmé and Monet among his friends. He died at fifty-one from complications caused by the amputation of a leg.

Brombert declares her intentions from the start. "You can be sure that a painter reveals himself in his work as much as and more than a writer does in his." This epigraph, from Diderot's *Salons,* leads directly into her argument. Brombert sets out the vivid relation between Manet's life and his art, not with a vengeance but with respect and affection for her subject. Brombert implies that Manet led a three-cornered life. He worked and saw his friends in his studio. After some irregular youthful years, he lived in a household presided over by his mother, along with his apparently childless wife and a much younger brother-in-law. And he lived also in still another realm—a realm of secrecy, tensions, and rewards difficult to locate in his biography and revealed in great part by his paintings.

IN RECOUNTING MANET'S life at the center of Parisian artistic turmoil, Brombert supplies the social and cultural background in appropriate detail. Her biography draws on vast resources to bring Manet to life against the backdrop of his era and in relation to his unconventional accomplishments as a painter. She provides a generally reliable introduction to Manet, and through him to the remarkable dynamism of nineteenth-century French painting. Brombert alternates chronological and thematic arrangement of her materials to good effect, and she only occasionally falls back on psychoanalytic clichés to provide explanations. She gives a full version of Manet's voyage to Rio de Janeiro at nineteen as a naval cadet, during which his vocation as an artist became even stronger. I find reasonable her conjecture, also made by the French biographer Eric Darragon, that Ernest Renan's widely read *Life of Jesus* (1863) directly influenced Manet's two early paintings of Christ from 1864 and 1865. But I find Brombert too uncritically reliant on the reminiscences of Antonin Proust, Manet's lifetime friend and chronicler. And sometimes Brombert just recycles stereotypes of the bourgeoisie: "the simpering virgins displayed by their mothers on the marriage market," or "the puritanical philistinism of the nineteenth-century middle class."

The principal (and unvindictive) purpose of Brombert's book is to demonstrate that Manet had some significant skeletons in his closet, and that those skeletons had an impact on his painting. At nineteen, Manet became the lover of Suzanne Leenhoff, his music teacher, and she gave birth to a son just as Manet turned twenty. From then on, Manet had to hide the fact that he had a mistress (until he married her after his father's death a decade later) and a son. Brombert accepts Adolphe Tabarant's conclusion that these machinations "pained and poisoned [Manet's] life."

And there was another secret, another shame. Manet's father, and Manet himself, died painfully of tertiary syphilis, an illness that stayed unnamed in public or private. Brombert insists that this poison spread far. The son's discovery of his father's transgressions, "along with his knowledge of his own, would serve him in his future portrayals of unspoken secrets, non-communication even between intimates, unfulfilled and unavowable long-ings, the inability to reach across silence, and the pretense of bourgeois propriety." And then there is the matter of Manet and other women. Almost all descriptions of the blond, witty, handsome, and soon-to-be painter por-tray him as "seductive." Three times Brombert tells us that Manet "knew how to talk to women." Yet we remain in ignorance of his love life—with his models, with his close friend Berthe Morisot, with others. Brombert writes as a discerning woman, not as a tendentious feminist. She does not state or imply that Manet was a rake and a seducer. She observes also that in his paintings, "Manet's women have a life of their own . . . not defined by their husbands or their children." About his relations with women, Manet remained as discreet and elusive as about his marriage and his disease. Brombert believes that Manet, "unfulfilled in his life and his profession," revealed himself in the symbolism of his works. Many of them are allegories of his personal life. Brombert plausibly points out a personal dimension, having to do with his uneasiness about his family and his artistic situation, in *La Pêche* (1861), *The Luncheon* (1868, with his son Leon dominating the composition), *Berthe Morisot with a Black Hat and Violets* (1872), and *In the Conservatory* (1879). In the latter picture, for example, Manet painted an elegant married couple, she seated on a bench and he leaning on its back, the husband looking uncannily like Manet; and so it appears that Manet is depicting himself in a composition that emphasizes the fact that, though placed at close quarters, the husband's and wife's hands and eyes do not meet. It is a portrait not of intimacy but of isolation. I am not convinced, though, by the personal allegories that Brombert proposes for *The Old Musician* (1862) and *Jesus Mocked by the Soldiers* (1865). Discussing *A Bar at the Folies-Bergère,* Brombert detects an antiheroic strain, and she sees the bemused barmaid as "a modern divinity, not of love, but of its illusion." Per-haps.

MICHAEL FRIED RESTRICTS *Manet's Modernism: or, The Face of Painting in the 1860s* to Manet's paintings of the 1860s, which were a turning point, he believes, in Manet's development as a painter and also in the development of modernism in painting. But Fried's purpose is far from restricted. This is the third and presumably the final volume in an overarching project dealing with depictions of "theatricality" and "antitheatricality" in painting. He launched his project in 1967, in an article in *Artforum* entitled "Art and Objecthood." Discussing contemporary minimalist works that rely on the presence of the beholder to rescue them from literal thingness or objecthood, Fried led up to a declaration of "theater's profound hostility to the arts" and of the need "to defeat theater." I found his pages abstruse; but they caused a stir, as did the appearance two years later of the bulk of his dissertation on Manet's sources in a special number of *Artforum*.

At that point, Fried decided to *reculer pour mieux sauter*, to establish the grounds of his interpretation by moving backward in the history of his subject. *Absorption and Theatricality: Painting and Beholder in the Age of Diderot* appeared in 1980, and it circles around Diderot's preference for paintings that show figures totally absorbed in unheroic activity and unaware of any beholder. A decade later *Courbet's Realism* examined, among other themes, how Courbet overcame this tradition of absorption in his figure paintings and often seemed to enter the painted scene himself as painter-beholder.

Fried's new book carries his categories of theatricality and absorption into promising terrain. In *Manet's Modernism,* he reprints and then reaffirms (with minor reservations) his dissertation, and he adds two powerful chapters on Manet's unique and guiding role in his own generation of 1863. (There is another addition that is not so welcome, a chapter originally written for a conference on Derrida's recent work, and it is less pertinent and more clotted in style than the other four.) The book accommodates a number of loosely interwoven topics—a lengthy commentary on nineteenth-century critics, careful and loving readings of individual paintings, a concern with redefining modernism, and more. Fried acknowledges "a certain absence of unity" and glancingly justifies it as appropriate to his subject matter. (It is inexcusable, in a book about theatricality, which is so considerably determined by size and scale, that Fried does not give the dimensions of the many paintings reproduced.)

This is a book composed at a very high level of intellectual communication. Its learning and its argument overflow into 170 pages of endnotes as well as into substantial footnotes, as if Fried's scholarly barque needs double outriggers. He sometimes overloads his sentences with the language of higher incoherence, which may impress some readers. At heart, however, Fried is not a mystifier. He wants to convince us with evidence and sound reason. Serious readers will take note of his running exchange with certain scholars and critics. Fried acknowledges three with graciousness. Nils Gösta Sandblad's *Manet: Three Studies in Artistic Conception* concentrates on the same decade of the 1860s. (It is, to my mind, the most satisfying single study of Manet.) Fried quotes at some length from his early mentor Clement Greenberg, whose influential essay "Modernist Painting" (1960) argues that painting since Manet has tended toward purity by paying attention to the nature of its own medium, particularly to its flatness. And T. J. Clark, whose studies of Courbet and Manet give primary place to a Marxian social-historical approach to painting, plays the role of Fried's hovering interlocutor and occasional adversary.

In the "Coda" of his book, his greater summation, Fried describes Manet's response to the crisis of antitheatricality, his shattering of the illusion of theatricality among the self-absorbed figures in a painting. Manet "courted unintelligibility" and employed "a kind of strikingness" and a "facingness" that reaffirm the presence of the beholder. The following paragraph, which nicely epitomizes his argument and his style, reaches all the way back to the first volume of the trilogy, and to Fried's earlier preoccupation with minimalist art.

All this [antitheatricality and unintelligibility] may be understood, as I say in *Courbet's Realism,* as an embrace of theatricality in the presentational rather than "actional" meaning of the term: Manet's involvement with Watteau, whose art Diderot had criticized as mannered, is altogether to the point. At the same time, I suggest there that the very extremity of the measures by which Manet's paintings acknowledge beholding as inescapably the fate of painting can have the effect of making the actual beholder feel excluded or supererogatory, and that it may be *that* experience that Manet's viewers have found more disorienting than any other. (I also describe Manet's intentions as at once theatrical and antitheatrical, hence as neither one nor the other in the sense I had been giving the terms until that moment.) In any case, Manet's modernism, with respect to the issue of beholding, consists precisely in the doubleness of its relation to the Diderotian tradition: on the one hand, marking the close of that tradition by insisting as never before on the "truth" about painting that the tradition had come about to deny or forestall; on the other hand, demonstrating by example that there could be no mere laying bare of that "truth" and therefore no entire extinguishing of that tradition, which is to say that "presentationality" in Manet's art is itself not simply presented (what could that have meant?) but rather is *represented* (not that the opposition "present/represent" is other than unstable, but precisely that constitutive instability is my point). For all its radicalization of theatricality, in other words, something in Manet's art was in the profoundest tension with the latter (cf. my discussion of his courting of unintelligibility, subversion of potentially absorptive motifs, denial of individual psychology, refusal of closure on the plane of technique; all such operations imply the "presence" of the suppressed term, as does Bataille's insistence that Manet's art "effaces" traditional subject matter). Painting after Manet would be severed from the Diderotian tradition that had made it possible (it would no longer be a requirement of ambitious painting that it defeat theatricality, though antagonism to the latter would remain a live option). But painting after Manet would not be liberated from the concerns of that tradition (it would not thereafter be indifferent to problems of beholding), least of all when a final step in a formalist-modernist evolution would purport to go beyond painting into Minimalist objecthood.

This is, obviously, pretty rough going. After weeks of reading Fried and tracking his arguments, I still cannot follow the fourth sentence, which begins "In any case. . . ." The structure (or structurelessness) of the sentence, the rhetorical question in parentheses, and the catch-up lunge toward meaning in the final parenthetical clause suggest that Fried is aware of his own distress. Using the word *precisely* twice does not help him.

Fried can write comprehensibly. When he reaches for powerful conclusions, he tends to produce convolution rather than clarity. Still, its style notwithstanding, both the passage that I have just quoted and Fried's argument generally strain toward significant distinctions. The problem, I fear, is that "theatricality," the pivotal term in Fried's enterprise, has buckled under the weight that he places on it.

The condition of theatricality arises out of what Fried calls in *Courbet's Realism* (and reaffirms in *Manet's Modernism*) "the primordial convention that paintings are made to be beheld." The convention can be served in two ways: actionally (or absorptively), by depicting human figures entirely wrapped up in what they are doing and therefore unaware of the beholder, like actors behind a transparent fourth wall; and presentationally, by depicting figures who look out at the beholder or at least face him in acknowledgment of his presence. According to Fried, Manet developed a presentational theatricality in opposition to the absorptive theatricality admired by Diderot in the paintings of Greuze.

Manet's "doubleness," I think, resides less in his paintings being "at once theatrical and antitheatrical" than in their successive alternation between facingness and absorption. Moreover, Fried's two forms of theatricality fail to clarify our relation to painting unless one adds a prior category not adduced by Fried, what I would call "histrionic theatricality." Many academic painters of historical and mythological scenes showed figures absorbed in their heroic actions yet performing them in so dramatic and expansive a way as to acknowledge and even play to the beholder. Consider Manet's largest painting, *The Execution of Maximilian* (Mannheim version, 1868–1869). Its censored political subject, its immense size (about ten feet wide), and its dramatic composition constitute the elements of a histrionic painting, not a presentational one. But comparison with related works by David and Goya reveals how carefully Manet eliminated emotional gestures and other forms of staginess. Without the contrasting category of histrionic theatricality, it is difficult for Fried to locate the muffled quality, the antitheatricality, of Manet's largest work.

Fried's grand comparison of painting and theater, in terms of their respective relations to the spectator, raises interesting questions about maintaining and breaking theatrical illusion in figure paintings by means of the glance, pose, costume, compositional anomalies, and the like. But the comparison is a little obvious. It is also somewhat misleading: It can lead to false philosophical quandaries about whether Niagara Falls makes a noise if no one is there to hear it. Finally, Fried does not convince me that "theatricality" should become the open sesame of art history and criticism. I am persuaded only that the notion has genuine, if limited, revelations to make about eighteenth- and nineteenth-century French painting, and about Manet in particular.

Fried's argument plants itself in a set of abstractions that have not been brought adequately into focus. Elsewhere he states that he is guided by ontological and epistemological preoccupations. An insistent part of his mind wants to do philosophy rather than look at paintings. The passage on pages 152–53, please note, refers to no works. He does not remain faithful to "the folds of flesh at the back of Victorine's neck," to which he paid fleeting homage a few pages earlier. Fried prefers to move toward the refuge, or the higher ground, that is found in much contemporary writing: doubleness, paradox, ambiguity, undecidability. He often leaves paintings behind for the Valhalla of big ideas and theories.

THESE TWO BOOKS, in markedly different ways, treat many aspects of nineteenth-century French art, including the rivalry between color and line, the politics of imagery, the social status of the artist, and the challenge of photography. Only one major force struck me by its absence: physiognomy. For the nineteenth century came to believe as deeply in the correlation between outer and inner characteristics as the twentieth century came to believe in the reality of the unconscious. Manet's figure paintings present a special case of physiognomy beginning to doubt itself. Derived from writings attributed to Aristotle and promoted by the Swiss pop-star intellectual Johann Kospar Lavater into a pseudoscience, physiognomy postulated a close relation between body and soul, between outward appearance and inner character. One can read a person's deepest qualities from facial features, head shape, and gestures. For some people, physiognomic correspondences (lifted by Baudelaire into vast analogies between the material and the spiritual) filled the gap left by the decline of Christianity. It is not too difficult to discern how a belief in physiognomy could provide strong underpinnings for portraiture or character reading, for realism (or things as they are without idealization), and for caricature (or things revealing their inner being through imaginative exaggeration).

Manet never worked steadily at caricature. But he would have known the doctrine of physiognomy from Baudelaire and Champfleury. And his whole project of painting the world "sincerely," from the Paris types of *The Old Musician* to the formal portrait of Antonin Proust, testifies to an uneasy faith that appearances will reveal the true nature of the world around us and the people in it. The theatricality that preoccupies Fried refers back to a venerable belief in the clues and the codes of physiognomy, in how people declare themselves in their deportment. We have by no means put this pervasive doctrine behind us.

Like some people, I sometimes have difficulty recognizing an unfamiliar painting by Manet. *Le Port de Bordeaux* looks like early Mondrian. *Le Linge* must have been painted by one of the mainline Impressionists. Certainly *Le Bon Bock* and *The Execution of Maximilian* do not fit easily into the category "Manet." For the remarkable and troubling truth about this painter is that he didn't have a style to apply to whatever subject presented itself. He was essentially restless, in his life and in his art; and this restlessness puts one in mind of Dürer and Balanchine, two other great impatients who also clung to their heritage. We keep looking at Manet and reevaluating his work not least because of this instability, this variety or unreliability of his style.

We return to him also because of his erratic relation to Impressionism, the only great popular school of modern painting. The impact of that style of painting on our notions of vision and our feelings for life may have been as great as that of stained-glass windows in Gothic cathedrals on the people of their time. Impressionism lays before us a sumptuous outdoor paradise of leisure and luxury, even as it installs us in the bar and brothel scenes of Degas, which seem to describe a fall from paradise. Generally, Manet stayed away from both these tendencies of his contemporaries. He painted an indoor world of posed figures not exactly at ease in their existence.

But then, at the end of his life, he gave expression simultaneously to Paradise and the Fall. In its all-devouring horizontal mirror, *A Bar at the Folies-Bergère* shows us Paradise Glimpsed in the ultimate Parisian setting of gaiety and display. In front stands a figure from the Fall in the person of a fully clothed Venus: the bemused barmaid. Unlike the nude Victorine in *Le Déjeuner sur l'herbe,* who looks boldly out at us, this human fixture casts her eyes just a bit down and off to one side, avoiding us. Standing between two worlds, dejected without being tragic, the barmaid resembles that other damsel of the mirror, Carroll's Alice, lost between reality and illusion. One recalls half-jokingly that Manet and Dodgson were born two weeks apart in January 1832. I say half-jokingly, since they both continue to haunt us with works that do not fit, or fit better than we know.

17

UNLIKELY PEN PALS:
GEORGE SAND AND
GUSTAVE FLAUBERT

LETTERS PROVIDE A high-fidelity tap into the stream of history, particularly when we have both sides of the exchange. And when two powerful writers are engaged, the exchange can deliver grade-A literature into the record. Chateaubriand called George Sand the Byron of nineteenth-century France. Perhaps Flaubert was its George Eliot. In any case their, ten-year correspondence records an astonishing friendship· it follows the events of a historic decade and takes up into the boiler room of literary production. Like everyone in France, Sand and Flaubert were deeply preoccupied by revolution—both political revolution in the search for a new form of government and the Romantic revolution in its heady attempt to substitute art for religion.

On these central questions of modern times, Sand and Flaubert did not agree at all. What gives their letters (*The Correspondence,* translated by Francis Steegmuller and Barbara Bray) passion and lucidity is the fact that, more than they recognized, they were trying to convert each other. As we shall see, Sand may have succeeded more than Flaubert—but barely. In one of the equally great and utterly different exchanges of letters between a man and a woman in the Middle Ages, Heloise revealed greater human love and a deeper Christian faith than her lover, Abelard. In this modern dialogue, the loving antagonists are so equally matched that one follows a few of the exchanges like a hard-fought deuce set in tennis.

Everything seemed to separate Sand and Flaubert. In 1866, when they began writing to each other after an exchange of books and a few casual meetings, Sand was sixty-two and still writing a novel a year, with plays and journalism on the side. Flaubert, at forty-five, was taking five years to complete *A Sentimental Education* (1869) and would soon be complaining of the "the onset of old age." Sand's sudden death ten years later cut off the exchange during one of its most absorbing moments. Sand had found comparative serenity with her extended family at Nohant, her estate 175 miles south of Paris. Flaubert was constantly in anguish over everything and divided his time between the irritations of Paris and his monastic retreat in Croisset, near Rouen. They were also separated by their pasts.

In the summer of 1833, Sand's scandalous third novel, *Lélia,* was given a rave review in the *Revue des Deux Mondes* next to a long poem, "Rolla," by the naughty boy of French Romanticism, Alfred de Musset. Sand, the mother of two children and recently separated from her husband, had already taken on Musset as her publicly flaunted lover. He was twenty-two, she twenty-nine. Sand survived this early summit of notoriety, and added to it by smoking cigars and wearing trousers. She wrote some sixty novels in all, and took half that number of lovers, some of them prominent like Musset and Chopin, few of them negligible. For several weeks, she turned out provocative pamphlets for the interim government following the 1848 revolution. Disillusioned by violent fanatics like the agitator Louis Auguste Blanqui, she let her utopian communism subside gradually into republicanism. She believed strongly in marriage and family and, in everything she did and wrote, promoted equal rights for women in marriage. She did not campaign for women to have the vote. Much of what she earned she gave generously to support needy friends.

In comparison, Flaubert had no profile at all. Born the son of a prominent doctor in Rouen, he weathered an obscure nervous condition and went on to sow his wild oats in Egypt and the Near East. After several false starts, he agonized for years over *Madame Bovary* (1857), which was given a rousing send-off by the government's unsuccessful attempt to censor it. Even though he had expressed weariness and even indignation about some of Sand's early writing, Flaubert could not overlook the fact that she had favorably reviewed both *Madame Bovary* and his Carthaginian extravaganza, *Salammbô.* In 1866, he introduced her as a regular member of the all-male dinners organized by Sainte-Beuve at the Magny restaurant in Paris. But they met only a few times each year and relied on letters. Soon they were intimate without ever becoming lovers. They regarded themselves as "old troubadours," between whom no subject was forbidden. Within a few months, they thought they had seen through each other. Sand called

Flaubert a "Benedictine . . . all alone in your delightful monastery, working and never going out." But she knew enough to add, "What his lordship needs are quicksands, deserts, asphaltic lakes, dangers and fatigues!" Later, weeping over her novel *Consuelo,* Flaubert wrote, "I can only compare you to some great American river: Vastness and Calm."

One constant preoccupation of these two correspondents is how the freelance writer-intellectual can earn a living and live with integrity in so strident and corrupt an era. Neither of them had any institutional connection or sinecure. They were good friends with Prince Napoléon, the emperor's cousin, but that connection did not exempt them from encounters with the censor. They wrote each other about every professional problem and did not neglect physical exercise, sexual abstinence, and religious sentiments. Sand insisted that the writer should serve a partly didactic role in showing virtuous actions resisting the basest human drives. Flaubert maintained that in his finely tuned fiction (totally unlike his impulsive and expostulatory letters) he tried to observe a disinterested attitude and not take any moral position at all. They both waxed eloquent.

Fortunately for us as readers, historical events in the decade 1866–1876 both imposed significant subjects on these lively letters and gave them the unexpectedly simple shape of a two-act play. Act I runs through 1871 and contains half the letters. It includes their first travels to each other's homes, Flaubert's delightful Christmas visit in 1869 to Sand's household of family, friends, and marionettes, the defeat and occupation of France by the Prussians, and the terrifyingly bloody violence of the Communé. The last fifty pages of act I stage an intense political debate between friends who respect each other and answer each other's arguments with care and conviction. Distrustful of universal (male) suffrage, Flaubert called for enlightened rule by mandarins who would, above all maintain justice undiluted by mercy and compromise. He had a strong sense of separation of church and state, no sense at all of separation of powers. Sand stood firm: "I've never been able to separate the ideal of justice that you speak of from love." She became so engaged in articulating her political position that three of her letters to Flaubert overflowed into widely read public letters published in the newspaper *Le Temps.* Together, they were advancing toward the position the Reverend Dr. Martin Luther King, Jr., defined superbly well: "Power without love is reckless and abusive, and love without power is sentimental and anemic."

Act II introduces deaths, financial problems, and other sources of distress for both writers. Then, suddenly, in the last twenty pages, they square off again on the only topic bigger and more urgent than politics: literature. It begins when Flaubert writes that he is receiving four regular Sunday visitors: Ivan Turgenev, Emile Zola, Edmond de Goncourt, and Alphonse Daudet. Such a caucus of realists did not please Sand in the slightest. "Art isn't merely painting or description. . . . It seems to me that your school of writers fails to concern itself with the depths, and tends too much to stay on the surface." The characters in Flaubert's novels, she told him, "are influenced by facts, but never grapple with them."

Flaubert protests that he has no "school" and that he deliberately conceals his own convictions and feelings as irrelevant to writing well. Sand raps out in response a long manifesto on the need to represent good as well as evil in literature, concluding that "supreme impartiality is antihuman." They next examine naturalness of style versus discipline.

A discussion of Zola provokes Sand to some ringing pronouncements. "Art ought to seek the truth, and . . . truth is not the depiction of evil." This time, Flaubert hits back with a famous manifesto of his own. He wonders if a harmonious work of literature cannot, as effectively as a patch of bare wall on the Acropolis, produce the effect of "an intrinsic Virtue . . . something eternal, like a principle (I speak as a Platonist)." A few days later, Flaubert suggests that Sand will recognize her influence in the goodness and humanity represented in his new story, "A Simple Heart." She did not live to read that beautiful homage.

These letters contain some of the most eloquent and impassioned writing of the era. Their rich historical tapestry calls forth a patter of odd endearments *(Chère Maître, Cher Cruchard, Je t'embrasse et je t'aime),* with which Sand and Flaubert framed and cushioned the pounding they gave each other on important subjects. In this extended collaboration, two superior minds rise to each other's challenges. These correspondents are almost never self-conscious or writing for posterity. Their concentration and frankness in more than four hundred letters has agglomerated into a remarkably shaped and unified work.

Facsimiles of a few letters would have shown the revealing contrast between Sand's neat writing, almost devoid of corrections, and Flaubert's wild scribbles, full of marginal inserts and revisions. And Sand's three public letters in *Le Temps,* growing directly out of her political tussle with Flaubert, belong to the correspondence as much as islands belong to a lake, marking where the submerged topography breaks through the surface to display itself in the air.

18

SARA BERNHARDT, THE
SACRED MONSTER

O WE HAVE reason to distinguish between a famous person and a celebrity? I suspect that the modern category "celebrity" connotes a significant degree of induced fame, of notoriety attributable not to high birth or attained position or heroic exploits, but to the operations of the new profession of publicity. Nobody called himself a publicist before the nineteenth century. The most colorful pioneer in the field was Félix Nadar, photographer, balloonist, adventurer, and protector of Impressionist painters. But whom can we identify as the first celebrity in the modern sense? Possibly Rousseau, who made his name by winning an essay contest with a polemic against progress and later rusticated his image by refusing to wear a wig, a sword, and white hose. And one of the purest of the early celebrities must have been the commoner who did nothing in life but cultivate perfect elegance in dress and decorum, frequent elegant friends, and run up large debts—the original dandy, Beau Brummel.

Closer to us, a strong case could be made for proposing Sarah Bernhardt (1844–1923) as the greatest celebrity of her era. Not because her accomplishments were so slender as Brummel's—quite the contrary, she had the talent and the discipline to become a very successful actress—but because the pillar of cloud and fire that went before her wherever she traveled was larger and denser than anyone else's. Every friend and enemy agrees that among Bernhardt's talents, self-promotion rated very high. Just listen to the stories.

At the height of her acting career, Bernhardt did not make bows after a performance; she held her hands under her chin or next to her cheeks, paused, and then threw her arms out in front of her to recognize and embrace the delirious audience. When she descended a spiral staircase, it looked as if she were standing still and the staircase were turning. She was boarded in a convent school and went home to a high-class brothel. In her youth, a band of Paris *galants* eagerly drank champagne from a tub in which she was bathing in their midst, and they were not perturbed to discover, in finishing off the wine, a pint more than they had poured in. Not to be outdone, the Bunyanesque Americans drank Lake Ontario dry after Sarah Bernhardt had swum in its waters.

In 1921, when Bernhardt was seventy-seven, a crowd of five thousand gathered to meet her train when it arrived in Madrid; by then, she had lost one leg, and the men laid down their coats in front of those who carried the actress to her hotel. She gave her admirer the Prince of Wales the role of a corpse in Sardou's *Fédora*. The great English actress Ellen Terry described her friend as "thin as a harrow." Cartoonists all over the world reveled in Sarah Bernhardt's famous S position—head facing one way, shoulders another, hips yet another. They drew her undulating like a serpent. On one of her several farewell tours in the United States, a cowboy who claimed he had ridden three hundred miles to see her tent show pulled a gun when he was told the performance was sold out; and pacified with a standing-room pass, the cowboy drawled, "Say, what does this gal do—sing or dance?" (We are not told whether he stood through a whole evening in French.) And, as everybody must have heard, she slept in her personal coffin, with or without her legion of famous lovers.

None of these anecdotes represents pure invention. All display, however, the fine art of embroidery. And these decibels of gossip invaded the domain of serious literature. Alphonse Daudet's roman à clef, *The Nabob* (1877), casts Sarah Bernhardt as a sculptress, an art that she had taken up with considerable success, and the notorious Duc de Morny as her lover, instead of her aunt's or her mother's. One of the best novels by Edmond de Goncourt, *La Faustin* (1881), follows the life of an actress based primarily on Bernhardt's career. And thirty years later, Marcel Proust modeled the acting of his fictional La Berma on Bernhardt's revival of *Phèdre* in 1893.

When Bernhardt herself wrote a weakkneed novel, *The Idol of Paris,* she refers to Esperance, her actress heroine, as "a force of nature, born only once in 100 years, like Joan of Arc." At the end of the story, a convenient medical diagnosis thwarts the panting dukes and counts who hope to end her stage career in marriage. If Esperance is not allowed to act, "neurasthenia or madness await her." She must have love *and* the stage. And quite emphatically, Sarah Bernhardt did just that.

The anecdotes and the escapades obscure the essential fact that Sarah Bernhardt seized total professional independence when she was thirty-six. She founded, administered, and inspired a large touring and repertory company with a home theater in Paris. Her impresarios worked for her, not vice versa. She raised money, read and chose plays, designed sets and costumes, set styles, directed performances, and starred in all of them: She was Diaghilev and Nijinsky rolled into one. *The Divine Sarah*, the biography of Bernhardt by Arthur Gold and Robert Fitzdale, opens brilliantly by plunging us with little delay into a full-page description by Edmond Rostand of a typical day from noon to near dawn—feverish administrative activities, rehearsals without compromise, an evening performance, studying a part before sleep, no lovers, lots of laughter.

The Divine Sarah was a one-woman institution. We should not assume the existence of male power, sinister or sugary, behind her scrim. And it all happened a century ago! Madonna has almost broken free of the entertainment industry. Streisand has her own production company. Admirers have tried to fly the designation "the Divine Miss M" for Midler. Oprah, having succeeded as an entertainer and an actress, has added the role of literary impresario. None of them rivals the total phenomenon of Sarah Bernhardt during more than three decades.

GOLD AND FIZDALE (Gold died in 1990) are completely at home in that era as a result of their activities as pianist-musicologists and research on their earlier book, *Misia, the Life of Misia Sert,* which appeared in 1980. In that companion of painters, close friend of Diaghilev and Stravinsky, wife of wealthy men, Gold and Fizdale picked a superb subject for surveying a teeming period. Little remembered because not an artist, Misia was a great fashion setter in her day and had the imperious taste to play a significant role in encouraging and in defending avant-garde art.

Misia carried the excitement of discovery, and of sympathy. *The Divine Sarah,* though it narrates the life of a prominent woman in the art world of the same period, does not have the same appeal. This time, the authors' subject has already been discussed in scores of biographies, memoirs, and studies. (All books on Bernhardt shamelessly plunder her memoirs, *Ma double vie,* though in that book she covered only the first thirty years.) Two other biographies in English strike me as in some ways better than this one. Behind its chatty surface, Cornelia Otis Skinner's *Madame Sarah,* which appeared in 1967, keeps a very cool eye on Bernhardt's accomplishments and escapades, and Joanna Richardson's biography of 1959 has the advantages of brevity and superbly chosen quotations.

Having no particular revisionist thesis and no startling new contribution, Gold and Fizdale retell the story with an enthusiasm that never comes to grips with the life of this amazing woman. And sometimes they overstrain for effect. On the first page of their prologue, for example, they quote George Bernard Shaw's acid remarks about the egotistical character of Sarah Bernhardt's acting and then produce this elaborate metaphor: "He was the rock of truth; she, the siren on the rock, her tail in the treacherous waters that surround it, her face turned to the moon." The double caricature is more grotesque than graphic, and it does not correspond to the generally evenhanded tone of the book.

At other times, Gold and Fizdale do not even try for effect. After Bernhardt resigned defiantly from the Comédie Française in 1880 and formed her own company, her future seemed to hang on the success of its opening performance in London. Gold and Fizdale settle for limp commonplaces in their description of that decisive night. "Sarah came through with flying colors. Furthermore, she behaved like an angel."

Precisely because she was the greatest international celebrity of her era from 1880 to 1914, Bernhardt's biographer must resist the temptation either to make her always larger than life or to reduce her to the proportions of puny mortality. Essentially, she lived a life of constantly renewed conquest, more like Napoleon on horseback than like Cleopatra on her barge. Many elements of her life, from her paternity to the nature of her acting, remain mysterious. Her mother, a blond Jewish seamstress from Amsterdam, had the looks and the astuteness to become a highly successful courtesan of Second Empire France. Half an orphan, the spirited young Sarah had protection and sponsorship from figures in high government and financial circles.

Farmed out to a nurse at age five, Sarah threw herself out of a window in order to oblige her visiting aunt to take her home to her mother. When she was fifteen, her career was picked out by her aunt's and her mother's lover, the Duc de Morny, the half brother of Emperor Napoléon III, who sat on the family council convoked to decide the future of this headstrong girl. She wanted to be a nun. But that night, Dumas *père* asked the family to his box at the Comédie Française. By Sarah's own account. Racine's *Britannicus* converted her to the theater. And the influence of the powerful and high-living Duc de Morny helped her to get started without delay at the Conservatoire.

Twenty years later, at thirty-six, having become one of the most applauded actresses in the Comédie Française, Bernhardt had the temerity to break her twenty-year contract and to set up her own touring company. In the 1890s, she seemed to discover new challenges on every side—new plays, new places to visit, new audiences. Her company went on a two-and-a-half-year world tour to four continents, taking twelve plays and an immense inventory of scenery and costumes. She cleared over 3 million francs to spend on her wastrel son and her own extravagant household. The profoundly theatrical spirit of la Belle Epoque seemed to preside at her day of triumph, the *journée Sarah Bernhardt,* in December 1896: at a seven-course banquet at the Grand Hotel, she sat between the minister of fine arts and the personal emissary of the president of the republic, and five poet-playwrights celebrated her in verse at the matinee performance. The grandiose occasion sounds like a parody of itself.

Three years later, at the age of fifty-five, she owned her own theater in Paris, which she completely refurbished in yellow and named after herself. For the next fifteen years, her huge profits came close to covering her losses. When her injured right leg was finally amputated in 1915, it looked like the end of her career after half a century on the stage. No prosthetic device would satisfy her. Still, in seated roles without entrances or exits, she performed courageously for troops at the front in 1916, and she made her last American tour in 1918. And when she was seventy-six, in 1920, she gave one of her most moving performances in an act of Racine's *Athalie.* It concerned an old woman painting her face "in order to undo the ravages of time." After that line, the audience is reported to have given her a spontaneous standing ovation. Old troupers earn a certain privilege of sentimentality.

What about the love life of this *monstre sacré,* this triumphant lioness of Western culture? Brought up to become a courtesan, Bernhardt soon reached the point where she could choose (and for a long time keep) her own men. Since she welcomed gossip and innuendo, there can be no accurate accounting. She claimed that the elegant Belgian Prince de Ligne marked her the most deeply and fathered her son. When she made Victor Hugo's plays shine again, the old satyr, forty-two years her senior, may have found his match. Coded entries in his journal could refer to nonconception or to impotence. The spirited painter-illustrator Gustave Doré filled several seasons of her avalanche like existence. When an unscrupulous Greek Don Juan eleven years her junior with a morphine habit seemed indifferent to her charms, she married him and tried to turn him into an actor. In later years, she was seldom without a younger man in tow.

Did she ever experience passionate love? Or were men merely part of the scenery that she arrayed around herself, the necessary decor for an extravagant life? On this point, Gold and Fizdale follow the responsible course and express skepticism about many of the anecdotes in circulation. They wisely advance no major claims to insight. For this reason, the information that they do supply opens up a few unexplored perspectives. A somewhat nasty book by a friend from her earliest days at the Conservatoire may or may not be accurate on Bernhardt's first major affair with Lieutenant Kératry.

> As for Sarah, though she was very attracted to him, she certainly did not love him, for she was one of those women who are incapable of love. After his passionate embraces, she liked him even less. Vague feelings of disgust and disillusion swept over her. Was *that* what love was about?

Such novelistic gossip takes on a different character, though, when linked to the remarkable letter that Bernhardt wrote to the magnificent tragic actor Mounet-Sully at the end of their tempestuous two-year battle of love:

> Besides, dear Jean, you must realize that I am not made for happiness. It is not my fault that I am constantly in search of new sensations, new emotions. That is how I shall be until my life is worn away. I am just as unsatisfied the morning after as I am the night before. My heart demands more excitement than anyone can give it. My frail body is exhausted by the act of love. Never is it the love I dream of.

Gold and Fizdale say only that the letter is "startlingly explicit . . . about her sexual problems." That leaves interpretation to us. Like the rich and powerful men who frequented her mother's salon, Bernhardt had her pick of lovers, plus the collective adulation of a voyeuristic public, before which she paraded herself every night. The verses that she shouted and whispered onstage infected her and her audience with the most overweening emotions. It is possible to imagine the tensions that such conditions would foster— and that those tensions would lead neither to nymphomania nor to frigidity, but to a Faustian insatiability. If love is always a dream, perhaps public lovers inhabit a dream within a dream. In any case, Bernhardt kept moving on all fronts.

T H E Q U A L I T Y A N D the appeal of Bernhardt's acting confront us with an even deeper mystery than her love life. The sheer mass of conflicting testimony overwhelms the memory and confuses the mind. A few episodes will illustrate. In 1881–1882, her newly formed company was received enthusiastically in Saint Petersburg and then faced a certain hostility in Moscow, where native Russian traditions held their ground. A twenty-one-year-old medical student wrote two lengthy articles in the Moscow *Spectator* in which he whipped himself into outrage over the notoriety and the publicity that preceded the actress. The young man was Anton Chekhov writing under a pseudonym. He had a hard time making up his mind about her acting in the famous nineteenth-century set piece by Scribe and Legouvé, *Adrienne Lecouvreur:*

> We watched Sarah Bernhardt and derived indescribable pleasure from her hard work. There were brief passages in her acting which moved us almost to tears. But the tears failed to well up only because all the enchantment is smothered by artifice . . . and Sarah Bernhardt is monstrously facile.

From other witnesses, we know that Bernhardt could underplay as well as overplay her roles; but Chekhov, from the bottom of his soul, resisted the spectacular.

Fifteen years later, in London, an even more revealing theatrical occasion took place. Both Sarah Bernhardt and her younger Italian rival Eleonora Duse performed a modern German play called *Magda*. Their respective champions, Max Beerbohm and George Bernard Shaw, seized the opportunity for a major critical joust. And their attacks show a curious resemblance. Beerbohm on Duse: "She treats her roles as so many large vehicles for expression of absolute self. From first to last she is the same in *Fédora* as she is in *Magda*. Her unpainted face and the unhidden gray hair are symbolic of her attitude." Shaw on Bernhardt: "Her lips are like a newly painted pillar box; her cheeks, right up to the languid lashes, have the bloom and surface of a peach. . . . The dress, the title of the play, the order of her words may vary; but the woman is always the same. She does not enter into the leading character: she substitutes herself for it." Was it great acting that these critics were watching? Or was it the systematic creation of a theatrical persona, a particular stage personality?

At the end of her career, Bernhardt obtained editorial assistance in assembling her book, *The Art of the Theater* (1924). In it, she declared herself emphatically on the emotionalist side of the great debate over Diderot's "paradox of the actor." (Lee Strasberg offered the most succinct formulation of the paradox: "To move the audience the actor must himself remain unmoved.") Instead of saying modestly with Olivier that "I just pretend," Bernhardt made more sweeping claims about how to fill a role. "It is necessary [for the actor] to feel all the sentiments that agitate the soul of the character":

How can an actor convince another person of his emotion, of the
sincerity of his passions, if he is unable to convince himself to the
point of actually becoming the character he has to impersonate? . . .
The actor cannot divide his personality between himself and his
part. He loses his ego during the time he stays on stage.

She was by no means the first actress or actor to describe the craft in terms
that, since Stanislavsky and Strasberg, we associate with Method acting.

In such passages, Bernhardt was also answering her critics, such as Shaw,
who saw her as vampirizing her roles. And her declarations in favor of emo-
tionalism are partially belied by other sections of *The Art of the Theater,* and
by everything we know about the care and discipline with which she chose,
prepared, rehearsed, and refined her roles. As Gerda Taranow has observed
in her clear-eyed monograph *Sarah Bernhardt, the Art Within the Legend,*
"She preferred to hide her art behind a histrionic persona." Her death scene
as the abandoned mistress in *La Dame aux camélias* (in English, it became
known as *Camille*) could reduce audiences all over the world to tears.
Watching her rehearse the part, Graham Robertson reported admiringly on
"the absolute precision with which she built up her apparently spontaneous
effects." But we also know that before every performance of Racine's *Phèdre,*
her greatest role, Bernhardt insisted on having an hour alone in her dressing
room with the lights lowered. Was she undergoing a complete metamorphosis of personality? Or was she running through all the tricks of the trade in
order to pretend convincingly?

Gold and Fizdale quote Freud's description of Bernhardt in 1885, when
he was, like Chekhov, a medical student:

After the first words of her lovely, vibrant voice I felt I had known
her for years. Nothing she could have said would have surprised me;
I believed at once everything she said.

For years, Freud kept a photograph of her in his Vienna waiting room. Gold
and Fizdale do not record that Yvette Guilbert, the French singer-*diseuse*
who regularly parodied Bernhardt's *voix d'amour* and serpentine movements, consulted Freud by mail in 1931 about her worries over being identified with the immoral, low-life characters that she impersonated and sang
about. Her letter elicited from Freud one of his rare discussions of acting:

This idea of the surrender of one's own person and its replacement
by an imagined one has never satisfied me very much. . . . I would
rather believe . . . not that the actor's own person is eliminated but

rather that elements of it—for instance, undeveloped dispositions and suppressed wishes—are used for the representation of intended characters.

The example that Freud offered was Chaplin, who "always acts himself as he was in his sad youth." Twice in the correspondence, Freud insists that "we know so little." Yet his notion of a projection based on inspired intro-spection partially resolves the paradox of the actor, and helps us to under-stand why this formerly kept woman of the demimonde, who had escaped into celebrity as an actress, made her surest appeal through plays of "chaste sensuality." Thus *Phèdre* offered just the right balance of sexuality tempered by magnificent classic poetry.

WE MUST NOT forget that Bernhardt, in the era of Ibsen, Strindberg, and Zola, avoided naturalism and remained loyal to the classic tradition—above all, to poetry. Her recordings can sound impossibly stilted to a contempo-rary ear. She never abandoned the Conservatoire training in declaiming lines, a studied intonation suspended between singing the sounds and expressing the meaning. Francisque Sarcey, her most faithful and exacting critic, declared very early that "her voice is music incarnate." He also cen-sured her severely—especially after her American tours—for excessive speed of delivery, singsong effects, and monotony. But neither voice recordings without image nor the handful of silent films that she made after 1900 will tell us much about Bernhardt's fifty-year grip on audiences from Auckland to Dakar to Constantinople. Her death scenes could last up to five minutes without a word uttered.

Two of the most time-consuming activities that human beings have invented, the most exhilarating and the most exhausting, are the preparation and the rehearsal of a stage role and a love affair. Bernhardt flourished by means of a grueling combination of the two—and had time left over for sculpture, tennis in the summer, and a succession of large pets (including trees with names). If, as I have proposed, Bernhardt has a claim to be the greatest celebrity of her era, do her life and her career give us further reasons for remembering her? The most evident factors in her success inspire a cer-tain respect, but they do not explain her legend. Despite uncertain health, she combined almost inexhaustible energy with a singularly strong will. She chose and flaunted her motto: *"Quand même."* Literally, it means "Even so." For her, it meant "To hell with the odds." And also "Don't get in my way." A good number of men along the way clogged the machinery for a time, but none ever stopped its advance.

This imperious forward movement of conquest was abetted by her instinctive sense of publicity. On her first American tour in 1880, the bishop of Montreal furiously attacked her and her roles, and he forbade Catholics to attend her performances. Her winning reply delighted the newspapers. "My dear colleague, why attack me so violently? Actors ought not to be so hard on one another." A few weeks later, when the bishop of Chicago fulminated against her company, her impresario had a letter ready—also for the newspapers. It has become famous:

Monsignor:
    It is my custom when I come to your city to spend five hundred dollars on publicity. But as you have done it for me, allow me to send you two hundred and fifty dollars for your poor.

A short time later, a scurrilous account of Bernhardt's life appeared with the names slightly changed. It bore the title *Memoirs of Sarah Barnum,* after the great circus producer, impresario, and publicist who was then at the height of his career. Everyone got the point, and the ensuing rumpus didn't reduce the income of anyone involved. (Many years later Barnum is reported to have offered to buy Bernhardt's amputated leg for the purpose of exhibiting it.)

ONE OF THE attractions of Gold and Fizdale's new biography is the illustrations, nearly one hundred of them in five signatures. Family photographs are followed by many publicity poses (including the celebrated picture of the actress "asleep" in her coffin); portraits of famous lovers and shots of the company on tour (one shows from the stage the waiting audience of five thousand packed to the visible rafters of the Convention Hall in Kansas City); photographs of her in a score of roles (including Phèdre, Cleopatra, Lady Macbeth, Hamlet, Joan of Arc, and Froufrou); and a color section of painted portraits, posters, cartoons, and caricatures. Out of this iconography comes a strong sense of how effectively Bernhardt used the publicity photograph and was shaped by it. Nadar photographed her in his vast clearinghouse of a studio (where the Impressionists held their first show in 1874) not after she had made her name, like his other famous sitters, but when she was sixteen. He posed her draped with classical column and then topless, with a fan hiding all of her face but one eye. Before the era of gossip sheets and *Penthouse,* these images made fortunes for the photographers and seconded the actress in her long triumph.

But energy and self-promotion, even when channeled into the theater, do not fully explain Bernhardt's legendary stature. Several other factors deserve consideration. I discern a powerful discrepancy, even a contradiction, between her resolute independence as a professional woman and her most successful roles as a doomed woman sacrificing herself for her love of a man. Yes, she succeeded in other roles, as different as Joan of Arc and Lorenzaccio. But in *Adrienne Lecouvreur, La Dame aux camélias,* and most of Sardou's plays like *La Tosca,* even in *Phèdre,* she played the victim and she usually died. In that manner, her roles seemed perpetually to underline the triumph of her own career. She surmounted precisely the fate that she made her living by representing.

Bernhardt's resoluteness appears to have been a matter of temperament and talent more than of inspiration by a mentor or an ideal figure. (By the time that she met George Sand, her first great woman hero, Bernhardt was already well launched on her acting career at the Odéon.) Above all, she wished to liberate herself from the dependent world of the courtesan in which she was raised. And her extraordinary reception was due in great part to the circumstance that there was a space waiting for her to enter. Two historical developments were at work in the mid-nineteenth century that favored her. The first was the enormously successful attempt by what we call the Romantic movement to raise artists to the level of a new priesthood of the secular sublime. (The literary historian Paul Bénichou has provided careful documentation of this shift.) The second was the change in the status of the actor from social outcast to culture hero, as represented by Talma and Rachel in France. Propelled by her gifts and instincts, Bernhardt entered the vast arena that waited to receive the actor as celebrity and the artist as priest. Everywhere she went, she carried with her a taint of scandal that lingered around the theatrical life, and an aura of the sacerdotal, the spiritual, to which the art of acting can grant us access. Her genius was to fill that space to overflowing.

Would we welcome her today? It is, of course, the wrong question. The right question is this: Who would Sarah Bernhardt *be* today? In this country, her mixture of temperament, talent, and buccaneering enterprise might have lured her into the world of high finance and stunning takeovers. Or she might be running for president. We may think we have outgrown our need for a figure like Joan of Arc, or Napoléon, but we could use at least a little of Bernhardt's spunk in the space that we call politics.

19

YUPPIES ALONG THE

SEINE: THE

IMPRESSIONISTS

T*HE WORKS OF* Goya and Turner offer us the boldest individual leaps of imagery and technique in nineteenth-century painting. Goya applied his late "Black Paintings" directly to the walls of his country house outside Madrid; their hallucinated subjects and bold style anticipated the innovations of Impressionism and Surrealism. Saved by Baron d'Erlanger, the paintings were exhibited at the 1878 Paris World's Fair, at the height of Impressionism. The English recluse Turner loved to finish his works in public performance on varnishing day. Helped by Ruskin's efforts to open an art-historical space for his new technique, Turner pioneered alone the path from the classical ideal, through realism, to a visionary art that approached abstraction.

Why do we open our eyes and our hearts more readily to a group of French painters who organized eight independent exhibits between 1878 and 1886 than to Goya and Turner? We welcome as close to our own the story of successful innovation by the Impressionists, with their vivid temperaments and contrasting social backgrounds. Drawing together painters, models, critics, novelists, poets, collectors, and dealers, they appeared to form an entire society of art. Their boating parties and dazzling brushwork seem to belong culturally and politically to our times, and they inspire a peculiarly personal nostalgia. Above all, the Impressionists reached beyond Goya and Turner and Delacroix to release cadenzas of light. The first large albums I remember seeing on pianos and coffee tables in the thirties were filled with the almost naked colors of Monet and van Gogh. And as time passed, Cubism, Expressionism, and abstraction never displaced Impressionism in public affection. We keep trying to explain to ourselves its continuing appeal, the meaning of its hovering smile. Are those blowsy street scenes idyllic? Are they ironic? Are they radical? Or all of the above?

Twenty-five years ago, scholars and critics emphasized the role of direct optical perception in Impressionist painting. Their preoccupation with light and color motifs directed attention away from the urban and social situations depicted; and there was a tendency to prefer the late, almost nonfigurative work of Monet. But an overwhelming number of major exhibits, catalogs, and books over the past twenty years has profoundly modified that approach by emphasizing context. "The New Painting," a large exhibition in San Francisco and Washington in 1986, partially reassembled the eight original shows of the Impressionists (of the Société Anonyme, at the start) in sequence. At the same time, the Musée d'Orsay in Paris decided to represent the total artistic output of nineteenth-century France, hanging the most blatant beside the most subtle in a Piranesi-like floating opera of art history. Recent scrutiny of the Impressionists has searched not so much for those painters' connections with twentieth-century tendencies as for their roots in their own era, and in the earlier work of the Barbizon School and of Realism. Monet, who lived on, actively at work, until 1926, was replaced as the swingman by Manet, who died in 1883.

ROBERT HERBERT is a seasoned scholar who has mounted exhibitions and published important writings on both the Barbizon School and Neo-Impressionism. In a famous article in 1979, Herbert exploded the notion that the blurred, "unfinished" surface effects of Monet's compositions arose from negligence or improvisation. For his major study, *Impressionism: Art, Leisure, and Parisian Society,* Herbert ranges far beyond painting techniques to draw on guidebooks, travelers' accounts, statistical reports, and other contemporary sources. He sets out for us broad swatches of daily life, primarily entertainments, and fashions.

Herbert's opening chapter argues that the Impressionists performed a "wrenching of painting into the present" by choosing as subjects the wide boulevards and elegant parks of Haussmann's redrawn Paris. Herbert examines the conflict between immediacy and detachment in Degas's backstage studies of dancers with hovering males and attendant mothers. Manet's comparable café scenes depict customers isolated in public, bereft of gaiety or even communication. Loneliness and commerce have infected all domains—except perhaps Renoir's not-yet-spoiled *Moulin de la Galette* (1876). Herbert provides us with fascinating information about the construction and financing of Second Empire parks and racetracks, where fashion and luxury found their stage, and where Degas and Manet followed them.

His longest chapter, on the sites along the banks of the Seine to which all classes of Parisians were attracted on holidays, supplies maps and notes on railroad travel, eating, swimming, and boating. This Sunday world, which has become familiar to us through Impressionist paintings, was being built up and industrialized throughout the 1860s and 1870s. Monet gradually turned away from the urban invasion of landscape and cultivated his own immense garden at Giverny. Manet and Renoir assimilated social transformation of the countryside with more equanimity. A later chapter, "At the Seaside," compares the responses of several painters to the scenes at summer resorts that were rapidly replacing fishing villages along the Channel coast in Normandy. (Herbert includes some superb pages on Berthe Morisot's suggestive compositions of vacationers at Fécamp and on the Isle of Wight.)

Thanks to a legion of devoted scholars, we probably know more about the social and personal background of the Impressionists than about any set of artists in history. Herbert has assimilated this vast domain of information, and he has searched out much more about the conditions of life in late-nineteenth-century France, especially the theaters and *cafés-chantants* of Paris and the attractions along the Seine. In an unavoidable paradox, Herbert frequently points out class differences (skating was a middle-class sport; horseback riding was aristocratic) in a book basically concerned with the blurring of class lines in modern urban life. Fortunately, he rarely refers to that great empty stereotype, "bourgeois values," and he does not overplay the term *modernity.* Just short of a foot square, this tightly designed book contains as many fine illustrations as two-column pages of text, along with a chronology from 1848 to 1886, ample notes, and a superb bibliography. In a practice now becoming common, reproductions of full paintings have margins and reproductions of details are bled to the edge of the page. (I have two quibbles: The dimensions of a painting are given not in its caption but in a separate list at the front, and the glue in the spine does not hold.)

BEFORE READING THIS thematically organized study, one should be familiar with the basic outline of Impressionism and with the lives and styles of its principal painters. Three quotations should reveal the connections Herbert sets out to establish, as tersely declared in his subtitle:

> Renoir's free brushwork . . . is an expression of his society's longing for signs of those values that were threatened by the organization of the urban-industrial world: spontaneity, individualism, and the freedom to find consolation among natural things.

> In this book I have tried to show that impressionist paintings cannot be separated from the history of the events, places, persons, and social institutions they represent: indeed, that to talk only of "style" and "motif" is to diminish the true richness of art by limiting the extent of its domain.

> Impressionist technique embodies an apparent spontaneity that suits the idea of life seized on the qui-vive, a lack of finish that leaves room for improvisation, a heightened color, and animated brushwork that appeal to the sensuousness of our leisure-oriented culture: in short, a way of working that springs from our "natural" depths, not from the authority-ridden dogmas that thwart true feeling.

Herbert's sociological research convincingly reinforces the paintings he reproduces to demonstrate that Impressionism must be inserted into history—above all, into the history of the emergence of leisure. Compared with the work of Millet and early Courbet, Monet and Degas paint a universe without work. The thesis is evident, yet it is essential. It combines uneasily with another of Herbert's principal themes: detachment, an aesthetic attitude displayed particularly by Degas and Manet and directed toward their subjects and their own style. The word *apparent* at the beginning of the third quotation above carries a heavy burden, for Herbert himself has revealed the careful calculations on which Impressionist technique relies for its spontaneous effects. And I hope "apparent" modifies the jejune generalization of the last part of the sentence. The book is not everywhere so "old-fashioned" as Herbert claims in his ill-conceived preface, in which he tries to review his own book.

Herbert has deliberately limited his history by stopping it around 1882, and by omitting Pissarro, Sisley, and Cézanne. Those painters dealt little with leisure motifs; they favored landscapes and portraits. The emphasis on leisure, consumer culture, and entertainment often leads Herbert to describe Impressionism as a near equivalent of Yuppie painting: works flattened and a bit blurred by their uncritical response to a self-satisfied society. Herbert never mentions the word; I use it reluctantly. For "Yuppie" remains an unsatisfactory category with an undeserved pejorative spin, and Herbert clearly loves and respects these wonderful paintings. The book attempts no sustained discussion of the optical, retinal, photo-influenced aspect of Impressionist style, or of the radical significance of studio practice versus plein-air practice. As William Seitz pointed out years ago, without the portable metal tube for paints that was developed in the 1840s, we would have a very different history of nineteenth-century painting.

THE TRUE TEST of a book like this lies not in theory but in ekphrasis. Herbert's alert eye first seeks an anecdote to explain the poses of the players in a scene, lingers convincingly over the structure, color, and brushwork, and finally consolidates the painting into a larger vision of the society. After a lengthy account of Second Empire racetracks, the discussion of Degas's *Jockeys in Front of the Grandstand* (1869–1872) does not hide Herbert's admiration for its tinted shadows and accented orthogonals. Then he returns to his task:

> [Degas's] pictorial devices were profound expressions of his class and his era because they literally gave shape to aspirations and anxieties that his society formulated in the races. Tracks, horses, and jockeys . . . [were] embodiments of industrial capital's drive for productivity and speed . . . investments whose risk was measured by split seconds, mobile stock coupons who gave life to the spirit of competition and enterprise.

Might there not be also an element of distraction and escape from business? Must the critic roll each work of art back into one immense social ball of wax? Herbert has here produced one of his more rhapsodic social passages, probably because he responds strongly to the painting. He calls Monet's *Bridge at Bougival* (1869) "one of the great landscapes of the era" and details how its double structure is integrated by "carefully dragged" brush strokes and by gray-purple tones. But am I wrong to hear a dutiful note in his conclusion? "In its complicated network of geometric shapes, [Monet's] picture expresses his generation's wish to impose order and regular intervals over nature. It speaks unwittingly for the Second Empire's diagrams of control."

In the following paragraph, Herbert acknowledges this statement to be an extreme assertion of the social meaning of art, and defends it. All art embodies "struggles between an individual's subjectivity and concepts of social organization." The adverb *unwittingly* in the previous quotation hints at Herbert's unwillingness to settle on a single agent for a painting. Every force counts for him. Class, commerce, generation, politics, fashion engulf the artist. At times, Herbert sounds as if he thinks society itself can paint a picture. When he begins talking directly about one of the several artists he values, he redeems himself by the trackings of his restless eye, by the aptness of his allusions.

The occasional lunges in Herbert's writing toward social determinism of art arise, I believe, from an oblique running dialogue he is carrying on with a book he mentions in the first paragraph of his preface, T. J. Clark's *The Painting of Modern Life: Paris in the Art of Manet and His Followers,* which appeared in 1985. Herbert states both that Clark's book has almost single-handedly reoriented the field and that, since he takes issue with much of what Clark writes, particularly with Clark's saturation in theory, the books have little in common. Still, they dance an elaborate minuet for us, to a music that many would call "revisionism" in art history.

Herbert dedicates his book to Meyer Schapiro and acknowledges him first among his "substantial debts." Clark opens his first chapter with a stunning full-page quotation from Schapiro's "The Nature of Abstract Art," which appeared in *The Marxist Quarterly* in 1937, on the objective forms of bourgeois recreation in the 1860s and 1870s. Both critics make extensive use of Georg Simmel's notions of detachment and the blasé, and of Thorstein Veblen's association of leisure and class. In both books, Haussmann's remodeling of Paris topography plays a major role as an instrument of social control. Clark does not make up his mind whether the Impressionists opposed or welcomed these changes. Herbert, more forthrightly, refers several times to the "complaisance" displayed by the Impressionists toward the organiza-tion and commercialization of leisure, "The history of Impressionism is in part the acceptance of, even the indulgence in these changes." The combination of delightful Seine-side setting and silken brushwork in Renoir's *Luncheon of the Boating Party* (1881), for example, creates a painting that "hovers on the edge of ecstasy." Precisely. Perhaps *Yuppie* is too weak a term for such complaisant painting.

Given their social and political outlook, and their deep suspicion of class as a structuring force in society, it strikes me as amazing that these two historian-critics never chide the Impressionists for having consented to a corrupt and destructive culture, and for having produced a highly decorative icing for a cake that revealed its rottenness as soon as you cut into it. In fact, the opposite is the case. They love the stuff. Herbert is a wonderful author to learn from, and to spar with. But, more the historian than the theorist, he reveals in himself "two guys," as Flaubert said of himself. One guy documents the exploitation that transformed every aspect of life in the era, and loosened class distinctions without destroying them. The other guy treasures the sturdily formed yet informal-looking canvases created by a few painters who witnessed these changes, and even sought them out to record. In the great ekphrasis playoff, the first guy hangs around, always turning up for introductions, transitions, and conclusions. The second guy wins hands down.

20

LIVING BY WORDS:

MALLARMÉ

IN THE FIGURES of Tennyson and Browning in England and Hugo in France, Romantic poetry traveled a long distance from its origins, in nature and in feeling. All three poets died around 1890, and with them disappeared much of the authority of poetry as a public voice. The developments that followed have given us the word *Symbolism,* and they arose primarily in France. Like the discovery of the calculus, the revelation happened twice, independently, and in close succession.

In 1867, a twenty-five-year-old lycée teacher in the provinces wrote a pair of letters reporting on an intense spiritual and artistic crisis over the past year. "My thought has thought itself through. . . . I have died perfectly. . . . Having felled God, I still have to look in a mirror to think. . . . I have become impersonal." Then, in 1871, a seventeen-year-old lycée student in the provinces wrote a pair of letters about his spiritual and artistic crisis. "It is false to say: I think. One should say: I am thought [*On me pense*] . . . *I* is someone else." Each of these young men was describing a partially induced fission of the self, the breaking apart of a consciousness no longer sustained by religious faith. Each of them went on to cultivate this crisis as his conversion, his ordeal, and the principal subject of his poetic work.

The first of them was Stéphane Mallarmé, who had already been recognized and published at twenty, though his career as a poet smoldered on underground until the 1880s and 1890s. The second was Arthur Rimbaud, the Mozart of modern poetry, who burned out in three dazzling years before he was twenty and abandoned literature for exotic languages and gunrunning in Abyssinia. Their method of highly individualized impersonality entered the mainstream of European poetry through the loose movement that came to be called Decadence, which was the reverse side of Symbolism. It is also significant that "The Drunken Boat." Rimbaud's earliest major work, was about a hallucinatory, catastrophic, yet somehow triumphant sea voyage. It matches "A Throw of the Dice." Mallarmé's great final work, which was laid out like a musical score to represent the immense sidereal shipwreck of poetic thought in the vacant ocean of the cosmos. With dramatically contrasting temperaments and careers, these two poets unwittingly collaborated to turn poetry toward the undermining of ordinary language and the cultivation of mystery and indirection.

It is also possible to make the case that these poets provided two of the strongest and most nefarious influences on modern literature. "Man may be democratic, the artist, taking another role, must remain aristocratic," wrote Mallarmé, ". . . poets, you have always been proud; go further, become disdainful." Mallarmé published this manifesto, "Art for All," when he was twenty. He believed that the cult of art is best expressed in works wrapped in obscurity, so as to dissuade the uninitiated reader. Under the influence of Poe's writings about literary composition, Mallarmé turned away from Romantic inspiration and cultivated poetry as a hermetic and self-conscious craft. And he moved beyond Poe toward a looking-glass phase of writing, in which every poem takes as its subject the composition of that poem. Mallarmé helped to lay the groundwork for the self-reflexive dogma that until recently hung like a cloud over contemporary literary criticism. For some readers, these Mallarméan traits condemn poetry to an intellectual narcissism far removed from its true purpose.

Hyperbole! de ma mémoire
Triomphalement ne sais-tu
Te lever, aujourd'hui, grimoire
Dans un livre de fer vêtu!

Car j'installe, par la science,
L'hymne des coeurs spirituels
En l'oeuvre de ma patience,
Atlas, herbiers, et rituels.

Hyperbole! from my memory
Triumphantly can you

Arise, today but a gramarye
In an iron-clasped book!

For I install through science
The hymn of spiritual hearts
In my patiently elaborated oeuvre,
Atlas, herbal or ritual.
(translated by Gordon Millan)

How does one begin to read such hermetic lines? A century ago, French critics were already attacking Mallarmé with ferocity. They mocked him as a mystifier and a charlatan, a High Priest of the Void. "Complete eclipse of the French language, of lucidity, of common sense! . . . Look, just take a hat, throw into it adverbs, conjunctions, prepositions, nouns, adjectives, pick them out haphazardly and write them down: there's Symbolism for you." This accusation by Leconte de Lisle, the chief poetic voice of the Parnassian school of poetry, was repeated almost verbatim twenty-five years later by the Dadaists as their battle cry. Both de Lisle and the Dadaists were wrong: The Symbolists were serious artists, not public pranksters. Their seriousness did make them vulnerable, however, to some wonderfully high-spirited pastiches and hoaxes, such as *Les Déliquescences d'Adoré Floupette* (1885), which parodied the jargon of poets like Mallarmé so resourcefully that many read it as a contribution to the new style.

The case against Mallarmé as a rarefied aesthete and an obscurantist thinker is not entirely trumped up. It sheds some light on why he was a disastrously ineffectual and boring classroom teacher of English in a succession of schools; but it also fails to reveal the genuine qualities of the man and the artist. The opposite of a self-absorbed *voyou* like Rimbaud, Mallarmé was devoted to his German wife and two children, held an onerous job for thirty years, and sacrificed much of his most precious resource—time—to his friends.

His often-unbuttoned letters display the unflagging stoicism of a studious poet. He deserved the love and the respect that he inspired. This upright citizen had too few skeletons in his closet to pique our prurience. (The best one can trot out is a late, fleeting, and discreet adultery with Méry Laurent, the celebrated model of his close friend Manet. Afterward, they remained chaste companions for ten years, until his death.) Sometime around 1880, Mallarmé began to keep up with his friends and admirers by receiving them in his tiny apartment in the rue de Rome on Tuesday evenings for a smoke and a grog and literary conversation salted with lots of gossip. These meetings were not monologues. Mallarmé may have floundered in the classroom, but literary manuals like to treat *les mardis de* Mallarmé as the last great literary salon of Europe.

Fame came to this mild, friendly writer in two stages, both of them closely implicated in the origins of what we now call "modernism." In the spring of 1884, by which time his writing had appeared only in reviews, two books almost simultaneously identified Mallarmé as the leader of a new literary movement. Verlaine, in *Les Poètes maudits,* chose him as one of three "absolute poets" or "accursed poets," along with Corbière and Rimbaud; his essay on Mallarmé included a number of new poems and a long autobiographical letter. And a few weeks later J. K. Huysmans, a naturalist writer and therefore a dissident, published *A rebours (Against Nature,* or *Against the Grain),* the novel that is now considered the masterpiece of Decadence.

In its fourteenth chapter, Huysmans's jaded aristocratic "hero," Des Esseintes, brushes away all the great works of nineteenth-century literature, except two personally printed and bound collections of poetry. They are both by Mallarmé, whose distillation of language into symbol and silence represents the final stage of literary Decadence. Des Esseintes smiles in exhausted pleasure over Mallarmé's slender volumes. The only other moment in the book when he smiles comes when he discovers the ultimate refinement for nourishing his delicate digestive tract: three peptone enemas a day. The two episodes furnish the crowning points of this experimental novel.

Seven years after these two books turned Mallarmé into a celebrity, the literary scene had become sufficiently agitated and polarized around Symbolism and naturalism to require what would now be a survey. The journalist Jules Huret interviewed sixty-four writers of all categories for the daily *L'Echo de Paris.* When Huret brought the interviews out as a book, he did not conceal his distaste for the vanity, the jealousy, and the egotism of most of his subjects. Still, Mallarmé's patient, good-natured answers made his interview the most informative in the volume. And the index revealed that he was one of the most frequently mentioned authors, ahead of Hugo and trailing Verlaine and Zola.

A few years later, when Verlaine died, Mallarmé was informally elected Prince of Poets. Mallarmé finally published two collections of his writings, retired from teaching in 1892, encouraged a new generation of writers at his *mardis,* including Valéry, Gide, and Claudel. He died in 1898, at the age of fifty-six. The cause was a laryngeal spasm; it cut off his breathing and suffocated him instantly, the way one silences the sounds of a bagpipe at the end of a piece.

Studies of Mallarmé's poetry have appeared steadily since his death, including important books by Albert Thibaudet, Emilie Noulet, Charles

Mauron, Wallace Fowlie, and Robert Greer Cohn. By common consent, the task of writing the life of the poet was left in the hands of the indefatigable French surgeon and man of letters Henri Mondor. In the 1940s, he published six books on Mallarmé; and for thirty years, students and scholars of Mallarmé learned most of what they knew from three of them. Mondor's *Vie de Mallarmé* is an eight-hundred-page saturation biography stuffed with quotations from the letters and with lively information on the backgrounds of Symbolism and naturalism. In *Propos sur la poésie,* Mondor collected in a slim volume the central passages from Mallarmé's letters on the theory and practice of poetry. And the Pléiade edition of Mallarmé's complete works collected every literary effort in sixteen hundred pages, with the exception of one important essay on Manet and Impressionism. (Its original French text has been lost.)

Mondor was a one-man Mallarmé industry until he died in 1962. (His biography of the poet has never been translated into English.) No one undertook another life until Gordon Millan, a Scottish scholar at the University of Strathclyde, recently produced *A Throw of the Dice: The Life of Stéphane Mallarmé.* Millan has given us a well-informed and workmanlike study in 350 pages. He carries out the pledge made in his introduction to restore the emphasis to Mallarmé's life and published poetry in preference to the more fashionable subjects of his poetic theories and his unfinished works. Millan has been able to draw on new materials from the correspondence, from documents assembled by his mentor Carl Paul Barbier, and particularly from an unpublished private diary by Henri de Régnier, one of Mallarmé's young disciples. We needed this full-length study in English.

Brushing aside Flaubert's famous growl to Louise Colet that one must live like a bourgeois and think like a demigod, Millan twice insists, at the beginning and the end, that Mallarmé's life and work are "an organic whole" and "truly inseparable." Better this effort to see the man whole than dubious speculations about alienation, schizophrenia, and disabling contradictions. Yet Millan's nine chapters partly belie his categorical thesis. For Mallarmé lived for thirty years with a split down the middle of his life between teaching, for him a livelihood without rewards, and poetry, a full-fledged secular religion with solemn rituals and bouts of despair and moments of ineffable vision.

Verlaine called him an accursed poet, but Mallarmé also enjoyed considerable protection in the Ministry of Education and in the literary marketplace. And this poet, whose name means "ill-armed," who called for the suppression of personality in submission to art, displayed a highly complex temperament. He was ambitious for his literary work, but in so meticulous a way as to be clumsy. Some of his letters on purity and obscurity in poetry may sound like the mouthings of a charlatan, but they were unquestionably sincere.

In a letter written when he was twenty-five, this poet so fixated on words (once, during a depression, he knelt down and prayed to the language itself) seems to confound his own aestheticism. "I think that to be truly a man, to be by nature capable of thought, one must think with one's body, which creates a full, harmonious thought, like those violin strings vibrating directly with their hollow wooden box." Above all, Mallarmé's relation to the act of writing was highly physical. Millan reports an incident of anxiety and depression in 1869 that took the form of hysteria not about the blank page but about writing with a pen. His doctor instructed him to dictate his letters, and he explained to a friend that "the thought of a pen writing through my will, even if it is by the hand of another, brings back my palpitations."

Millan does not establish an organic unity of life and work, of aestheticism and physicality, in Mallarmé's case. As I shall argue, even the uncertain unity of Mallarmé's writings eludes him. But Millan does better in dealing with the major poems. The extended commentary comes first as preparation; then Millan gives the French text and his English translation as if he really expects us to read the lines aloud in one version or another, preferably both. This respect for the integrity of the poem redeems many of the book's weaknesses, not the least its regrettable wanness, which misses the intensity at the heart of Mallarmé's universe.

Millan's writing is frequently at fault. It is characterized by awkward sentences, a weakness for cliché, and a misplaced urge to anticipate events to come. He never flashes a sentence so incisive as Sartre's on Mallarmé: "More and better than Nietzsche, Mallarmé lived through the death of God." Millan's blurred instinct for detail leads him to throw into the notes at the back of the book important details about Mallarmé's finances, and about his feeling for language. And he makes periodic attempts to introduce into Mallarmé's thinking "the presence/absence paradox" without explaining this dubious borrowing from deconstructionist criticism.

Millan's biography will serve many readers who have little French, but it does not displace the crabbed, craggy mountain of a biography by Mondor, where one can revel in the bursting anecdotal background of the period. Mondor registers the importance of the poet Laforgue, unmentioned by Millan. And Mondor has a good nose for stories. (To wit: Mallarmé told Valéry one day that he thought he had seen Baudelaire in his last year riding on the upper deck of a three-horse omnibus, wearing a top hat, and holding, perhaps, "The Painter of Modern Life," his essay on Constantin Guys.) The best complement in English to Millan's biography is the selection of Mallarmé's letters translated by Rosemary Lloyd in 1988. Our new Plutarch, whenever he or she arrives, could do worse than to include in a modern *Parallel Lives* a pairing of the gentle Mallarmé with the aggressive Rimbaud.

Beyond his sweetness as a person and his difficulty as a poet, Mallarmé remains so extreme and so important a figure in literature that it is important to get things right about him. There has been too much fuss made about the period of his youth in the provinces, when he turned to language as to a new religion. His major personal and artistic crisis occurred in the nineties, when he achieved fame and entered his fifties. By then he had become fully aware of the two poles of his talent. The collection of his complete works contains fifty pages of serious poetry and one hundred pages of "occasional verse"—postal addresses written on letters in the form of rhymed quatrains (and actually delivered by conscientious mail carriers), ingenious inscriptions for ladies' fans and New Year's gifts, and similar froth.

At this juncture, Mallarmé had also fallen into what looked like contradictions in his pronouncements about his art. He seemed to be calmly working both sides of the street. Which has priority, speech or writing? The final words of an interview in 1891 are categorical: "Basically the world is made to end up in a book." But following his lifelong attraction to everything theatrical and performed, Mallarmé also insisted that "nothing will remain without being spoken." What about the question of naming things in poetry? In 1886, he stated that to say the word *flower* releases the pure musical notion or idea absent from any real bouquet; yet five years later, in one of the major definitions of Symbolism, he pronounced that *"to name* an object is to suppress three-quarters of the poem's pleasure, which consists in divining little by little: suggest, that's the dream." Mallarmé, as much as Whitman, contained multitudes. But the accumulation of such statements leads to a certain precariousness.

THE GREATEST CRISIS was formal. Following Baudelaire, Mallarmé remained faithful in his poems to the conventions of French versification and also wrote prose poems, his own and his translations of Poe's verse. But something happened to make him reconsider his own position. After the death of Hugo in 1885, as if his mere presence had held back the flood, free verse made its appearance in French through translations of Whitman, through poems by Rimbaud and Laforgue, and through works by a flock of young poets. They more or less declared themselves Symbolists in 1886, and they made *La Vogue* their house review. They were all friends and admirers of Mallarmé, and they expected approbation from the master. But free verse was not Mallarmé's natural impulse. In a lecture given at Oxford and at Cambridge in 1891, Mallarmé raised a warning finger: *"On a touché au vers."* Verse has been tampered with.

How would he react? Would he encourage or resist the innovation? As the leader of the new school, would he write free verse himself, in the way that, say, Stravinsky would finally succumb to serial composition? Mallarmé's most challenging decisions came at the height of his fame, in 1892, just after he had published *Vers et Prose,* his first book for the general public. His response was a masterful maneuver, neither capitulation nor attack, in which he discovered in himself new resources. Millan conveys little sense of this crucial moment, which was so important for Mallarmé and for the development of European poetry.

Mallarmé produced, for a start, a few poems that strike a rare balance between his most obscure and forbidding style and his lighthearted occasional verse. For a banquet of poets at which he was asked to preside in early 1893, he composed "Salut," a toast in the form of a sonnet. Every line refers directly or metaphorically to the literal scene of an older poet standing, champagne glass in hand, at one end of a tumultuous banquet table like a captain standing on the poop of his ship in stormy seas. The analogy of the dangerous sea voyage is both an elaborate joke and a serious literary device for making a toast to great poems still to be written. (The translation that follows is mine.)

Rien, cette écume, vierge vers
A ne désigner que la coupe;
Telle loin se noie une troupe
De sirènes mainte à l'envers.

Nous naviguons, ô mes divers
Amis, moi déjà sur la poupe
Vous l'avant fastueux qui coupe
Le flot de foudres et d'hivers.

Une ivresse belle m'engage
Sans craindre même son tangage
De porter debout ce salut

Solitude, récif, étoile
A n'importe ce qui valut
Le blanc souci de notre toile.

Mere froth, these virgin verses
Cut like glass to hold the void

Where mermaids gambol to avoid
The drowning scenes my eye rehearses.

We set our sails, my motley friends,
I standing on the wintry poop
To watch young poets on the prow usurp
The pomp this thundering night portends.

Tipsy upon a tossing deck
Yet fearless of pitch I now elect
To make this stern freestanding toast

Solitude, or reef, or star
To lines our empty sheets disbar
From sounding at this gay repast.

At the end of his life, Mallarmé chose "Salut" to open the collection of all his poetry. He realized that in this poem he had fused the full range of his gifts, from the down-to-earth to the ethereal. And in 1895, when the newspaper *Le Figaro* conducted a survey on free verse, Mallarmé answered by giving not a statement, not a free-verse experiment, but a playful sonnet composed of seven-syllable lines. "Toute l'âme résumée" treats the action of smoking—breathing, smoke rings, combustion, ash—as an analogy for poetic creation. The last two lines restate and parody the whole Symbolist aesthetic: "Anything too clear will blow away/Your entire literary play."

But on one occasion, almost as if he foresaw his death, Mallarmé accepted the challenge of free verse, and he produced an utterly unprecedented work independent of any known genre or form. "A Throw of the Dice" lays out on eleven double-page spreads fragments of verse and prose in different fonts, so as to form a flowchart and a score for a live reading by many voices. The virtually sculpted lines seem to trace the narrative of an enigmatic thought doomed to shipwreck. Mallarmé creates, aurally and visually, the arresting interference and the booming override of an echo chamber. He observes, in his preface, that "this experiment engages, with uncertain results, in quests particular and dear to our time—free verse and the prose poem." The traditionalist outperformed, in one try, the most obstreperous avant-gardists.

Mallarmé's third response to the vexed state of poetry was to write, in 1896, "Crise de Vers," his most dense and important essay, to evaluate the situation. The allusion to *crise de nerfs,* or nervous seizure, was inescapable. The essay belongs among a handful of major documents in modern literature. The exalted tone sounds religious. "We are witnessing, as finale to this century, but not like the previous one, great shifts, far from the public eye: a trembling and even a tearing of the veil of the temple." He is talking about poetry. Mallarmé welcomes the "polymorphous" rhythms of free verse, refers to the blank spaces and the "total word" of his own "A Throw of the Dice," and asks that poetry reclaim from music the purity and sonorousness that are its own original properties.

In these three concrete responses to the "exquisite crisis" that Mallarmé discerned in literature during the nineties, he was taking also one further and more subtle step: He was allowing a glimpse of his own ultimate project in poetry. He had declared, in his early twenties, that he worked by indirection and suggestion, and that Poe was his master in obtaining singleness of effect in a poem. Now he set down unmistakable hints about an almost heretical goal, and it had to do with the nature of language.

In "Crisis in Verse," Mallarmé deplores the fact that the post-Babel diversity of languages in the world deprives any one of them of authority, of the possibility of offering perfectly expressive words. In French, for instance, a certain perverseness has given to *jour,* or day, a dark sound, and to *nuit,* or night, a bright sound. Something must be amiss. Then he adds a crucial comment on this lapse from ideal expressiveness in language: "But, we must remember that if we had the ideal language, *verse would not exist*—for verse redeems the sins of individual languages by providing their superior complement." At nearly the same time, in a letter to Gide, Mallarmé explained the layout of "A Throw of the Dice" by insisting on the appearance of the work on the page: "The rhythm of a sentence about an act or even about an object, makes no sense unless it imitates them, unless by its outline on paper . . . it renders some aspect of them."

In these three places, Mallarmé reveals what he believed to be the true purpose of poetry. It is to rectify the arbitrary and often perverse results of there being many languages and no perfectly expressive one. In the inconclusive *Cratylus,* Plato's discussion revolves around the question of whether names of things are natural or conventional; and the German dramatist Lessing recapitulates and decides the entire discussion in a sentence: "Poetry must try to raise its arbitrary signs to natural: that is how it differs from prose and becomes poetry." Lessing anticipates Mallarmé's project in which the studied visual arrangements and cultivated musicality of poetry can introduce a higher onomatopoeia, a new Cratylism into language, to reach beyond the arbitrary conventions of ordinary language. Through a renewed fusion with sound and appearance, poetry can surpass the limits and the contingencies of any national tongue and attain a higher form of speech.

It is a serious mistake to permit deconstructionists and other theorists of language to co-opt Mallarmé into the view that language is the sole reality, excluding any external world, and that literature is an arbitrary, authorless construction of signs. On the contrary, Mallarmé sought a seamless correspondence between language and reality in the form of poetry, a universal language directly incorporating the senses and the referential world into "a total word." This near-mystical vision of a universal poetic language resembles the discovery of colors for vowels by Rimbaud and the casting off by Khlebnikov of the exigencies of Russian and his invention of *zaum,* meaning "beyond sense."

In an undertaking close to magic and practicing some of its rituals and mysteries, Mallarmé wished to invoke—almost to convoke—the real world by discovering the privileged speech of poetry. It is in this context that he spoke of "ceding the initiative to words" and in the next sentence of "eliminating chance." He sought the true names of things, not the idle play of signifiers. He would surpass the painful deficiencies of *jour* and *nuit.* And unlike Rimbaud and Khlebnikov, Mallarmé remained modest in his Faustian undertaking and good-humored in his daily dealings. The secret life of his mind was intense beyond our knowing.

If poetry is not the mere creature of language but its redeemer, we have good reason to listen again to the two best-known anecdotes about Mallarmé, both omitted by Millan. Degas once sought out Mallarmé at Berthe Morisot's house to complain about the impossible art of sonnet writing. "I spent the whole day on a sonnet without going anywhere. But I have ideas coming out of my ears—too many ideas." Mallarmé didn't try to console the painter: "You don't make sonnets out of ideas, Degas. You make them out of words." And at another gathering Mallarmé was approached by Debussy, who was twenty years younger, with the information that he was setting *Prelude to the Afternoon of a Faun* to music. "Well, Debussy," said the poet "I thought I had already set it to music."

21

THE PRESENT PLACE

OF FUTURISM

B Y ABOUT 1905, the cultural solution of *la fin de siècle* in Europe had reached supersaturation. In many major cities, linked by good trains and rapid postal services into a surprisingly close community, artistic circles were both exhausted and expectant. Out of a rich mixture of naturalism, Symbolism, Decadence, and anarchism, of Bergson, Nietzsche, Jarry, and Sorel, there emerged before World War I a series of movements that explored the most significant modern tendencies in the arts. Fauvism, Cubism, (Italian) Futurism, (Russian) Cubo-Futurism, Der Blaue Reiter, (English) Vorticism—they succeeded and overlapped one another in an unprecedented display of artistic energies. Among these schools, however, historical circumstances have tended to keep Futurism in the background.

The hegemony of Paris in the art world has obscured the stunning success of Filippo Marinetti's international tours between 1912 and 1914. A master of self-promotion, Marinetti performed brilliantly onstage as an agitator for his Futurist movement, launched with a manifesto in 1909, and for the half a dozen uninhibited painters who accepted his leadership. Confusion and rivalry ensued around 1911, when newspapers started calling Russian artists and writers Futurists; like the Italians, the Russians practiced tactics of public performance and scandal. In the yeasty years that led up to World War I, both groups announced a program of reconstructing the world according to a fanatical utopian program that would place the artist's imagination in charge of society. Italian Futurism went on to make an uneasy contribution to Mussolini's fascism. In Russia, after a few years of collaboration with the revolutionary government, Cubo-Futurism was ground to nothing by the Soviet state: It ended in a series of suicides.

In the United States, we tend to distrust such utopian programs, as well as any organized, self-promoting artistic movement that engages in bombast. For these reasons, we have favored looser and less political schools such as Cubism, and individual artists who kept their distance from faction— Pasternak, Klee, Valéry, Eliot, Matisse. Gradually, however, scholars have been informing us about the half-forgotten Futurisms, even the discredited Italian brand. The pioneer works in English are Joshua Taylor's informative catalog that accompanied the Museum of Modern Art exhibition in 1961 and Marianne Martin's superb *Futurist Art and Theory* (1968). They opened the way for R. W. Flint's edition of *Selected Writings of Marinetti* (1972), for a major exhibit and catalog at the Philadelphia Museum of Art, *Futurism and the International Avant-Garde* (1980), and for a wonderful small show and catalog on "Word and Image" at the Yale University Art Gallery, *The Futurist Imagination* (1983). These publications establish a judicious perspective on the participants' inflated statements about their goals and accomplishments.

Two substantial books from the late eighties make two very different contributions to the fortunes of Italian and Russian Futurism. Marjorie Perloff has written studies of Robert Lowell, Ezra Pound, Frank O'Hara, and modernist poetics, always with increasing attention to the visual arts and to European backgrounds. The Futurist "moment" that she examines in her book encompasses all the prewar avant-gardes. She lumps them together in their ambition to overthrow the past and seek a new age. In *The Futurist Moment: Avant-Garde, Avant-Guerre, and the Language of Rapture,* the wide angle of her lens glimpses the whole European scene between 1905 and 1914, and the vital connections of the arts today to that resurgent moment. Pontus Hulten's *Futurism and Futurisms,* by contrast, catalogs the inaugural 1986 exhibition of over twelve hundred items at the Palazzo Grassi in Venice. The Swedish scholar and museum director Pontus Hulten, formerly of the Pompidou Center and the Los Angeles Museum of Contemporary Art, directed thirty scholars in producing a presumably definitive record of Futurism as an international movement in every aspect of culture, including dress and furniture.

Perloff subordinates her wide-ranging research on Italian and Russian Futurism to a pervasive thesis. The prewar moment of "remarkable rapprochement between avant-garde aesthetic, radical politics, and popular culture" furnishes the true origins of "our own postmodern urge to break down the centered, hierarchical orders of the past." The intervening, reactionary chapter of high modernism separates us from this essential period, in which collage, "Words Set Free," and other devices were invented. I concur that literature and the arts in the 1980s have a special affinity with the 1905–1914 period; I remain skeptical about the name and nature of "our own postmodern urge."

Perloff begins with a lengthy examination of "the first simultanist book," the seven-foot-tall *La Prose du Transsibérien* (1913)—poem by Blaise Cendrars, "simultaneous colors" by Sonia Delaunay. Perloff's rhapsodic discussion does not convince me that this curio is Cendrars's best poem (I would vote for *Dix-Neuf Poèmes Elastiques*), or that he was "the prototype of the new 'total' Futurist artist." Perloff's second chapter, on "The Invention of Collage," gives a superb account of the way the Futurists, Italian and Russian, transformed the Cubist technique. She argues that collage's rejection of representation and of individual consciousness liberated both painting and poetry. The juxtaposition of fragments in Picasso and Giacomo Balla, in Cendrars and Marinetti demands more attention to composition than to subject matter. Perloff perceives and welcomes the essential theatricality of the Futurist manifestos.

A chapter on the uncoupling of the word from its conventional meaning in Russian Futurism leads into a convincing demonstration of the impact of Futurist "Words Set Free" on Pound's poetic style. The conversational prosody and scorelike typography of his *Cantos* took shape precisely in 1913–1914, when he and Wyndham Lewis were developing Vorticism and publishing *Blast*. The final pages of *The Futurist Moment* deal with public monuments as they represent the Futurist ambition to reach a mass public. Apollinaire, Cendrars, and Barthes all celebrated the Eiffel Tower in their fashion; and the monuments that the late Robert Smithson discovered and imagined and recorded in Passaic, New Jersey, or erected in an abandoned quarry in Holland, revive the Futurist "spirit of invention, or rupture, of the concept of art work as something that can actually *change* our landscapes and our lives."

Perloff combines solid scholarship with enthusiasm and provides a fine selection of reproductions in black and white and in color. She does not waste her time on old debates over priority (Italian versus Russian Futurism, Apollinaire versus Cendrars) or on the political collapse of Futurism into fascism. She studies the Futurist movement because she believes it is still with us. At times, her concern with the contemporary deflects or distorts the discussion of her chosen historical moment. She consistently favors the dynamic and disruptive over the decadent and reflective. The surface of her exposition remains very busy, fitting in cross-references and citations of recent critics. But she makes no reference to two books closely related to her topic, John Berger's *The Moment of Cubism* and Max Kozloff's *Cubism/ Futurism*.

My principal reservation concerns a central omission, reflected in Perloff's choice of title. Futurism mounted an enormous international campaign for speed and motion, for war and violence, for "Words Set Free," for the rejection of the past, for the appeal to the masses. But the "moment" that Perloff wishes to set before us in all its excitement participates equally in a different ism—primitivism. Though this current was never organized into a school, it affected all artists of the epoch. Yet many important elements of the period—not just African and Oceanic sculptures but also children's art; the art of the insane; a powerful wave of interest in the occult, the spiritual, and magic; and the constant presence of Bergson's philosophy of nonrational ways of organizing experience—are not discussed and barely mentioned in *The Futurist Moment*. The incompleteness of the account may be attributable to Perloff's eagerness to establish postmodernism as continuous with her version of Futurism, and to get off a few whacks in passing at high modernism and its accompanying New Criticism. But primitivism burns as bright as Futurism in the relations of the arts today with the pre–World War I decade. Perloff's writings ask us to remain attentive to three levels of analysis: to abstractions, such as textuality and theatricality; to the complex dynamics of artistic schools and movements; and to the qualities of individual works. Her eye, her ear, and her store of knowledge work best together in the last category.

I did not visit the Venice exhibition of Futurism. The evidence of Hulten's volume confirms other accounts about the scope of that event and its organizers' resolve to project the international side of the movement. *Futurism and Futurisms* does not follow the art-historical format that has become the norm for exhibition catalogs in recent years: a handful of scholars contribute careful essays to the catalog and collectively propose a revisionist understanding of the works displayed. Hulten offers something both more and less ambitious. Instead of several scholarly essays, he opens with eight sketchy pages of his own that provide a little background information and standard answers to a few critical questions.

In affirming the neglected influence of Futurism, he fleetingly mentions the Baroque as a model for the grandiose projects of the Italian artists. The analogy will not bear scrutiny. There are probably more Futurist manifestos than masterpieces, a proportion that does not hold for the vast category of Baroque art. Hulten observes that "Cubism was individualistic and contemplative; Futurism was social, political, and aggressive," but he leaves himself no space to refine this generalization. The intellectual climate of 1900 is schematically presented in a list of fifteen "revolutionary books." Without commentary the list signifies very little. The genuine problems of Marinetti's personality, his megalomania and his sexual obsessions, go by in a paragraph. "Eros and Thanatos were confused in Marinetti's imagination, as they were in the Marquis de Sade's and Lautréamont's. . . . The incompatibility of power and love seems not to have been clear to [him]." Hulten's introduction, in sum, does not support its last sentence: "Futurism has profoundly changed our ideas about ourselves and about history."

Yet the four hundred pages of beautifully reproduced and carefully labeled color illustrations that follow establish without any accompanying commentary the achievement of the Futurist painters. Particularly Giacomo Balla, Umberto Boccioni (who died at 34), and Carlo Carrà worked steadily to evolve a style that moved beyond the depiction of movement into exploring the frontiers of the nonfigurative. Almost a quarter of this superb visual documentation deals with Futurist paintings outside Italy, from Argentina to Sweden, and above all in Russia and Great Britain. Both Cubism and Futurism challenge the viewer to engage in decipherment and detection in order to grasp the composition, but the immense Venice show reveals that as a rule the Futurist painters maintained a compositional element that the Cubists jettisoned very early: frontality. A Futurist painting often registers successive images seen from a single perspective; a Cubist painting superposes several different perspectives.

The remainder of this mammoth volume is composed of two hundred three-column illustrated pages of a "Dictionary of Futurism," contributed by thirty art historians; an international chronology from 1900 to 1930; a catalog; a bibliography; and an index. If you know what to look up, the dictionary synthesizes a large fund of information on the artists, the writers, and related subjects: for example, Café-Cabaret; Cinema; Futurist Soirées; Mass Audience; Typography and Layout; Women, Futurist. Some of the most important discussions are tucked away in unpredictable entries. The longest of them, "Ideology," argues quite properly against "the hasty reduction of Futurism to the category of Fascism" and goes on to prevaricate about Marinetti's political and personal ties to Mussolini. "On the whole Futurism had no ideology." We are told to look instead for "an attitude toward life." Later, you may discover another entry, "Reconstruction of the Universe," and read about the Futurists' "global aspiration . . . [to] revolutioniz[e] the surrounding environment." You will also find a partial list (not given under "Manifestos") of the fifty-odd manifestos that laid plans for revolution, including two political manifestos (1909 and 1914). Under "Settimelli, Enrico," you will come upon the 1914 document "Weights, Measures, and Prices of Artistic Genius":

> The Futurist measurement of a work of art means an exact scientific determination expressed in formulas of the quality of cerebral energy represented by the existent impression which people may have of the work. . . . We therefore ask the state to create a body of law for the purpose of guarding and regulating the sale of genius.

Having founded their own political party, the Futurists joined Mussolini at the very beginning of fascism, in the hope that the state would implement their utopian program. It was an uneasy relationship. The entry "Marinetti" states bluntly that Futurism "is animated by a 'totalitarian' impetus. . . . From the beginning, politics were inherent in the movement's ideology." On Marinetti as leader and artist, the entry is defensive and inadequate. One has to look under "Mayakovsky" to find the Cendrars quote that best captures Marinetti and Mayakovsky (and Tzara): "Poetry = Advertising."

To find any illumination of the famous sentence from Marinetti's first manifesto, "We will glorify war . . . and contempt for women," you have to look under "Love and Sexuality." That article quotes from Marinetti's books *Against Love and the Parliamentary Process* and *How to Seduce Women*. It also prints the full text of the *Manifesto of Lust* by the Futurist poet and superwoman Valentine de Saint-Point, which appeared in 1913. "The satisfaction of their lust is the conquerors' due. . . . It is natural for the victors, proven in war, to turn to rape in the conquered land, so that life may be recreated." Like Marinetti, she believed in the elimination of all "sentiment" from relations between men and women. These two Futurist writers carried on the nineteenth-century antifeminist ideas trenchantly and wittily traced by Bram Dijkstra in his recent *Idols of Perversity*. The brief reference in this article to "Marinetti's masculine hysteria" may seem puzzling, unless one knows from other sources how forcefully he admired Gabriele D'Annunzio as a "distinguished seducer," opposed marriage and family, and envisioned war as a gigantic act of coitus.

Though packed with detailed accounts of an important cultural movement, the written parts of *Futurism and Futurisms* remain incomplete, tendentious, and poorly edited. The absence of cross-references diminishes the book's usefulness as a reference work. Nothing tells the reader that thirteen Futurist manifestos are reproduced in full in various entries. The short bibliography, which lists only books published since 1974, does not mention the two books a curious reader should consult first: Joshua Taylor's *Futurism* and Marianne Martin's *Futurist Art and Theory, 1900–1915.* But the reproductions in this volume constitute the best existing record, in quantity and quality, of Italian Futurist painting.

WAS THERE A discernible "moment" in the years before World War I for which we should have a name and a definition? For two important London exhibitions, Roger Fry chose the term *Post-Impressionism.* It could not stick. Pound's and Lewis's "Vortex" is far more apt and descriptive; but it is too late to transfer it from a part to the whole. The descriptive difficulty lies in the tight intertwining during the prewar decade of at least three strands. In Paris and Russia, artists and writers grafted disembodied formal relations onto primitive visions to produce Cubism. In Italy and Russia, a quest for velocity, collective action, utopian ideas, and mass audiences coalesced as Futurism. Overlapping these two currents, and particularly strong in German movements like Der Blaue Reiter, was a third current composed of artists who abandoned the representation of reality in order to express an inner, universal spirituality. Books by Wassily Kandinsky, Clive Bell, Wilhelm Worringer, and P. D. Ouspensky contributed to this tendency, which ultimately became Abstract Expressionism. All these styles shared one compositional principle: the juxtaposition of states of mind, of different times and places, of different points of view. Metaphor, montage, collage, the inter- , penetration of planes—all these devices can best be subsumed under the term *simultanism.* Just before the war, various artists squabbled over who had used the term first. Berger, Perloff, and Kozloff have opened up space for a book that might usefully be called *The Simultanist Moment.*

Still, our desire for synthesis and unity should not blind us to an uncomfortable discrimination that Perloff's and Hulten's books oblige us to make. A large segment of art and literature moved through collage and free verse toward a preoccupation with manipulating the medium itself. The masterpieces of high Cubism and Russian Rayonism and Suprematism seek a condition of autonomy in art far removed from social change and popular appeal. Another segment, linked most directly to the paired figures of Mayakovsky and Marinetti, moves through the cult of energy in the direction of theater and the rally as a means of manipulating crowds. Art in their work leans toward mass seduction, toward the reconstruction of society through ritual violence and war.

But the greatest artists have, I believe, avoided both extremes. In 1925, Hans Arp and El Lissitzky published an odd trilingual pamphlet entitled *Die Kunstismen.* They identify fifteen art movements by short quotations from their champions. The entire enterprise of distinguishing among art movements is set by Arp in the right perspective with two unsigned articles, written in his deadpan style and faltering English:

EXPRESSIONISM
From cubism and futurism has been chopped the minced meat, the mystic german beefsteak: expressionism.

METAPHYSICIANS
To represent the immaterial by the material is the problem of the metaphysicians. As futurists they would put fire to the museums, as metaphysicians they are happy to use museums as asylums for the old age. This is the punishment for having wished to measure eternity with three cowstalls.

22

EARLY PICASSO:

MAILER'S VERSION

T*HE TWENTIETH CENTURY* in Paris opened with a curious lull, almost a whimper. During the previous century, each generation had staged at least one political upheaval, culminating during the 1890s in a spate of anarchist bombings and the near revolution of the Dreyfus Affair. By organizing their own exhibits, the Impressionist painters had found a detour around the Beaux Arts–Salon system. With their recently developed prose poetry, free verse, and stream-of-consciousness style, writers had abandoned the authority of the Académie Française in literature. But the seething activity designated by the loose term *avant-garde* seemed to slow down as the new century opened.

At the Salon d'Automne of 1905, one central room housed the color-saturated works of Matisse, Derain, Braque, and Vlaminck along with a huge predatory jungle scene by the Douanier Rousseau. A journalist named it "the wild animal cage," *la cage aux fauves,* and the movement known as Fauvism found a name. But it flourished for only two years before it flickered out. Scores of talents were hard at work in the Latin Quarter and on the slopes of Montmartre. But in literature Zola's naturalism and Mallarmé's Symbolism appeared to hold everything at a standstill. In painting, the unprecedented work of Cézanne, van Gogh, Gauguin, and even the aging Monet would fall awkwardly into the makeshift category of Post-

Impressionism. It was Virginia Woolf who, on seeing their paintings in London, wrote: "On or about December 1910 human character changed." What was happening in these years? Were the first two decades of our century an intermission or a turning point?

A bold simplification would focus on three forces affecting the cultural life of Paris during this period. The new technologies of automobiles, airplanes, electricity, telephones, phonographs, radios, cinematography, and bicycles led to an ethos of speed, belligerence, and scientism to be proclaimed in Paris by a group of Italian artists as Futurism. The best self-promoters and publicists in Europe, they persuaded the Paris daily *Le Figaro* to publish their manifesto in 1909.

At the same time, other artists, writers, and musicians were discovering the appeal of African and Oceanic masks along with children's drawings, the art of the insane, jazz, and folk music. No one wrote a counterpart manifesto of primitivism, but the ingredients were there for the taking. Many of them became associated with the amorphous movement soon to find a name: Cubism.

A revived spirituality tending toward occultism and exotic religions ran even deeper through these years than Futurism and primitivism. This was the era of a revived Rosicrucianism, Mme. Blavatsky's Theosophy, cosmic consciousness, and similar doctrines, many of them considered in William James's *The Varieties of Religious Experience* (1902). In Paris, as all over Europe and the United States, these spiritual currents left a deep mark on the arts.

Today, because of founding works by Stravinsky, Debussy, Schoenberg, Braque, Picasso, Matisse, Kandinsky, Proust, Apollinaire, Lawrence, Joyce, Chekhov, Mann, and Rilke, we see this pre–World War I interlude not as a lull but as an astonishing new beginning. Its impetus was only temporarily interrupted by World War I. Then it assimilated a disciplined *rappel à l'ordre* in the twenties and projected its energies up to the thirties, until stopped by the stultifying directives of socialist realism.

THE OPENING DECADES of the twentieth century in Paris remain an alluring period, often explored, still not definitively mapped. But why would Norman Mailer, contender for the heavyweight fiction title and journalist of contemporary events, take it into his head to devote a full-length book, neither novel nor journalism, to this century-old period? He does not hide the answers, and they give us a certain insight into the present state of mind of one of our most ambitious writers, who likes to alternate between the roles of Old Testament prophet and New Age confidence man.

In an imaginary interview of 1960, "The Metaphysics of the Belly," Mailer speaks of how looking at Picasso reproductions relieved the severe eyestrain from which he was suffering. As *Ancient Evenings* grew out of studying ten volumes of Egyptian hieroglyphics at the New York Public Library, he wants us to believe that *Portrait of Picasso as a Young Man: An Interpretive Biography* grew out of eight weeks spent at the Museum of Modern Art turning the pages of Zervos's thirty-three-volume catalog of Picasso's work. In both cases, the pictures cast a magic spell. Years later, Mailer translated the Egyptian spell into a thousand-page first-person narrative, and the Picasso spell into a medium-size illustrated monograph. So much, he tells us.

The dust jacket Mailer must have approved suggests a slightly different tale. With this book, Mailer wants to pin his tail on Picasso's donkey. He cannot contrive to make the name Picasso mate cabalistically with the name Mailer (as he mated Marilyn with Mailer, thus displacing Arthur Miller). Instead, he and his publisher display on the jacket the photograph of a young man framed top and bottom by poster-size lettering of the two names. And, lo, the level-gazed likeness could belong to either contender. A photograph of Mailer at twenty-six shows an almost spectral resemblance to the picture actually printed of Picasso aged twenty-three in his corduroy suit. In writing about eight critical years out of Picasso's lengthy career, Mailer is creating another opportunity to write about himself.

WHAT MAY HAVE clinched the deal after Mailer reneged on his first contract for a Picasso book becomes clear when one wakes up to the fact that Mailer fell in love—both literally and literarily—with Fernande Olivier, Picasso's mistress, *la belle* Fernande, who wrote two books about that heady period. A couple of photographs of her clothed and hatted, plus scores of drawings of her in nude poses, make her charms convincingly real. And she writes about bohemian life and art and sex with an economy and a directness that must have impressed Mailer as often surpassing his own rodomontades on the same subjects. He quotes close to twenty pages of his own translations of her second book, *Souvenirs intimes* (1988). She was also the first to use the expression "White Negro," when she described Braque in her first book, *Picasso et ses amis* (1933). Mailer's most succinct statement of his story line gives Fernande an essential role.

This Spaniard, of weak and intermittent machismo, drenched in his own temerity, full of sentiments of social and intellectual inferiority, short in stature, was possessed of the ambition to mine universes of the mind no one had yet explored. His female companion for these most creative years of his life was a woman who is not without interest in her own right. While their love would suffer the fate of most passionate relationships, she is, nonetheless, the first of those women who will love him for all of his life. Since it is more than likely that she gave him the dignity to believe in himself as a man, so, too, did he acquire that indispensable buttress to extreme ambition, a measure of self-respect in the social world. Of course, she is worth our close attention!

A less narcissistic author might have used a different photograph on the jacket—one showing *two* figures—and called the book *Pablo and Fernande.*

I shall have a good many criticisms to make of the prose, the lazy assumptions, and the tangled purposes of Mailer's book. But it remains the serious, sometimes impassioned undertaking of a major writer who wishes to restage events that took place almost a hundred years ago. We cannot dismiss this book because Mailer has moved out of his lane or because he has no eye. He offers a fast-moving synthesis of views on a subject that naturally and inevitably includes him.

MAILER'S "INTERPRETIVE BIOGRAPHY" does its duty by Picasso's early years in Spain and his three preliminary trips to Paris. He traces the depression and dread of the Blue Period compositions primarily to Picasso's sexual uncertainties lurking beneath the macho exterior, including the possibility of impotence, homosexuality, and syphilis. Thus preoccupied, Mailer pays disproportionate attention to Picasso's running output of small erotic drawings, particularly of vulvas and penises, and he barely looks at the large allegorical painting *La Vie* (1903) with its motifs of maternity and fidelity. In this regard, Mailer should have borrowed even more heavily from one of his principal sources, John Richardson's *A Life of Picasso*, volume 1, 1881–1906 (1991). Richardson's fine chapter on *La Vie* examines the multiple symbols consolidated in the composition, including tarot cards, Gauguin's *D'où venons-nous? Que sommes-nous? Où allons-nous?*, and exorcism by magic imagery.

Mailer's story gets fully under way only in part 3 (of eleven), entitled simply "Fernande." On his fourth trip to Paris, Picasso settled into the Bateau Lavoir, a building that resembled a Seine barge for washerwomen grounded on the high hill of Montmartre. (Recently, it was destroyed by fire.) A year later, Fernande, an artists' model, moved in with him. Mailer reproduces the lovely lyric watercolor *The Lovers* (1904), which celebrates "the profound beginning of an affair." He fails to observe that this most fully erotic work in the whole book—two lovers "floating away on a sea of peace"—finds no need to display penis or vulva or the male visage. Starting a new life with Fernande, Picasso learned French, made Parisian friends like Max Jacob, Apollinaire, and André Salmon, and distanced himself somewhat from his Spanish past.

Almost all Mailer's comments on the paintings are anecdotal and fall within the confines of his biographical narrative. Writing about the works in themselves is not his forte. His one painterly preoccupation is to remark on the resemblance of one shape to another. When a painter renders an object,

> he transfers it to another existence, he initiates a line that becomes a particular form. Soon enough, the painter is aware that one form can often represent more than one kind of object. The figure 7 can always be seen as a nose upside-down.

For Mailer, these natural resemblances provide more than amusing visual puns. They make magic, and "Magic offers priceless energy." Mailer woefully overstrains his theory of mimetism when he relies on it to transform both a Baroque wall mirror in *Science and Charity* (1897) and a candle flame in *Head of the Dead Casagemas* (1901) into vaginas. On the other hand, I believe he is not far off the mark in finding this magic mimetism in early Cubism. "Now [Picasso] will try to interchange torsos and trees." By 1908, "Picasso will demonstrate that one form can turn into another as soon as one uses a moving source of light."[1]

EVER SINCE HE wrote *Marilyn* in 1973—on commission and against a crushing deadline—Mailer has at times faced allegations of excessive borrowing and quotation to the point of plagiarism. As in the case of *Marilyn,* threats of legal action arose over earlier versions of this book. It changed publishers more than once before the threats were allayed. Precautions have been taken. The preface lays claim to "no original scholarship," and *Portrait of Picasso as a Young Man,* complete with a title lifted from Joyce, arrives fitted with dutiful acknowledgment of "quoting other authors at greater length than is customary."

The systematic derivativeness of Mailer's biography of Picasso may account in part for the nervous fumblings in his style. They begin in the brief preface, where Mailer uses the pronouns *I* and *one* in alternation to designate himself as author, as if the first-person singular and the standard impersonal pronoun have the same meaning. This casual switching of point of view creates a yodel effect in the syntax that I find inept. Soon the reader begins to hear a recurring chorus of exculpatory phrases: "Be it said that . . ."; "It's safe to assume that . . ."; "One ought to add that . . ." Mailer sometimes cannot restrain himself from anticipating events, thus weakening the element of suspense. In discussing the resemblances of Picasso's and Braque's work in 1912, Mailer even loses track of grammar.

> They had been dealing with death and decomposition, with motion through time, with modern city uproar—transcendentalism and near-chaos had no need of a signature until it did. But then it did. Anonymity was growing cold.

What is the antecedent of "it"? There is no reason for us to look the other way when one of the most resourceful purveyors of the English language stumbles needlessly. A copyeditor should have used the blue pencil.[2]

In telling his tale of bohemian artists living in the grungy studios of Montmartre, Mailer gets a substantial number of things right: the use of opium, the appeal to magic and the occult encouraged by Max Jacob and Apollinaire, circus and cabaret motifs, the rivalry with Matisse, the intense and somewhat impersonal collaboration with Braque, and the self-serving friendship (on both sides) with the Stein circle. Mailer has a sense of anecdote almost as strong as Vasari's when the latter described Renaissance painters. Because Mailer has narrowed his story to the years between 1903 and 1914, the climax comes not at the end but in the middle of the book, with the composition of *Les Demoiselles d'Avignon* in the spring of 1907.[3]

In the section called "The Brothel" after an early working title of the project, Mailer convokes all his resources in order to burrow inside the painting. He begins disastrously by comparing its greatness to that of Fidel Castro "in the wilds of eastern Cuba in 1956." Then he moves to the conventional analogy of "the equal in modern art to the relics of a saint." After quoting substantially from Roland Penrose, Pierre Cabanne, Daniel-Henry Kahnweiler, André Malraux, Patrick O'Brian, and himself (a passage from *Of a Fire on the Moon* about loss of human scale in Cézanne), Mailer confronts the question of why, chronologically and compositionally, in the middle of *Les Demoiselles,* Picasso transformed its style by introducing African masks for the two figures on the right. Then he quotes O'Brian's troubling account of Fernande and Picasso adopting a child and soon after returning her to the orphanage. Mailer now has his answer: The fright masks in the painting will exorcise the failed attempt at adoption.

> For Picasso, however, what a disaster! It must have taken no small march over the rocks in his Spanish soul to accept the idea of raising another man's child with his barren mate, yet he came that far. Then Fernande gave the child away. Speak of curses. He was ready to practice exorcism.

This story of adoption and repudiation is of no relevance to the

Negro masks unless both events took place in the spring of 1907, but if so, not only is much accounted for, but it can also explain why, a few months later in that summer of 1907, Picasso decided to separate from Fernande. But there we anticipate.

The problems and latent strengths of this book converge here. The novelist's imagination has discovered a possible, perhaps even a plausible, biographical explanation for the wrenching shift visible along the central axis of *Les Demoiselles*. Some see it as the major fault line of Western art since antiquity. But neither the journalist nor the historian in Mailer has exerted himself to disinter the facts and to verify the proffered solution. The structure of the chapters and the significance universally attributed to this painting designate this section as the high point of the book. The banquet held in Picasso's studio for the Douanier Rousseau, the collaboration with Braque, and Picasso's alleged complicity in the theft of the *Mona Lisa* all belong, for Mailer, to an intense yet diminishing aftermath. He may be right that the combination of painterly and personal circumstances he describes carried Picasso up onto the watershed of *Les Demoiselles* and then down again by another path. But there is a hole here in the middle of the story (mostly filled in by Richardson's second volume published in 1996). Mailer's elaborately conditional formulation of his solution to the big question about Picasso as an artist undermines his own slender guess. He has moved a short distance inside the mind of the artist who produced *Les Demoiselles*. But even an "interpretive biography" must hunt down the pertinent facts.

AS I READ him, Mailer develops three nested theses. First, Cubism between 1906 and 1914 represents the greatest achievement of Western art, a dazzling breakthrough to a new vision. Mailer quotes Cabanne to make the case. "For so perilous an enterprise one had to sacrifice the entire illusionist apparatus of painting, that is, everything the public was used to, everything it judged a picture by." Second, not single-handedly but more persistently than anyone else, Picasso found his way to this high frontier. He had swiftly absorbed academic and Post-Impressionist practice, and in 1907 glimpsed a magic link between the stark bone structure in the head of Fontdevila, an imposing old smuggler in Gósol, and the awe-inspiring deformation of human features in African religious masks. Third, the figure who facilitated this achievement, who was soon revulsed by it, and who almost alone understood that the shift was undertaken willfully against the grain of Picasso's fundamental classicizing temperament, was Fernande Olivier.[4] None of these theses is original. No one else has assembled them in the same manner. And even Mailer never sets them down in this stark form.[5] I list the theses not because they afford us new insights into Picasso but because by default they call attention to aspects of Mailer's subject he fails to cover.

Attentive to lives and social currents immediately surrounding Picasso, Mailer still misses several important elements of that milieu. There is no discussion of the philosophical, political, and criminal appeal of anarchism, a doctrine that spread wide and deep in both France and Spain during that period. Mailer does take account of the art dealers who spotted and stalked Picasso from his earliest visits to Paris. But he never mentions the little band of private buyers who formed a modest holding company called La Peau de l'Ours (the Bear's Skin) and bought directly from the most advanced artists beginning in 1904. Their public auction in 1914 quadrupled their investment; Picasso's *Les Saltimbanques* (1905) fetched almost twelve times what he had received for it in 1909. A fifth of the profits was returned to the artists. Money was probably more important than magic for Picasso. It would soon allow him to live exactly as he pleased.[6]

PART 5 OF *Portrait of Picasso as a Young Man* collects many amusing stories about the bohemian antics of Max Jacob, Apollinaire, Alfred Jarry (whom Picasso admired without ever meeting), and others. In the following sections on *Les Demoiselles* and the birth of Cubism, Mailer leaves such high jinks behind. He concentrates instead on Picasso's exorcism of personal terrors and on aesthetic considerations. However, no careful art critic or historian can discount the fact that the attitude of *blague d'atelier,* of studio joke and mystification and elaborate hoax, contributed its leaven to the development of avant-garde experiments. That ebullient attitude originated as much among Beaux Arts students as in artists' studios. The Futurists from 1909 on deliberately and defiantly mocked artistic and individual conventions in order to scandalize the bourgeois. The press's wariness about being taken in by publicity stunts from artists working in mockery or in bad faith was not just a form of philistinism. By 1912, Théodore Duret, the sturdy supporter of Impressionism, was warning his readers that the snobbish new art lovers were "ready to swoon in front of any eccentricity." The hint of a grin hovered on the face of Cubism and complemented its audacious formal experiments. Mailer does not allow enough for the impulses Picasso felt, along with his fellow artists, to try out a series of impish sight gags along with his serious exploration of a new visual space.

Instead of humor and farce, Mailer insists on a cluster of ideas closer to his own career than to Picasso's. "It is the essence of middle-class intuition that art is reckless, art is putatively criminal." Presumably, the fact that Fontdevila was "a noble outlaw" gave his prominent cheekbones an added liberating force to release Picasso's style from realist representation. And the last summation of Picasso's character as an artist turns us firmly back toward the author.

> If he was a monster, we have no alternative but to accept him. We ought to know that violence and creativity all too often connect themselves inextricably. . . . He was not only the genius of us all, but a prisoner in the structure of his character.

To a large extent, Mailer is writing here and elsewhere in the book about his own moral dilemmas since he wrote "The White Negro," the 1957 essay that defends the psychopathic hipster and the "apocalyptic orgasm" of criminal violence. He is trying to maneuver Picasso sideways until he lines up with Gary Gilmore, the murderer-artist of *The Executioner's Song,* and with Jack Abbott, the prisoner whose cause Mailer took up in the early eighties and who was later convicted of manslaughter. In so doing, Mailer is surrendering to the prevailing romantic dogma of two centuries—that the artist must be an outlaw and pariah engaged in transgression, violence, and crime in order to plumb the depths of his genius. The life and work of contemporary artists like Matisse and Braque and Arp tell a different story; regrettably, they provide smaller advances for their biographers, precisely because they do not conform to the outlaw convention.

Mailer remains deaf to the powerful case that can be made for the artist as someone who can probe the subtle and elusive condition of the normal because of his own superior normality. Somerset Maugham argues toughmindedly along these lines in *The Summing Up.* George Eliot and Tolstoy and even Proust reveal that ordinary people, imaginatively portrayed, are rarely uniform or shallow or even ordinary. Mailer has been too impressed by the unreliable and compromising stories in Arianna Huffington's biography of Picasso. And Mailer can hear very little over the song of his own theories about the artist as the enemy of all social institutions and constraints.

FOR THOSE ATTENTIVE to the history of art in its largest aesthetic and cultural significance, Mailer's most grievous failure concerns neither the pre–World War I era nor Picasso as a young artist, but the early years of Cubism as a movement—more exactly, their outcome. Did Cubism go anywhere, accomplish anything? In order to grasp the trajectory of Cubism, we have to know more than Mailer tells us about what was going on outside the Bateau Lavoir, both in Paris and in other cities of Europe. For it was precisely between 1905 and 1914 that Kandinsky in Munich, Malevich in Russia, Mondrian in Holland and Paris, and Kupka and Delaunay in Paris crossed the line into nonfigurative or abstract painting. A series of influential books accompanied this defining step: Worringer's *Abstraction and Empathy* (1908), Kandinsky's *Concerning the Spiritual in Art* (1912), and Clive Bell's *Art* (1914). Kandinsky reached the widest audience among artists. Bell launched the immensely useful phrase "significant form." By a powerful visual and philosophic logic, "pure art" emerged out of Impressionism and Post-Impressionism, renounced the world of objective appearances previously rendered as the very essence of art, and turned to a domain of pure form, line, and color linked to inchoate interior feelings and to the spiritual.

Publicized through journalists' mockery of "little cubes" and producing some of what were regarded as the ugliest and most grotesque paintings ever submitted to the public gaze. Picasso and the Cubists provoked such a rumpus in the prewar years that many people did not notice that these painters chose *not* to go over the brink into nonfigurative, abstract painting. It looked as if they would take that leap. But persistently in the depths of the most severe, most stripped-down autopsylike compositions of Braque and Picasso in 1911, there remains the armature of a human figure along with shards of pipe, book, or bottle. And, until their respective deaths as the last grand masters of nineteenth-century painting, Cézanne (d. 1906) and Monet (d. 1926) dwelt bravely on this outermost frontier of representation and refused to go over the top into pure forms. In his own sector, Matisse also kept the faith with appearances.

A number of historical circumstances have helped to obscure the significance of this withdrawal from the abyss by most artists of the prewar Paris School. World War I brought a serious hiatus, followed by the long variety show of Dada and Surrealism, accompanied by a neoclassic reaction, followed by the dictates of socialist realism, followed by another world war, followed by the New York School displacing Paris and establishing the triumph of Abstract Expressionism. In such a jumbled sequence, Cubism appears to figure as an important early step along the inevitable road toward nonobjective painting. In the fifties and sixties, the powerful critics Clement Greenberg, Harold Rosenberg, and even Meyer Schapiro hectored us into accepting this version of progress in art. In reality, Cubism undertook a highly varied holding action, neither a great leap forward nor a retreat. The fault line visible in *Les Demoiselles* alludes not to where Picasso went over the edge but precisely to how he refused to do so by adapting the expressive distortion of African masks and the vertiginous plastic resources of four-dimensional space-time, however seriously misunderstood.

Félix Fénéon's reported response to Picasso on seeing *Les Demoiselles* was to advise him to devote himself to caricature. That remark points to one of the paths by which the Paris School found its way down from the mountain, not back to earlier practices but obliquely into new plastic territory where the world of objects and figures still counts. Some, like E. H. Gombrich, have argued that the exciting nineteenth-century practice of caricature had a crucial part in bringing a new expressiveness by distortion into twentieth-century art. And caricature is not unrelated to African masks and *la blague d'atelier.*

MAILER HAS PICKED out the most challenging episode in modern art—challenging both to the artists themselves and to us in our attempt to grasp what happened. I believe he fails to see that Picasso was a Moses in reverse. Having reached a point where he could look over and hear what voices around him, like Apollinaire's, were proclaiming as the Promised Land of pure light and of forms liberated from the contingent world of appearances, Picasso was not too old and weak to complete the journey. He was too young and vigorous to relinquish his belief in the sensible world. Therefore, he neither strode on nor turned back. He found a companion and rival in Braque, with whom he could occupy the embattled terrain of appearances until other paths emerged. For all their simplifications and smoothings out, Arp and Brancusi remained on the near side of the great divide. Drawing deeply on the reverberations of the studio joke and caricature, Duchamp, Klee, de Chirico, Ernst, and Magritte all explored their separate ways along the uncertain slopes of easel painting following the Cubist explosion. We do not yet know what terrain lies ahead of us in the next millennium. But the refusal of these artists to renounce appearances will not be ignored or forgotten.

Mailer has found his way to an exciting geographic and chronological site in the landscape of modern art but fails to see the whole picture. Some have called Montmartre in the pre–World War I decades "a new Acropolis." There, a handful of young artists and poets collaborated in a successful attempt to stir up the eerie lull that followed the turn of the century. They founded a new artistic movement soon named Cubism. It also carried the markings of a sly cultural prank trumped up out of Pataphysics and high spirits, of a magic trick performed in the face of grinding poverty and disastrous personal lives, and of an unbelievably successful financial enterprise at least for one of their number and for a few dealers. Because his own persona often stands in his line of vision, Mailer gets the picture only partly right. In a shorter book without the trappings of scholarship, I believe he would have avoided the gaucheries of style and the wavering artistic judgments that now obstruct his account. *Portrait of Picasso as a Young Man* tells us that Mailer's intelligence is still turning over and that he can lay out the plan of an enterprising book, however derivative, however skewed. Is he now going to devote himself to "masterpieces of ugliness" of the kind he says became Picasso's trademark? I don't think so. Mailer cannot convincingly pin his tail on Picasso's donkey. Their careers do not run parallel. And "ugliness" hardly does justice to Picasso's post-Cubist works.

Mailer uses an epigraph in which Picasso refers to his intent "to revolutionize [people's] way of identifying things." Yes, truly. But let's not forget the essential fact that in Cubism, and in Picasso's works for the rest of his life, "things" remain there to be seen. In a half-facetious "Practical Guide for the Amateur of Cubism," written for a 1912 show in Barcelona, Max Jacob gives us advice on how to identify those things. "Pick out a detail that contains the key to the whole, stare at it for a long time, and the model will appear." Thanks to such artists and such poets, the world is still very much with us.

NOTES

1. Twice Mailer alludes to the revelation of looking at a composition on its side or upside down. On page 257, he inverts an early Cubist figure to make his point about the interchangeability of torsos and trees. In these passages, it would have helped if Mailer had more background in the history of art. Turning a painting has long been a traditional device for testing its formal composition more than its representational powers. And in the case of Kandinsky, as told in his *Reminiscences* (1913), his failure to recognize the objects first in a Monet haystack and then in one of his own paintings standing on its side encouraged him to eliminate objects altogether from his work.

2. A copyeditor should also have caught a number of mistakes in French: e.g., *Le Violin* (p. 304), and *Feneon* (p. 247 and passim). And how did color plate 8 pass inspection with the huge copyright line imprinted in white right across its face?

3. The book's forty-eight color plates appear to be of fair quality for the modest price. An expert on color, Patricia Lambert, compared three of the plates with their originals on display at the Museum of Modern Art and found discernible but not excessive variations in value and balance. Of the three, *Les Demoiselles* comes off best.

4. This third thesis is best documented in Madame Olivier's own writings, some of which have not been translated. Mailer is right in implying that Fer-

nande Olivier's letters and recollections provide a more significant source on Picasso and Cubism than Mailer himself.

When Alice Toklas invited me to tea in 1948 to meet Fernande Olivier, I was too young and timid to ask to take French lessons from this legendary woman with a beautiful voice. She was in her late sixties. Wearing a large hat, she sat calmly among the Picasso paintings lining the walls in the rue Christine apartment, flirted without conviction, and shook her handsome head over my benightedness.

5. Nor does he confine himself to them. He cannot keep his eyes off Picasso's late obsessive drawings of women's privates and of male death heads, both from the last months before his death. They fall awkwardly outside Mailer's chronology.

6. All purchases were made for La Peau de l'Ours by André Level, a remarkably gifted banker, collector, and speculator. He told his own story in *Souvenirs d'un collectionneur* (1959). Michael Z. Fitzgerald's *Making Modernism: Picasso and the Creation of the Market for Modern Art* (Farrar, Straus and Giroux, 1995) documents the market-driven aspects of Picasso and Cubism.

23

CAPTIONS OR

ILLUSTRATIONS?:

BRAQUE'S HANDBOOK

ORTY YEARS AGO in a Paris bookstore near the Odéon, I happened
upon a large, slim volume of intermingled writing and drawing. That
book was the first object I acquired for purely aesthetic reasons. I
could not use it or wear it or consume it, only peruse it and share it with a
few other people—very few. In later years after I stumbled into teaching, the
rare students I showed it to never reacted with the awe or enthusiasm I con
sidered appropriate. I would put the book back on the shelf to wait for a better day. No one else seemed to know about it. Like a child who discovers a
magic rock and wants to keep it to himself, I hesitated to write about what
attracts me to this hybrid work of art. It exists on the high unmapped frontier that separates and unites word and image. The written parts practice an
economy of means that associates it with the maxim, even the joke. The
drawings show the crudeness of a master. It is full of fine flaws, even spelling
mistakes.

SELECTIONS FROM *CAHIER
DE 1947* BY G. BRAQUE*
Translated by Roger Shattuck

2. Nature does not give a taste for perfection. One cannot conceive of her either better or worse.

5. Art is a mode of representation.

12. Do not imitate what you want to create.

15. The artist is not misunderstood; he is barely recognized. People exploit him without knowing who it is.

18. I cherish the rule that corrects emotion.

22. The painter does not try to reconstitute an anecdote, but to constitute a pictorial fact.

33. Limited means engender new forms, invite creation, make a style. Progress in art does not consist in extending its limits, but in knowing them better.

44. To protect their illusions, people hold on to words. Today people are convinced they can fly.

53. You have to choose. Something cannot be both true and a likeness.

70. Seek the common element, which is not similarity. That's how the poet can say: A swallow stabs the sky, and change a swallow into a dagger.

80. A painting is finished when it has effaced the idea. The idea is the launching cradle of the painting.

93. With age art and life grow together.

*Numbers refer to pages in Braque's Notebook reproduced here.

La nature ne
donne pas le goût
de la perfection,
On ne la conçoit
ni meilleure ni pire.

L'Art est un
mode de
représentation

5

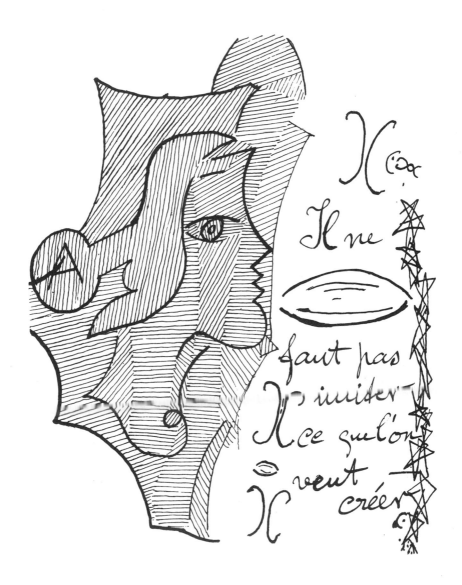

)(c'est

Il ne

faut pas
)(imiter
)(ce qu'on
)(veut
créer

L'artiste
n'est pas
incompris
il est
méconnu

On l'exploite
sans savoir
que c'est lui.

15

J'aime la
règle
qui corrige
l'émotion.

Le peintre ne tâche
pas de reconstituer
une anecdote

mais de
constituer
un fait
pictural

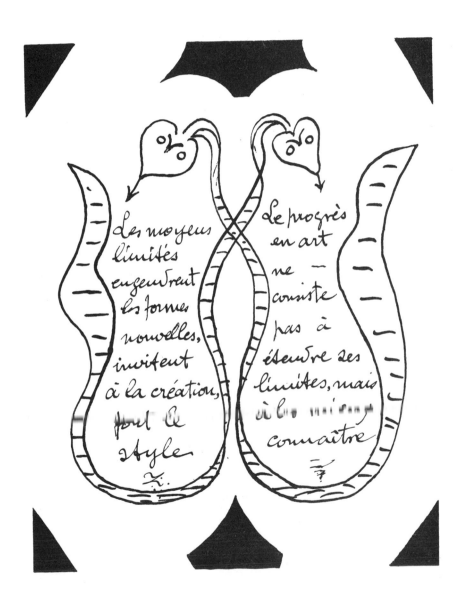

Les moyens
limités
engendrent
les formes
nouvelles,
invitent
à la création,
font le
style.
X.

Le progrès
en art
ne —
consiste
pas à
étendre ses
limites, mais
à les mieux
connaître

Pour protéger
son illusion
on garde le
mot.

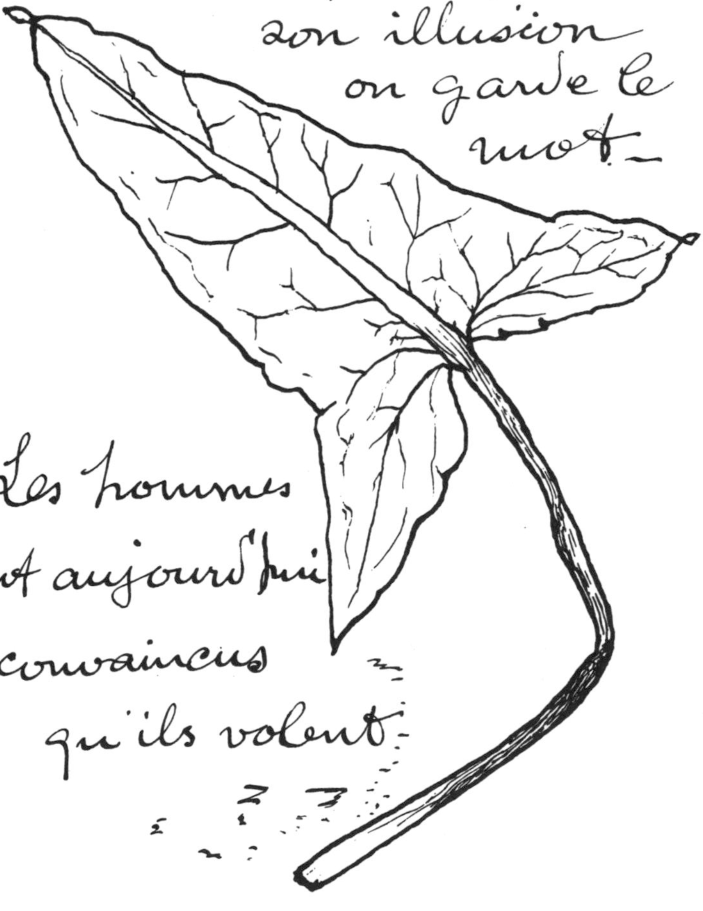

Les hommes
sont aujourd'hui
convaincus
qu'ils volent.

Il faut
choisir.

Une chose
ne peut être
à la fois vraie
et vraisemblable

53

Rechercher le
commun qui n'est
pas le semblable.
C'est ainsi
que le poëte
peut dire :
Une hirondelle
poignarde le
ciel, et fait
d'une hirondelle
un poignard

Le tableau est fini,
quand il a
effacé l'idée.

L'idée est
le ber du tableau

Avec l'âge
l'art et la vie
ne font qu'un

An informative monograph recalled these events to my mind. Renée Riese Hubert's *Surrealism and the Book* (California) examines with an intelligent eye some remarkable and little-known works that resulted from the collaboration between an artist (painter or photographer) and a poet. Intent on exploring collective consciousness, a number of Surrealists working in pairs transformed the nineteenth-century illustrated book into an instrument for probing the furthest reaches of the imagination. Hubert provides the historical background that is missing from *Artists' Books: A Critical Anthology and Sourcebook,* edited by Joan Lyons (Peregrene Smith, 1985). In twelve packed chapters, Hubert (herself a fine poet in French) practices the ancient art of ekphrasis on about thirty Surrealist books. I find most rewarding the discussions of Ernst and Eluard's *Répétitions* (1922), of Miró and Breton's *Constellations* (1959), and of two books for which Arp served as both artist and poet. Hubert describes at some length how in these double-barreled volumes words and images do not illustrate or caption or represent or refer to one another or even display a discernible connection. Figuration and mimesis lie far behind us in this domain of pure transformation. The opening chapter evokes "a dialectic of paradox," the technique of collage, and deliberate mystery as explanatory principles for these alluring books. Hubert has written a profoundly responsive study on a neglected subject.

She omits any reference to the historical irony that surrounds and almost obscures these works. Surrealism started out in an attempt to subdue artistic production in favor of scientific and social goals and to reach the everyday life of ordinary people. (See "The D-S Expedition" in my *The Innocent Eye.*) During its development and diaspora before and after World War II, Surrealism did affect the culture in contrasting ways. *Animal Crackers* (George Kaufman and the Marx Brothers, Broadway, 1928, Hollywood, 1930) and sassy advertising styles show the influence of Surrealist experiments, often close to the popular forms like the wisecrack and the cock-and-bull story. At the same time, the most original and the most truly beautiful—the word is not out of place—products of Surrealism may never find a wide audience. These *livres de peintre,* or artists' books, in highly limited editions at astronomical prices exist only in the rare-book rooms of wealthy libraries and in a few private collections. The untraditional aesthetic they celebrate reaches a bare handful of readers and appeals only to sophisticated tastes. These esoteric works make the Surrealist "revolution" look like a very restricted affair that does not tally with their political and proletarian declarations.

In the last chapter, on "Specificity of the Surrealist Book," Hubert quotes from an auction catalog a sentence by Georges Braque to point up the antimimetic stance represented by these collaborative volumes. "The painter does not try to reconstitute an anecdote but to establish a pictorial fact." We nod sagely and think we understand. Powerful tides of abstraction, nonreferentiality, and textuality seem to carry us in the direction of autonomous art. Many assent to it as to a religion, less by demonstrated truth or superiority than by faith or conformity. But I light on Braque's sentence for a different reason. Hubert seems to be unaware that the words come from a very particular self-illustrated book of Braque's, not Surrealist nor Cubist nor Expressionist—simply Braque. It is the book I found in Paris in 1948, *Cahier 1916–1947* (Maeght, 1948).

The ordinary trade edition I bought is a photographic reduction to twelve and a half by nine and a quarter inches of a deluxe numbered original edition (19 1/2 x 12 1/2 inches) of 845 copies on fine papers, each with a color lithograph. The ordinary edition comes in a white dustcover with a blue schematic woman's head in silhouette and in black type "G. Braque." Generally in india ink, the artist drew and wrote every mark in these ninety-three pages, including title page and page numbers. Typeface appears nowhere inside. The binding is of sturdy beige simulated cloth. I find the volume an inexhaustible object to manipulate, to read sequentially or at random, to flip through only for images, and to meditate on slowly. Braque uses few tricks. Each page forms a self-contained unit, contrasting with the design, density, and meaning of the facing page. For the most part, drawing and writing are kept in separate areas and carefully measured out to fill the space. With two exceptions (numbers 21, all drawing, and 89, all words) writing and image frame one another in a variety of patterns. Braque never tries Steinberg's witty device by which the curlicue of a written word turns into its referent—bird, hand, et cetera—and vice versa. Nor do Braque's words form pictures as in Apollinaire's *calligrammes* and some concrete poetry. Braque asks for our divided attention to his apothegms and to the visual motifs that circulate through and around them. The *Cahier* demonstrates once again Braque's *pondération* (equilibrium, sense of measure, not ponderousness) often contrasted with Picasso's *virtuosité*.

Two periods of incapacitation impelled Braque toward the notebook form and toward these terse meditations on art, on life in art. Trepanned after a serious head wound in combat, Braque spent several months in bed during 1915 and 1916. At this time, he composed "Thoughts and Reflections on Art"; his friend the poet Pierre Reverdy published a group of them in the little review *Nord-Sud* in 1917. These twenty short pronouncements of one to six lines stand alone without images in this first appearance. Widely reproduced, translated, and quoted, they have been treated by Braque's critics as the most reliable source of his aesthetic.

Thirty years later, serious illness incapacitated the artist again in 1945 and 1947. During those intervals, he turned to the notebooks he had been drawing and writing in ever since 1917. "I always have a notebook within reach," he told Dora Vallier. Now he selected and recombined and redrew to produce the single deluxe *Cahier* published in 1947 by Galerie Maeght, his new dealer. After the unadorned copy that appeared in *Nord-Sud* (somewhat edited by Reverdy, as the manuscripts show), Braque chose this time to mix his media. The twelve pages reproduced here suggest the variety of the full collection. He also chose to present the *Cahier* with no introduction, no front matter, not even a copyright page. My brief comments will be impressionistic. They serve no thesis.

In number 2, following the simple title page, Braque opens the notebook with the word *nature,* the only given, represented here perhaps by an amorphous worm or bug. It underlies two emblems of art, pages of poetry and a musical instrument, themselves included in a conventionalized drawing. Though invaded in the world and in this album by the rival realms of art and ideas, the original given of nature will never be pushed out of the picture, will resist excessive manipulation. Here on the first page, do words serve as captions for images? Do images illustrate words? Either way, or both at once, on succeeding pages the basic elements will not remain in the same traditional layout of image above, words below.

The words of number 5 seem to confound the great insights of Braque's career since early Cubism and the *papiers collés* of 1912—unless one puts the emphasis on *mode.* In that case, the superimposed drawings, figurative and decorative, exploratory and incoherent, recapitulate that career. The zigzag rising from the bottom center recasts a motif from the previous page, reminding us that "It's not enough to make people see what you paint. You must also make them touch it." In such ways, this book presents itself as belonging to the class of *livres-objects* designed to be handheld. We are told in number 11 (not reproduced) that "The painter thinks in forms and in colors. The object is his poetics." The words are accompanied by, perhaps illustrated by, a single large form at the top, bone or footprint. Then comes the apparent retraction or revision of it all in number 12. Limitation bows before creation. The head is schematic, not rendered. Do the squiggles at the right echo the touch-feel theme? What are we to make of the pairs of cheek to cheek curves? They will recur often.

Number 15 plunges us into a cartoon version of the artist's studio—conventionalized palette and brushes held by a ghostly artist shape facing his easel. The easel holds a squashed window-in-the-wall emblem of traditional painting. Butterflies and debris fill the air. The most clogged of all the compositions and the closest to caricature almost overwhelms the two sentences about mistaken artistic identity.

Braque uses the first person only four times in this highly personal volume. In number 18, the *je* utters the most quoted declaration in the collection. Art leads to a disciplined restraint. The dancing plant has a voracious mouth. It seems to covet a variation on the reversed parenthesis motif and to protect the words. In number 22, an inchoate, heavily hatched figure—paper cutout? human torso?—accompanies another famous sentence. (Maurice Denis, Mécislas Goldberg, and Apollinaire were among the first to formulate this attitude.) The pictorial fact here constituted seems slender compared to what Braque accomplished elsewhere in works of paint on canvas that make the same point. Are these words or is this book necessary?

The sense of constraint and discipline continues in number 33, where the serpents and the six black shapes form a symmetrical decorative frame. Why isn't the message just as effective in the unillustrated *Nord-Sud* version? Our eyes linger longer here and oblige the mind to track the coiled structure of notions like "limit" and "style."

The following page carries us back to the artist in his studio, speaking in the first person about fervor. On first glance, I saw an ithyphallic figure. Is Braque putting us on after all? Perhaps, for he has doctored the evidence and led us into error. Number 34 reproduces the left-hand section of the lithograph that accompanied the deluxe edition, one of a series showing Helios in his chariot driving the winged horses. The palette shape is one of the horses' wings. There's a muted reversal or joke at work in number 44 also. An impeccably rendered drawing of a leaf separates the two sentences about illusion and seems to diminish the tranquil confidence of language. At the same time, the trompe l'oeil drawing undermines its own illusion. The false leads and verbal-optical contradictions in these pages induce a gentle mental giddiness.

Number 53 may provide enlightenment. The Greek Goddess (cf. numbers 5 and 12) looks down on the inexorable and momentous choice facing the artist. The flow of Braque's work since Cubism suggests that he sees the art object not as the representation of truth or of nature but as an object in its own right—what Arp called "a concretion." By now, the recurring pair of curved lines seem to represent the ever-present dilemma of art as representation (number 5) and as independent creation (number 12). Number 70 presents the Greek head again, embedded in a magnificent jug or urn. Do the two nested objects have something in common, like dagger and swallow? Braque is entering the modern debate on the nature of metaphor. Lautréamont wrote that one of his characters was "as handsome as the fortuitous encounter on a dissecting table of a sewing machine and an umbrella." Braque's friend Reverdy gave a pocket definition of metaphor in *Nord-Sud* in 1918. "The image is a pure creation of the mind. . . . The more distant and exact the links between the two things brought together, the stranger the image." By now, we do not expect to find any drawing of either swallow or dagger. Is Braque suggesting an analogy: head is to jug as swallow is to dagger? Possibly. I think he is relying more on a principle embodied in all his work, verbal and plastic, and stated in number 13: "In art only one thing counts: what one cannot explain." (The drawing reproduces the mysterious crosshatched form of number 22.)

Long a resident of the busy port and shipbuilding center of Le Havre, Braque knew what a *ber* (launching cradle) looks like and how a ship floats out of it after launching. Number 80 offers the most succinct form of his antiintellectualism, parallel to Mallarmé's telling Degas that one writes a sonnet not with ideas but with words. Even more than a poem, a painting is concrete, specific, material. Braque's finger is constantly wagging at us. "To define a thing is to substitute the definition for the thing" (number 35). "One must always have two ideas: one to destroy the other" (number 59). Number 2 belongs in this company, but what about number 5? In number 80, why is the visual element so sparse? The twin curlicues now suggest disjunction, separation between abstract and concrete. But on the facing page, Braque confounds us and himself again. "A lemon next to an orange ceases to be a lemon, and the orange an orange, to become pieces of fruit. Mathematicians follow this law. So do we" (number 81). Is this the cradle from which the painting launches itself?

An answer may hover discreetly in number 93, the last page. A jagged half frame, schematic cup, cut lemon, and knife, all implying the conventions of still life. No Cubist reconstitution of space and perspective, form and color. Very few words, the cryptic simplicity of an adage. Does "age" mean mature experience or the rediscovery of the direct sensibility of the child? After a long series of binary oppositions in the preceding pages, Braque abandons them all for this great gesture of reconciliation. No paired curlicue of dissent and division floats here. Just the things of this world simultaneously *vraies* and *vraisemblables*. The ninety-three successive pages, composed and recomposed during thirty years of an artist's life, embody age, embody time enough to subsume and surpass the contradictions of a lifetime. Call it a generation. The interval of Proust's constant.

CURT VALENTIN DISTRIBUTED the Braque *Cahier* in the United States with an insert of translations by Bernard Frechtman (1949). In 1952, Gallimard published *Le Jour et la Nuit*, the text only of Braque's notebooks with additions since 1947. The 1956 Maeght illustrated edition of the *Cahier* contains twenty-one new pages. Dover Publications issued the latter (1971) in facsimile with translations by Stanley Appelbaum. The Dover edition keeps the basic size of the French edition but crops all four margins by half an inch, enough to make most pages look overcrowded and unbalanced. The pages added after 1947 lean heavily toward the written word and show less vigor and variety in the drawing than those in the 1947 *Cahier*. Unfortunately, the inexpensive Dover edition went out of print in 1998.

Perused unhurriedly, the *Cahier* contrives to be both calming and unsettling. Its paradoxes and volte-faces never allow the gnomic pronouncements to settle into a system. Braque did not participate in the revived classicism of the twenties that provoked sharp stylistic shifts in the work of Picasso, de Chirico, Malevich, Cocteau, and many others. The *Cahier,* which bridges these post-Cubist years, follows its own dialectic of consolidation and exploration.

Running a count on its visual and verbal motifs does not clarify everything. The largest visual category consists of decorative, nonfigurative elements—linear and curvilinear and planar, including the opposed curve emblem, usually in combination with figurative elements. Next comes the human head, followed by leaf forms, bird-fish shapes, still lifes, and artist's studio themes. I find it difficult to classify the written elements more systematically than my scattered comments so far. The most limpid aphorisms often become the most elusive. "I seek to put myself in unison with nature more than to copy her" (number 25). The sentence relates to a large set of observations about truth and representation and about rejecting the idea, the definition, in favor of the thing itself. It also belongs to the other major category of Braque's thought: Artistic creation, like the good life, arises from a carefully adjusted state of mind. Above all, the artist avoids stultification. "Let us be content with provoking reflection and not try to convince" (number 9). "Freedom for ordinary people is the free exercise of their habits. For us it means going beyond what is permitted" (number 87). "Never join up" (number 88). The last item ("Ne jamais adhérer."), accompanied by a stern face resembling that of Marianne, symbol of the French nation, applies to political affiliations, artistic conventions, and personal habits. This sober studio artist trained as a housepainter concerns himself primarily with staying out of the pack and out of a rut.

He succeeds. The *Cahier* contrasts as dramatically with other major written documents we have from a painter's hand as with "illustrated" books. Leonardo's *Precepts of the Painter,* Reynolds's *Discourses,* Delacroix's *Journal,* and van Gogh's *Letters* fall within familiar prose genres and include only an occasional figure. After the *Nord-Sud* test run without drawing, Braque challenged himself to keep word and image together, not merely within the same covers but on every page, in a kind of insistent domesticity or reciprocal uxoriousness. And he limited himself to a condensed style related to the proverb, the maxim, the inscription. It seems beautifully suited to his artisan's temperament. It also parallels a tendency toward terse, pithy utterance among modern French poets. Valéry's *Cahiers,* Eluard's early permutations of proverbs, Michaux's and Char's late works seek the oracular. A comparable attraction to the adage appears occasionally in William Carlos Williams and Wallace Stevens.

Such a style entails a risk. Admiration for the oracular, for the enigmatic style of the koan, may lead to artificiality and straining for effect. Among French artists and intellectuals I have known, the most ambitious often scorn the lightness of esprit for a pretentious speech tending toward mystification. No culture has a monopoly on intellectual fraudulence. We hear it often in our own surroundings. Braque's seemingly casual drawings and remarks, his thirty-year selection of elegant-crude doodles, can become precious. What does number 15 really mean? Several pronouncements rely on uninspired puns and wordplay. (*"Découvrir une chose c'est la mettre à vif"* [number 26].) A few I have quoted teeter on the edge of emptiness, imposture. There's nothing like a paradox to convey the impression of profundity. "The true materialist is the believer" (number 74). The *boutade* or quip was supposed to be Cocteau's specialty. Braque ventures very close. "The artist's temperament is not the sum of his tics" (number 8).

In spite of the risk and the lapses, Braque offers us a rare stereographic or bifocal device in which words and images overlay and counterpoint one another. The distance and obliqueness of angle at which they "illustrate" one another requires a considerable effort of reflection to take in the full range of meaning and vision. For Braque, I believe, the *Cahier* (and all the pages he drew and rejected in order to arrive at the final selection) represent a safety valve. The uncomplicated yet rare genre allows him to engage in ideas, definitions, concepts, while remaining skeptical of their role. Here the artist who read many poets and listened to Maurice Raynal explain the aesthetic ideas of Kant and Schelling could escape for a short space into the magic world of words. Representation and figuration present no problem for words. Meaning arises through agreed-upon convention, not through likeness. This culturally determined aspect of language may explain why the verbal component finally dominates in the *Cahier.* The visual artist is taking a rest without abandoning his craft. I find myself looking at the drawings first, then at the inscriptions, and then trying to discover the path from the former to the latter, not vice versa.

This direction of flow does not mean that the drawings are superfluous. Without them, the album would collapse, leaving a collection of quotes we would read only to inform ourselves about the artist Braque. As they stand, I believe they would pass the test of anonymity. One would spot genius without the certification of a famous name. Take one of the longer ones, sparsely and mysteriously illustrated. It gives us a whiff of Chaplinesque humor. "You cannot always have your hat in your hand. That's why hat racks were invented. In my case, I discovered painting as a nail to hang my ideas on. That allows me to change them and avoid fixed ideas" (number 46).

Because he did not follow the interstates, traveling with Braque becomes a sustained adventure.

24

THE STORY OF

HANS/JEAN/KASPAR ARP

T*HERE IS A* city on a great river. The river is the natural frontier between two countries that keep having wars. Some years the city belongs to one country, and some years to the other. The river is called the Rhine, and the city is called Strasbourg. The people in Strasbourg speak three languages. One is French, the language of the country to the west, and one is German, the language of the country to the east. The third language is their own. Outsiders call it a dialect. The people of Strasbourg use their dialect to talk to one another and to the good natured, mischievous imps and goblins who live in the forests.

Years ago during a long interval between wars, a child was born in Strasbourg with bright eyes, nice big ears, and a wonderful egg-shaped head. All his life, he liked egg-shaped things—clouds, pebbles, jars, fruit. His father owned a cigar factory with the family name painted in big letters on the outside. It was not a prosperous factory. The boy dreamed through most of the time he spent in school, and for a while his father turned him over to a tutor. The tutor read poetry aloud and walked with him in the mountains. The boy also loved a vast stone building in the city, called the cathedral. When he walked there, the brightly colored figures in the windows seemed to walk along with him. The gesturing statues came to life. He never forgot the cathedral. Later, he said he would write 1,001 poems about it.

Since the boy loved to draw in big notebooks, his father sent him to a school of arts and crafts. The stuffed birds and dried flowers were so dull that he wrote poetry instead of drawing. Before he was eighteen, he had a whole book of poems in German and sent them east to a publisher. The publisher lost the poems, but some of them appeared in a magazine. People called him a poet now.

> *Ein rote Beere wachst in der Stille des Waldes.*
> *Sie ist gross wie ein Menschenkopf.*
> *Sie hat zwei leuchtende Augen*
> *und einen Mund daraus eine lange rote Zunge schiesst*
> *die nach winzigen denkenden Blitzen hascht.*

> *A red berry grows in the still of the woods.*
> *It's as big as a man's head.*
> *It has two shining eyes*
> *and a month. Out of it shoots a long red tongue*
> *that snatches at tiny reflective lightning flashes.*

When the young man was twenty-one, he went to Paris to study art and to see what was going on in the city for artists. But he found he was not ready for Paris. He made himself ready by going to a tiny Swiss village and living alone for a long time—more than two years. He looked out of the window at the snow and the forests. He read folktales and the work of mystic philosophers. He drew pictures that people could not recognize and shook their heads over. Later, he destroyed them. Then he began to travel again, to Paris, to Zurich, and to Munich. He exhibited his pictures along with those of other young painters. These groups had curious names, like the Blue Rider, the Cubists, the Storm. Maybe it was all poetry. The young man had a name, too. Or rather, he had three names. Hans Arp in German. Jean Arp in French. The third name was a deep Alsacian secret, which we now know. Kaspar. Kaspar means "imp" or "goblin."

> *weh unser guter kaspar ist tot.*

His most famous poem starts this way. German is full of capital letters, but Hans began to use only small letters, especially for good goblins, for himself.

Then came the Great War. Hans caught the last train from Strasbourg to Paris and became Jean. He was ready now for Paris. He found a room in a sprawling, funny-looking building that floated on a hill above the city. This place had a name, too: the Laundry Boat or Wash Boat, le Bateau Lavoir.

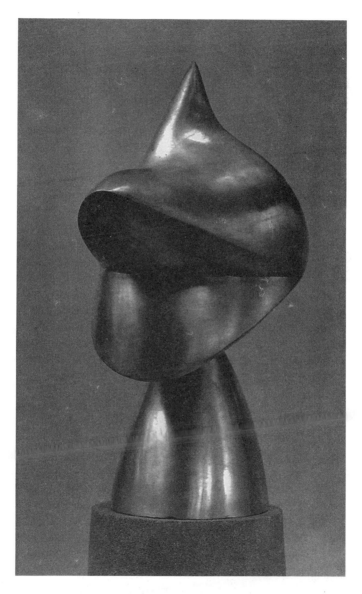

Hans (Jean) Arp, *Gnome (Kaspar),* 1930, bronze, 19¾ in. Palm Springs Desert
Museum, California.

Many writers and painters lived there in tiny rooms. In studios and cafés, he met painters with names much stranger than his: Modigliani, Delaunay, Picasso. After several months, Jean had no money. It was not easy to live in Paris as a German during the Great War with no money. So Jean took a train to Zurich, in Switzerland, and became Hans again. Zurich was like the calm space in the middle of a storm. But the German consul wanted to put him in the army. When they asked his age, clever Hans wrote down 16 September 1887 at least thirty-three times, drew a line, and added it all up to make millions and millions. The consul decided Hans would not make a good soldier and let him go.

That year, people came to look at his pictures in a Zurich gallery. And two wonderful things happened. First, he met Sophie Taeuber. She was a painter and a dancer. They fell in love and painted together and never separated as long as they were both alive. And second, he met Hugo—Hugo Ball. This gaunt poet and cabaret piano player and man of the theater had run away from German like Hans and from one of the stupidest of all wars. There in Zurich during the worst days of the Great War, Hugo and Hans invited refugee poets, painters, and musicians to meet in a little beer cellar in Looking Glass Lane. They called it the Cabaret Voltaire. They performed together and made joyful yet bitter noises against what was happening all around them in Europe. Somebody found a name for this rumpus: Dada. It was a great success. Dadadadadada. Anyone could say it, including Tristan Tzara and Hans Richter and Richard Huelsenbeck. It might mean anything. "Dada is for nature and against art," said Hans. Years later, he said it another way: ". . . the Dadaists despised what is commonly regarded as art, yet put the whole universe on the lofty throne of art. . . . The whole earth is art." All over the world, people began paying attention to Dada—too much attention. It became a craze.

Hans produced drawings and designs, on paper and cut out of cloth. Art happened to him like fingernails growing, like fruit maturing, like clouds drifting by. He was always full of fun and played with everything, including words.

Ich bin der grosse Derdiedas
Das rigorose Regiment
Der Ozonstengel prima Qua
Der anonyme Einprozent.

I'm the authentic la-di-da
The Razzle-dazzle regiment
The mighty spaced-out ozone stalk
The anonymous one percent.

Some said he let everything happen by chance. Some said he heard voices. He never stopped.

After the war, Hans traveled again, mostly to German cities where people were interested in Dada. They worked with him on magazines and strange drawings and wood reliefs. Many of his friends had now gone to Paris to participate in big meetings and demonstrations. But Hans stayed on in Switzerland, until he could make a living selling his works and Sophie could give up her job as a teacher. Jean and Sophie now settled in Paris. Outside the city on the hillside of Meudon, they built a simple house, all white, with a big garden and a low shed in back where Jean worked. It was sculpture now. He shaped things out of stone and metal, wood and plaster. Wherever they stood, outside or inside, his objects seems at home. He said they belonged to nature, like trees and stones. He called them "concretions," not abstractions. Art dealers showed his smooth rounded forms in their galleries.

In Paris, artists love to sit in cafés and organize movements. Jean didn't need movements to work, but he didn't mind them. After all, he and Hugo had founded Dada. Now he joined them all: Surrealism, Circle and Square, Abstraction-Creation. Joining all was probably the same as joining none. This was a period called the 'thirties. He was writing his poems in French more often than in German. His friends say that every morning he redid the same drawing—to see what would happen. Sophie's garden became more and more beautiful. They were very happy. Living was like swimming. Or like walking in the snow on a clear day in the mountains. They were very happy.

Then another Great War came. Jean and Sophie went south with some old friends, the Delaunays. When the war spread, they went back to Switzerland. Quietly one day, Sophie died in her sleep because of fumes from a stove. For five years after that, Jean made no more sculpture. But he wrote poems and he drew shapes. Finally, he began carving and modeling again back in Meudon. By now, his work was known all over the world. He found a special shape for a big public square in Venezuela. He made a dancing mural relief to gladden the spirits of graduate students at Harvard University. He won prizes and received commissions. In the garden-studio in Meudon, the forms seemed to become purer and simpler. He said Christopher Columbus discovered America by going the other way around. "When we tried to paint the other way around, we discovered modern art."

At seventy-nine, Hans/Jean Arp died. He had never stopped working. He had never lost faith in his work. He had never boosted himself through tricks or publicity. He had never become fanatical about money or sex, fame or politics. He was a gentle man. Arp's work was forever new, and forever the same, like a freshly laid egg. He seemed as alive and as old-fashioned as a mother hen. Change one letter of his name, Arp, and you have his calling.

It's almost magical. Yet he always had his doubts about art and tried to turn his works back into natural things. No pedestals, he said. No frames. He signed his works like other artists. His name was on the books of his poetry that kept coming out in two languages, French and German, with his sly illustrations. A tiny name like that, of course, almost disappears before you notice it. That was as it should be. Hans/Jean/Kaspar came as close as any modern artist to being himself and remaining anonymous at the same time.

COCTEAU, NATIVE SON

OF PARIS

*I*N THE WINTER of 1904–1905, two journalists for *Gil Blas* inter- viewed—in person or by letter—ninety-seven French and Belgian writ- ers. During its piecemeal appearance in the Paris newspaper, the survey provoked enough interest to earn publication by the distinguished house that represented many of the authors interviewed.* To the inevitable ques- tions about "the dominant tendency" in literature at the moment and about the shape of things to come, the eminent writers answered with a lengthy, uninspired mishmash of naturalism, Symbolism, revived classicism, and new social concerns. They commented without heat on the importance of "schools" to organize and activate the literary scene. The only subject they disagreed about with any real vehemence was free verse—its contribution to poetry and its chances of survival. (The nays had it.) Explicitly or by their listless tone, they all bore witness to the stagnant condition of French letters after the decline of naturalism and Symbolism and after the wrenchings of the Dreyfus Affair. The most influential figures, Anatole France and Mau- rice Barrès, had little to say. Gide and Claudel, among the youngest inter- viewed, succumbed to the generally mournful tone. Valéry, Proust, Jarry,

*Georges Le Cardonnel and Charles Vellay, *La Littérature Contemporaine: Opinions des écrivains de ce temps* (Paris: Mercure de France, 1905).

Apollinaire, and Bergson, all of them active, were neither interviewed nor mentioned in the four hundred pages of literary trivia. It looked like a dead calm.

We know now, of course, how fast the rebound came in the arts and literature. The Fauves—with the Douanier Rousseau cast into the same cage—were identified and named in the fall of 1905, and they pushed Impressionism further into the past. Within four to five years Cubism became the most dynamic new movement in painting, and Diaghilev captured *le tout* Paris with his Russian operas and ballets. At the same time, Gide and Copeau's new literary review, *La Nouvelle Revue Française,* signaled the entry of a new generation of writers, and in 1912 Apollinaire's review, *Les Soirées de Paris,* gave the avant-garde painters and poets their own lively organ. What burst forth between 1905 and 1914 in Paris was a dynamic compound of renewed classicism, unbridled experimentation, cool scientific nihilism, and a rash of primitive devices and attitudes derived from African, Oceanic, folk, and ancient sources, as well as from the art of children and the insane. Particularly in the prewar seasons of Les Ballets Russes, these manifestations found an enthusiastic public ready to be astonished and to respond. The artistic impetus that arose in the first decade of the century carried right through World War I to spawn Dada and Surrealism and the experiments of the 1920s. It required the political and social preoccupations of the 1930s to slow it and divert it. The avant-garde of the early twentieth century in Paris thrived as much in the traditional institutions of salon, theater, and café as in the more recent institutions of cabaret and cinema. All of them increasingly fostered collaboration among the arts, subject to no established hierarchy. In their survey, Le Cardonnel and Vellay had consulted the wrong oracles.

Many of the greatest participants in this upsurge of activity in Paris were foreigners—Picasso, Apollinaire, Stravinsky, Arp, Stein, de Chirico, Man Ray, Ernst. The cordial welcome they all ultimately received points up an irony about one certified native son of Paris, Jean Cocteau. Intimately identified with this juncture in the arts, chronologically, geographically, culturally, temperamentally, and aesthetically, Cocteau nevertheless could not ever feel easy and secure at its shifting center. Probably he was too close, had too many advantages. Some fate or trait debarred him from unqualified admission to his own rightful domain. Still, he flourished for half a century in Paris and left an important mark in several arts. All these circumstances have made Cocteau one of the most revealing artistic and historical figures of that remarkable era.

Cocteau was brought up in the heart of Paris, between the boulevard Haussmann and Pigalle. An acute sense of fashion in all things, of the theatricality of life, and of the fickleness of the public, highbrow and lowbrow, came to him very early from his hothouse environment. "La comédie est fort avancée" ("The play is far advanced") was the way he expressed the idea of getting older.

Cocteau was also both helped and hampered by having too many talents. A prolific writer in every known genre, he tells us that the formal act of sitting down at a desk stopped his flow of words. Consequently, he wrote anywhere, anytime, on his lap, unstintingly. From the start, he was a nonstop conversationalist—or rather, monologist. Anna de Noailles—a close friend in private—refused to see him in public for fear he would outtalk her. Drawing and design apparently came naturally to him, sometimes with pleasing results. His grandfather's collection of Stradivarius instruments and his family's familiarity with scores and concerts gave him an easy entrée into the world of music and musicians. Some undefined combination of talents made it possible for Cocteau to become a serious filmmaker, as both author and director, after the age of forty. From the start, he was endowed with a vivacious disposition and compulsive intelligence that enabled him to form friendships with people from all walks of life. Others, reacting against his social connections and public posturing, considered him an incorrigible arriviste. Gide painted an unsympathetic portrait of him as Robert de Passavent (Windbreaker) in *The Counterfeiters.*

We distrust extreme versatility. We nod wisely on hearing that the universally gifted Leonardo could never properly finish any task. Cocteau aroused immediate suspicion because he always played the child prodigy, who knows too much too soon and cannot grow up or grow old without loss of face. Charlatanry cannot be far off; yet the accomplishments are many, and some of them lasting. All in all, Cocteau presents a complex figure. It is appropriate and inevitable that one of the most probing accounts of his life and art can be found in Frederick Brown's unsparing biography, *An Impersonation of Angels.*

My own introduction to Cocteau's work has helped me come to terms with his many shapes. In the spring of 1947, I went to Paris as a young man with a commission from Ezra Pound to carry out two errands. I was to hunt down the sculptor Brancusi and report on his health and work—a story for another occasion. And I was to obtain a copy of Cocteau's latest book of poetry, *La Crucifixion,* and send it to Pound at St. Elizabeth's Hospital. At the same time, I came upon the short volume of essays, *La Difficulté d'être (The Difficulty of Being).* Up to that time, Cocteau had been little more to me than a name. Now I discovered two of his most striking and successful works. Four years later, while conducting me through the magnificent ruins of ancient Thebes near modern Luxor, where he was in charge of French excavations, the brilliant Egyptologist Alexander Varille told me that one visitor had understood that the only way to "translate" the laminated meanings of hieroglyphics into a contemporary idiom would be by means of film. That man was Jean Cocteau, who had visited these same sites only a few months earlier. His eye had encompassed the subtle interrelations of inscriptions, architecture, landscape, season, Nile level, the heavens, and cosmic juncture. No system of writing as we know it can register all that information. Cocteau had proposed that a series of films could begin to do justice to it. It is perhaps this kind of overreaching, unitary vision that induced Cocteau to classify everything he produced as "poetry."

In the dazzling versatility of his career, however, his poetry—as opposed to his "plastic poetry," "ciné poetry," and so forth—is perhaps in danger of being overlooked. Somewhat unexpectedly, this pursuer of fame and fashion could produce poetry that combines verbal agility approaching playfulness with genuine spiritual urgency. Before sending *La Crucifixion* to Pound, I read its twenty-five short stanzas. Without resolving the poem's enigma, the last stanza displays its pulse and several of its themes.

A genoux à droite
et à gauche. Seul hélas
de mon espèce (il n'y a pas de quoi
être fier) sous une cotte
de maille faite en chiffres sous
une armure de vacarme
seule à genoux à gauche
à droite—la neige aux mains d'aveugle
mettant la nappe—je ferme
à genoux seul de mon espèce
hélas dans cette chambre où le crime
eût lieu la bouche
jaune de ma savante
blessure capable
de prononcer quelques mots.

Kneeling to right
and left. Alone alas
of my own kind (nothing here
to quicken pride) beneath a coat
of monogrammed and ciphered mail beneath
a clanking suit of armor
kneeling alone to left

and right—blind-handed snow
spreading the altar cloth—I close
kneeling alone of my own kind
alas in this room where the crime
took place the yellow
mouth of my knowing
wound just able
to pronounce these words.

Cocteau has written a rhythmic chant for a personal reenactment of an unrepeatable and ever-present event. His conversion to Catholicism under the influence of Jacques Maritain and their public exchange of letters do not pertain here. The poem uses a flat diction and repetitious structure to transform familiarity into mystery. It is one of the least typical and most convincing of Cocteau's writings.

One other aspect of Cocteau's talent I wish to recognize is as well known as the first is neglected.

"The Truth is too naked; she does not inflame men."

"Victor Hugo was a lunatic who thought he was Victor Hugo."

"Nothing is more difficult than to sustain a bad reputation."

"The tact of audacity consists in knowing how far to go too far."

"The Louvre is a morgue; you go there to identify your friends."

"Living is a horizontal fall."

Cocteau's adeptness in coining a *boutade,* or quip, at the proper moment—in conversation or in writing—goes a long way toward explaining his public success. Effortlessly, it seemed, he could advertise with one-liners whatever he did, whether he was managing the comeback of a bantamweight boxer, or adapting a Greek tragedy with Stravinsky, or helping to launch a new nightspot. His skill at reducing ages of wisdom to the dimensions of a maxim loaded with paradox and irony corresponds to the sense of *velocity* that made Cocteau run. The film *The Blood of a Poet* is framed, start and finish, by successive shots of a factory chimney collapsing—stock trope for instantaneity or simultaneity. But the device seems to belong to Cocteau as his own, without cuteness or contrivance. For in his universe everything is going on at once, breathlessly, at cross-purposes or with miraculous harmony, the way he glimpsed it in the ruins at Thebes, the way he reveals it in his films.

In work after work, Cocteau tells us that it is very difficult to exist, above all because we don't know how to attune ourselves to our most precious and ominous gift: time. He never conquered that difficulty, but he lived closer to it than most.

CONFIDENCE MAN:

MARCEL DUCHAMP

I.

For fifty years after he had avowedly ceased painting, Marcel Duchamp spent much of his time advising friends what art works to collect. He helped Katherine Dreier form the one-woman museum of modern art called the Société Anonyme, Inc. When plans were made to donate the collection to Yale University in the forties, Duchamp wrote thirty-three one-page biographical and critical notices on artists from Archipenko to Jacques Villon. If he had decided, not uncharacteristically, to include a notice on himself as one of Dreier's artists, he would probably have produced an astute blend of truth and fable, like the others he wrote. Let me imagine such an account by lifting terms and phrases from the notices he did write.

A tournament chess player and intermittent artist, Marcel Duchamp was born in France in 1887 and died a United States citizen in 1968. He was at home in both countries and divided his time between them. At the New York Armory Show of 1913, his *Nude Descending a Staircase* delighted and offended the press, provoked a scandal that made him famous in absentia at age twenty-six, and drew him to the United States in 1915. After several exciting years in New York City, he departed and devoted most of his time to chess until about 1954. A number of young artists and curators in several countries then rediscovered Duchamp and his work. He had returned to New York in 1942 and during his last decade there, between 1958 and 1968, he once again became famous and influential.

With the strong personality of a pioneer, he navigated his own way around the Cubist and Futurist creeds and away from theories of abstraction during the "heroic" period of 1912–1913. An able cartoonist, he also concerned himself with physics and mathematics. From an early age, Duchamp addressed himself to two questions: Can one produce mental works of art not reliant on primarily retinal effects? Is it possible to produce works that are not works of art? His series of manufactured objects—chosen, signed, exhibited, and named "readymades"—and his *The Large Glass* (*The Bride Stripped Bare by Her Bachelors, Even,* 1915–1923, accompanied by extensive published notes and drawings), display a restless, playful intelligence that sometimes sought a refined aesthetic state. Duchamp demonstrated that new forms of art could be invented after the domination of Impressionism. An aloof person, he nevertheless enjoyed the loyalty and affection of many friends.

Can we do better than this bare synopsis? The most probing short assessment of Duchamp's accomplishment can be found in a dozen double-column pages near the opening of William Rubin's *Dada and Surrealist Art.*[1] Since about 1960, a mass of writings has appeared on every aspect of Duchamp's life, works, and influence. One discovers, whatever it means, that he never learned to swim, drive a car, dance, or type, that his family supported his becoming an artist even though at eighteen he failed the entrance examination for the Ecole des Beaux-Arts in Paris, and that this alleged loner left behind an extensive correspondence with family, friends, admirers, and critics. The young Duchamp comes to life again during the brief chess-playing sequence in René Clair and Picabia's superb avant-garde film *Entr'acte* (1924). In it, he makes the awkward unrestrained gestures of an adolescent, the way Julien Levy described him two decades later and the way I observed him during a few encounters in the sixties.

ONE WAY TO locate Duchamp's singular case history in the development of modern and modernist art is to enumerate the different roles he maintained quite comfortably and naturally through many social circumstances.

1. Detached and laconic by temperament, Duchamp behaved with an ironic serenity that increased with age. Some considered him a true dandy in the Baudelairean tradition of turning oneself into a work of art, a new postrevolutionary aristocrat. His friend Henri-Pierre Roché gave him the most alluring endorsement: "His most lovely work is his use of time."

2. In both word and deed, Duchamp was an incorrigible joker. He produced a huge collection of verbal puns and anagrams, among them a few gems (*objet dard;* anemic cinema). His few mature works of art could be considered visual-verbal puns.

3. These aesthetic puns arose from Duchamp's role as a frontiersman who thrived on the two borders that he helped make central to the whole modernist foray: the border between art and nonart and the border between art and life. On these unmapped and now overmapped frontiers, he served as pacifist agent provocateur, tour guide, and tolerated smuggler.

4. As a chess player, Duchamp competed internationally and spent huge segments of time studying chess moves. All his life, he trained himself in long-term strategy, exercising his imagination within the inflexible rules of an ancient game.

5. Duchamp was a lady-killer—handsome, slender, quietly good-natured, non-predatory, enjoying the field more than playing it. He could have married many an American heiress. Instead, his first, brief marriage to an unlikely French girl confounded his friends. His second marriage, at age sixty-six, lasted until his death and radiated warm sentiments in all directions. Women formed an important part of his life.

6. Duchamp learned how to withdraw from projects to which he appeared committed. In his mid-twenties, he stopped making traditional paintings and devoted himself to irregular enterprises along the outskirts of art. The central theme of *The Large Glass* appears to be the nonconsummation of an intricately proffered and reciprocally desired sexual act. The three women closest to him through most of his life, two of them presumably his mistresses, testified to a "certain deadness," and to a "strange tendency . . . to be neutral in relationships." The benign lady-killer did not conceal his lack of what the rest of us might call a heart. This Tin Man may have found his Dorothy once—but too late.

7. As an adviser to art collectors and galleries and museums, Duchamp had a large influence on the art market in the United States during half a century. John Quinn, Walter Arensberg, Katherine Dreier, Julien Levy, Peggy Guggenheim, Sidney Janis, and Walter Hopps listened to him with confidence. In general his recommendations were sound and free of petty jealousy. Only the more doctrinaire forms of Abstract Expressionism from the New York School provoked him to tart remarks.

This noncombatant abstainer contrived to position himself in the eye of the storm that is still traversing modernist art. Was it luck or canniness? During his lifetime, his example supplied an essential impulse for Dada, Surrealism, Pop Art, and Conceptual Art. He gave his blessing to Happenings. For the quarter century since Duchamp's death, his cultural stock has continued to rise. Amid the flood of specialized studies, catalogs, and collective volumes devoted to him, no reliable full-scale biography had appeared in either French or English until recently. Now we have two new books in English for the intelligent general reader. They carry on the Duchamp saga with effects that I shall have to approach slowly.

2.

A New York and *New Yorker* writer, Calvin Tomkins published an admiring sixty-page essay on Duchamp in 1962. Three years later, the essay led off his book *The Bride and the Bachelors,* in which Duchamp appears as the bride or paragon of four avant-garde artists: John Cage, Jean Tinguely, Robert Rauschenberg, and Merce Cunningham. Through chance, humor, and courtship of the commonplace, they all break down the boundary between art and life. The fleshing out of Tomkins's sixties tribute has produced a readable, well-documented account, *Duchamp: A Biography,* of an elusive figure. The book as a whole argues that Duchamp is an exemplary artist who shaped his life more successfully than his art. Why, then, does Tomkins open with a chapter on *The Large Glass,* since he feels obliged to tell us near the start that this multimedia work "sheds relatively little light on the mystery of Marcel Duchamp"? Things become clearer when Tomkins begins at the beginning and goes on to describe Duchamp's life in workmanlike narrative prose.

Proceeding chronologically, Tomkins divides the life into thirty chapters or clusters of events; they convey the sense of an episodic career, alternating between withdrawal and renewal. Tomkins has discovered a considerable amount of new information from interviews with survivors and offspring of those who were involved with Duchamp and from archives at the Philadelphia Museum of Art, the Smithsonian Institution, and elsewhere. These materials concern Duchamp's personal life more than his work as an artist.

Of the six children born to the prosperous Normandy notary Eugène Duchamp and his withdrawn wife, four became artists with parental approval and a modest allowance. At seventeen, with his baccalaureate behind him, Marcel followed his two older brothers to Paris. He took up with the *artistes humoristiques* and produced cartoons before settling down to paint his way through a two-year recapitulation of the major styles since Impressionism: Fauvism, Cubism, and Futurism. In a chapter entitled "The New Spirit," Tomkins surveys the churning intellectual background of the pre–World War I years, from Henri Bergson's élan vital to Alfred Jarry's grossly destructive Père Ubu. One of Tomkins's sentences here merits attention: "For the most sensitive artists of the period, moreover, the effort to turn life into art might have seemed like the only hope of sanity in a world where Ubu had gained control." Tomkins sympathizes with the aestheticizing tendencies of the avant-garde in the face of rising political violence. He does not consider how much those tendencies contributed to the development of fascism in Italy and Germany and of Soviet communism in Russia.[2]

Three chapters on the crucial years from 1911 to 1914, chapters that cover Duchamp's productive two-month visit to Munich in the summer of 1912, assemble the events in a somewhat confusing chronological sequence. We regain our bearings with Duchamp's triumphal arrival in New York, the sudden extension of his social life, and his decision to go public with his recent invention, the "readymade." Its disruptive force gradually overtook that of *Nude Descending a Staircase.* The readymade is an ordinary manufactured object, like a snow shovel, chosen by the artist, whose signature presumably transforms it into a work of art worthy of public display and admiration. A studio prank grew into a revolutionary gesture directed at the heart of the institution called "art."

Tomkins treats Duchamp's first three-year visit to New York in vivid detail. It included the brouhaha over the refusal by the unjuried 1917 Independents exhibition to display a urinal on a pedestal signed R. Mutt, Duchamp's dummy sculptor. With this piece, called *Fountain,* Duchamp entered art history for the second time in three years and then withdrew to Buenos Aires and Europe. He spent most of the interwar years in France, playing serious tournament chess, publishing copies of his notes and miniature facsimiles of his early work, and keeping the women who were in love with him out of his monastic apartment. Without dwelling on either the scurrilous or the scandalous, Tomkins traces Duchamp's lazy womanizing as a symptom of his character. While all his presumed intimates complained of his aloofness, none seems to have given up on him as a companion. Tomkins unearthed a letter from Janet Flanner to Kay Boyle concerning Mary Reynolds, Duchamp's mistress of forty years, in her final days. Dying painfully of cancer, Reynolds could not stand having people with her, even friends—except Duchamp. Flanner reports Reynolds's explanation: "Marcel is the only person I ever met who was not people. He could be in a room with me and I still felt alone." Tomkins comments aptly that this was a strange tribute.

Tomkins's most startling pages concern a beautiful, flamboyant forty-three-year-old sculptress, Maria Martins, wife of the Brazilian ambassador and a successful Washington hostess. In the years after World War II, she became the one infatuation in Duchamp's laid-back life. Among other works, he gave her an amorphous abstract painting, *Faulty Landscape*. Later analysis established that one of the media used was human semen. Yet Martins's daughter considered the affair "more cerebral than physical." In any case, Martins apparently gave new impetus to Duchamp's last major project, *Etant donnés . . .* , or *Given: 1. The Waterfall 2. The Illuminating Gas*, a peep-hole display of what Duchamp referred to in his letters as "my woman with open pussy." He sent the preliminary drawing for the faceless frontal nude to Martins in 1947 and worked on the project in secrecy for twenty years.

During the final decades of his life Duchamp overcame some health problems, married an American divorcée close to the art world, registered his lack of enthusiasm for Abstract Expressionism as too retinal,[3] and witnessed the strong resurgence of his status and influence as an artist. Books accomplished the shift, not exhibits. Michel Sanouillet collected Duchamp's notes and writings of every sort in *Marchand du sel* (1959); Robert Lebel published the first comprehensive study and illustrated catalog, *Sur Marcel Duchamp*, in 1959; and in 1960, the full notes for *The Bride Stripped Bare by Her Bachelors, Even*, or *The Large Glass*, appeared in a typographic version designed by the British artist Richard Hamilton and translated by the American art historian George Heard Hamilton. It looked like a conspiracy. The Duchamp retrospective exhibition in 1962 at the Pasadena Art Museum curated by Walter Hopps drew enormous press and critical attention. By this time, Duchamp's gaunt figure moved easily from lecture platform to gala openings to photo opportunities to television interviews. His charmingly accented English had become fluent. The Tate Gallery in London accorded him a major show in 1966.

Two years later in Buffalo, during the last year of his life, he attended the opening of *Walkaround Time*, a dance by the Merce Cunningham company based on *The Large Glass*. The set by Jasper Johns reproduced icons from the *Glass* in inflatable painted plastic shapes. Later, Cunningham described how Duchamp came up the stairs to the stage to join the others for curtain calls: ". . . Eyes bright, head up, none of that looking down at the steps. . . . He was a born trouper." Duchamp died suddenly and quietly that fall in his Paris apartment.

TOMKINS DOES NOT hide his sympathies for Duchamp's habits of discretion and restraint. *Duchamp: A Biography* combines a wide knowledge of both figure and ground with a style that usually handles forward-moving narrative as adroitly as analysis of persons and artworks. When appropriate, Tomkins knows how to distance himself from foolish manifestations of the Duchamp cult. In the following quotation he turns his attention to the artist's admirers (and overlooks the dangling modifier at the start).

> Dazzled by his example, it was all too easy to fall into the seductive fallacy that anything goes. Anything does go in art, as Duchamp had demonstrated with the readymades, but only when art is approached in the way he approached it: not as self-expression or therapy or social protest or any other of the uses to which it is regularly subjected, but as the free activity of a rigorous and adventuring mind. The failure to grasp that essential point about Duchamp's work and Duchamp's life has given rise to a prodigious amount of tiresome and self-indulgent art in our time, and in that sense it is certainly possible to argue that Duchamp has been a destructive influence.

Tomkins's portrait does not abandon common sense. His biography will not soon be displaced. I shall come back to the matter of freedom.

3.

A history professor at New York University, Jerrold Seigel has published a book on Marx and a fine cultural history, *Bohemian Paris: Culture, Politics, and the Boundaries of Bourgeois Life, 1830–1930.*[4] *The Private Worlds of Marcel Duchamp: Desire, Liberation and the Self in Modern Culture* is shorter and more ambitious than Tomkins's. Seigel offers not a biography that follows a peregrine life but a thematic study of Duchamp's work "to show that his career forms a coherent whole . . . of identifiable and interrelated ideas and impulses, linked to a set of personal themes that persisted throughout his life." Only the Italian dealer and author Arturo Schwarz, touting incest and alchemy in his lavish volume *The Complete Works of Marcel Duchamp,*[5] has made so sweeping a claim to coherence. Seigel maintains he has cracked the Duchamp code and can lay it before us in 250 pages. In spite of a few lapses in expository prose,[6] *The Private Worlds of Marcel Duchamp* deserves attention beyond the specialized field of Duchamp studies.

Chapter 2, on the nineteenth-century background, and chapter 4, on *The Large Glass,* and much of chapter 8, on the artist's sense of self, sustain the reader's attention. On balance, they outweigh the two weak chapters, one on readymades and one at the end, "Art and Its Freedoms." Seigel has important things to say about the history of modern art, but his unified Duchamp theory will not staunch the flow of commentary in years to come. One of Seigel's first moves is to explain the enormous fame of *Nude Descending a Staircase* at the Armory Show by attributing it to the Weberian charisma of Duchamp's persona. I find this explanation misleading. Duchamp did not arrive in New York to parade his persona until two years later. His character then struck people as relaxed, attractive, and secretive, the reverse of the divine gift of charisma. Seigel argues pertinently that Duchamp can be seen as the culmination of a long avant-garde tradition from Baudelaire to Jarry, a tradition that includes proneness to a personality cult and scorn for ordinary work and morality, and that offers status as an artist without one's necessarily producing art. The subtitle of the book enumerates the three familiar subjects it takes up: desire, liberation, and the self.

Early on, Seigel defines desire in Duchamp by quoting and frequently referring back to his cryptic 1913 note about yearning to possess an object displayed behind a shop window and the disappointment that must follow if one obtains that object. In other words, fantasy, imagination, and desire yield a higher reward than their consummation. Then, in the last chapter, Seigel restates the attitude with a new emphasis.

> Duchamp's pure freedom requires that the inner play of fantasy meet the world of material things wholly on the former's terms: it is lost when one breaks the shop window and discovers that the objects which beckon there only yield to possession by imposing the actuality of their limitations on desire's infinite wish. Such freedom cannot be experienced through direct interaction with the world, but only at a remove, in the Large Glass's perpetual delay, the chessboard's abstraction from social relationships, or the protected enclosure of the *Boîtes en valise* [i.e., the boxes containing miniature reproductions of sixty-nine of his own works that Duchamp assembled in 1939].

Such freedom is "pure" because undiminished by any encounter with the contingent world. Freedom through abstention, through abdication. Is this a new asceticism? A higher hedonism? I am in no sense mocking this line of thinking and behavior.[7]

SEIGEL SUCCEEDS IN showing how the principle of separateness corresponds to parts of Duchamp's personal life, particularly his relations to women. And the chapter on *The Large Glass* presents an ironic, even silly, yet impressive work that enacts and celebrates the pure freedom of non-completion—a high-minded version of coitus interruptus (Seigel does not use the term). As other critics have done, including Tomkins, Seigel envisions *Given,* Duchamp's lewd "environment" of a faceless woman sprawled in a bed of branches in a field, as the exact opposite of *The Large Glass.* In the former, one finds nature, an encounter with contingency, consummation, disappointment, disaster. In the latter, one finds a mental world, aloofness, noncommunication, heightening of tension, a permanent standoff. ". . . Desire's ability to lift human beings, male or female, into the realm of imagination turns to disillusionment once they settle for mere physical possession."

Yes, the contrast is clear between the early *Glass* and his final *Given,* and Duchamp surely intended it. But Seigel omits an equally important aspect of the *Given* peepshow. For years, the waters had remained calm around the man whose name was made famous by the scandal of the Armory Show and again by *Fountain,* the urinal on a pedestal. Was he really abdicating his niche in art history? It appeared so, for almost no one knew that Duchamp was planning twenty years ahead of everyone else. It took him that long to construct a semiposthumous explosion that would carry out his most elaborate and carefully timed slap in the face of public taste. *Given* does display a few features of a moral tale—like a scene of the morning after from *The Rake's Progress.* But *Given* primarily represents a return to Duchamp's earliest ribald social cartoons. He remains a boy hiding a vulgar word in an acrostic. One anticipated response is laughter—laughter at the private foundation that bought *Given,* laughter at the curators and trustees of the Philadelphia Museum of Art who installed it as a full-fledged work of art. "The Emperor's New Clothes" is enacted daily in an august municipal edifice dedicated to monuments of culture. But laughter rarely breaks out.

Duchamp's better-known challenge to the boundary between art and nonart took the form of the readymade—the reductio ad absurdum of the creative process in which the artist affixes a signature to any designated object. (For example, he canonized a bicycle wheel, a dog's comb, a bank check, and a typewriter cover.) Duchamp exercised this labor-saving short circuit a limited number of times; he never (except in cases of loss) chose the same object twice, but allowed facsimiles to be made and sold. How, then, do these artist-sponsored objects belong to the "coherent whole" of ideas and impulses that Seigel beholds as Duchamp's life and work? How are readymades related to elaborately conceived, planned, and constructed works like *The Large Glass,* which "strongly links art with transcendence and with freedom from material existence"? Seigel's answer relies on a phenomenon central to Duchamp's mental universe: the homophone, or pun. "Readymade" equals "ready maid" means the Bride eager to attain her long-anticipated "blossoming." Language alone forges the link. Seigel acknowledges its conjectural nature.

> Strangely, no evidence seems to exist that Duchamp was aware of the pun that linked the Large Glass with his turn to ordinary objects: a bride stripped bare is a ready maid. But it seems impossible that he did not know.

I find this a tenuous basis on which to enclose the readymades within the same aesthetic and personal universe as the works over whose manufacture Duchamp took great personal pains. More than punning, I believe, lies behind the craftsmanlike works and behind the seemingly offhanded yet devastating gestures that produced the few dozen items cataloged as readymades. It will take a good deal more probing to reach bedrock.

Increasingly in chapters 6 and 8, Seigel speaks of Duchamp's "aspiration to the experience of transcendence," attested to by his language experiments. The next step in the argument associates Duchamp with Arthur Rimbaud, the precocious poet who abandoned poetry in his early twenties for fortune hunting. Seigel affirms that through calm detachment "purified of the residues of ordinary life," Duchamp achieved "a radical wholeness like that Rimbaud sought in his more desperate program of sensory derangement." This insistence on transcendence in a down-to-earth artist makes me uneasy. *The Private Worlds of Marcel Duchamp* overflows with keen observations and unforeseen historical perspectives. But the thesis of radical wholeness based on transcendence rests finally on a common misreading of Duchamp. In his notes and sketches and mechanical drawings, Duchamp does begin to look uncannily like Leonardo da Vinci and to encourage our treatment of him as a master. Still, we should step carefully. It is possible to take the court jester of modernism too seriously.

4.

In both Seigel's study and Tomkins's biography, Duchamp's exemplariness for modern artists consists in the freedom he created for himself—for Seigel, freedom to probe his deep self; for Tomkins, freedom to make art. The latter, in his final pages on Duchamp's liberating influence, declares that Duchamp "demonstrated by his own example that the goal of art is not the work itself but the freedom to make it." Insofar as the traditions of the avant-garde and bohemia have led us to believe in a myth of personal license without social constraints, they have benefited neither life or art. For in that direction lies not so much the lightness and detachment Seigel and Tomkins envision as the possibility of selfishness, cruelty, and havoc to which they close their eyes. Rimbaud's life, fully understood, could have enlightened them.

Tomkins and Seigel reconstruct reliable accounts of the fall of 1912 and the spring of 1913. Those months precipitated Duchamp's decision to abandon the conventions and innovations of Western painting, which he had partially learned, for art by other means. Both books insist on the somewhat mad fascination of Duchamp for Jarry, creator of Père Ubu and the grandiose science of "Pataphysics," and for Raymond Roussel, whose plays and novels enact a world of pure verbal fantasy. But Tomkins and Seigel deal only glancingly with an important aspect of turn-of-the-century culture. It receives full treatment in a chapter of a recent book by Jeffrey Weiss, *The Popular Culture of Modern Art: Picasso, Duchamp, and Avant-Gardism.*

Drawing primarily from daily and weekly newspapers, Weiss outlines the history of *blague* (studio joke, practical joke) and *mystification* as common accusations brought against artists in France, roughly from Manet to the Cubists, and not sparing writers. A notorious spoof of decadent poetry, *Déliquescences, poèmes décadents d'Adoré Floupette* (1885) duped so many people that it remains a chapter in literary history. As much to enjoy as to mock the unbridled freedom of the juryless Salon des Indépendants, some wags from the Lapin Agile cabaret submitted a canvas painted by the switching tail of Lolo, a donkey. Displayed complete with Impressionist title, the work was attributed to a non-existent painter, Boronali. The *blague* was leaked to a guffawing press and, a few years later, inspired one of Russia's avant-garde group shows. It was called "The Donkey's Tail." Cartoons and columnists treated Fauve, Cubist, and Futurist artists as pranksters and charlatans peddling worthless goods.

In 1912, the French Chamber of Deputies was the scene of a highly publicized dispute about the alleged disgrace to the nation and to the Grand Palais of allowing Cubist "criminals" and "thugs" to exhibit their works there in the Salon d'Automne. Weiss documents the fact that the spectacle of an artist signing a blank canvas and fobbing it off as a work of art had a music-hall and cartoon history going back to 1877. The mock school of Amorphism claimed substantial space in the daily *Paris-Midi* and advocated "leaving it up to the observer . . . to reconstruct the form." Duchamp and others would echo those words half a century later.

Francis Naumann's near-definitive 1994 monograph, *New York Dada 1915–23,* as well as the catalog he edited two years later for the Whitney

Museum's exhibit, gives extensive attention to the motif of humor in both the European and the American contributions to the antics in New York. But Naumann does not look beyond a machine-age, sexualized euphoria and leaves unexplored the darker realms of *blague* and *mystification*. It falls to Abraham A. Davidson, who contributes a brief essay to the Whitney catalog, to detect "a deadly seriousness," a strain of nihilism, beneath the mischief of such European Dadaists in New York as Duchamp and Picabia. The more lighthearted American Dadaists such as Man Ray and Joseph Stella were creating a buoyant state of mind rather than undermining a tradition.

The European substratum of *blague* and *mystification*, some of it good-natured, some of it conspiratorial, is essential to our understanding of an episode that neither Tomkins nor Seigel treats adequately. Duchamp helped to found the New York Society of Independent Artists, whose exhibitions would be juryless and prizeless, like its French predecessor's. He served as chairman of the hanging committee for the first mammoth exhibit in April 1917, just as the United States declared war on Germany. One hour before the opening, he resigned from the board in protest when the sculpture entitled *Fountain*, was refused admission as "by no definition a work of art." Alfred Stieglitz photographed the troublesome fixture and thereby certified it as an aesthetic object. The papers carried the story; the urinal then disappeared from view. Duchamp's little magazine *Blind Man* gave a detailed inside account, reproducing the Stieglitz photograph and carrying an editorial and two signed articles defending the sculpture against this exclusion. Only gradually did word get around that Duchamp had planned and executed the incident as a test of the Independents' good faith.

A published collection of talks entitled *The Definitively Unfinished Marcel Duchamp* (1991) devotes 150 pages to two studies covering every facet of the *Fountain* episode. William Camfield summarizes his extensive research on the subject and establishes that, for Duchamp's admirers, the upstart urinal displayed, like most of the other readymades, formal aesthetic appeal that led to its being called both "the Buddha" and "the Madonna" of the bathroom. Art history writing has heaped itself high around the hoax called *Fountain*, treating it as fetish, antiart, an occult symbol, pure sensuous form, and art as philosophy. Camfield is convinced of its evolving place in art history.

In the same collection, a Belgian-Canadian art historian, Thierry de Duve, dwells heavily on how Duchamp "put everyone in his pocket" through guile and slyness in the *Fountain* affair. Waxing enthusiastic in the discussion following his talk, Duve celebrates the fact that a urinal can become art and nominates Duchamp as the "lever with which to lift the aesthetic world again." Duve goes on to wonder inconclusively about the source of legitimacy for an artist who signs such a work as *Fountain* into being (are we all artists?) and for curators and institutions who might accredit it.

In the mountain of recent publications about him, Duchamp is presented to us still surrounded by quandaries.

5.

In order to cut through these quandaries, I am prepared to propose that through the long undisturbed stretches and occasional noisy incidents of his eighty-one years, Duchamp accomplished three things. I put them in order of increasing art-historical significance.

1. Before he turned forty, Duchamp produced a few highly personal and original works of art, very different from one another and almost all on exhibit now in one place: the Philadelphia Museum of Art. The bare-bones list includes *The Bush* (1910–1911); *Nude Descending a Staircase, Number 2* (1912); *The Bride* (1912); *Tu m'* (1918); *To Be Looked at (from the Other Side of the Glass) with One Eye . . .* (1918); and *The Bride Stripped Bare by Her Bachelors, Even* (1915–1923). I have omitted all readymades and his last elaborate construction, *Given* (1946–1966). Those who know the works I have listed will not have to be reminded how insistently they take as their theme the sensuous act of looking. This artist of the mind could never tear himself away from the eye he wished to subdue.

2. Working from the casual, underplayed toy of *Bicycle Wheel* (1913) through the crafty subversiveness of *Fountain* to the naughty rebus of *L.H.O.O.Q.* (1919) (Mona Lisa defaced with mustache and goatee), Duchamp devised the readymades as a challenge to the sovereignty of Western art. I continue to see them in a carnival tradition as works of art for a day, which then subside into a collateral status of works in the history of art. They could be collected in an equivalent of the Smithsonian Institution. As the Smithsonian houses Lindbergh's airplane, which no longer flies, we could construct a museum of disparate objects that used to be art.[8]

The idea of counterfeit art or art by mere fiat represented by the readymades has bewitched a number of philosophers like Arthur Danto and turned a considerable segment of art criticism and history toward aesthetics and the abstruse discipline of ontology. But in reality, the readymades belong to a simpler and more fundamental category of art in general and of Duchamp's art in particular. When associated with his compulsive verbal and visual punning as a means of jump-cutting between frames of reference, and with unfamiliar media like glass and wood, the readymades come together and flow into a principle of universal metamorphosis. Duchamp is our machine-age Ovid of the industrial object and of everything else within reach. A French window, through carefully controlled yet offhand permutations, including talking with a head cold, turns into *Fresh Widow* (1920). Duchamp constructed a mock-up of a window glazed with black leather that obstructs rather than permits vision. Using verbal, visual, and metaphysical punning, one can transform anything into anything else. Because they apply the principle of metamorphosis in the highly sensitive area of aesthetics, the readymades locate a collective funny bone. We laugh at our own discomfort about what is and what is not art.

3. Tomkins and Seigel and other reliable writers on Duchamp do not depict him as driven by the search for money, for women, for power, or for an ultimate esoteric or alchemical truth. He turned down contracts from art dealers and proposals from rich women in order to live, like a latter-day Thoreau, with a minimum of needs. He appeared to be content with his lot and to float along responding to requests from others. The rest of his time— several hours a day through most of his adult years—he devoted to an activity in which any inattention courts defeat: chess. In one segment of his life, Duchamp was an amused nonparticipant in the politics, therapies, and binges of self-expression that have importuned artists from the twenties on. He claimed to have taken early retirement. In another segment, he trained himself unflaggingly to be a victorious commander in a warlike contest requiring vigilance and planning.

Did he ever unite these two sides of his temperament and his life? I believe he did, quite evidently, in the overall strategy of his low-keyed, occasionally scandalous, and stunningly successful career. At some juncture between the unexpected fate of *Nude Descending a Staircase* (first rejected in 1912 by his own family circle of Cubists, then singled out the following year to become the most publicized work in the Armory Show) and the *Fountain* episode in 1917, Duchamp decided to make a wager with himself about the artistic and intellectual culture he belonged to. He wagered that he could beat the game by doing virtually nothing, by just sitting around. His minimal, carefully planned tactic required that he sign only a few carefully selected objects. Deftly used, that tactic would bring him the one thing he wanted—fame. And the move coincided with his already-formed scheme to abandon painting in the traditional sense. Draped in arcane notes and irreparably cracked in transit, *The Large Glass* fit easily into this lifelong mystification. Duchamp, a canny deadpan operative beneath these antics, never gave himself away. The strategy worked perfectly. Yes, he put us all in his pocket.[9]

He even conned his friends and the Philadelphia Museum of Art into believing that the indecent peekaboo diorama *Given* should be considered a work of art. After all, he had kept it mostly under wraps for twenty years. Half a century after *Fountain* was excluded from an exhibition, *Given* was embraced without opposition by a distinguished museum. I continue to believe that the work represents the "ultimate and most daring art-history hoax, perpetrated (with their connivance) upon museums, critics, art historians, book reviewers, stunned public, and himself."[10] Clement Greenberg's anxious and discerning comments soon after Duchamp's death suggest that Greenberg entertained a similar view but had no stomach for calling Duchamp a *blagueur* and mystifier.

BUT WE HAVE learned to respect the tricksters, the Till Eulenspiegels of our civilized condition. In his notes for an unwritten preface for *The Flowers of Evil,* Baudelaire advised the artist not to reveal his innermost secrets—and thus revealed his own.

> Does one show to a now giddy, now indifferent public the working of one's devices? Does one explain all those revisions and improvised variations, right down to the way one's sincerest impulses are mixed in with tricks and with the charlatanism indispensable to the work's amalgamation?

In such a passage, *charlatanism* comes very close to becoming a synonym of *imagination.* The two great novels of charlatanism that portray a confidence man, Melville's 1857 work of that title and Thomas Mann's unfinished *Confessions of Felix Krull, Confidence Man* (1955), convey a latent admiration for the human being who can metamorphose himself into multiple identities. The stranger on Melville's riverboat performs a wonderfully Duchampian prank on himself, on the other passengers, and on the reader by posting

> a placard nigh the captain's office, offering a reward for the capture of a mysterious impostor, supposed to have recently arrived from the East; quite an original genius in his vocation, as would appear, though wherein his originality consisted was not clearly given.

No one ever catches up with Melville's strange impostor—or with Duchamp.

Felix Krull takes pleasure in seeing the world as a chessboard on which he can manipulate the pieces at will and in cultivating his ambition and his knowledge of the ways of the world by spending whole days peering into elegant shop windows. Once again, a novel sheds light on Duchamp's camouflaged universe. Duchamp's formation as an artist does not preclude his prowess as an impostor.

Duchamp's cool achievement lay, beyond his art and nonart works, in the wager he won that he could dupe the art world into honoring him on the basis of forged credentials. On the other hand, they were authentic credentials if examined in the light of the alternate tradition of *blague* and *mystification*. I can hear Duchamp still laughing among the celestial plumbing fixtures not only at our gullibility but also at inferior con men who seek their reward not in laughter but in money or sex or power—or in conventional fame. When Duchamp climbed up onstage at the end of his life to take his bows, he did not have to look down at the steps. From long and careful calculation, he knew exactly where they were. He had planned it all like a master.[11]

NOTES

1. Abrams, 1969.

2. See "From Aestheticism to Fascism," Chapter 28 in this book.

3. Much has been made of Duchamp's declaration to James Johnson Sweeney in 1946, in which he attributed to Courbet the modern emphasis on the physical aspect of painting. "I was interested in ideas—not merely in visual products. I wanted to put painting once again at the service of the mind." Duchamp referred frequently to the undesirable "retinal" side of painting.

These opinions citing Courbet for removing painting from the realm of the mind and subordinating it to the retina draw verbatim from the opening page of Gleizes and Metzinger's 1912 essay *"Du cubisme."* Whatever their source, the opinions do not do full justice to the socially radical and intellectually searching work of Courbet. And Duchamp's remarks imply a simplistic distinction between mental and retinal that is difficult to sustain in Duchamp's case, and in the cases of most modern painters from Turner to Cézanne to O'Keeffe to Clifford Still. The mind and the eye are close to inseparable in any seeing person, particularly in an artist.

4. Viking, 1986.

5. Abrams, 1969; revised edition, 1996.

6. For example, on page 161 an essentially sound observation drowns in a sentence whose awkward construction is compounded by a solecism ("are" instead of "is" toward the end): "But the deeper reason for not joining in the deconstructionist attempt to make 'delay' and 'deferral' the principles of reading Duchamp's career or anyone else's is that there seems to me little reason to believe either that the verb 'to be,' or the commonsense notion that human beings inhabit a world stable enough to be named by our ordinary words and concepts, are as oppressive as Duchamp and Derrida believe them to be, or that subverting language could offer liberation of the sort they claim."

7. I examine the importance of this theme in Emily Dickinson and Madame de Lafayette in chapter 4 of my book *Forbidden Knowledge: From Prometheus to Pornography* (St. Martin's Press, 1996).

8. See my remarks at the 1961 symposium that included Duchamp, "The Art of Assemblage." The full proceedings are published in *Studies in Modern Art,* no. 2 (1992). On this occasion, Duchamp read his definitive half-page treatment of the subject, "A propos of Readymades."

9. For contrast and comparison, I shall mention three other reputed hoaxes.

James Joyce's *Finnegans Wake* (1939) was eighteen years in the making. His close friend and principal literary rival, Oliver St. John Gogarty (the model for Buck Mulligan in *Ulysses*), mocked admirers of the book as "the victims of a gigantic hoax, of one of the most enormous leg-pulls in history."

In 1984, a book appeared in French—*Le Miroir qui revient*—that traced the origins of the French school of the New Novel to an imposture. This clever mystification was allegedly launched by Alain Robbe-Grillet and seconded by the academic critic Roland Barthes. Devotees of *le nouveau roman* preferred to look the other way, since the author of the exposé was Robbe-Grillet himself. He describes the ease with which he and Barthes discredited the notions of author, narrative, and reality and refers to that maneuver as "the terrorist activities of the years 55 to 60."

By confessing to his astute calculations in the 1950s about how to stake out and claim a prominent place in French literary life, Robbe-Grillet does not demean himself. He outstrips himself as confidence man. With dignity and assurance, *Le Miroir qui revient* takes a new heading toward fictional autobiography. Robbe-Grillet, a masterful player of the literary game, never misses a beat as he allows his whole corpus of new novels to assume the status of a wager or a bluff. The fact that they represent a winning number in the literary sweepstakes does not detract, he implies, from the high quality of their writing. Adoré Floupette eked out one slim book of hoked-up Decadent verses. Robbe-Grillet composed more than a dozen new novels; they "took" so well that the impostor can now tell the story on himself in perfect security. He comes close to bragging.

Ten years later, two New Zealanders, Heather Busch, an artist and photographer, and Burton Silver, an art critic, collaborated on *Why Cats Paint: A Theory of Feline Aesthetics*. The magnificently illustrated book treats the history, theory, psychology, and phenomenology of cat painting—a dozen cases of feline marking behaviors, from Tiger "the spontaneous reductionist" to Rusty "the psychometric impressionist." A graphically illustrated section toward the end studies curvilinear patterns cats draw in their litter boxes to hide or to highlight their feces. Through six reprintings, the volume has enchanted TV and documentary producers, a few animal-rights defenders, and savvy critics. Some readers appear to have swallowed the hook whole. Its high professional standards rarely falter, not even in the selected bibliography of imaginary titles, which includes "Ciacometti [sic], A. 1989. *Forget the Cat, Save the Art. A Reappraisal.* Raspail, Schwitters & Prat, Lyon."

Why Cats Paint sustains through nearly one hundred pages a hilarious, deadpan triple send-up: of the inflated jargon and grotesque theory churned out by art critics and historians; of some animal lovers' overinterpretation of instinctive behaviors as linguistic communication; and of the commercial coffee-table book as high culture. Busch's and Silver's canniness rivals that of Alan Sokal's recent spoof of social scientists in the pages of *Social Text.*

Have we now wandered too far away from Duchamp? I think not. For we have bumped against a gnawing question: Which of the following propositions is true? The better the bluff, the more important it is to call it. Or: The better the bluff, the more important it is to let it stand. I find no record of Duchamp having played poker, but he knew how to bluff.

10. Roger Shattuck, *The Innocent Eye* (Farrar, Straus & Giroux, 1984), p. 70.

11. I wish to thank Hellmut Wohl for his comments on a draft of this essay. He by no means concurs with all my comments and interpretations.

27

THE LAST CAUSE (AN
EXPERIMENTAL PLAY)

A *PLAY,*" *THEY* call it. No need to look for better billing. "Musical" would be claiming too much. *The Last Cause* plays off everything, including theater, art history, the culture itself, and, above all, the audience. For now, I'll call it an absurdist history play that sets out to explore the neglected wellsprings of modern art. Without inventing a single person or place, Phyllis DeForest has written a three-act semidocumentary with a new set of characters for each act. Aristotle's dramatic unities do not preside here. For all its grab-bag ingredients, this episodic musical play provides generous entertainment, especially if you know a few random facts about modern art after Impressionism and have undertaken an annual pilgrimage to your regional museum of modern art. In case you don't or haven't, I supply program notes from the *Playbill* at the end of this review.

Don't expect artists' studios and attics. *La Bohème* lies far away across several mountain ranges. *The Last Cause* chooses public places in which to present a culture inversion—a phrase I model on "temperature inversion" in meteorology. While following the circuslike action, you keep wondering precisely what elements have reversed themselves in this world turned upside down. I cannot summarize the story, not having found one. Here's what happens on the stage of the Bethany.

Act 1. It is summer 1912 inside the Simplicissimus Cabaret in

Schwabing, the artists' suburb of Munich. The high walls are crowded with paintings in all modern manners from Impressionism to Expressionism. Before the evening's entertainment begins, two young men are excitedly comparing notes about how much is happening all over Europe. In Paris, Cubism and primitivism and Simultanism and a new group called the Section d'Or. Then there's "The Donkey's Tail" exhibit of all the crazies in Moscow. Marinetti touring his Futurist circus to one capital after another with thunderous advance publicity. Rumors of a committee of American artists scouring Europe in search of works to include in a major show in New York the next year. Above all, both young men are excited and puzzled about developments right in Schwabing. One name keeps coming up: the Russian Kandinsky, who has lived and worked here for fifteen years. The thin, handsome one with a French accent and slick hair says that even Apollinaire praised Kandinsky's *Improvisation* at the Salon des Indépendants in Paris that spring—called it "Matisse's theory of instinct carried to the point of pure chance." The other young man, with soft features, and a soft voice, quotes from the book Kandinsky has just published, *Concerning the Spiritual in Art*. Every artist in Europe is talking about it. Since the wave theory of the electron has annihilated matter, objects can no longer be represented as solid. We have come to the turning point, Kandinsky claims. Painting will be like music, like the poetry of pure sound.

Meanwhile, on the tiny stage of the Simplicissimus, a slender young woman has started singing dark songs about whores and criminals. A cousin of Frankenstein's monster accompanies her on the piano. A third young man rides right into the cabaret on his bicycle to join the others, one of whom he met here yesterday. They sing elaborate bantering introductions that provide the information we need. The jaunty cyclist in his thirties is Paul Klee, a Schwabing regular from Switzerland. On a recent trip to Paris, where he visited Delaunay's studio, Klee heard about the young Frenchman Marcel Duchamp, whose painting *Nude Descending a Staircase* had just been excluded from the Indépendants. They now shake hands. Asked to explain what he's doing in Munich, Duchamp sings an aria about the fourth dimension, alchemy, circular motion, and getting away from Paris. The third young man, Hans, or Jean, Arp, recites strangely shaped lines of poetry about clouds and goblins and produces weightless stone sculpture from under the table. Klee introduces the visitors to the singer in her pageboy bob, Emmy Hennings, and to the dour pianist, Hugo Ball, avid anarchist and dramaturge of the municipal theater.

At this point, the action develops some momentum as the cabaret fills up. The famous playwright Wedekind wanders in with his guitar and accompanies Emmy in a set of his sexy, sentimental torch songs. Quantities of beer and wine disappear. Duchamp dances with several girls. Klee laughingly tells his friends two anecdotes. At an exhibit of French Impressionist art in Moscow several years ago, Kandinsky looked at a painting and saw not a recognizable object or place or person but just forms, pure painting. The power of the canvas was all the greater for this disappearance of the subject. (The catalog stated that it was a haystack by Monet.) Later, here in Munich, Kandinsky came into his studio one day and couldn't recognize, couldn't identify one of his own works. (It was standing on its side.) Same reaction: The subject can be dispensed with. Pure spiritual forces and forms will take its place.

Klee seems impatient with these claims and points out one of his own paintings hanging on the wall of the Simplicissimus. Immediately, we see it blown up on a scrim hanging in front of the set. Works by Arp and Duchamp follow Klee's. Arp talks softly and passionately about concrete art, like pieces of fruit, like pebbles in a brook. The scrim fades out. A portly man in a well-cut suit, smoking a cigar, comes in and sits with the three younger artists: It is Kandinsky. He talks like a book, like his book. "Our most ordinary actions become solemn and portentous if we don't understand what's going on. Imagine several men preparing to lift a heavy weight. Their movements appear mysterious and dramatic—until you have the explanation. Then the charm disappears. Functional meaning negates abstract, spiritual meaning. Just look at this scene. If you didn't know we were in a cabaret, you might think it was a church service. Or the end of the world."

The celebration becomes frenetic. Before long, only Klee, Duchamp, and Arp are left, slightly tipsy. They make a solemn three-sided wager. Arp bets that he will make art objects so self-contained and pure that they can be placed out in the woods or in a field without frame or pedestal. Concrete art, natural art. Klee cannot stop talking about his illustrations for Voltaire's *Candide*. He will make it impossible to tell the difference between children's drawings and the most avant-garde painting. Duchamp does a ritual dance in front of Klee's bicycle, which is still leaning against the wall. "I'll put a stool under one of those wheels and pass it off as a work of art. The claim will be enough. It's impossible to make something that is *not* a work of art." The three artists are resolute and exultant at the same time. Their handshake seals an historic pact, which they swear to reveal to no one. Their conspiracy will change the path of painting. As the curtain goes down, they are laughing wildly, their arms around one another.

Act 2. Set in a New York hotel dining room during the twenties, DeForest's second act does not allow the energy released in the first to subside for long. Gradually, the places at a round table center stage fill up with actors wearing names on their backs like football players. Ordinary diners at the surrounding tables form a gawking audience. Dorothy Parker chassés in on point singing "I'm Always Chasing Rimbauds." Amiable and worried, Marc Connelly has barely sat down before George Kaufman ambles by and rubs Connelly's bald pate. "That feels just like my wife's bottom." Connelly reaches up to touch the same spot and performs a mock Eureka. "It does, by golly, it does!"

H. L. Mencken introduces a French artist on his third trip to New York. Marcel Duchamp testily corrects Mencken and identifies himself as a professional chess player. Out of his sleeve, he pulls a folding chessboard.

"I'll give you a sentence with horticulture," Parker announces to no one in particular. Everyone freezes. She savors the silence before going on. "You can lead a whore to culture . . ."

A stout pixie with glasses and a sign saying ALEXANDER WOOLLCOTT arrives in time to cut her off at the pass. ". . . but you can't make her think. You must work on your timing, darling. This is my new friend, Harpo Marx from the vaudeville *I'll Say She Is*. It opened last night on Broadway and fills my column today in the *Times*. You all have orders to go see it. Orders."

Harpo, fully accoutered, simply beams at everyone.

Now launched on a course it never followed in history, the Algonquin Round Table careers from prank to wisecrack to slapstick. Woollcott orders every item on the menu not containing the letter *e*. Duchamp charms Parker into a chess game. The diners at the other tables have given up all pretense of eating in order to gape and applaud. Harpo and Kaufman smile at each other across the table like two conspirators. "How do you manifest yourself onstage, Mr. Marx?" Kaufman asks. Harpo holds up a warning finger, honks a horn hidden under his garments and summons his three brothers from the wings. Groucho swings in on a chandelier. Their attempt to save Harpo from the denizens of Broadway and the high priests of *The New Yorker* is foiled by a gargantuan figure who holds everyone at bay by just windmilling his arms. "I saw them first, in Rhode Island," he sings. "They're mine." The sign on his back says HERMAN MANKIEWICZ.

When an unsteady order has returned with the four Marxes standing like captive slaves on the table, Woollcott and Mankiewicz auction them off to Kaufman and S. J. Perelman, who has sneaked in while no one was looking. The two writers declaim in unison that they will transform vaudeville into a film medium that will lift American culture to new heights of the ridiculous. The four brothers perform a ritual slow-motion hat-changing routine—it could be from *The Cocoanuts* or *Waiting for Godot*. Woollcott starts a toast. "This is more than a gala day for us all." Groucho squelches any effusion. "A gal a day is enough for me. I can't handle any more." His volcanic clouds of cigar smoke put everyone to sleep, including himself, thus closing the act.

Having laughed uproariously, the audience looked puzzled during the second intermission. Almost everyone came back to see where it was all going. What can you extrapolate from two such widely separated points? ·

Act 3. After the high jinks of the Algonquin Round Table, the third act starts off as a solemn courtroom hearing. In the Café Cyrano in Paris, the Surrealist André Breton sits as a red-robed judge to settle several disputes. It must be about 1929 or 1930. This time, there's a tourist guide with a megaphone strapped to his face to identify the players. He seems to be bringing a Hirschfeld caricature to life. In one corner, Jacques Prévert is singing protest songs and accompanying himself on a concertina. A dandified Aragon holds a book by Lautréamont in his right hand and one by Lenin in his left, then narrates a long, elaborate dream about the top deck of a bus to Marcel Duchamp, who is bolting a crank to his bicycle wheel while he plays chess with Man Ray. Hans Arp, the perfect egghead sculpted by his own fine hand, is arm wrestling without much conviction with Dalí, costumed as himself. The handsome version of Dr. Caligari prowling upstage is Antonin Artaud. The walls are covered with generic Surrealist paintings. Throughout the act, young ladies in the café play musical chairs to soft tango music.

After Breton has gaveled the meeting to doubtful order, the poet Paul Eluard stands up to give the report from the Committee on Proverbs. Suitably scrambled, they come out along the lines of "One good mistress deserves another." Politics raises its head. Several members vehemently protest their leaders' having recently joined the Party, thus surrendering the Surrealist revolution to the Communist revolution and Party directives. Aragon defends the Soviet experiment as a glorious anticapitalist vision that will transform the world. From the rear, Artaud growls that no illusory change in the class system will contribute one iota to the spiritual salvation of a single individual in the room. Breton announces his decision by quoting scripture. " 'Transform the world,' Marx said; 'Change life,' Rimbaud said. These two watchwords are one and the same." Mixed cheers and boos.

The next order of business is the role of art. An earnest young Surrealist, Max Morise, gives a historical report. Breton himself originally attacked all forms of art. He called art a "lamentable expedient," an "alibi" distracting us from more important activities like transforming everyday life and liberating love. The term *artist* can be attached to no true Surrealist. Duchamp abandoned all forms of art years ago for chess. Pierre Naville, another Surrealist, said it most trenchantly: "Everyone knows by now that there is no such thing as Surrealist painting." Cheers. Morise sits down.

Man Ray—for some obscure reason displaying a French accent—rises to croon a laconic blues song called "The Objects of My Affection." Paintings, photographs, sculptures, mere things—they amuse, annoy, bemuse, bewilder, mystify, demystify. It turns into a jingle with "Art without art" as the refrain. Duchamp joins in with a single repeated obbligato, "Object o' fart. Object o' fart." It's not clear that anyone has paid much attention. Chess, arm wrestling, and some heavy flirting have been going on throughout.

Artaud, a professional ham actor, strides forward now and brushes everything aside with a Mephistophelian sweep of his cloak. Forget about art. The greatest work of the Surrealist revolution, a veritable hymn to anarchy and intellectual liberation, is not any book or painting or even any work produced by this bunch of café lizards in Paris. Artaud's voice has developed great power. The Marx Brothers films *Monkey Business* and *Horse Feathers* elevate sight gags and word games to a level of magic that becomes both terrifying and beautiful. How is it that the American sense of humor can send us the most extreme and original works of our era? The Marx Brothers have tapped the poetry of our insanity the way Dan mask carvers express the terror and beauty of African magic. We're never going to find the Surrealist spirit in a café any more than in the Ecole des Beaux-arts or in the weekly meeting of a Communist cell. "I move that the meeting be adjourned!" Artaud shouts. "I move that Surrealism be adjourned! I move that Paris be adjourned so that we can go see the Marx Brothers!

> "Klaver Striva
> Cavour Tavina
> Scaver Kavina
> Okar Triva."

Artaud's chant of bruitist poetry accompanied by African drums gathers momentum and goes out of control. Morise and Aragon escort him out of the café.

With noble gestures, Breton sings a powerful baritone aria to calm the waters, while off to one side a series of disturbing Surrealist paintings appear on the scrim. "Literature and art accompany us into adult life like toys we cannot give up. All around us as we speak, reality itself is at stake. The great modern painters—Chirico and Ernst, Arp and Masson, Miró and Man Ray, even Braque and Picasso without their Cubist price tags—have taught us to abandon the bird in hand for anything stirring in the bush, to elect shadow over substance every time. That way lies black humor, lies the marvelous."

Amid acclamations, Breton proposes a toast to the marvelous. Helped by Man Ray, Duchamp pedals his captive celestial bicycle wheel to unprecedented speeds. The whole café and its occupants disappear behind the scrim, which shows a clip of comic-apocalyptic war footage from the end of *Duck Soup*. Final curtain.

By canny costume changes, the fourteen actors in *The Last Cause* create the impression of a cast of hundreds. The director falls back on the same crescendo effect in each act and succeeds in keeping our attention. The Marxian invasion in the second act provides the only burst of dramatic action. No one seems to take the occasional musical numbers very seriously. Spoof is king. Nor did the producer budget much for sets. The most stunning visual effects occur when the projection of immensely enlarged modern paintings on the scrim engulfs the stage. For a short interval, the actors' voices eminate from behind a delicately trembling veil of images—fantastic yet familiar. These moments create the kind of spectacle dreamed of by German Expressionists and Russian Futurists, and by the French Symbolists before them. On this huge scale, lyricism and farce cohabit without tensions.

WHAT, THEN, SHALL we do with this drunken sailor of a play? Where did it come from? Where is it going? What does it mean? In great and small museums all over the Western world, carefully worded placards accompany traveling exhibits in order to explain to an obedient public shifts in style and recognized stages in artists' lives. Phyllis DeForest has copied down some of the wall signs and rewritten them for the stage. In the process, she has woven a message into the play, a view of events approaching an art-historical agenda. Behind the entertainment lies a fairly simple thesis about the flow of the arts since what we like to call the "turn" of our century. Her thesis goes something like this: "A widespread outbreak of wit, children's art, chance, and primitive forms squeezed high seriousness out of painting without removing the spiritual element. Some groups became impatient with the whole privileged category of art." A manifesto? An entertainment for savvy intellectuals? Writing about his collaboration with Picabia and Satie in 1924 on the film *Entr'acte*, René Clair lifts a corner of the curtain draped over a large segment of twentieth-century art. "I hope that one day a future doctoral candidate will write a thesis on the role of mystification in contemporary art." By having so many jesters around, DeForest seems to be signaling us that she is really in earnest. We shall have to scrutinize how she put this pageant together.

Is DeForest our Vasari writing another *Lives of the Artists*? Better question: Can she get away with shuffling and dealing her file cards so whimsically? For she has read modern art history like a buccaneer seizing treasure on the high seas. Duchamp did travel to Munich in the summer of 1912 and produced there the major early studies for *The Large Glass* in his new mechanical, visceral style. We do not know what else happened to him there—whom he met and where he stayed. But Paul Klee, a Munich resident since 1906, had gone back to Switzerland that summer, and Arp's Munich visit had come the year before. Hugo Ball worked in Munich in 1912, but not as house piano player at the Simplicissimus. Though he reigned during the twenties and thirties over a large province of American letters, H. L. Mencken never attended an Algonquin Round Table luncheon and regarded New York as a suburb of Baltimore. When in New York during the twenties, Duchamp played his practical jokes with the Arensberg crowd, not in the Algonquin, and made visits on the side to Man Ray's place in New Jersey. On the other hand, Harpo Marx (not his brothers) did play poker and vigorous croquet with the Algonquin group and even turned up for lunch. Don't ask me to straighten out Surrealist membership in the early thirties in Paris, a period of constant turnover and bickering about politics and women. The Café Cyrano served as a Surrealist headquarters for many years, but at a slightly earlier period. So far as I can tell, the dialogue in all three acts is based on available sources—once or twice removed. DeForest has invented nothing and altered everything. It's quite a feat.

There's one act missing from *The Last Cause*. All prewar European art movements flowed into Zurich during World War I as into the neck of a great funnel. In 1916 at the Cabaret Voltaire, Hugo Ball and Jean Arp and (later) Tristan Tzara submitted all these movements to the fusion process they named Dada. Later, Dada flowed out again into the European bloodstream. There may be good reason why DeForest didn't write this act. In an oblique, differently weighted play called *Travesties*, using Joyce and Tzara, Tom Stoppard has "done" Zurich. But Stoppard explores only that one moment, not a hypothetical culture curve covering two decades.

The Last Cause has the skewed documentary quality of good caricature. The telescopings and displacements do not distort the truth. They reveal a flow of events that we might not otherwise perceive. DeForest brings to life for us three successive artists' hangouts where the conversation circles around a displacement of art toward verbal wit and language games. She picks two strands to hold her package together: Duchamp and the Marx Brothers. Where does the supremely unflappable Duchamp, who never succeeded in turning his back on art, intersect the unstoppable Marx Brothers? Even in real life, the brothers began emptying the contents of the inkwells when they visited their own bank on East Sixtieth Street in Manhattan. To find the link, you don't have to seek out a big word like *Surrealism.* Duchamp and the Marxes spot the visual and verbal anomalies of life as they go by and capture them in displays of unmatched waggishness.

The first act leaves things somewhat unclear. It is true that Duchamp, Klee, and Arp refused to follow Kandinsky into the new high seriousness of pure abstraction. But they did not for that reason reject spiritual content. For all his jokes about "ironic causation" and his elaborate hoaxes, Duchamp never gave up alchemy and a special relation to the fourth dimension. Klee's high-wire act between cartoon and abstraction never carried him away from a region of the imagination devoted to sacredness, mystery, and childhood. Arp, perhaps the greatest artist of the three by traditional standards of form and execution, was also an original and influential poet writing in both German and French. Like his sculpture, his poems create a fairy-tale universe, which hovers between the pastoral and the preposterous. In all three artists, the pervasive deployment of *blague,* of joke, leaves intact the spiritual and the aesthetic dimensions of art. Duchamp, Klee, and Arp bring art down to earth without lowering it a centimeter.

Nothing new here. I remember that my college art-history textbook by E. H. Gombrich carried a schematically posed illustration of *Christ in the Temple* from a medieval English Psalter. After looking at it for a moment, you notice in the wide lower margin a beautifully rendered graffito of a hunting scene with horses and a trained hawk catching a duck. The naturalistic drawing—lower on the page, and lower in the artistic hierarchy established by religion in that era—is wonderfully joyous. That joy keeps peeping through the details of Renaissance painting as facetiae and bizarrerie until it surfaces fully in Brueghel and Rabelais. Crowds of people and objects overflow their works, the way multiplying things fill a Marx Brothers film and an Ionesco play.

By now, we should be able to tell what, if anything, is going on in the three acts of *The Last Cause,* and whether it all arises from more than mere mystification. I suggested at the opening of this review that DeForest is examining a culture inversion, a world turned upside down. But what has been reversed? A century and a half ago, by writing a preface to his romantic drama *Cromwell,* Victor Hugo produced one of the early manifestos of the modern. In that preface, he identified the two elements that have been reversed in our culture inversion.

> It is the fertile union of the grotesque with the sublime that gives birth to the genius of the modern, so complex and varied in its forms, so inexhaustible in its creations, and in that respect clearly opposed to the uniform simplicity of ancient genius.

In the ancient epic, Hugo argues a little perilously, the ideal and the sublime leave little room for comedy and buffoonery. Falstaff, Harlequin, Scaramouche, and Goethe's Mephistopheles have brought us myriad new forms of humanity tending more toward the grotesque than toward the sublime. Hugo sees this reversal as the essence of the modern spirit.

A generation later, developing his ideas on the "Grand Style" of painting in volume 3 of *Modern Painters,* John Ruskin seized on the same term that Victor Hugo made much of:

> A fine grotesque is the expression, in a moment, by a series of symbols thrown together in bold and fearless connection, of truths which it would have taken a long time to express in any verbal way, and of which the connection is left for the beholder to work out for himself; the gaps, left or overleaped by the haste of the imagination, forming the grotesque character.

In these two quotations, Hugo and Ruskin offer us a way of understanding both the episodic structure of *The Last Cause* and its message about the grotesque and the comic infiltrating the realm of the sublime in modern art. High and low have changed places.

DeForest has assembled into a play three widely separated, half-imaginary incidents in the story of the modern arts in order to suggest a new dispensation between sublime and grotesque. It all turns, she implies, on freewheeling wit and unhousebroken imagination. Despite his moments of thralldom at Kairouan in deepest Tunisia, Klee refused to give up the vocabulary of children's art. The Marx Brothers—above all, Groucho, backed by the impressive battery of Algonquin writers who thought up his rapid-fire one-liners—anchored themselves firmly to the age (eight to ten?) when nothing trembles a child's reality and tickles its funny bone so seismically as a stupid pun. "What's that in the road? A head?" The Marx Brothers thrived on such fare. Correspondingly, DeForest didn't have to invent the doctored proverbs the Surrealists throw at one another in her third act. In 1920, the poet Eluard put out a little magazine called *Proverbe,* to which every loyal Dadaist contributed travestied proverbs. Then they all tried to figure out the originals. Even the first sentence of Breton's long sermon known as the Surrealist Manifesto transposes a well-known proverb.

I find myself welcoming the fantasy conspiracy hatched in the first act of this roller-coaster play. Three young artists turn up one night in 1912 in a Munich cabaret and make a tipsy compact that will change the course of modern art. Yes, Vasari and Apollinaire would have approved of DeForest's principle of dramatic composition: One good mystification deserves another. The following two acts, while hilarious in spots, do not attain an equally convincing level of art-historical whimsy. I assume that DeForest's title refers to the vital role of comedians and artists in an unsettled world. While all around us compulsively interviewed pundits propose wildly contradictory solutions to our crises, *The Last Cause* suggests that only artful comedy can save us from ourselves. Good tonic.

PROGRAM NOTES FOR
THE LAST CAUSE

Apollinaire, Guillaume, d. 1918. French modernist poet, journalist, critic, early champion of Cubism.

Aragon, Louis, d. 1982. French poet and novelist, founder with Breton of Surrealism in 1924, abandoned it for Communist party.

Arensberg, Walter and Louise, d. 1953–54. Major American collectors and patrons of Duchamp, Picabia, American Dada group.

Artaud, Antonin, d. 1948. French actor, director, poet, active in Surrealist group during early years.

Ball, Hugo, d. 1927. German writer, dramaturge, cabaret musician, poet. Founded Cabaret Voltaire in 1916 with Arp.

Clair, René, d. 1981. French film director and writer. Close to Dada and Surrealism in early years.

Connelly, Marc, d. 1981. American playwright and Hollywood scriptwriter. Early collaborator of George Kaufman.

Delaunay, Robert, d. 1941. French painter, launched Simultanism with Apollinaire.

Donkey's Tail. Large Moscow exhibit of Russian avant-garde art organized in 1912 by Larionov, Goncharova, Malevich, Tatlin.

Eluard, Paul, d. 1952. French Surrealist poet, wrote often on painting.

Hennings, Emmy, d. 1948. German cabaret singer and occasional poet. Accompanied Ball to Zurich.

Hugo, Victor, d. 1885. French romantic poet, dramatist, novelist.

Kaufman, George S., d. 1961. American playwright, screenwriter, leading Broadway figure for thirty years.

Mankiewicz, Herman, d. 1953. American screenwriter and Hollywood producer, began as journalist in New York.

Man Ray, d. 1976. American photographer and artist. Moved to Paris in 1921 and worked closely with Dada and Surrealist groups.

Marinetti, Filippo, d. 1944. Italian poet and writer. Organizer and champion of Italian Futurism.

Mencken, H. L., d. 1956. American journalist, critic, lexicographer.

Morise, Max. Minor early Surrealist.

Naville, Pierre. Surrealist and political journalist.

Parker, Dorothy, d. 1967. American poet, fiction writer, and acerbic journalist.

Perelman, S. J., d. 1979. American journalist, short story writer, Hollywood script writer.

Picabia, Francis, d. 1953. French painter and author, a founder of French Dada.

Prévert, Jacques, d. 1977. French poet, song- and screenwriter, early Surrealist.

Rimbaud, Arthur, d. 1891. French prodigy-poet. Author of "A Season in Hell" and "Illuminations."

Ruskin, John, d. 1900. English writer on art, architecture, and literature. Champion of Turner.

Satie, Erik, d. 1925. French composer and musical wit.

Section d'Or. An eclectic group show in October 1912 of painters who dissented from the Braque-Picasso version of Cubism. Included Gleizes, Metzinger, the Duchamp brothers, and Kupka.

Tzara, Tristan, d. 1963. Roumanian writer, carried Zurich Dada to Paris.

Wedekind, Frank, d. 1918. German dramatist in Munich, forerunner of Expressionism.

Woollcott, Alexander, d. 1943. American journalist and powerful New York drama critic in 1920s and 1930s.

BIBLIOGRAPHY

Artaud, Antonin. "Les Fréres Marx au cinéma du Panthéon." *Nouvelle Revue Française,* ler janvier 1932.

Adamson, Joe. *Groucho, Harpo, Chico and Sometimes Zeppo.* NY: Simon & Schuster, 1973.

Appignanesi, Lisa. *The Cabaret.* NY: Universe, 1976.

Arp, [Jean]. *On My Way.* NY: Wittenborn, 1948.

Der Blaue Reiter, ed. Klaus Lankheit. Munich: Piper, 1965.

Breton, André. *La Clé des champs.* Paris: Pauvert, 1967.

————. "Le surréaliste et la peinture." *La Révolution Surréaliste,* 1925–27.

Case, Frank. *Tales of a Wayward Inn.* NY: Frederick A. Stokes, 1938.

Clair, René. "En guise d'épigraphe." *Cinéma d'hier, cinéma d'aujoud'hui.* Paris: NRF, 1970.

Gehring, Des D. *The Marx Brothers: A Bio-Bibliography.* NY: Greenwood, 1987.

Goldstein, Malcolm. *George S. Kaufman, His Life, His Theater.* NY: Oxford, 1979.

Gombrich, E. H. *The Story of Art.* London: Phaidon, 1951.

Harriman, Margaret Case. *The Vicious Circle.* NY: Rinehart, 1951.

Hugo, Victor. "Préface de *Cromwell.*" 1927.

Kandinsky, Wassily. *Concerning the Spiritual in Art.* NY: Wittenborn, 1947. Also "The Problem of Form" (1912) and "Reminiscences" (1913).

Klee, Paul. *Diaries 1898–1918.* Berkeley: U. of California, 1964.

Lanchner, Carolyn, ed. *Paul Klee.* NY: Museum of Modern Art, 1987.

Lebel, Robert. *Sur Marcel Duchamp.* Paris: Trianon, 1959.

Man Ray. "Preface." In *The Art of Assemblage,* ed. William Seitz. NY: Museum of Modern Art, 1961.

Marcel Duchamp, ed. Anne d'Harnoncourt and Kynaston McShine. NY: Museum of Modern Art, 1973.

Matthews, J. H. *Surrealism and Film.* Ann Arbor: U. of Michigan, 1971.

Mencken, H. L. *The American Scene: A Reader,* ed. H. F. Cairns, NY: Knopf, 1969.

Mencken, H. L. *Selected Prejudices.* NY: Knopf, 1927.

Meredith, Scott. *George S. Kaufman and His Friends.* NY: Doubleday, 1974.

Nadeau, Maurice. *The History of Surrealism.* NY: Macmillan, 1965.

Read, Herbert. *Arp.* London: Thames and Hudson, 1968.

Ruskin, John. *Modern Painters,* vol. III, part IV. NY: Wiley & Halsted, 1856.

Shattuck, Roger. *The Banquet Years.* NY: Harcourt, Brace, 1959.

Stoppard, Tom. *Travesties.* NY: Grove, 1975.

Willett, John. *Expressionism.* NY: MacGraw-Hill, 1970.

28

FROM AESTHETICISM
TO FASCISM

I

In culture if not in medicine, homeopathy has subdued allopathy. No one reads sermons anymore, or *Pilgrim's Progress*. TV evangelists use seamy case histories—all too often their own—to point the way to virtue. Horatio Alger stories have disappeared from high school shelves. The popular classic status of *Catcher in the Rye* demonstrates how completely we have accepted a principle of catharsis in education. It is better to present the naked truth than to arrange discreet drapery. We act as if we do not fear the poison of vice and evil, as if we can use it to inoculate ourselves against it. In a suitable environment and in proper proportion, reading does not corrupt. It immunizes us to the dangerous temptations of life about us. Without this belief, the case for freedom of speech would be weaker.

Every so often, we would do well to reexamine the fundamental opposition of allopathy and homeopathy as it affects not only medicine but also education, morality, and virtue. (We squeamishly avoid the last two words in favor of what must sound to many like a less theological term: ethics.) The second half of the nineteenth century in Europe set out to reinvigorate our post-Enlightenment immune system with an audacity we have not yet caught up with or assimilated. Distancing himself from Romanticism,

Baudelaire chose a title (*The Flowers of Evil,* 1857) that suggests a form of therapy or redemption by vice and blasphemy. Poems of Baudelaire's like "The Irremediable" and "The Heautontimorumenos" revel in venom, more than they recoil from it. In Baudelaire's writings and in that of many later authors, much moral exploration took place in and near the claims made for the doctrine of art for art's sake and for life lived as art. In his master fable of the heroism of modern life, "The No-Good Glazier" (1862), Baudelaire has his protagonist and alter ego respond to a mood of boredom and pent-up energy by dropping a flower pot out of his window on the poor glazier's entire stock of panes. Sheer "caprice" is the only motive proffered. The prose poem closes with a question: "These nervous pleasantries are not without peril, and often one pays dearly for them. But what does external damnation matter to the person who has found in an instant the infinity of sensual pleasure?" Two years later, Dostoevsky's *Notes from Underground* explored the perverse pleasure of "caprice" as the only form of individual freedom remaining in a piano-key world of determinism. Chapters 8–9 of part 1 read like an expansion (in large part ironic) of Baudelaire's fable, complete with boredom and energy, the Crystal Palace as symbol of blind progress, and a mood of joking mystification surrounding the whole undertaking.

After this apparent convergence of Baudelaire and Dostoevsky on a morality of caprice, one can trace how the art for art's sake aesthetic was steadily displaced by everyday living. The Franco-British figure of the dandy embodied the shift particularly well. Then the haughtiness of the dandy was retempered in flagrant hedonism by the "Conclusion" Walter Pater felt he had to remove from the second edition of *Studies in the History of the Renaissance* (first edition, 1873). The mild-mannered classics scholar proposed an unadorned amoralism of sheer intensity.

Not the fruit of experience, but experience itself, is the end. . . . To burn always with this hard, gemlike flame, to maintain this ecstasy, is success in life. . . . Of this wisdom, the poetic passion, the desire of beauty, the love of art for art's sake, has most: for art comes to you professing frankly to give nothing but the highest quality to your moments as they pass, and simply for those moments' sake.

Anthologies still carry these incendiary pages. Does anyone find them scandalous today? The last sentence of Pater's "Conclusion" quoted above has calmly dispensed with the question mark Baudelaire saw fit to use in the last sentence of "The No-Good Glazier."

From here on, art for art's sake and aestheticism fuse into an intensely blurred morality of Decadence. We tend to know the amalgam best in

Huysmans' fictionalized version of *Against Nature* (1884). But Huysmans restricts and confines his hero's universe where others extend and expand the dimensions of decadence. "It is only as an *aesthetic phenomenon* that existence and the world are eternally justified" *(The Birth of Tragedy, 1872, #5).* "L'art pour l'art means 'The devil take morality.' Art is the great stimulus to life" *(Twilight of the Idols,* 1888, "Skirmishes" #24). In his first book, as in one of his last, Nietzsche was aestheticizing experience. From him and from Pater, the new gospel passed with a strong infusion of energy into Wilde's seductive dialogues.

> Gilbert. There is no sin except stupidity.
> Ernest. What an antinomian you are!
> Gilbert. . . . To be good, according to the vulgar standard of goodness, is obviously quite easy. . . . Aesthetics are higher than ethics. . . . [Through aesthetics we shall attain to] that perfection of those to whom sin is impossible . . . because they can do everything they wish without hurt to the soul. ("The Critic as Artist," 1890)

Following such an extreme point of antinomian, decadent aestheticism, which ran rife across Europe at the turn of the century, the events of history seem to move in two different directions. In England and France this mood affected large segments of society without undermining the parliamentary system and democratic freedoms and without utterly subverting the bases of public morality. In Germany and Italy, the same mood contributed to forms of irrationalism, racism, and nationalism that produced the most vicious and destructive aberration of modern times, perhaps of all time. One could, at least, propose this double hypothesis. What happened in Russia is not unrelated.

To my knowledge, no one has undertaken a thorough examination of this cultural and political lineage. In Germany, it runs parallel to a philosophic line that connects Hegel on "the political work of art" and Burckhardt's reflections on "the state as a work of art" with Walter Benjamin's exasperating essay "The Work of Art in the Age of Mechanical Reproduction" (1936). Its last paragraph has attained a certain notoriety. Quoting Marinetti, Benjamin describes fascism thus:

> The consummation of "l'art pour l'art." . . . Its self-alienation has reached such a degree that it can experience its own destruction as an aesthetic pleasure of the first order. This is the situation of politics which Fascism is rendering aesthetic. Communism responds by politicizing art.

Those ringing sentences leave it uncertain whether Benjamin wished to suggest that the Communist response saves us from fascism or plunges us into an equal horror. It is a question on which our ideas should by now be clear.

II

One of the least satisfying forms of eating consists in trying to consume a sandwich that will not hold together, in which the filling too easily slips out of its casing. Just such an awkward disintegration affects a 1989 book about many of the above-mentioned aspects of the arts and culture in the first half of our century. Modris Eksteins, a history professor at the University of Toronto, calls his ambitious study *Rites of Spring: The Great War and the Birth of the Modern Age.* The publisher printed on the dust jacket unstinting praise from Paul Fussell and Alfred Kazin. Reviewers were generally respectful, and the book enjoyed the customary half-life of a paperback edition and adoption in a few history courses. But even with toothpicks, the advertised sandwich will not stay in one piece. Few will be able to consume the whole.

Eksteins' preface and final chapter frame the book in a deeply disturbing and potentially important thesis about the relation between avant-garde movements in the arts during the first quarter of our century and political events in Germany during the second quarter. In the central chapters, Eksteins sets before us a series of episodes that highlight very diversified aspects of the era. The preface sketches in the thesis a bit cryptically after a glance at "the whole motif of liberation . . . and of rebellion" in avant-garde attitudes and in modernism.

> Very few critics have ventured to extend these notions of the avant-garde and modernism to the social and political as well as artistic agents of revolt, and to the act of rebellion in general, in order to identify a broad wave of sentiment and endeavor. This book attempts to do so. Culture is regarded as a social phenomenon and modernism as the principal urge of our time. The book argues in the process that Germany has been the modernist nation *par excellence* of our century.

The last sentence comes too early in the book to carry the necessary tone of irony. As a result *"par excellence"* fails to convey Eksteins' true purpose of showing how post-Weimar Germany transformed the avant-garde call for liberation into the horrors of the Third Reich. The last chapter presents his case more clearly.

Outside Germany, too, there was much interest and sympathy in intellectual and artistic quarters for the experiment [of Nazism] taking place in central Europe, as there had been earlier for the advent of Bolshevism in Russia and then Fascism in Italy. All these experiments seemed to capture the mystique of the avant-garde movements of an earlier day: to embrace life, to rebel against bourgeois sterility, to hate respectable society, and above all to revolt—to bring about a radical revaluation of all values. Misfortune became grace; need became salvation; despondency, intoxication; weakness, strength. In April 1917 Paul Morand had heard Misia Sert, Diaghilev's admirer and patron, "speak enthusiastically of the Russian Revolution, which appears to her like an enormous ballet." Her friend Serge Lifar, one of Diaghilev's early proteges, who was to be made director of the Paris Opera Ballet under the German occupation, would repeatedly refer in conversations to a meeting he had with Hitler: "Only two men in my life have caressed me like this," he would say as he slid his hand down the arm of his interlocutor, "Diaghilev and Hitler!" The vitalism, the heroism, the eroticism of first Bolshevism and then Fascism produced a very strong brew indeed for artists and intellectuals. Nietzsche had asserted that the only way to justify the world was as an aesthetic phenomenon, and Benn thought in 1933 that Germany was about to realize the meaning of that statement. (326)

[Post–World War I] Germany inherited from the imperial era, especially its last decades, an aggressive urge to expand, to establish its predominance, at least on the continent of Europe, which was still regarded as the center of the world. She had been in the pre-1914 age the national incarnation of rebellion against the bourgeois Anglo-French epoch of materialism, industrialism, and imperialism. At the same time, she was also its offspring: the personification of youth, rejuvenation, and technical efficiency. Her defeat in the war paralleled the death of a young generation, and her frustrations were emblematic of the frustrations of the confused, neurotic, rebellious survivors who in droves everywhere in the twenties took up the torch of the prewar avant-garde and turned rebellion against the hated bourgeois into a matter no longer of individuals, or even of one nation, but of an entire generation. Germany remained the foremost national representative of the revolt. The Great War was the psychological turning point, for Germany and for modernism as a whole. The urge to create and the urge to destroy changed places.

The urge to destroy was intensified; the urge to create became increasingly abstract. In the end the abstractions turned to insanity and all that remained was destruction, Gotterdämmerung. (328)

My earlier pages on Decadence and aestheticism should suggest the sympathy I feel toward Eksteins' claims. Few aspects of the recent past deserve scrutiny more urgently than these, which intimately link political and cultural history.

In my estimate, Eksteins has failed to do the job he lays out for himself. The variegated filling sandwiched between his opening and closing formulations of the thesis does not present adequate evidence for that thesis. In part 1, Eksteins discusses the "aesthetic imperialism" of Diaghilev represented by the Stravinsky-Nijinsky *Rite of Spring* (1913), the enthusiasm with which Germany welcomed war in 1914, and the spontaneous fraternization between opposing troops in the trenches at Christmastime in 1914. The second part concentrates almost entirely on the "transvaluation" of social and cultural norms in Germany brought about by the terrible yet exalting experience of World War I. The two chapters before the last are devoted to the figure of Lindbergh symbolizing the new man of action and to the popularity of the revisionist war novel *All Quiet on the Western Front* (1929). In these three hundred middle pages, Eksteins has narrated some lively scenes and case histories. His most enterprising research assembles remarkable letters from English, French, and German troops in the trenches.

But Eksteins' sampling of forty years of swarming history does not hold together and does not build a sustained and convincing demonstration of his ambitious theses. The elements of his book remain curiously isolated or seem to connect by chance or by verbal association. The word *spring* is the single thread that links many of the pieces, particularly the epigraphs, and carries us from Diaghilev's *The Rite of Spring* to the last dangling sentence of the book: "A popular German song in 1945 was entitled 'Es ist ein Frühling ohne Ende!' " Midway between, in a chapter about war entitled "Sacred Dance," we are told: "Invigoration by death: such was Germany's 'rite of spring.' " In his conclusion, Eksteins makes much of the fact that the staff confined in the canteen of the Führer's bunker began, in the last hours before the end, to frolic in a dance, presumably a striking parallel to Diaghilev's opening ballet in 1912. Are these genuinely significant details or mere coincidences? Eksteins has not shown cogently that, as his subtitle affirms, the Great War represented the turning point that led important parts of Europe from aestheticism and Decadence down the path of fascism. I would argue that, if we must have a turning point, it comes later, when the Great Depression and the new "open arms" policy of international communism prepared for the Red Decade and gave an opportunity to Hitler's tactics. And Eksteins leaves unsupported his other major contention, stated in the prologue. "If there has been a single principal theme in our century's aesthetics, it is that the life of imagination and the life of action are one and the same."

The initial promise and ultimate failure of *Rites of Spring* leave us with an incoherent book that has one great virtue. It identifies an important subject. How, in at least two European countries, did a highly refined cultivation of the arts turn into kitsch and political subservience? How did a culture of liberation yield to nihilism and state terrorism? Are these the right questions to ask about the most significant events of our era? I hope other historians and scholars will improve on Eksteins' confused but essentially right-minded attempt to deal with the subject.

As I tried to imply earlier, Eksteins is not the first to address the question. Some minds were troubled very early. In 1895, a book appeared that foresaw many of these dilemmas. H. G. Wells's *The Time Machine* describes the desperate condition of the human race in the year 802,701. Human beings have by then split into two opposed strains living in a state of perfect symbiosis—or perfect war. The frail, aesthetic, almost idyllic Eloi living on the overgrown surface of the earth turn out to be cattle slaughtered for food by the subterranean simian Morlocks. Wells was extrapolating from what he saw in radical proletarian protest and in decadent aestheticism at the turn of the century. Eksteins, writing in the eighties, could look back at an even more terrifying set of events: history as it actually happened. Not a college or a university in the land today goes without several courses on the avantgarde and modernism. I fear that Eksteins's book is not well enough constructed to startle these professors and students into asking the truly searching question about enticing cultural movements that are still with us.

AMERICA, AFRICA,

AND ELSEWHERE

29

AN AMERICAN ROMAN-
FLEUVE: *THE BEULAH*
QUINTET

T*HE BEULAH QUINTET* does not fit. But it works. It works superbly as a set of sustained and exciting narratives that probe a history about which we know far too little—our own.

These five novels in sequence by Mary Lee Settle do not fit our expectations of the roman-fleuve.* They do not belong to a single era as in Balzac, or to one central character as in Proust, or to one Mississippi county as in Faulkner. They relate time, place, and persons in a looser and larger structure than that of any of those masters. Furthermore, Mary Lee Settle's lengthy and fruitful research into the web of occurrences we offhandedly call "the past" has produced stories that do not lie easily under the label "historical novel." History bathes and floats the events, yet it never overwhelms the restless characters as they learn about the ways of the world, pause long enough to love, and pursue their ideals to unexpected ends.

The five novels work—singly, and even better in sequence—because Ms. Settle blends tone, texture, and timing in paragraph after paragraph of strong yet unobtrusive prose. It is where all good stories start.

---

*Prisons (1973); *O Beulah Land* (1956); *Know Nothing* (1960); *The Scapegoat* (1980); *The Killing Ground* (1982). *The Beulah Quintet* has been reissued in a uniform edition by Ballantine Books (1981), Scribner Signature Editions (1987), and the University of South Carolina Press (1996).

I saw him then, mighty Cromwell, setting his horse high above me, followed by only a few officers. He had dirty linen, and his hands and face were streaked with mud from hard riding. He was smiling down on Gideon. It was a sweet smile that belied the stern lines of his face. His eyes looked as a man's who falls into secret melancholies, apologetic, sodden eyes, with much need in them. I would have said a drunkard from them and from his swollen face, but it is not so—not for so common a lover as strong drink.

Johnny Church's fresh voice in *Prisons* evokes the violent paroxysms of the English Revolution as well as its lulls. After his death at twenty by firing squad, Johnny's "democratical notions" reverberate through the four succeeding volumes of *The Beulah Quintet*, set in the Virginia Territory. As Virginia wins independence from the Crown and later undergoes painful division into two states in the Civil War, Johnny's ideals of freedom and charity pass through the turmoil of history in successive generations and modified form, yet somehow unchanged. The power of Ms. Settle's saga grows out of her sense of the heavy odds against which this continuity has been won—and against which, as well, every major American novel has been written.

These odds are caused by the scattered way in which American culture has evolved and by the difficulty American novelists have had in finding a world to fictionalize that is as rich in social and individual meaning as that of the great English and European masters. When he wrote about his visit to the United States in 1830, Tocqueville made frequent use of the French word *formes*. What struck him was the absence of *formes* in the new democracy—of customs, rituals, and conventions of behavior that give a culture character and coherence. In the same vein, Lionel Trilling has pointed out how Cooper, Hawthorne, and James each said in his way that American society is " 'thinly composed,' lacking the thick coarse actuality which the novelist, as he existed in their day, needed for the practice of his craft." Ms. Settle is descended from these writers and has their needs. In the closing pages of the last novel in *The Beulah Quintet,* she refers to "the price of freedom" that has dogged her principal characters. She means something closely akin to the absence of *formes* on this continent.

This is the challenge Ms. Settle has met head-on. For her subject in *The Beulah Quintet* is the direct opposite of American society as thin gruel. The pivotal events around which her story takes shape are ritual, almost primordial happenings: feasts, public ceremonials, formal balls, marriages, battles, violent deaths, funerals, and even mysterious descents far underground into the darkest entrails of the earth. The crucial scenes of the series give mythic scope to the classic American pioneer story. Through three centuries, we can follow the full-bodied conflicts and tensions of characters who both value the constraint of such *formes* as they find around them and fret to get rid of them in a recurring quest for freedom and a better life.

The quest begins in seventeenth-century England. In *Prisons,* Johnny Church, a sixteen-year-old boy, leaves home and his father's hard-won land in 1645 to fight on Cromwell's side for freedom and conscience. In those tumultuous times, the new experiences of love and battle reach him almost simultaneously. Johnny comes to understand his revolutionary ideals only when his superiors, including Cromwell, betray them—and him. At the end, facing execution along with his friend Thankful Perkins, Johnny achieves serenity enough to reflect that the "metaphor" the two of them have lived is also a "kind of lie"—not a vain lie, but an essential one.

A hundred years later, in *O Beulah Land,* Johnny's ideals come back to the land and to a homestead. Johnny Lacey, his descendant, moves his family from the Virginia coast to a valley west of the Endless Mountains. His wife never loses her nostalgia for elegant Tidewater ways. With few slaves, and threatened by both Indians and white frontier bandits, Johnny establishes a flourishing estate that his tenants name "Beulah" after dipping into the Bible for guidance. When he is elected to the House of Burgesses in 1774, he knows he has founded his "dynasty."

On the eve of the Civil War in *Know Nothing,* the ideals and the dynasty have been partly compromised. Peregrene Catlett, descended from both Johnnies, is troubled about the slaveholding that allows him to survive in a changing economy. Yet he cannot change his way of life. All his children abandon the estate. When the second son, another Johnny, returns to Beulah from the West, his sense of duty binds him to the land and permits him only a brief interlude of tenderness with the cousin he has always loved. Johnny resigns himself to fighting the war for the Confederacy, knowing that some of his family and some of his loyalties are on the Union side. He leaves no heir.

The Scapegoat portrays several reduced offspring of the Beulah dynasty facing one another in 1912 during a bitter strike in Lacey Creek, a down-river coal-mining community. They are barely aware of their shared past and blood. The arrival of the fiery agitator Mother Jones precipitates a confrontation between miners and strikebreakers, followed by fleeting violence, into which everyone is swept. Mother Jones's earthy speeches revive ideas of freedom and conscience in a society corrupted by southern resignation and eastern money.

Hannah MacKarkle, the central figure in the last volume, *The Killing Ground,* has left her comfortable heritage in West Virginia for the sophisticated pleasures of New York. The inexplicable death of her brother Johnny in jail one Saturday night brings her home and turns her into the chronicler of Beulah's collective history—the people, the land, the ideals. Gradually, she discovers that both sides of her family go back to seventeenth-century England and to Johnny Church's facing the firing squad. Her battle consists in the work of assembling that confused and half-obliterated past into a story, a story close enough to truth and significance to be told with conviction.

The themes that span and unite this extended narrative necessarily have epic dimensions. They also assert themselves in very down-to-earth ways. For instance, you cannot read these volumes comfortably without a map, for the larger action turns on a constant awareness of the surrounding land—the whole territory. The colorful names (Fluvanna County, Dunkard Valley, Fort Necessity) underscore the high relief of the countryside that shapes the lives of the people on it. But far more than beautiful or rugged landscape is at stake here. *The Beulah Quintet* takes its title from a well-known gospel hymn whose words are adopted from Isaiah 62.

O Beulah Land, sweet Beulah Land,
As on they highest mount I stand,
I look away across the sea
Where mansions are prepared for me,
And view the shining Glory Shore,
My Heaven, my Home, forevermore.

For early settlers, the Virginia Territory represented the Promised Land, the dream of establishing freedom and a life of plenty in the wilderness. *Beulah,* the Old Testament tells us, means "married." At the end of *O Beulah Land* (the second volume), the carefully chosen Beulah estate founded by Johnny Lacey does for a time permit a marriage of the real and the ideal in a reasonably harmonious community.

As the hymn implies, the myth of America has always been, above all, a myth of land. The land one struggles to reach and to prepare for future generations holds out the promise of a better life. Alas, the counterpart truth is too often forgotten: Land corrupts as well as inspires. The burden of land one owns and has settled can soon stifle ideals and promises. Ms. Settle does not flinch from telling the whole story. The Beulah estate under Peregrene Catlett in *Know Nothing* goes sour because of slavery and because of a smug and constricting sense of duty in a landed gentry that has lost touch with freedom and even love. When later applied to the bustling commerce of West Virginia with its coal mines and country clubs, the stirring words of the Beulah hymn turn ironic, even bitter. The most searing sentence in the whole series comes from Cousin Annie in the middle volume: "The satisfied are unjust." The Promised Land, when we settle there, brings our undoing.

This cycle of restless quest, settling down, and renewed quest spreads out into a temporal sequence—the ancient and irreconcilable conflict between Antigone and Creon, between rebelliousness and security. Ms. Settle's narrative alludes several times to the classic figures. She has even pointed out—a little impishly, I suspect—that during the Revolution there were two American folk heroes: Brother Johnny, the legendary colonial soldier representing youth, equality, and freedom; and Uncle Sam, the father figure of authority and age. Antigone and Creon appear in surprising guises. *The Beulah Quintet* traces the story of Brother Johnny's gradually losing out to Uncle Sam as the frontier froze into "real estate." The series also shows how we have kept Brother Johnny quietly with us—as we must.

In effect, Ms. Settle recasts the bipolar Antigone-Creon conflict into a more complex situation, closer to those of us who are not rulers or noble orphans with a king for uncle and guardian. The successive generations of *The Beulah Quintet* set before us not two but *three* closely related antagonists: American history with its interlocking opportunities and oppressions—our version of fate; the lone individual seeking his place within these engulfing forces of history; and the intense cluster of persons we call "the family" doing its best to mediate between society and the individual and usually caught itself in a strong seesaw motion between stability and instability. The three antagonists are evenly enough matched to keep our eyes open, as readers, to all aspects of the action. In the stunning barroom brawl near the end of *O Beulah Land,* the tall stranger is challenged and finally silenced without bloodshed after he calls Johnny Lacey "a diehard Tuckahoe Episcopal ruffle-shirt Tory king-lover." The situation that gives the scene far more than ordinary cinematic tension fuses strong political convictions about what the colonies should do in 1774, the dominant place of the Lacey family in the valley, and the ornery individuality of two frontier mavericks willing to risk a fistfight and a shoot-out over words. *The Beulah Quintet* enlarges the Antigone-Creon conflict without reducing its drama.

Ms. Settle composes her story with a remarkable freedom and variety of narrative styles. *Prisons* is told in the first person by a young man, living and remembering his own story as he goes along. The first-person mode does not return until sections in the last two volumes. Elsewhere, the action is told in a flexible third-person voice that moves at will into the minds of the characters and back out again, sometimes to tell us explicitly what they do *not* know. This multiplicity of points of view is appropriate to the semi-independent nature of the five volumes. It also coheres around the clear line of the action in its Virginia setting and around the depth of perception that lurks everywhere in the detail. In *The Scapegoat,* headstrong Lily, daughter of the local mine owner, has taken up a young Italian miner in order to educate him. Eduardo is fascinated by the blond girl, always dressed in white, and equally wary of her. "After the black-haired women with their dark pools of eyes made huge by shadows under them like tearstains, she seemed the color of disappearance." Such touches create a texture of writing that is finally the signature of the whole quintet.

Much of the striking detail in the writing comes from the relentless instinct for concreteness that has closeted Ms. Settle at frequent intervals for solid months of reading in the British Museum and in libraries and archives throughout Virginia. A 1980 interview suggests the thoroughness and imaginativeness of her historical research.

> In the state library in Charleston, I found 5,000 pages of records of a Senate investigation into the West Virginia mine wars and the Holly Grove Massacre. Instead of taking notes I recorded fourteen hours of tape by reading key testimony aloud. That way I could hear the language. Everyone said there was no record of Mother Jones' speeches because she always spoke extemporaneously. Right at the end I found stenographic transcriptions of three of her speeches to the miners. A court reporter made them for Brown, Jackson, and Knight, the coal owners' law firm. They wanted to indite her for sedition. They didn't get her on sedition, but they left me the clues to Mother Jones' rhythms, her phrasing, her vocabulary. From that I could build both her character and her speech.

When investigative research and the imagination work hand in hand, the resulting fiction allows us to perceive the events of history from inside. Mother Jones comes to life with the grainy vividness that makes Cromwell fully convincing in *Prisons.*

The pacing Ms. Settle uses in her constantly renewed tale of settlers and wanderers constitutes another element of stylistic texture in the quintet and also of its form. The action of *Prisons* covers two days and two nights in 1649, during which the retrospective narrative draws out of itself the essential scenes of one man's short life. *O Beulah Land* moves in great strides from the American wilderness back to the streets of London, then over again to Tidewater Virginia, and finally out to a western settlement defending itself against the elements, Indian raids, and other hardships. In *Know Nothing,* three sequences each twelve years apart portray the pathetic-heroic tribulations of the last two generations before the Civil War. The events of *The*

Scapegoat converge, sometimes at breakneck speed, sometimes at a near standstill, in seventeen hours on June 7–8, 1912. *The Killing Ground,* reaching the "present" of its own composition in 1980, shuttles back and forth across a twenty-year interval, whose gradually revealed content transforms a woman's character and establishes the narrative context for the preceding volumes.

The restless movement of this three-hundred-year chronology carries a significance very different from that of Faulkner's convoluted narratives. He rarely allows a major event to happen straight out, onstage and on schedule, before our eyes. It is usually retrieved from an elaborately reconstructed past, sometimes by a character thrust suddenly forward to a future-perfect consciousness in order to supply this backward perspective. Whenever the story line ventures close to a crucial occurrence, the narrative pressure collapses or is interrupted in such a way as to prevent the stream of time from flowing into a simple present. The sometimes-frustrating fascination of *Absalom, Absalom!* lies in the frequency with which Faulkner engages in a narrative equivalent of coitus interruptus. Sutpen, a self-made man of mysterious ambitions and innate courage and shrewdness, never achieves a moment of satisfaction. The shape of the story, as much as its content, tells us that this larger-than-life adventurer cannot touch life long enough to grasp it.

In Ms. Settle's novels, on the other hand, the swerves and jumps in the story do not deprive time of its ability to catch up finally with the present at a point where, for a rare bright interlude, it coincides with the character's consciousness and experience. Like parts of a liturgy, her deliberate narrative gestures certify the occurrence of a few major events following an interval of high suspense. "My mind twitters," Johnny says to himself near the end of *Prisons,* as he waits to be shot. In spite of his intense anguish, both he and we are there, in full awareness, when his death comes in the form of three brief and fully eloquent sentences on the last page. In *Know Nothing,* Johnny Catlett and Melinda desire each other through thirty years and four hundred pages of obstacles raised by themselves and the society they live in. When finally they can come to each other, just once, in full physical embrace, there is not one shred of uncertainty or narrative evasiveness in the sentence that records the moment. "After the longing they hardly needed to move."

Both Faulkner and Ms. Settle would reject Parmenides' perennial notion that "True being is timeless." Faulkner's entire universe suggests that even the most imaginative, or energetic, or reflective of human minds has no access to "true being"—if indeed it exists. His characters spend their lives circling around it in exhausting, sometimes spectacular loops that constantly breed further loops of memory and speculation. In *The Beulah Quin-*

tet, Ms. Settle's narrative loops—rarely so compulsive or so extravagant as Faulkner's—establish a distance and a perspective from which the action can at intervals return to the straightaway of experience. True being is not timeless. Rather, we come upon it when the stream of individual consciousness coincides briefly with the stream of time shared with others. These interludes are not hushed epiphanies as Proust and Joyce celebrated them, moments projected out of the domain of contingent consciousness. They remain *in time.* After long preparation and many missed turns, a perceptive individual may participate fully in a recognizable event of genuine significance to him and to others. It is a rare accomplishment in modern fiction.

Thus Ms. Settle's free treatment of narrative form and individual time leads the story intermittently to the same ceremonial, almost archetypal happenings of celebration or loss that testify to her sense of *formes.* The convergence has a tightening effect on the economy and power of her novels. Part of the writing creates a kind of ontological suspense around the events it depicts, because the characters themselves cannot endow them with full reality, full existence. In other, rarer passages, the action approaches certain heightened, ritualized moments and enters them long enough to give us a glimpse of "true being" as well as a sense of social custom. Both the private and the public sides of *The Beulah Quintet* contribute to one insight: life, or perception, comes in strong flashes. The corollary: Don't fall asleep in the intervals.

At no point in her writing does Mary Lee Settle become an antinovelist or a player of literary games. Be of good faith, she says quietly, for I can help you see that everything is significant—the shape of a girl's fingernails; the way a man sits his horse or his car; the excited gestures of frontier children as they smoke snakes out of a rock pile. We may not be able to notice everything, as Henry James counseled us; but Miss Settle, patiently and convincingly weaving history into her roman-fleuve, reveals that nothing has to be lost for good. *The Beulah Quintet* represents an act of faith in the novel, less as vicarious experience than as a source of energies we can carry back to life itself, to our lives. Literature in its highest form does not distract us. It puts us on our mettle.

30

"THE GREAT AMERICAN
THING": O'KEEFFE AND
STIEGLITZ

ARL, THE GLASSBLOWER, was closing his shop in the dusk. A slight man with a shock of gray hair, he looked grim and a little frail as he fastened the shutters. He knew that soon he would no longer be opening the shop in the morning and closing it at night.

People had loved the carafes and pitchers and vases he made as a young man. Then he had begun to display in his shop the pottery and silverware and wood ware of many other craftsmen. Carl's shop was small but central, and the craftsmen liked the way he showed their wares. And they often visited his shop because there was something special about the way Carl talked. Sometimes he was like an inspired preacher. Sometimes he went on and on like a great wind. Sometimes he could put magic into words like spirit and freedom and feeling. "Beauty begins where thinking ends," he would say. The objects he sold became treasures for the wealthy citizens of the town. Carl himself did hardly any more glass blowing. He said everyone should be able to live content with a few beautiful things. He made many converts.

Now Carl was soon going to lose his shop. For months his trade had dwindled. A great international fair had made people forget about Carl. Many artisans opened their own shops. New fashions influenced everything. And a terrible war had started that changed the way people lived. The landlord said Carl could not stay in the building. As he fastened the shutters, Carl sighed heavily. He was *not accustomed to being alone. He would soon have to move everything out of the shop. But where? He had no place to go. And he still had so much to do and to say.*

In the dusk, Carl noticed a young woman carrying a sack and looking at the row of shops. In a firm voice, she asked him where to find Carl the glassblower. He made a noise between a bark and a laugh.

"I suppose you have things to show me."

His scorn changed to admiration when he saw the objects in her sack. She had animals and flowers woven out of reeds and grasses. She also had stark, beautiful shapes that did not resemble anything real.

"Who taught you to make these?"

"I was apprentice to the best basket makers. These are my own."

"Why do you come to me?"

"People say you will understand them."

"Bah! People want to get rid of me. What difference does it make now if I understand?"

But Carl could not turn Miranda away. She was dark and resolute like a gypsy. During the few days Carl had left to occupy the shop, he cleared out the pots and carvings and laid out all Miranda's work. Her things combined the jaggedness of bones with the softness of summer clouds. Carl's friends did not say much about Miranda. He let her sleep in the shop. He had a little apartment upstairs. Not many people bought her things. But Carl talked differently now. He talked as if something were beginning in his life, not coming to an end.

Miranda went away for a time. They wrote long, excited letters to each other about what they saw and felt. When she came back, Carl took her into the tiny attic where he had moved. The new place had to be their shop and their home in one. His friends still came to hear him talk and to find out about the dark, silent woman who had changed his life. For Carl was working again. He was blowing nude figurines in a bold new style. He said it was really one figure in many poses. Often he did not include the head. He never said who the figure was supposed to be. But everyone knew. And everyone in the town came to see the figurines.

Carl and Miranda were very happy now. For the summers, they found a little place in the country next to a lake and invited their friends to visit. Carl always had plans for the future of their group and he loved to explain the meaning of the things they were making. Miranda remained remote and dignified. She was weaving larger and more brightly colored objects. Once, Carl and Miranda showed their work together. Of course, the gossip did not stop. Some people in the town said they had always known that Carl was a dirty old man. And they said anyone could tell that she was witch. It would all come to a bad end.

For several years, Carl and Miranda lived and worked together. They had become man and wife. Though he was growing old and white, Carl kept his place open. Friends came by to hear him talk about the links between music and beauty, between the beautiful and the spiritual. Wealthy citizens in carriages came to visit his shop and to buy the things he had there. It was as if Carl and Miranda had changed people's taste. Pitchers and glasses had a firmer shape. Many husbands bought her woven flowers to give to their wives.

After a time, Miranda became restless. She missed the distant land she came from and the quiet she had known before. It was never quiet around Carl. He loved noise and made lots of it himself. She could no longer work well in town. Miranda went away for longer and longer periods—sometimes for a whole season, even for a year.

No couple can live without quarrels and jealousies. But these two needed each other, and Miranda always came back. His small glass pieces did not look at all like the bigger and bigger things she was making now—colored screens, sumptuous hangings. Once every year, Carl showed Miranda's things in his shop. She became rich and famous.

When Carl died quietly, a few people in the town believed they had lost a special person, possibly a great man. Even those who had been annoyed by all his talk recognized his gifts. But many of them said that Miranda's work was more beautiful than his. Her strongly colored tapestries conveyed a new sense of form and space. Discussions about how much Carl and Miranda had contributed to the reputation of the town went on and on. But the town council never named a street or a square after either of them, or even after both of them together.

Then, a few years after Miranda died, a strange thing happened not in the town but in the capital city. Someone decided that Carl's glass objects and Miranda's woven works should once again be shown together in one place. Ordinary people as well as learned scholars wanted to find out how much the two had inspired each other and how good their work really was. Can lovers collaborate? Does collaboration make lovers? Or should we forget about all that and just look at the objects? During the exhibit, some visitors said they could hear Carl's voice speaking to them from hidden corners of the galleries. Other visitors whispered to one another about a dark Indian-looking girl who walked slowly and alone through the rooms. She must have Miranda's blood in her veins. Or was it Miranda herself?

There is still no Carl-Miranda square, not in their town, not in the capital. But in many homes you can find flowers woven by Miranda or one of Carl's figurines. Those things have made a difference to the way people live.

AS A COUPLE, Alfred Stieglitz and Georgia O'Keeffe are often portrayed as representing the ideal of a romantic union, artistic and erotic, whose very privacy seemed to radiate notoriety. From cooler accounts, we learn the extent to which their selfish plottings, publicity stunts, and occasionally shady dealings reveal two opportunists working in cahoots to exploit others—and each other. The outward facts pose no problem. Their collaboration, which lasted from 1917 to about 1930, reached a high point in their joint exhibit in February 1924 at the Anderson Galleries. It is artistically more than biographically that their association makes a difficult act to chronicle and to understand.

Anyone concerned with the development of the arts in America must form some opinion of this founding couple of the modern. As much as T. S. Eliot and Ezra Pound worked for a time together toward a new prosody and a new principle of association in poetry, O'Keeffe and Stieglitz supported an art that would be defined by its Americanness, a quality associated in their day with provincialism. Things were happening fast in the opening decades of the twentieth century, and we should have the story straight.

I

When Virginia Woolf flatly affirmed that "on or about December 1910 human character changed," she was alluding to the shock of the first Post-Impressionist exhibit in London. It included works by Manet, van Gogh, Cézanne, Gauguin, Redon, and many others. Yet this shock was only the beginning. Between 1905 and 1930 and barely interrupted by the events of World War I, a surge of experiment carried painting in France, Germany, Russia, Holland, and Italy up to and sometimes across the threshold of abstract art. This radical combination of primitivism and Futurism in plastic form gathered force early in the century while American Impressionist painters were having their great period of success and while the Ash Can School of early social realism was organizing independent shows as "the Eight" (1908, 1910). In a period still characterized by the sinuosities of Art Nouveau style and by the semicaricaturized ideal of the Gibson girl, the United States turned out to be surprisingly responsive to the great wave of European modernism—provided it remained European.

For the 1913 Armory Show had an even greater impact on New York than the 1910 Post-Impressionist exhibit had had on London. Enthusiasts have claimed that the Armory Show opened up America to European innovations the way Commodore Perry opened up Japan to trade with the West. Two-thirds of the sixteen hundred works were American, but the European rooms drew the crowds, the press, and the hecklers. In spite of many mocking reviews and cartoons, the show had a remarkable artistic, commercial, and fashion success. New galleries offering European art opened in New York, and the style of Cubism, Fauvism, primitivism, Expressionism, and abstraction began to infiltrate the art schools. When Joseph Albers wrote catalog copy for a group show at the Addison Gallery in 1937, he was repeating a doctrine that had been welcomed since 1913. "Abstract Art is the purest art; it strives more intensely toward the spiritual. Abstract Art is Art in its beginning and is the Art of the Future."

The man who had done more than anyone to prepare the way for the Armory Show and might have been expected to welcome it called it instead "a circus" and played only a reluctant role on the organizing committee. Stieglitz realized that his small, tastefully arranged gallery offerings of new European artists were being engulfed in one of the earliest blockbuster shows. How is it, then, that in looking back on the years that followed, O'Keeffe did not refer to European tendencies but used the slightly amused expression, "the Great American Thing"? The answer will lead us in several directions.

Stieglitz's Little Galleries of the Photo-Secession at 291 Fifth Avenue, founded in 1905, served virtually as a cover for other activities. He maintained a gathering place for artists and patrons, a major art publication called *Camera Work,* a growing concern with painting, and the strong sense of a group with a leader and a high mission. Within a short time, the gallery became famous enough to be known simply as 291.

By 1910, Stieglitz had won his campaign to establish pictorial photography, photographs that imitated the motifs and the formal arrangements of traditional European painting, as an art worthy of recognition by museums. But at the time of this first triumph, he was already in hot pursuit of other causes—primarily in Europe. He came back to New York in 1911 in the full glow of one of his enthusiasms.

> I felt the way Tannhäuser must have felt when he returned from Venusberg and lost his patience listening to his colleagues theorizing about love. There is certainly no art in America today, what is more, there is as yet no genuine love for it. Possibly Americans have no genuine love for anything. But I am not hopeless. In fact I am quite the contrary.
>
> *(Letter to Sadakichi Hartmann, December 1911)*

The last two sentences reveal his plan. The shows at 291 of Cézanne, Picasso, Braque, and African art were the first of their kind in the United States. The critics, the public, and artists responded passionately, if not always favorably, to these revolutionary exhibits. So much so that by May 1912, Stieglitz could take quite a different stance. "Isn't my work for the cause about finished?" he wrote to Heinrich Kuehn. Stieglitz was exaggerating, as usual, but he had reason to think that the Armory Show that would open the next year would merely be following his lead. This second triumph led him to correct his course again—not by going to Europe for new candidates but by affirming America. The constant convert first mounted an exhibit of his own "straight"—that is, nonpictorial—photographs to run during the Armory Show and then gave unwavering support and attention to his American artists.

In 1917, in large part because of the war, Stieglitz lost everything—his headquarters, his gallery, *Camera Work,* and the new avant-garde review *291.* It would be years before he found another place to call his own. But just before the catastrophe, as if by some compensating mechanism or benevolent providence, two young artists entered Stieglitz's life and lifted him professionally and emotionally into a new orbit. A twenty-six-year-old New Yorker, Paul Strand, began to produce strongly rhythmic photographs that renewed Stieglitz's dedication to photography as an independent artistic activity. And a twenty-eight-year-old Wisconsin farmer's daughter, from her teaching posts in South Carolina and then Texas, sent to New York works that vindicated Stieglitz's new Americanist cause. Georgia O'Keeffe would soon become his inspiration and his competition. The Spirit of 291 did not die; it found a new direction. Four years after Stieglitz closed the two famous rooms on Fifth Avenue with O'Keeffe's small first show of drawings and watercolors, he began at the Anderson Galleries a series of exhibits of a group that was to become almost a family. Demuth, Dove, Marin, and Hartley were all Americans. Now approaching sixty, Stieglitz placed his own work and that of his publically proclaimed model, consort, and prospective wife at the center of his project.

1921. For the first time in eight years, Stieglitz exhibited his own photographs, forty-five of them forming a section entitled "A Woman." O'Keeffe posed both primly attired (as herself) and stark naked (always headless), sometimes in front of her own strikingly abstract pictures. The photographs spoke most clearly in the way they fused the language of design with the language of eroticism.

1923. "Alfred Stieglitz Presents One Hundred Pictures: Oils, Watercolors, Pastels, Drawings, by Georgia O'Keeffe, American." Swirling, bursting abstractions hung beside closely seen still lifes of fruit and leaves. In the accompanying pamphlet, Hartley called her work "volcanic"—implying powerful sexuality. Her own statement sounded a note of resolute independence. The critic for the *New York Herald,* Henry McBride, who would soon become a good friend, praised her as "unafraid."

That spring, Stieglitz exhibited more than one hundred of his own works, including *Music: A Sequence of Ten Cloud Photographs* and a large number of portraits.

1924. Stieglitz and O'Keeffe's only joint exhibit combined sixty-one four-by-five-inch cloud photographs with fifty-one mostly figurative paintings, many of them very large. The implied equality of photographs and paintings generally persuaded the critics and led to a number of purchases.

1925. "Seven Americans: 159 Paintings, Photographs & Things Recent & Never Before Publicly Shown" mixed the media even more resolutely than the previous show. Two photographers (Stieglitz and Strand) consorted on equal terms with five painters (Marin, Dove, Hartley, Demuth, and O'Keeffe). It was the largest exhibit Stieglitz ever mounted. By endorsing photography as an art and by certifying the acceptance of his protégée O'Keeffe as the unchallenged peer of the men, it also marked the apogee of his career as artist and impresario.

Still hard at work, he wrote to Sherwood Anderson, "I feel I am still needed on the bridge." He did work on after 1925 in New York and at Lake George, if not quite on the bridge. But the spirit of 291 made its most important contributions between 1921 and 1925, after it had lost its headquarters and twenty years after its founding. How can we explain this vigorous survival during a period of rapid social and cultural change?

Stieglitz's initial project of leading a group toward the religion of art had little originality other than its association with the comparatively new medium of photography. The value he attached to purity of means and to constant experiment, and his ostentatious refusal to yield an inch to commercialism had their roots in the European doctrine of art for art's sake and in Symbolism. Maeterlinck, Bergson, and Kandinsky had impressed him deeply with their writings on the spiritual. Why, then, did Picabia, the unofficial spokesman for the most rebellious faction of the European avant-garde during the Armory Show, declare that nothing in Europe could compare with what Stieglitz was doing in New York?

I believe that what impressed Picabia was Stieglitz's extroversion, the perpetual group discussions that spilled over into daily roundtable lunches at a nearby restaurant. Stieglitz had hit upon the awkward yet sturdy counterinstitution called 291—clubhouse, chapel, laboratory, and salon, as it was variously called—because of his compulsive need to collaborate. Stielitz lived and worked in public. The impresario in him sometimes overwhelmed the artist. It was Edward Steichen, fifteen years his junior, who conceived of, designed, and provided the early contents of *Camera Work*. Steichen also promoted the idea of Little Galleries of the Photo-Secession in 1905 and discovered space for it in the studio he was vacating at 291 Fifth Avenue. In the following decades, Stieglitz worked closely with a whole contingent of artists and writers, principally with Paul Haviland, Marius de Zayas, and Paul Strand.

But the O'Keeffe-Stieglitz collaboration appeared to overshadow and outlast all the others. The famous couples of art offer us few useful precedents or comparison for this prickly union. The extramarital literary and domestic union between George Eliot and George Henry Lewes brought them closer and for longer than this American couple. Robert and Sonia Delaunay reinforced each other's experimental painting and for a time headed an informal household of poets and artists. But the dynamics of artistic life in London and Paris differed widely from those in New York. We marvel at O'Keeffe's relation to Stieglitz, almost twenty-five years her senior, because she resisted submission. In maintaining her personal and artistic independence, she also gave impetus to his work. Their principal collaboration took place during the extended sittings for *Georgia O'Keeffe: A Portrait.* For over a decade, she increasingly posed herself for Stieglitz's voracious camera eye.

I am prepared to concede that there is little new under the sun. Yet I recognize something unique in the ten-year working union of O'Keeffe and Stieglitz. In the most intimate poses of "A Woman"—some images in that exhaustive exploration reduce her to a direct frontal view of heavily furred pudenda—she never loses her dignity as a human being. When the time came in 1927 for her to pay public tribute to Stieglitz, she painted his name into the New York skyline of *Radiator Building—Night, New York.* It is not a neon sign, as some have suggested; an oblong ruby-colored emanation reveals his name hovering below a single vivid star. Such a tiny point of light punctuates many of her compositions, figurative and abstract, and marks an intersection between form and meaning. O'Keeffe and Stieglitz acknowledged each other artistically in powerful ways.

The sexual excitement that obviously drew them together at the start deserves recognition primarily because the intimacy it provoked modified their artistic development, separately and together. The electric current around them in New York and at Lake George was generated by a dynamic of strong differences. Beyond contrasts in age, sex, and culture, Stieglitz's gregariousness and exhibitionism sometimes grated on O'Keeffe's need for privacy. One of her descriptions of Stieglitz conveys the tensions among which they lived together and, for a surprisingly long period, worked together. "His power to destroy was as destructive as his power to build— the extremes went together. I have experienced both and survived, but I think I only crossed him when I had to—to survive" (O'Keeffe, introduction, *Georgia O'Keeffe: A Portrait by Alfred Stieglitz*).

II

In the 1990s, some museums began to rehang their twentieth-century collections, interspersing paintings, photographs, and graphic work. I wonder if in such an integrated gallery a sensitive eye, yet an eye unfamiliar with the historical background and ignoring the labels, would spot a connection between O'Keeffe's and Stieglitz's works. Many other loops and links in modern art, like the upended picture plane, the Cubist grid, and biomorphic forms, would probably strike that eye first. Yet I believe there is a fruitful line of inquiry here. Let us try to look at several works without necessarily following prior art-historical promptings.

The title of Stieglitz's familiar photograph *The Steerage* (1907) implies a document that comments on social class and economic condition. Its depiction of respectable poverty in shawls and shirts soon yields, however, to juxtaposed diagonals with circular shapes at key points and to dramatic contrasts of light and dark. An even more defiant combination of content and composition strikes us in O'Keeffe's painting *Black Abstraction* (1927). The near-photographic outline of thigh and calf confounds the title and then reveals an ominously black concentrically circular pattern overflowing the frame. The bright dot functions as an almost ironic node to pin together the two parts—figurative and abstract, photographic and painterly. The graceful line of what I read as an allusion to O'Keeffe's own body photographed by Stieglitz achieves secure coexistence with the pulsing target shape like a dark halation trying to engulf the leg.

The above description of *The Steerage* does not conflict with Stieglitz's account of how he found and caught "shapes related to each other" as well as a view of "the common people." But my interpretation of *Black Abstraction* departs from O'Keeffe's explanation of the painting as images of a skylight, and arm motions in a dark room occurring just prior to anesthesia for an operation. Whatever the genesis of the painting, I see its contrasting elements as a symbolic double portrait of herself and Stieglitz. Her own words reinforce that interpretation. Soon after writing the lines quoted at the end of the previous section, O'Keeffe went on to write two sentences that illuminate the menace and the exaltation reconciled in *Black Abstraction*. She was still talking about Stieglitz. "There was a constant grinding like the ocean. It was as if something hot, dark, and destructive was hitched to the highest, brightest star."

In *Black Abstraction,* O'Keeffe alludes to the *Thighs and Buttocks* series (1923) that forms a little-known segment of *A Portrait*. The photographs vary an *a tergo* motif that Stieglitz repeated with greater insistence in the 1932 *Buttocks and Thighs* series. Shot close-up and severely framed to exclude head and extremities, these rear-view photographs represent an ambiguous mix of naughtiness and abstraction. In the elegant composition *Line and Curve* (1928), painted the year after *Black Abstraction,* O'Keeffe acknowledged the abstraction and rejected the naughtiness of the *Thighs and Buttocks* photographs even though she had been and would again be a willing party to them. Pictorial evidence tells us something about the width of the gap between her life as a model and her life as an artist.

What is the significance of the fact that, with limited exceptions, the human figure disappeared from their pictures? It happened for O'Keeffe after the 1917 *Nude Series* of watercolors. For Stieglitz, except for the portraits, it happened after *The Steerage*. The bulk of their work depicted landscape, cityscape, and still-life motifs all tending strongly in the direction of pure form and abstraction. Even animals are excluded except in the inanimate form of bones. More than context or subject, formal composition offers the most revealing way in which to compare and group their works.

When contemplated side by side, O'Keeffe's handsome *Madison Avenue (White Abstraction)* (1926) and Stieglitz's *Spiritual America* (1923) seem to acknowledge each other's tonal nuances, visual geometry, and elusive-allusive titles. I find no evidence that O'Keeffe was thinking about the Stieglitz composition when she painted hers. But once made, the association abides. Even more starkly than *The Steerage, Spiritual America* presents a clearly etched linear geometry contrasting with subtle nuances of texture and shadow. No other title of Stieglitz's insists so emphatically on the symbolic interpretation of a close-up. We are approaching the blurred universe of Antonioni's *Blow-up,* in which proximity brings not recognition but disorientation. Does the title imply that the sturdy white horse Stieglitz referred to as a gelding and whose privates he shows us as carefully framed as O'Keeffe's stands for the deprived state of artistic sensibility in the United States? What does it mean that the horse is unhitched and the traces attached above the breaching to the hip straps? There's an obscure joke or curse in the framing and naming here that recalls works by Picabia and Man Ray.

Considered without its full title, O'Keeffe's *White Abstraction* approaches the starkness of a Malevich. With "Madison Avenue" pinned on, it tempts one to look for witty realism, like Mondrian's *Broadway Boogie Woogie.* But I believe O'Keeffe was simply identifying the figurative origin of the formal composition. And then we find the pattern or remember it portrayed in *New York, Night* (1928–1929). Starting from the dark mosaic of cityscape with its partially masked diagonal, white rose window, and bright pagoda, she has transfigured the colors, eliminated the massive and detailed signs of city life, and retained only the major stress lines and the round nodal point displaced downward. This pair of paintings shows us one of the clearest versions of her bifocal vision. She could paint both ways, abstract and figurative, convincingly.

On one rare occasion when O'Keeffe decided to leave her vegetarian world and to paint an animal, she posed and framed the poor creature more radically than Stieglitz had done with her body. I doubt that *Cow* (1922), if found unidentified in an attic, would be attributed to O'Keeffe. Dove seems more likely as the creator of this strange emblem of the bovine, bellowing at the moon or gagging on its immense tongue. On first encounter, it provokes a double take. Then one discovers the magnificent eye, schematic and terrified, and the black snoutlike shape turning into a purely formal element on the green ground. *Cow* is one of O'Keeffe's most impressive and puzzling paintings.

At this juncture, Stieglitz had just begun photographing clouds. Many European and English painters and photographers had preceded him. Stieglitz presented these works simultaneously as straightforward documentary images of nature, as lyric expressions of personal states of feeling, and as formal compositions as controlled as any painting. Since there was nothing candid or spontaneous about the photographs, the first claim and the last stand up best. Any expression of emotions has to be interpreted not as momentary and impetuous but as an aesthetic attitude built up toward natural forms over a long period of time. Cumulatively, Stieglitz's several cloud series achieve a unity in variety that the many images of the O'Keeffe portrait achieve only intermittently.

It was an intense awareness of formal relations in their pictures that first gave O'Keeffe and Stieglitz the confidence to work alone on the frontier of their respective arts and then brought them together as associates. If it is possible to identify a common element of design in O'Keeffe's *Evening Star* series (1916–1917), I would attribute it in part to European influences and in part to a widely recognized system of teaching design in the United States. When O'Keeffe referred to "the idea of filling space in a beautiful way," she was repeating principles identified with Japanese *notan*. She had heard about these "darks and lights in harmonic relation" directly from Arthur Wesley Dow at Columbia Teachers College and from one of his students in Virginia. Both O'Keeffe and Stieglitz could read the six chapters on *notan* in Dow's hugely successful book, *Composition: A Series of Exercises in Art Structure* (1899; revised 1913). Dow praised the elements of composition in *notan* by emphasizing their ability to create visual music. Stieglitz called the earliest series of cloud photographs *Music*. O'Keeffe used the same title for a set of ropelike pink-and-blue abstractions in 1919. Whatever the source of their devotion to formal design in their pictures, during the crucial years of their association, Stieglitz and O'Keeffe sometimes worked as closely together as mountain climbers or trapeze artists.

III

For over a decade the founding couple of American art collaborated in a stubborn effort to hold out against invasion from abroad and to keep Amer-

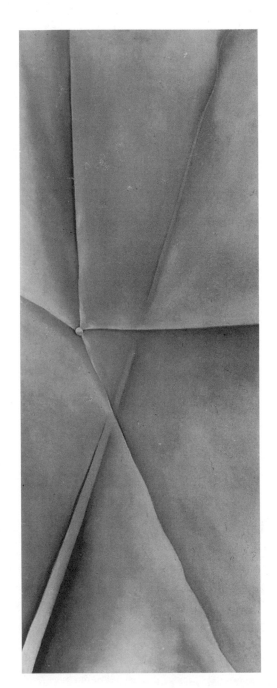

Georgia O'Keeffe,
*White Abstraction
(Madison Avenue),*
1926, oil on
canvas, 35½ × 12
in. Museum of
Fine Arts, St.
Petersburg,
Florida.

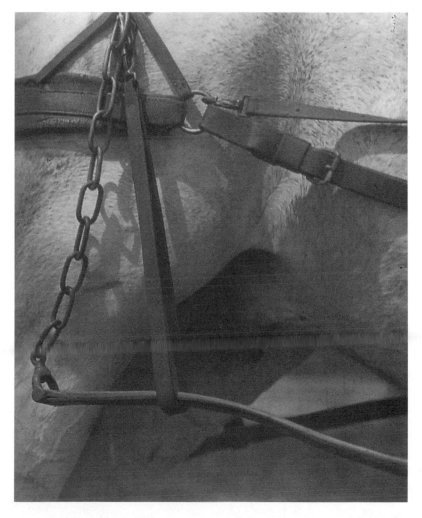

Alfred Stieglitz, *Spiritual America,* 1923, gelatin silver print, 4½ × 3½ in. The J. Paul Getty Museum, Los Angeles.

ican art safe for Americans. In first welcoming and then resisting Post-Impressionism, Fauvism, Cubism, Expressionism, and Futurism, Stieglitz and O'Keeffe were maintaining the position stated by Stieglitz in a letter to Steichen. "[Despite the] Ballyhoo at the Armory, 291 is still the stormcenter." It sounds like a fit of petulant jealousy, but the claim had merit. Even though the 291 gallery folded four years later, the spirit lived on in a series of chauvinistic exhibits at the Anderson Galleries. The brief autobiographical note for Stieglitz's 1921 show of his own new works, including "A Woman," opened with two defiant sentences. "I was born in Hoboken. I am an American." The announcement for the 1923 exhibit of one hundred pictures identified the artist as "Georgia O'Keeffe, American." When the whole 291 group showed their work together in 1925, the event was publicized a little belligerently as "Seven Americans." In 1929, Stieglitz finally found a tiny space in which to work and talk and show a few things. He named it An American Place. What O'Keeffe named "the Great American Thing" gradually took shape in the environs of a New York collaborative enterprise that lost its space and kept its spirit.

The history of American literature generally accepts the Concord Transcendentalists as the first significant literary movement or school to assemble a set of talents and gifted writers and to declare full independence from European models. Emerson's early addresses and essays read like manifestos of the movement, particularly "The American Scholar" and "Self-Reliance." After the first phase, promoting pictorial photography, and the second phase, championing European avant-garde art, Stieglitz's 291 entered a third period, in which it fulfilled in the arts much the same function as that of the Transcendentalists in literature. Stieglitz combined a stirring message of artistic independence with a vague spirituality that never quite became a religion. His ideas in many ways resembled those of Emerson and influenced not only artists' attitude toward their art but also impressed successful writers about America like Sherwood Anderson, Waldo Frank, Paul Rosenfeld, and Lewis Mumford.

The most surprising element of the comparison between the Transcendentalists and the later years of 291 lies not in the general similarity of circumstances and ideas but in the association of two specific incidents. Among the few people to whom Walt Whitman sent the first slender 1855 edition of *Leaves of Grass* was Emerson. Not many recipients reviewed the book or responded to the author. Emerson wrote back a historic letter to the boldly American poet and warmly praised his undertaking. From Concord, the dean of Transcendentalists and celebrated platform lecturer sent this message to the unknown thirty-six-year-old poet. "I greet you at the beginning of a great career." It constitutes one of the most stunning acts of recognition in the history of our literature.

In the history of American art, the words Stieglitz said in 1916 to Anita Pollitzer on first looking into O'Keeffe's drawings stand as the approximate equivalent of Emerson's greeting to Whitman. "Finally a woman on paper." Stieglitz welcomed O'Keeffe as the unspoiled voice of America, a child of the West, a kind of savior whose very sex would help rescue art from the embrace of European influences and doctrines. The cosmopolitan Stieglitz converted to an almost ethnic Americanism in great part because of O'Keeffe's nonfigurative compositions. They hid their many sources (including European) as effectively as Whitman hid his. But whereas the Emerson-Whitman encounter led to no further exchanges, the Stieglitz-O'Keeffe encounter detonated a burst of artistic activity on both their parts. As a result of their union of equals for over a decade, we will do well to regard them twice—separately and together.

REFERENCES

Beyond the vast bibliography on O'Keeffe and Stieglitz, a few recent publications have helped me greatly in writing this essay:

Bram Dijkstra, "America and Georgia O'Keeffe," in *Georgia O'Keeffe: The New York Years* (New York: Calloway/Knopf, 1991); Benita Eisler, *O'Keeffe and Stieglitz: An American Romance* (New York: Doubleday, 1991); Sarah Greenough and Juan Hamilton, *Alfred Stieglitz: Photographs and Writings* (Washington, D.C.: National Gallery of Art, 1983); Sara Whitaker Peters, *Becoming O'Keeffe: The Early Years* (New York: Abbeville 1991).

Benita Eisler, Merry Foresta, and Phillip Timbert contributed valuable comments and criticism.

CANDOR AND
PERVERSION: MAN RAY

MAN RAY HAD connections. He moved as easily from one social group to another as from one country to another. He seemed to be always on familiar ground. When this short, determined American arrived in Paris in 1921 at the age of thirty, he brought with him an old theatrical trunk full of works of art. He also had with him a few hundred borrowed dollars, no knowledge of the language, and hopes that a French friend he had known for five years in New York would meet the boat train. The friend, Marcel Duchamp, was waiting on the platform at the Gare Saint-Lazare and took him that afternoon to the Café Certa in a dusky glassed-in *galerie* near the Opéra. The Dada group of moonlighting medical students and writers met there every afternoon, dressed like Man Ray himself in suit, tie, and fedora. It was 22 July, a date he later changed to Bastille Day. At the Certa, André Breton, Louis Aragon, Philippe Soupault, Paul and Gala Eluard, Jacques Rigaut, and Theodore Fraenkel welcomed Duchamp's friend more with gestures than with words. Age meant a great deal to this exuberant band. Breton, the oldest at twenty-five, was nine years younger than Duchamp and five years younger than Man Ray. The Dadaists were eager to add to their number an experienced American who had found his way in New York to an artistic dissidence and extremism close to their own. Always independent, more protected than hindered by being an outsider, Man Ray stayed with the French group through the next twenty years of unruliness and adventure.

To the young men in the café Certa, the summer of 1921 was the doldrums. In 1919, Breton, Soupault, and Aragon had launched an antiart review, ironically named *Littérature,* and devoted themselves to automatic writing and discovering the secret street life of Paris. In January 1920, they invited to Paris from Zurich the Romanian Dada poet and notorious public agitator Tristan Tzara. For two seasons, the self-constituted demolition squad outraged or entertained the art world and themselves with a series of manifestos, public meetings, and violent demonstrations. In May 1921, they threw their full support behind Max Ernst's first Paris exhibit of collages; to much of the French press, a German artist was still *un sale boche.* Ten days later in a crowded concert hall and with full judicial robes and procedures, Breton staged a mock trial of the eminent author Maurice Barrès.

But such a trial raised awkward problems. If Dada stood for the flaunting of all constraints and for total freedom, in the name of what law could anyone accuse anyone else of an infraction? By the autumn that followed Man Ray's arrival, the raucous yet fragile, Dada movement had fallen apart into three clusters around Tzara, Breton, and Francis Picabia. Breton was himself virtually put on trial for proposing a plan as serious as a huge international congress to consider the state of European culture. It took three years to construct out of the ruins of Dada a new enterprise that would be called Surrealism.

During the interval, which was both slack and tense for the Dadaist-Surrealist group, Man Ray simply followed the connections he found within his reach. Before he had unpacked the works in his trunk, his new friends proposed that he provide the first exhibit at the Soupaults' Librairie Six gallery. Through Picabia's first wife, Man Ray met the fashion designer Paul Poiret and began taking commercial photographs for him. By the time of his December opening, May Ray had started the portrait photography that brought him growing celebrity and a stream of famous sitters—French, American, English, and Irish. He had also begun learning French from Kiki, the popular artists' model and Montparnasse figure who became his mistress for eight years.

In the catalog of the Librairie Six show, the Dadaists rivaled one another in their fabulous descriptions of Man Ray as a gum-chewing millionaire turned artist who had come to Paris to bring a new poetic springtime. Among the densely packed balloons at the opening, Man Ray met the fifty-five-year-old composer Erik Satie. They went out to warm up with a grog in a café. Coming back, Satie helped Man Ray buy a flatiron and tacks for the self-defeating *Cadeau* he constructed on the spot and added to the items on exhibit. Also at that opening, Man Ray's guest Matthew Josephson met Louis Aragon and through him the rest of the Dadaists. Because he could speak reasonably fluent French, Josephson became the only other American who participated in the group's discussions and celebrations. Also at this time, Tzara became enthusiastic about Man Ray's cameraless rayographs. The Romanian contributed the influential preface to the album in which the first rayographs were published, *Les Champs délicieux* (1922). (Two years earlier, Breton and Soupault had called their automatic writings *Les Champs magnétiques.*) When Breton gave a talk in November 1922 at the Atheneum in Barcelona on the state of the arts in France, he devoted as much time to Man Ray as to Duchamp and Picasso. Within a short while, living what he called a double life between commercial photography and art, Man Ray had arrived. His sense of humor and his genius inspired André Thirion to write the most succinct of all biographies: "Man Ray had an important position in Montparnasse because of his inexhaustible inventiveness, his friendliness, and the new use he made of the camera. He dazzled us all with his cars. And the girls he went out with were beautiful."[1]

NEITHER WEALTH NOR social standing gave Man Ray the connections that opened his way to success in Paris. He had earned them during twelve hard years as a fledgling artist in New York. While he was steadily employed as a draftsman for a map publisher, his own work recapitulated the stages of Western art up to the 1913 Armory Show. That huge display of the latest European work seemed made to order for this young American who had chosen art as his calling. At twenty-two, already a habitué of Stieglitz's 291 gallery of photography and painting, he left his Jewish family and moved to a house in rural New Jersey. He took a new name, married a young Belgian woman with a child by a previous husband, and found a set of new friends among writers, artists, and anarchists.

Everything pointed to Man Ray's independence and resolute purpose. Through Stieglitz, through his well-read wife, Donna, and through his new friend Marcel Duchamp, Man Ray educated himself spottily in literature, art history, and philosophy. In *Self Portrait,* he states that in 1913 or 1914 Donna produced out of a crate of books works by Baudelaire, Mallarmé, Rimbaud, Lautréamont, and Apollinaire and translated them for him. His chronology may waver a bit, but there is no denying that he picked up an impressive French background without knowing the language. The three single-issue avant-garde reviews he published, the "Ridgefield Gazook" (1915), *TNT* (1919), and *New York Dada* (1921, with Duchamp), display his own spirited originality and anarchist humor more than they reveal the influence of reviews from Zurich and Paris. Appropriately, Duchamp took the ferry from Manhattan to look up Man Ray in New Jersey, not vice versa. By the time Man Ray finished *Revolving Doors* in 1917, he had assimilated the formal innovations of Cubism and Futurism, of machine art, abstraction, and collage. He was working on his own. "I couldn't go back; I was finding myself."[2]

Displayed with all their provoking titles as the centerpiece of his third one-man show at the Daniel Gallery in 1919, *Revolving Doors* remained renderings on paper and were never translated into the series of paintings he had once planned. But they represented Man Ray's state of mind at that time better than the large-scale painting *The Rope Dancer accompanies Herself with Her Shadows*. The colored cutouts of *Revolving Doors* developed a brand of geometric-anthropomorphic fantasy that we can associate either with nineteenth-century caricaturists like John Tenniel and Grandville or with modern makers of the whimsical grotesque like Paul Klee and Max Ernst. Aerographs and photographs, which he conceived of not as mere records but as independent works, would soon give him further opportunities to distance himself from traditional easel painting.

Two photographs of 1920 have particular significance. One shows a large lumpy object covered with a rug or heavy matting and firmly tied with rope. Its title, *The Enigma of Isidore Ducasse*, underlines the uncertain identity of the shape, which could be vaguely human, or animal, or mechanical. The famous simile from Lautréamont's *Les Chants de Maldoror*, "lovely as the fortuitous encounter on a dissecting table of a sewing machine and an umbrella" *(chant sixième)*, has led many observers to see in the round projections the form of a sewing machine. In any case, Man Ray assembled the amorphous object in his New York studio, photographed it, disassembled it, and kept only the print for exhibition. The cropping and title of another photograph, *Dust Raising*, exploit ambiguity in a different fashion. En route to identifying the dust-covered shape as Duchamp's *The Large Glass (The Bride Stripped Bare by Her Bachelors, Even)*, we respond to various cues that suggest both landscape (oblique perspective, straight lines like roads) and cloudscape (clumps of dust in the foreground). The photograph masks its subject more than it displays it. In both cases, since the original assemblage or object has ceded its existence to the photographic image, we adopt an aesthetic attitude toward the photograph. These are not identification pictures, but works of art in themselves.

Because of the presence of these two photographs in his luggage, along with several paintings, Man Ray arrived in Paris as an involuntary smuggler. He relates in some detail the misleading explanations he gave the customs inspector about the strange objects in his trunk. The works, however, cleared the severe inspection of not only the French customs service but also that of Breton and the Dadaists. They had strict regulations, based in part on the attitudes of Rimbaud and Lautréamont and, more recently, Jacques Vaché, who "kicked any work of art away from him with his foot." The Dadaists excluded from their universe art for art's sake. According to Breton, Dada works had to "lead somewhere"—to a revision of moral and aesthetic values, to a new spark of lucidity, even to a nihilistic "nothing."[3] Max Ernst's collages passed inspection as antipainting, and in the catalog preface to Ernst's first Paris show in 1921, Breton referred in his first sentence to the moral blow administered to painting and literature respectively by photography and automatic writing. Man Ray's collection passed Dada muster for similar reasons. Objects and photographs figured prominently among his works; few were easel paintings. He often chose enigmatic and humorous titles. These factors prompted the Dadaists to accept Man Ray as a fellow antiartist who had liberated himself from traditional art.

Despite appearances, Man Ray introduced into the Dada movement works that obliquely or covertly incorporated principles of design and form, color and line long associated with Western art. The sackcloth texture, diagonal trussing, and looming relation between figure and ground in *The Enigma of Isidore Ducasse* are carefully arranged within a conventional frame to suggest, precisely, the fetishism of an undivulged work of art. *Dust Raising* does not mock the category of "art"; rather, it suggests the buildup on Duchamp's work-in-progress of a special kind of reverse patina or aura, not a rich layer of color but a sedimentation that evokes burial and archaeological rediscovery. Furthermore, Man Ray's prints seem to have convinced the Dada group almost overnight that the unpredictable results he obtained from a partially mechanical process were particularly appropriate to their antiart stance in *Littérature* and later in *La Révolution surréaliste.*

Late in life, Man Ray made a statement that applies to his whole career: "Everything is art. I don't discuss these things anymore. All this anti-art business is nonsense. They're all doing it. If we must have a word for it, let's call it Art."[4]

THE QUIET, CONTRABAND artist who supplied Dada and Surrealism with art in the form of photography and displaced objects like *Cadeau* had three interchangeable garments in his wardrobe: the garments of mystery, humor, and the erotic. He sometimes wore all three at once. "Mystery—this was the key word close to my heart and mind," he said.[5] His objects were "designed to amuse, bewilder, annoy." Many of his self-portraits served a similar function of mocking provocation. One of them shows the artist, with only a bathrobe to cover his nakedness, standing next to a bed and close to a nude photograph (could it be a mirror?) of the beautiful Lee Miller on the door beside him. Sensuous floral wallpaper fills the rest of the composition. In another self-portrait, he lounges in double-breasted suit and tie, smoking a cigarette, in what is obviously a lighting setup for dress models. He called it *Fashion Photograph*.

This tendency toward spoof declared itself very early in Man Ray's freewheeling use of language. The one irrepressible number of the "Ridgefield Gazook" in 1915 reveled in puerile puns and portmanteau formations: "How to make tender buttons itch"; "Soshall science"; "Art Motes." This low level of wordplay became somewhat more subtle after he met Picabia and especially Duchamp, whose style of sophisticated verbal invention increasingly displaced the plastic components of his antiart objects. Man Ray's titles, however, do not reliably endow his works with undertones of mystery, as Magritte's and de Chirico's titles do, or with innuendos of eroticism and humor, as Duchamp's do. Only *Le Violon d'Ingres* sets off an inexhaustible series of associations that combines mystery, humor, and the erotic. I cannot help wondering which (presumably French) collaborator helped him find the multiple visual-aural pun that rhymes violin shape with woman's torso, with the French expression for hobby, with a famous composition by Ingres—and more. Does the title of this photograph that apes a painted nude tell us that photography was only Man Ray's hobby? In any case, Man Ray never gave up on words. At the end of *Self Portrait*, he twice refers to reversing the Chinese proverb to produce the notion that one word is worth a thousand images. "In a life devoted to the graphic arts, I have felt more and more a desire to supplement my work with words."[6] He wrote those words in the book that represented that very supplement.

Man Ray's wardrobe was not his only resource. Another reason why he won a place for himself as an artist in several media is that he was handy—handy not so much with brushes and words as with things and devices. As a young boy, he built a soapbox cart that looked like a locomotive and devised a sheet-brass lamp shade with decorative perforations made on his mother's sewing machine. He excelled more in mechanical than in artistic drawing. Throughout his life, he never stopped selecting objects from his environment and displaying them with titles intended to generate a steady cultural-aesthetic current of the unexpected. One of his first creations in Paris was *L'Hôtel meublé*. The small wooden assemblage (a combination bookshelf/ floor plan/cabinet) crosses the seamy connotations of life in furnished rooms with a neat structure suggesting the niches and categories of the mind. One of his last objects, *Etoile de verre*, is a fragment of glass glued onto painted sandpaper *(papier de verre)* to make a dim pun and a striking facsimile of a

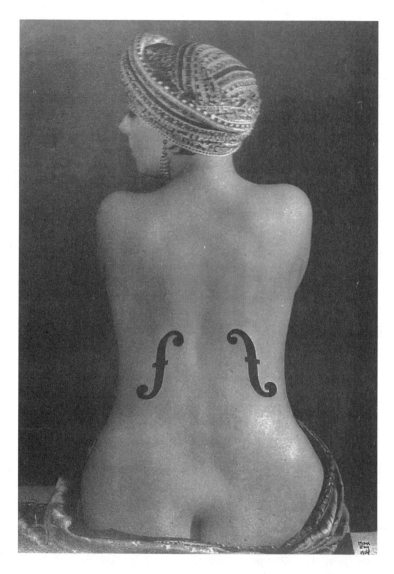

Man Ray, *Ingres' Violin (Le Violon d'Ingres)*, 1924, silver print, 9¹³⁄₁₆ × 7⅝ in. The J. Paul Getty Museum, Los Angeles.

seascape. This handyman worked steadily at his chosen tasks and achieved the rewards he deeply desired. The most ingenuous and unpretentious sentence he ever uttered describes his carving out a new life for himself in Hollywood during World War II: "Well, now I had everything again, a woman, a studio, a car"—a down-to-earth version of "A Jug of Wine, A Loaf of Bread,—and Thou," without the sentimentality.[7]

By the time Man Ray walked into the Café Certa in Paris, he had also found his pace. Here more than anywhere he revealed himself as a cultural and artistic crossbreed. His formative years in and around New York City gave him many of the characteristics of a young man in a hurry. Most of the early incidents in *Self Portrait* illustrate the rapidity with which Man Ray wanted to work through the stages of art-school training and reach the contemporary scene. By the end of his life, he perceived that swiftness arose out of long years of discipline, as in the case of the Chinese artist who spoke of the lifetime of practice required to draw one adequate dragon. "In painting, with skill and new techniques," he said, "I sought to keep up with the rapidity of thought, but the execution still lags behind the mind as it does behind perception."[8] To a large extent, Man Ray learned such patience and wisdom from his French friend in New York, the artist who retired from active painting before he was thirty. Duchamp's coolness and detachment left a deep mark on Man Ray. The word *leisure* keeps recurring in *Self Portrait* in an unself-conscious fashion. One of the few significant reasons he gives us for not devoting himself more to film had to do with the tension generated by its limited period of screening: "I prefer the permanent immobility of a static work which allows me to make my deductions at my leisure, without being distracted by attending circumstances."[9] Not unexpectedly, he projected this pace, this sense of being a spectator of life and art, even a certain laziness, onto the ethos of Paris.

> I'd go into hiding [during World War II], I thought, until I could return to my accustomed haunts: to the easy, leisurely life of Paris, where one could accomplish just as much and of a more satisfying nature—where individuality was still appreciated and work of a permanent quality gave the creator increasing prestige.[10]

He preferred to take his time. But he could also respond swiftly to commissions like Tzara's urgent request in July 1923 for a film to be used during "Soirée du coeur à barbe," or to unexpected situations like forgetting the lens when he went to photograph Matisse in the painter's studio. (He substituted a pair of eyeglasses.)

Man Ray worked at a steady, leisurely, almost lazy pace of invention that arose both from a certain detachment from his surroundings—always the American in a foreign culture—and from confidence in his materials—always the handyman and jack-of-all-trades.

MAN RAY CHOSE to live peacefully with two anomalies. He was an American living and pursuing a prominent career in a foreign country, and he was an artist who practiced two creative careers that were widely considered incompatible. The parallels between his situation and that of other historical figures apparently never occurred to him and have rarely occurred to his critics.

After becoming one of the most celebrated and enthusiastic supporters of the American Revolution through his pamphlets *Common Sense* and *The Crisis,* Thomas Paine carried his revolutionary zeal back to England. Two years later, his stinging reply in *The Rights of Man* to Burke's *Reflections on the Revolution in France* (1790) was condemned as seditious libel. Paine had already escaped to Paris. There, he participated in the French Revolution as an elected delegate to the National Convention and later to the Assembly, and as an appointed member of the Committee of Nine to frame a new constitution. Unable to speak French, imprisoned for ten months as an enemy alien (that is, of English birth) until James Monroe obtained his release as an American citizen, aging and sick from a malignant fever contracted in prison, Paine remained one of the few international figures who played a significant role in French revolutionary history. He had the courage to oppose on humanitarian grounds the death penalty for Louis XVI. In prison, he wrote the first part of *The Age of Reason,* a powerful deistic pamphlet that attacked the superstition and repression of revealed religion. Later, Paine wrote two more books of political criticism and theory. When he returned to the United States in 1802, he did not fare as well as Man Ray in 1940 in California. Paine's religious and economic iconoclasm exceeded the limits of the new democracy.

We tend to forget that during the crucial decade of the French Revolution, Paine was welcomed into the official assemblies of a new government seething with radical ideas about the transformation of society and everyday life. These bodies contained the intellectual ancestors of the young men who welcomed Man Ray to the Café Certà in 1921. Amid the excitement, both men protected their special status by remaining *bricoleurs* and inventors. Paine's schemes to design and promote iron bridges resemble Man Ray's discoveries in photography. Their lack of linguistic fluency as well as an incorrigibly independent, even "American" strain in their characters kept them—for a time at least—at a safe distance from the Parisian battles. It seems inevitable that, at the end of their careers, both men would fall from notoriety into comparative obscurity.

James McNeill Whistler provides a counterexample. His early drawing skills earned him a job in cartography, as later did Man Ray's. But having learned fluent French in Russia as a boy, the dandified and witty Whistler was at home immediately in France and in England. Working first in Paris, he made a name for himself at the Salon des Refusés in 1863 and appeared in a group portrait with Delacroix, Fantin-Latour, Baudelaire, and Manet—all before he was thirty. In London, he participated in the Pre-Raphaelite movement as independently as Man Ray collaborated with the Dadaists and Surrealists. But in almost every respect, Whistler's and Man Ray's approaches to their artistic calling differed. Whistler sought every opportunity for outrage, publicity, conflict. His fierce gregariousness and taste for adventure inevitably led him to courtroom disputes, scandal, and debts. Man Ray apparently got along with everyone—except a few envious Americans in Paris who thought he must be a fraud or a snob to know so many French artists. He systematically avoided politics, crowds, demonstrations, arguments. He was responsible with money, whereas Whistler was a spendthrift. They practiced two different ways of succeeding as an American abroad.

The revolutionary journalist John Reed represents a third way, based on near-total identification with a foreign cause. Three years older than Man Ray, he reached Russia at age thirty in 1917 and immediately wrote *Ten Days That Shook the World.* He approached closer to revolution than Paine, worked for the Soviet propaganda bureau, and welcomed appointment as Soviet consul in New York. (The United States turned down the arrangement.) Reed was buried in 1920 in the Kremlin. In his case, the man, in both his professional and personal life, was devoured by conversion to a virtually religious cause. Man Ray loved Paris deeply but kept his feet firmly planted on the ground of his career as an artist and photographer, serving no cause more limited or limiting than individual freedom. He was admitted directly into high-party councils of Dada and Surrealism, as Reed was welcomed by Soviet leaders. But Man Ray refused to be an idealogue and maintained a special status, in which he was not subject to party discipline and politics. Partly through his own temperament and his experience in New York, benefiting from the example of Duchamp as independent senior partner to everyone, Man Ray succeeded better than Paine, Whistler, and Reed in remaining patiently himself, an uninsistent American. He sustained the role through two of the most turbulent decades of artistic activity in the history of Paris. The fact that he was neither an intellectual nor middle-class probably protected him against the temptations of ideology and snobbery.

NEAR THE END of his life, in a series of interviews with Pierre Bourgeade, Man Ray pointed out in passing: "In my first film, *Etoile de mer (Star Fish,*

1928) there are no doors. Doors have disappeared. People disappear without going through doors because there aren't any."[11] Man Ray's memory failed him about the film, two scenes of which prominently feature a door. Yet the motif of a universe without boundaries, without compartments, remains significant. Duchamp, by building a mock-up of a two-way door in a tight corner of his Paris studio, proved that a door can be simultaneously open and shut. In his early writings especially, Breton speaks of leaving doors open so that people can come freely in and out of his life. Through out-of-focus shots and unfettered editing, Man Ray went a long way in *Etoile de mer* toward eliminating barriers. Nonalignment functioned from the beginning as a principle of his artistic conduct. He moved unrestrained among nationalities, social classes, artistic genres, and rival schools.

One aspect of this openness was his willingness to collaborate. A lot could be said about his prolonged collaboration with Duchamp, and about the works he produced with Tzara and Eluard. Reversing the usual order of events surrounding the French *livre d'art*, poets set down words to "illustrate" images that Man Ray had already created. Breton relied on him as house photographer for *La Révolution Surréaliste* and used him to illustrate his most important literary works, principally his novel *L'Amour fou* (1937). Man Ray's relations with Kiki, Lee Miller, Adrienne, and Juliet add colorful chapters to the history of the manifold form of collaboration known as "the artist and his model."

Yet his principal collaborations may have been with artists he never met in the flesh. In 1925, Breton had the aging poet Saint-Pol-Roux "Le Magnifique" visit Man Ray's studio for a portrait photograph. Some twenty-five years before, the poet, in his flamboyant early days, had been photographed in the Nadar studio. Man Ray cannot have lived very long as a photographer in Paris without coming up against the figure of Félix Tournachon. Under the name of Nadar, he drew caricatures, wrote journalistic pieces, developed the photographic portrait into a stunningly successful and subtle art form, and constructed his own balloon for aerial photography and publicity. Man Ray and his biographers never mention Nadar, but it is hard to believe that his blend of art, technology, and self-promotion did not play a role in Man Ray's career decision six months after he arrived in Paris: "I now turned all my attention to getting myself organized as a professional photographer."[12] His portrait photographs of famous persons, particularly in the twenties and thirties, practiced a combination of straightforwardness and sensitivity to the sitter's personality and vocation that lies close to Nadar's work. The miniature shots of the Surrealists pasted up as a chessboard refer obliquely to Nadar's Rogues' Gallery displays of painters and fashion models. The blurred nude photograph (probably of Kiki) that appears in the second issue of *La Révolution surréaliste* (1925) occupies an artistic space close to that of one of Nadar's rare nudes.[13] Nadar's model is traditionally identified as Christine Roux, the inspiration for Musette in Henri Murger's *Scènes de la vie de Bohème* (1845–1849). In both photographs, the model holds her arms over her head and reveals her shapely body in a pose reminiscent of Ingres's *La Source.*

Much more has been made of Man Ray's collaboration with Lautréamont. On several occasions, Man Ray stated that his first wife, Adon Lacroix, introduced him to *Les Chants de Maldoror* in 1914. Unless she had among her books a very rare early edition, it seems more likely that he encountered the tortured imagination of Lautréamont in 1919 in the pages of *Littérature* or in the following year in the edition published by La Sirène. In fact, 1920 is the date assigned to the unidentified wrapped object now known as *The Enigma of Isidore Ducasse;* Man Ray was still in New York.[14]

Man Ray's claims to have been marked by Lautréamont several years before the Dadaist-Surrealist group discovered him ring less true than his statements about the importance of his discovery of the Marquis de Sade. In his conversations with Bourgeade, Man Ray told how one of his neighbors in the Montparnasse building where he had his first studio, barely a year after his arrival in Paris, was the devoted Sade editor and expert Maurice Heine. Heine asked Man Ray to photograph the fragile fifty-foot roll of paper on both sides of which Sade had written *The 120 Days of Sodom* in prison. Intrigued, Man Ray investigated Sade's career more thoroughly than he had that of any other historical person. And he went on to read all of Sade's novels:

> above all *Aline and Valcour* which is in my opinion the most important because all political questions are treated in it with very little pornography. It's a bit boring to read, that's true, but I read it from beginning to end. In this book Sade talks already of a United States of Europe! He solved all the problems![15]

In 1940, Man Ray "waxed fervid and eloquent" about "his hero" to Henry Miller in Hollywood: "Sade represented complete and absolute liberty."[16]

Man Ray's respectful opinion of Sade's imaginary African country of Butua makes one wonder if he understood the language of *Aline and Valcour.* Butua's "incredible liberty" consists of the total, institutionalized subjugation of women to men's pleasure (female orgasm, considered dereliction of duty in servicing a man, merits the death penalty), absolute tyranny of the sultan, human sacrifice, and cannibalism. "Sade showed what you could do if you had power."[17]

Man Ray's blind enthusiasm when he talked about Sade disappears in the images he devoted to the writer-philosopher. Their subtlety points to a whole different circuit through which he could channel human fantasies about power and pleasure. The series of photographs and paintings, executed over a twenty-five-year period, turns on three primal scenes. In the earliest scene, later restated in the oil painting *Aline et Valcour,* an artist's articulated mannequin reclines in the foreground between a cone and a sphere. Out of the background looms a lovely (severed?) head of a blindfolded woman, her chin resting on a green book, the whole encased under a gleaming glass bell that stands on a bureau. From Sade's novel of systematic repression of everything except male pleasure, Man Ray distills a cryptic, almost lyric dream image. Only the faint decapitation motif suggests the carnage and algolagnia of Sade's narrative. The painting conveys the impression of a code, a rebus. The book is closed, as is the drawer. The woman's eyes cannot see. The wooden mannequin is only a replica of a human being. All communication seems blocked.

One assembles the cues of *Monument à D. A. F. de Sade* with greater reward. The folds of naked flesh are framed by the cutout of an inverted cross. It takes a moment to recognize that the soft folds belong to the buttocks of a person seen close-up from behind, with left cheek lifted slightly out of alignment. The superimposition of a rigidly ruled cross over delicate asymmetrical shadings from a particularly private part of the human body shouts with connotations: beauty, excrement, vulnerability, asininity, intimacy, sodomy, black magic, incongruity, blasphemy, and more. Here the simplicity and familiarity of the elements combined suggest that Man Ray was spoofing the myth of Sade as an author who attracts by corrupting and whose perversion some would equate with innocence. *Monument* remains one of Man Ray's most successful and witty compositions.

In 1938, he painted another striking work that identifies the marquis as its inspiration: *Imaginary Portrait of D. A. F. de Sade.* A massive masonry head (with red lips and one blue eye) bursts out of the semblance of a masonry body in the foreground and looks toward the Bastille, which is in flames in the background. In the middle ground, small figures lit by the fire enact scenes of struggle and defiance—or perhaps celebration. The great stone face missing one eye and labeled below in large capitals "S A D E" conveys a menacing authority as it contemplates the holocaust. The composition—a humanoid figure on the left imagining or witnessing a possibly frightful and enigmatic scene in the right background—recurs in *Aline et Valcour.* Paradoxically, the seemingly indestructible figure of stone decrees in the subscription painted on the canvas below that the "traces of my tomb shall disappear from off the face of the earth, as I hope my memory shall be wiped out in the minds of men"—the last sentence of Sade's will. Those words deeply impressed Man Ray, who seems to be implying the opposite result. As the stones of the Bastille were looted and reused in hundreds of other structures, Sade's teachings will "disappear" into the subconscious musings of mankind. Man Ray's response to Sade is troubling and more ambiguous in his images than in his words.

Man Ray described Maurice Heine, who devoted most of his life to rescuing and publishing Sade's work, as a sweet and gentle man. I read this description as an involuntary anti-Sadean self-portrait, another of his major genres. For Man Ray's favorite collaborator was himself. Among his self-portraits, there is a brief series worth lingering over. In 1937, Man Ray experimented with a variation on the rayograph, this time using a camera with the shutter open in the semidark. Sitting in front of it with a small flashlight, Man Ray "drew" in the air and thus onto the film. The white arabesques of movement between blobs of rest have a physical scale that corresponds to the reach of the arm of the blurred, yet recognizable, artist whose body fills the frame. We discern in the background works by Man Ray and other artists. In *Space Writings,* the photographer has recorded himself as an easel artist painting in framed space, a proper tribute of the photographer to the painter. It is almost a spectral portrait.

THE RAPID TEN-YEAR evolution of Man Ray's art in New York records his discovery of flatness, of the picture plane as reaffirmed by at least a half a century of European painting, culminating in Cubism. What happens in *Space Writings* replicates a tendency visible in many of his early works like *Dance, The Rope Dancer,* and *Revolving Doors.* By inscribing movement through an overlay of images, as suggested by Cubism, Futurism, and Duchamp's famous *Nude* in particular, Man Ray began to flatten out not only space but time, as well. The long exposure time that remains undeclared and unfelt in *Dust Raising* cannot be overlooked in *Space Writings.* A major segment of Man Ray's best work, encompassing both machine motifs and the human figure, studies movement or narrative crossed with a static freeze-frame image. He apparently never reproduced Etienne-Jules Marey's and Eadweard Muybridge's experiments with multiple cameras and motion study. But in works like *Revolving Doors* and *Space Writings,* he expressed a desire to test Lessing's law: The image describes; the word narrates. The format of *Revolving Doors*—images hinged to a vertical stand, permitting the viewer to flip through the plates easily and rapidly—suggests a narrative sequence. At the same time, each separate colored plate in the group forms a freestanding multiple overlay of elements that project the tracery of their possible permutations. A single well-chosen image encroaches on narrative time. As a photographer, Man Ray never lost a powerful sense of the *instan-*

tané, or snapshot that both arrests and affirms motion. Some of this quality was evident early on in the plates of *Revolving Doors.* The precisely drawn spiral that forms the vertical armature of *The Meeting* lays out around itself the space and time for the two caricatured male and female cutouts to turn and maneuver as on a carousel. Thirty years later, Man Ray followed similar principles in painting his other important series, *Shakespearean Equations.* Photographs taken in the Poincaré Institute of artificial objects constructed to illustrate mathematical formulas provided him with templates, which he varied and combined freely. By letting the "abstraction" reside in the mathematically generated models, Man Ray could first photograph and then paint their convenient concreteness. A mixture of playfulness and formalism propels *Shakespearean Equations* and—more successfully—*Revolving Doors.* Those images iron time flat and present it as a laminated series of stencils.

Man Ray remained a studio artist. Except for a few commissions (it was Tzara who dragged him to photograph Proust on his deathbed), he did not work as a journalistic or candid photographer. His late statement about his hybrid vocation rings true: "I paint what I cannot photograph, something from the imagination, or a dream, or a subconscious impulse. I photograph the things that I don't want to paint, things that are already in existence."[18] He never confined himself to bed like Proust with his manuscripts banked around him. But his life and work centered in the restricted city spaces he designed for himself in New York, Paris, and Los Angeles. After two years in rural New Jersey, he never again aspired to work *en plein air.* His location of choice was a personal downtown quarterdeck, or headquarters, where his handiness, his freedom, and his penchant for collaborations could find their mutual compatibility. Apparently, he never developed studio fever; his photography, his painting, and his three-dimensional constructions fed and foiled one another in ways that kept Man Ray constantly on the move artistically. He may have been right in considering himself lazy. But his laziness was shot through with an insatiable restlessness. "Man Ray has one fault. He never does the same thing twice."[19] No, Bourgeade was wrong. That's a description of Duchamp, the cat that walked alone. Man Ray repeated himself often, always with enough variation in medium and approach to produce a new work. For instance, the self-portrait he offered as a frontispiece to his autobiography is a modified and reversed replica of *Monument à D. A. F. de Sade.* Instead of a backside seen through an inverted cross, he presented his own full face with crosshairs running through his pupils and aimed to catch him precisely between the eyes. I am, the image says, a camera-rifle-captive-model-eye-target-prey-witness-hunter-artist come out of America to explore the no-man's-land between art and photography. Nothing could be more candid than my self-portrait. Nothing could be more perverse than some of my works.

NOTES

1. André Thirion, *Revolutionaries without Revolution*, trans. Joachim Neugroschel (New York: Macmillan, 1972), p. 134.

2. Man Ray, *Self Portrait*, (Boston: Little Brown and Company, 1963); p. 71.

3. Vaché quoted in Breton, *Les Pas perdus* (Paris: Gallimard, Idées, 1969), p. 75; for Dada artistic principles, see Breton, "Maldoror" in *Les Pas perdus*, p. 69.

4. As quoted in "Interview with Man Ray," in Jean-Hubert Martin et al., *Man Ray Photographs* (Paris: Philippe Sers, 1983), p. 36.

5. Man Ray, *Self Portrait*, p. 76.

6. Ibid., p. 395.

7. Ibid., p. 335.

8. Ibid., p. 397.

9. Ibid., p. 287.

10. Ibid., p. 323. Merry Foresta commented on this quotation: "What do you think was the source of Man Ray's laziness—courage or fear? Was the camera the tool of a lazy painter? The quote is a 1962 Man Ray writing about his thoughts in 1940s California about the Man Ray that had existed in 1930s France. The 1930s Man Ray—well known, fashionable, traveler to the South of France—was a different Man Ray from the defiant experimental artist of the 1920s."

11. Pierre Bourgeade, *Bonsoir, Man Ray* (Paris: Belford, 1972), p. 52.

12. Man Ray, *Self Portrait*, p. 119.

13. See Nigel Gossling, *Nadar* (New York: Alfred A. Knopf, 1976), p. 69.

14. The photograph carried no title when published on the first page of the first issue of *La Révolution surréaliste* (1924).

15. Quoted in Bourgeade, *Bonsoir, Man Ray*, p. 76.

16. Miller quoted in Arturo Schwarz, *The Rigor of Imagination* (New York: Rizzoli, 1977), p. 322.

17. Quoted in Bourgeade, *Bonsoir, Man Ray*, p. 78.

18. Quoted in Martin et al., *Man Ray Photographs*, p. 35.

19. Bourgeade, *Bonsoir, Man Ray*, p. 5.

32

BORN-AGAIN AFRICAN:
LÉOPOLD SENGHOR

(This essay was coauthored with Samba Ka.)

I.

On July 7, 1928, the graduation ceremonies of the new French lycée in Dakar, Senegal, were dignified by the presence of the governor general of West Africa. Primarily the children of white colonial administrators and businessmen, the school's hundred-odd students included about fifteen Africans, only one in the graduating class. They had been put through their paces for the baccalaureate by examiners sent from Bordeaux to maintain French standards. After the speeches, when the prizes were finally awarded, the same student walked forward time after time to receive the book prize in each academic subject and then one last time to receive the outstanding-student award conferred by the governor-general himself.

The student who thus swept the field was neither French nor a Creole with French citizenship from one of the four original colonial settlements, but a black Serer from the bush. The triumph of Léopold Sédar Senghor over all his more privileged classmates soon became a legend in West Africa. Ahead of him lay more than ten years of higher education in Paris. His ensuing sixty-year career as Francophone poet, promoter of negritude, and elected president of Senegal comes close to realizing two different dreams: the Western dream of philosopher-king or poet-legislator, and the African dream of the sage celebrating his people in song and story under the palaver tree. Yet there is an unexpectedly tragic side to this life, a side we shall approach slowly.

BORN IN 1906, Senghor was nearly the youngest of some two dozen children by several concurrent wives of a successful Serer tradesman and church-going Catholic. Missionaries in West Africa tolerated very latitudinarian forms of Christianity. Senghor was brought up until the age of seven in a small riparian village by his mother and maternal uncle according to local pastoral traditions and without a word of French. Then his father sent him for six years to a French missionary school. He excelled in his studies, grew in piety, and moved on to a Catholic seminary in Dakar. After three years, the white Father Director turned Senghor down for the priesthood. This first deep disappointment redirected Senghor's career into secular education without shattering his religious faith.

In 1945, seventeen years after his brilliant lycée graduation, Senghor brought out his first collection of poems, *Chants d'ombre*, with the estimable Seuil publishing house in Paris. At the same time, recently elected a representative from Senegal to the French Constituent Assembly, this Sorbonne-educated black man from Africa was chosen to oversee the grammar and style of the newly drafted Constitution of the Fourth Republic. By 1960, he had become known worldwide as a founding father of negritude, the black consciousness movement of the Francophone world, and as an effective champion of independence for the French colonies. After the failure of the short-lived Mali Federation, the Republic of Senegal elected Senghor its first president. He was regularly and honestly reelected for the following twenty years and helped to establish a remarkably liberal democracy with continuing ties to France. Senghor is the first African head of state in modern times to have turned over power peacefully and voluntarily to his successor. In 1984, the French Academy elected him to membership on the basis of his accomplishments as poet, scholar, and statesman.

RESOLUTE AND REMARKABLY gifted as a boy, Senghor benefited enormously from the French presence in his country and then was instrumental in transforming that presence. Every stage of his career throws light on the decline of the French colonial system and on the difficult birth of a post-colonial African polity. As he entered his thirties, this elegiac poet and seasoned veteran of the French university system decided that his skin color carried responsibilities beyond attaining success in the white man's system.

The courage of that decision emerges clearly when one understands the itinerary by which a black Frenchman became a born-again African.

In a letter to a white friend, he states explicitly that he was "born again" as "a New Negro," a term he borrowed from black Americans he was reading in the thirties. He had lived through a period of intense assimilation to French culture, to the point of choosing Proust as bedside reading. Then in the years before World War II, a combination of European anthropology about Africa, American authors like W. E. B. Du Bois, and discussions with West Indian friends in Paris like the Martinique poet Aimé Césaire and the Guyanan poet Léon Damas reconverted Senghor to his earliest origins and his African culture. Behind his cosmopolitan exterior, he remained very much a split identity and never tired of quoting Du Bois on "double consciousness." Out of this crisis of conscience came the influential but awkward notion of negritude, developed with Césaire and Damas.

Senghor's forty years of public life also oblige us to consider anew what he referred to as "the Balkanization of Africa," its self-confinement within frontiers arbitrarily imposed on it by the European colonialist powers at the Conference of Berlin in 1885. Those fragile frontiers of national security are also fault lines of weakness and disunity within larger regions. Between 1958 and 1960, black leaders spoke excitedly of the United States of (West) Africa, but one hears little of this idea today.

And finally, Senghor sets before us once again an old refrain in history and mythology: the solitude of the chief, the leader alone in his tent or his study. Africa may signify to some people another race, another set of cultures; but situations like that of the revered statesman losing touch with his people are universal and help us to understand that the truly important race is the human race.

THE IMMENSE JOURNALISTIC and scholarly attention paid to Africa in the past fifty years has produced no comprehensive biography of an important African leader. We may, for example, recognize the names of Nkrumah, Nyerere, Houphouet-Boigny, Sékou Touré, and Senghor. But the best studies devoted to them remain partial in one or both senses. Two probing books on Senghor's political career and thinking make little attempt to deal with his poetry.[1]

An Africanist and Sovietologist of long standing, Janet Vaillant has written *Black, French, and African: A Life of Léopold Sédar Senghor.* It overlooks no aspect of his life. She has drawn on many new sources in Senegal about his youth and organizes her thirteen chapters firmly around the stages and turning points in his complex international career. Vaillant's evident respect for Senghor sometimes leads her to avoid frank discussion of personal and social matters, even though there are few skeletons to hide in this dedicated life. Her political and intellectual judgments seem generally sound but unevenly documented.[2] Of the several future Third World leaders who resided in Paris during the twenties and thirties, including Ho Chi Minh and Chou En-lai, Senghor was the least seduced by Communist revolutionary ideology and traveled the furthest toward nonviolent democratic institutions and toward the reconciliation of racial and cultural differences. Today, when the fading of the Cold War is forcing us to look at many local and often ethnic conflicts, this exceptional life has much to suggest to us about the significance of early personal backgrounds and the depth of ideological conflict among leaders of emerging democracies.

2.

Since antiquity, the figure of the black has played far more than a walk-on part in Western culture. A cluster of recent books on the black in Western art has given us a cornucopia of particulars from that history.[3] When did the black as Negro begin to raise his or her voice in the pandemonium of Western thought and literature? Unable to get an education in the United States during the middle of the nineteenth century, the West Indian black Edward W. Blyden moved on to Liberia to write his five remarkable books. This powerful missionary-educated mind occupies the place of Aristotle for African studies and black consciousness.

Blyden's isolation, even while he represented Liberia at the Court of St. James, was probably exceeded by that of W. E. B. Du Bois, who, after taking a Harvard M.A., was denied a doctoral degree in Germany for not fulfilling the residence requirement. (He earned it later at Harvard.) After 1900, Du Bois devoted much of his energy to organizing congresses of the Pan-African movement, interracial in principle, pan-Negroist in practice, as the British historian Basil Davidson points out. However, in spite of the congresses, of the intellectual capacities of the leaders, and of the genuine circulation of black elites in the early part of the twentieth century, the voices of Blyden, Du Bois, Martin Delany, James Africanus Horton, and many other blacks were never able to gain the international hearing they deserved.

What happened in Paris in the 1930s and 1940s resembles the rapid forming of a critical mass, composed not only of black intellectuals from the West Indies, the United States, and West Africa but also of white artists, poets, and intellectuals already halfway to Africa because of their responses to primitive art, jazz, blues, and Josephine Baker. Gide, Camus, Emmanuel

Mounier, and Sartre joined Senghor, Césaire, Damas, the Senegalese writer Alioune Diop, and Richard Wright as sponsors of the new review *Présence Africaine* (1947). Sartre contributed a lengthy manifestolike introduction to Senghor's *Anthologie de la poésie nègre et malagache* (1948). Through such activities, the black voices that represented negritude laid claim to and were granted a new cultural prominence. The term *negritude* represents a set of claims as significant and complex of those of Surrealism and existentialism.

Senghor, Césaire, and Damas maintained in the 1930s that blacks throughout the world have a different psychological makeup from that of whites. Blacks, they said, have retained profound human values that whites have lost. Black artists share a characteristic style. Africa, the mother continent, possesses a rich culture qualitatively different from that of Europe. Senghor and his friends set out to convince black intellectuals to take pride in the fact of being black and to inform the world about black character, black history, and black civilization.

It was a daring and ambitious goal, which soon faced charges of counterracism. Today, anyone can amass references and quotations to prove that Africa and the Africans have a long history and that prejudice against color is a sign of intellectual backwardness. But in the early years of the twentieth century, blacks had been written out of history both by much evolutionary theory and by writers on culture. There is a debate today over whether ancient Greeks and Romans were racist. But about the eighteenth and nineteenth centuries, the evidence is overwhelming. "Enlightened" scholars were shaped by a reverence for science, progress, and the preeminence of European thought. The absence of these values, they called "savagery," as many statements of Voltaire, Hume, Hegel, and Darwin attest. The ideology of conquest in the nineteenth century became the next logical step. The American historian and political scientist Robert W. Tucker summarizes that continuity when he describes how Europeans judged colonization to be "both inevitable and just—inevitable because reciprocity could not necessarily be expected from those lacking in civilization, just because the primacy of the European states serves to confer upon the backward the benefits of civilization."[4]

One can imagine the distress of the brilliant black students in European universities sitting quietly and listening to charges brought against the color of their skin and against the African peoples from whom they had sprung. How could they respond? Their equality of opportunity was compromised by theories of race and culture that still went unanswered and by the incontrovertible color of their skin. Even those black students who mastered Greek and Latin were reminded by many true sons of Europe that they were illegitimate children of Western culture.

By the mid-1930s, Senghor and his friends had had enough. In essays and in poems, they began to declare their version of "Black is beautiful." But they were not just writing slogans in public places. Vaillant's book traces their long voyage of cultural self-discovery and discusses several sources of the negritude movement. A special place is accorded to Senghor's debt to the intellectual vigor of black American poets, writers, and academics such as Countee Cullen, Claude McKay, W. E. B. Du Bois, Alain Locke, and Langston Hughes. The Nardals, a black American family established in Paris who held open house, provided the crucial link among black intellectuals of all shores living in or passing through Paris in the 1930s, Vaillant could have provided more information on the two Nardal sisters, particularly on Jane. We are not told that her unpublished article "For a Negro Humanism" launched many of the ideas that Senghor and Césaire would present to the world with such brilliance.[5]

In these pages, Vaillant should also have given some attention to Edward W. Blyden, the remarkable Liberian precursor of negritude mentioned earlier. Between 1857 and 1903, his writings opened up the whole field of "the African personality." A letter Blyden wrote to William Gladstone from Liberia makes "this little Republic, planted here in great weakness" sound like Plymouth Plantation.[6]

The second debt of negritude traced by Vaillant is not to other blacks but to European anthropologists and artists. Leo Frobenius, Maurice Delafosse, and Robert Delavignette were the first anthropologists to do archaeological work on African cultures. By revealing the antiquity and significance of African precolonial history and civilization, they outlined a new picture of black achievements. In the same period, artists who "went native" in their spiritual quest, from Rimbaud to Gauguin to Picasso to Chirico, left a deep mark on the Western psyche. They also provided a stimulus for Senghor in his rediscovery of Africa. In a few cases, like that of André Gide, Vaillant mentions a highly important name and passes on with no further discussion.[7]

When young black intellectuals in Paris in the 1930s assembled all these resources to reach for a new way of looking at themselves, they did not use the word *negritude*. Borrowing an expression from American blacks, they called themselves "new Negroes" after Alain Locke's anthology, *The New Negro* (1925). Only later did Césaire coin the term *negritude*. It has remained an evolving concept whose definition varies from writer to writer and whose focus shifts, particularly in the case of Senghor.

At the start, Senghor defined negritude as "the sum total of qualities possessed by all black men everywhere." This definition comes very close to the way in which Blyden, in the previous century, described the "black personality movement": "the sum of values of African civilization, the body of qualities which make up the distinctiveness of the people of Africa."

Later on, during the struggle for independence of African colonies, Senghor presented negritude as a political ideology designed to promote liberation and self-rule. In a third stage, after independence, Senghor expanded negritude to emphasize blacks' contribution to a coming civilization of universal values. Themes of cultural exchange were always present in his notion of negritude, and Vaillant gives a full account of *métissage* in Senghor's thinking.

Negritude, or black consciousness, has at least a 150-year history and has taken many forms, starting well before the name was invented in the 1930s. Senghor's contribution, whose evolution we have traced above in three stages, has lost influence since the late 1970s for a number of reasons. It was difficult for him to put aside "the racial premise," as Vaillant phrases it, of his early declarations, the premise of a genetic distinctiveness. Even Richard Wright, Jacques Stephen Alexis, and many other black intellectuals insisted on the primacy of geographic, cultural, and economic factors—as opposed to genetic ones—in discussing the fate of black people. When generalized into communitarian African socialism for local consumption in Senegal, negritude lost its edge and its appeal. When later grafted onto the cloudy thinking of Pierre Teilhard de Chardin, it sank into a sea of universal spirituality. All along, Senghor clung to a static, idealized notion of precolonial African history as essentially "traditional." Historians can now demonstrate that Africa, including West Africa, has for centuries absorbed cultural and political shocks, including the arrival of Islam in the tenth century.

There will be more to say about negritude.

3.

After Senghor's retirement as president of Senegal in 1980, the Bibliothèque Nationale in Paris mounted a large exhibition in his honor. Senghor welcomed the event on the condition that the exhibition emphasize his intellectual and literary work rather than his political career. The Senegalese, however, remember Senghor the shrewd politician and charismatic leader better than Senghor the poet and essayist. Other African heads of state sometimes criticized Senghor's ideas, but rarely his integrity and his skill. He learned early to navigate in a political system molded by three conflicting forces: precolonial political traditions, the Muslim Brotherhoods, and political institutions inherited from France.

Senegal borders on both the Sahara and the Atlantic Ocean. Because of the early advent of Islam, most Senegalese are Muslims (83 percent), and Muslim leaders, called Marabouts, play an important role in the political process. Although the Marabouts do not make policy, and although attempts to build an Islamic party have failed in Senegal, the support of the Marabouts is essential for the stability and even the viability of any government. The question then becomes how Léopold Senghor, a Catholic, managed to be accepted by the Islamic religious leaders.

Senegal has also had long and continuous contact with Europe by way of the Atlantic. A French colony from 1850 to 1960, Senegal was the only region in black Africa where France fully implemented its assimilationist policies. As early as 1879, black residents of the major cities along the coast were granted French citizenship and were allowed to elect their own mayors, municipal council, and a representative to the French Chamber of Deputies in Paris.

This disparity in colonial status between citizens and subjects gave rise to two very different styles of political leadership. In the cities, the political leaders were the urban, Western-educated Senegalese, beginning with Blaise Diagne. In the countryside, leadership came from Islamic and traditional chiefs. In a colony so divided, it was very difficult for political thinking to evolve toward nationhood and unity. After World War II, the Senegalese deputy in Paris, Lamine Guèye, obtained passage of a bill extending the vote and rights of free association to all Senegalese citizens, including women. He picked Senghor to seek election as deputy of the newly enfranchised citizens. By accepting, Senghor faced two political challenges. How was a Paris professor and poet born in a rural village to earn recognition as a leader from the black Senegalese political elite of the towns, a turbulent group with habits of unfettered political debate and considerable skills in party organization and campaigning? At the same time, how was a Catholic intellectual educated in Paris to establish a constituency in an essentially feudal system of local Islamic rulers whose power and prestige were determined by the number and the loyalty of their clients? The concept of one man, one vote was utterly alien to the rural parts of the country, where the majority of the population lived.

Comparing archival sources and her own interviews with participants, Vaillant traces Senghor's political career from winning that first election in 1945 to his resignation from the presidency in 1980. The story is marked by successes, serious mistakes, and resounding defeats. Against all odds, Senghor and his friends succeeded in dominating the old Senegalese urban elite, and early in his career he was able to win the support of the

Muslim leaders by promising them a higher price for peanuts and by including them in the nascent political process. By the mid-1950s, his party, the Senegalese Democratic Bloc (BDS), was able to articulate the political demands of the majority and to represent them vigorously to the French colonial administration.

The growing demand if not for independence at least for greater autonomy pushed the Fourth Republic to issue the *"loi cadre"* of 1956, which established partial self-government in the black African colonies. At the same time, the BDS turned left as it incorporated young radical intellectuals, and its name changed to the Senegalese People's Bloc, or BPS. The BPS won again in 1957. Mamadou Dia, an able technocrat and Senghor's political alter ego, became the head of government while Senghor was conducting the battle for autonomy in Paris. A new situation was created by de Gaulle's return to power and the beginning of the Fifth Republic. De Gaulle held out two options to French African colonies: political autonomy within the framework of the French Federation or immediate independence. Senghor, the coalition builder, was obliged to make some tough choices.

Vaillant misses this dramatic juncture, in which a political defeat became one of the two most searing personal crises of Senghor's life. At the Cotonou Congress he convoked in 1958 to consider de Gaulle's offer, he declared in a fifty-page report that the French colonies were not yet ready for independence. The delegates to the congress, including those of Senghor's own party, rejected his report and voted unanimously for independence. Senghor retreated in humiliation to his wife's property in Normandy. His political career was saved by a small change in the constitution, allowing an affirmative vote for association with France within the Community to lead eventually to independence.[8]

In 1958, Senegal, like all other French colonies except Guinea, rejected immediate independence and stayed with the French Community.[9] But not for long. Senegal and the former French Sudan[10] became sovereign as the Mali Federation in 1960. The Mali Federation represented an attempt by Senghor to avoid the fragmentation, or, as he said, the "Balkanization" of Africa. The Mali Federation, however, collapsed six months later when Senegal seceded from it. This happened because the increasingly radical Sudanese could not work with the conciliatory diplomacy of Senghor. In August 1960, he was proclaimed president of Senegal by the National Assembly and later elected.

Senghor dreamed of being president of a federated country extending from Dakar to Lake Chad, from Nouakchott to Cotonou. Instead, he ended up being president of a country the size of South Dakota, with a population of 3 million in 1960, basically a peasant-dominated society overwhelmed by problems of poverty and illiteracy. Discouraged by the collapse of the Mali Federation but still confident, Senghor and Dia, his prime minister, launched a strategy to overcome economic problems by developing the agricultural sector while building schools and hospitals. But soon, another grave political crisis erupted, a power struggle with Dia.

Vaillant describes this conflict carefully and vividly. The two men held diverging concepts of nation building and of the way in which the peasants should participate in politics and the economy. For Dia, the purpose was to build a modern state without the Muslim Marabouts as middlemen between the government and the peasants. Dia's socialist and nationalist-minded programs also antagonized French interests. Senghor, on the other hand, wanted to maintain and enhance the connection with the Marabouts as intermediaries and to strengthen French interests in Senegal. He believed that a French economic presence was essential for the country's future and adopted a relaxed open-door approach. Dia remained a conscientious technocrat and tried to protect the country's limited resources. Senghor won the struggle with the support of the Marabouts. But he lost a close friend and his most valuable political ally.

Without Dia, Senghor ran a lax economy based on the peanut crop. When successive droughts decimated the harvest, he had to take strong measures to maintain the legitimacy of his government. In the mid-1970s, Senghor decentralized the administration, brought young technocrats into the political process (including Abdou Diouf, the current president of Senegal), and made political institutions more democratic by instituting a controlled multiparty system. Among the many one-party governments in Africa since independence, this move by Senghor in 1975 represented the first U-turn from authoritarianism to a relatively open political life.

SCHOLARS ARE STILL debating the significance of these developments in Senegalese politics. Vaillant thinks that Senghor, with his long experience of negotiation and compromise, was more at ease with an open political system than with a one-party system. "Senghor's final political wish was to commit Senegal firmly to representative democracy." The trouble with this line of argument is that it reflects a "patrimonial" conception of politics: Democracy is a gift from an enlightened leader or powerful elite to a powerless part of society. Vaillant's explanation overlooks the long fight by peasants, trade-union workers, and intellectuals for an open system, and it omits Senghor's resistance to that change. As noted by Vaillant herself, beginning in 1962

Senghor advocated a new authoritarianism, whose basis he found in negritude. When circumstances obliged him to make changes, Senghor helped bring democracy to Senegal. He was not its sole agent.

4.

No published photograph shows Senghor wearing a boubou, the flowing costume of his region. His elegant single-breasted suits and tan gloves signified the degree to which he adopted the role of a Frenchman. After three years of special preparation for the Ecole Normale Supérieure, he had failed the oral examination in 1931, whereupon he switched to the Sorbonne. Continuing study of Latin and Greek and writing a thesis on Baudelaire did not interrupt his vast reading, including the archnationalist Maurice Barrès along with Proust and Rimbaud. After obtaining French citizenship in 1933, he became the first African to attain the highly competitive *agrégation.*

But by this time, in 1935, Senghor knew that he was swimming in a river that flowed in two directions. While his formal studies were making him more and more French, or "Hellenic," as he liked to say, a strong countercurrent in French intellectual and artistic life was propelling him back toward "primitive" cultures. Senghor later proposed the name Revolution of 1889 for the Bergsonian antirational tendencies in philosophy and anthropology that, before and after World War I, accompanied the African influences at work in Apollinaire and Cendrars, in Cubism and Surrealism. These currents received their official apotheosis in the Paris Colonial Exposition of 1931. That was exactly the moment when Senghor met the Nardal family and, through them, the militant group of West Indian poets living in Paris.

Amid these Parisian buffetings, Senghor exhibited a double uniqueness compared with Césaire and Damas and the other West Indian writers. His jet black color left no doubt about the purity of his African origins. He occasionally went so far as to refer impishly to an imaginary drop of Portuguese blood in his veins. At the same time, his enduring Catholic faith, though several times profoundly shaken, set him apart from the others, some of whom were lapsed Catholics.

Here, then, is the turbulent confluence of cultures within which Senghor, entering his thirties, tried to establish a place for himself in France. One current carried him to a high plateau of French education and on to a position teaching Latin at a lycée in Tours, and then into the French army as World War II broke out. The reverse current, issuing from different forces in

French cultural life and from his West Indian friends, pushed him insistently back toward the country he had left behind. In a poem he wrote in 1940 while in a German prison camp, Senghor used a military metaphor to describe his moral turmoil:

> *Europe has crushed me like a warrior flattened under the elephantine feet of tanks.*
>
> *My heart is more bruised than my body used to be coming back from distant adventures along the enchanted shores of Spirits.*

("NDESSÉ")[11]

A French reader hears in these lines the long Biblical verses used by Claudel with sidelong glances at Rimbaud.

But Senghor also wrote in a very different mode:

> *Mbaye Dyôb! I wish to proclaim your name and your honor.*
> *Dyôb! I wish to run your name up the flagpole of homecoming, to ring your name like the victory bell.*
> *I wish to chant your name Dyôbène! You who called me your master and Warmed me with your fervor on winter evenings around the red-hot stove, which made me cold.*
> *Dyôb!*

("TAGA FOR MBAYE DYÔB")

A Senegalese can hear the dithyrambs of a village singer improvising in formulaic patterns to honor his noble patron. Senghor's poetry seems sometimes to combine the European and the African traditions, sometimes to alternate between them. "Springtime in Touraine," an early poem, mixes lyricism echoing Apollinaire with an undercurrent of violence out of Rimbaud. Then it ends abruptly with the jokey, menacing line *"On ne badine pas avec le Nègre"* ("Don't kid around with a black"), which rides piggyback on the title of a Musset play, *On ne badine pas avec l'amour.* Some of his best-known and most moving poems, like "Nuit de Sine" and "Femme noire," are no more African than European in diction and form. As time went on, Senghor composed increasingly in a strong elegiac mode with a loose sweeping line that hovers among its sources—Lautréamont and the Surrealists; the *guimm,* or ode, of the Serer people of West Africa; Whitman; the blues. At his weakest, he took refuge in the travelogue style of a self-appointed United Nations poet, a first-person universal that does not reach the power of true incantation.

Like the Surrealist André Breton, Senghor maintained that all great poets write with the ear. He gave clues about how to recite his poems by printing directions on musical accompaniment: "For flutes and balafong"; "Ode for kôra." "Elegy for the Trade Winds," a powerful suite illustrated by Marc Chagall in a deluxe edition, cries out for declamation. The language swells through ten pages celebrating childhood, winds and tornadoes, and the alluring place names of West Africa. Out of the night and the rain, the poet performs ritual insistent gestures:

> *My negritude has nothing to do with racial lethargy but with sunlight in*
> *   the soul, my negritude is living and looking.*
> *My negritude goes trowel in hand, a lance clenched in its fist. . . .*
> *The smell of spring green white gold, smell of albizzias.*
> *I say lemon smell where one embalms hearts and passions have been*
> *   embalmed.*
> *And I salute their spurt into the joyous Tradewind.*
> *Let the old nigger die and long live the new Negro.*

Senghor's militant affirmation of negritude turns up in his most expansive poems. He strove neither for epic narrative nor for lyric intensity. His poems celebrate life as directly as songs can.

5.

Senghor, a short, slender, courteous, public man, must sometimes become annoyed at how often he is expected to refine and redefine the notion of negritude. Yet since the 1930s, that term has helped black intellectuals gain confidence in their cultural and racial identity. Unfortunately, Duvalier in Haiti appropriated it to justify his tyranny. But negritude also helped guide Senegal into independence with a pride and steadiness that blocked many of the evils to which other African countries fell prey.

As Senghor entered his mideighties, two books appeared in French to complete his career. *Oeuvre poétique* is a compact four-hundred-page volume, sections of which have already been translated into a dozen languages. The poems express emotions and convictions familiar to readers throughout the Third World and are fully accessible in their rolling rhythms and vivid figures to all of us.

In *Ce que je crois,* Senghor collected five essays that swing in gradually expanding orbits around the original kernel of negritude. After drawing ambitious conclusions about the significance of African prehistory and the elements of a native African philosophy, he delivers both subjects into the arms of what he hopes the future will bring: *"La Civilisation de l'Universel."* This naïve and undefined ideal seems to designate a kind of apolitical multiculturalism on a global scale.

Senghor cannot write many pages without evoking the word *métis.* Sprung himself from Serer, Malinke, and Fula ethnic roots, he means primarily cultural intermixture, as in his own career he crossed passionate negritude with passionate Frenchness. But he also makes much of the special gifts of Maurice Béjart, the dancer-choreographer of mixed white and African birth. And Senghor himself, after observing an early vow to marry a black wife, later married a white Frenchwoman and had a son by her.

One half-hidden suggestion in *Ce que je crois* should interest those concerned with the relation between primitivism and modernism. First implicitly in discussing the syntax of Wolof poetry, and later explicitly in commenting on the influence of Negro arts on Cubism, Dada, and Surrealism, Senghor identifies the common terms, the essential exchange, as the style of "parataxis"—placing words in sequences without explicit connection or transition. Precisely. We have really known it all along. But it takes a grammarian of European and African languages to go to the heart of that great cultural intersection at the opening of the twentieth century and find the precise word. More precise than the modernist alternative: *montage.*

BEHIND THE BEAUTIFULLY dressed public man, a private individual had disciplined himself all his life, through regular physical exercise and a demanding work schedule, to remarkable habits of concentration and punctuality. How, then, considering his many accomplishments, could we have spoken in our opening paragraph of a tragic note in Senghor's life? In her biography, Vaillant refers frequently to challenges and difficult decisions, less often to any lasting defeats. To what degree has Vaillant the biographer found her way not only through the swarm of events around Senghor but also into the mind of this dedicated man? What is the tone, the inner sound of his life?

The younger of Senghor's two sons by his first wife and the one son by his second wife both died before their father, one by suicide and the other in an automobile accident. The fate of his sons has brought great sorrow into Senghor's later years. Vaillant tells us virtually nothing about his family life, or about how a good Catholic was able to "dissolve" his first marriage and marry again.

For thirty years, from his early twenties to his early fifties, before he became president, Senghor lived with few interruptions in Paris and, along with the Nardal sisters, served as the great agent of exchange among West

Indian, American, and African blacks. Every West African intellectual in Paris accepted his hospitality and sought his friendship. Yet today Senghor, once again living primarily in France, has few close Senegalese friends. After retirement, when he built a house in a suburb of Dakar, he asked the city council to rename the adjoining streets for Aimé Césaire and Léon Damas. His closest friends are still West Indians whom he met early in Paris. When Mamadou Dia broke with him two years after independence, he lost his most valued Senegalese friend. The extroverted African intellectual now finds himself thrown back on his French connections.

In Senghor's early political career, even his enemies marveled at his ability to find a way to speak directly to any group, however remote, however destitute, even if he barely knew their language (in a country of six national languages). A Catholic from a trader's family in an Islamic nation intensely aware of noble lineage, Senghor made his way not by violence and military coups but by essentially democratic means of persuasion, compromise, and free elections. What rewards has he reaped?

A few years ago, the Senegalese government decided to rename the University of Dakar, the most respected university in French-speaking Africa. Thirty years earlier, Senghor had been the moving force behind the university project and its principal fund-raiser. The government finally chose the name of Université Cheikh Anta Diop, after Senghor's chief political and intellectual rival. In Dakar, where everything in sight carries the name of a colonial administrator or a national hero, people are wondering what is left to name for the country's great leader.

FIFTY YEARS AFTER its launching, the term *negritude* has by no means disappeared. Every black African intellectual and politician has had to find a satisfactory response both to "subjective negritude"—the way an individual black wears his or her color—and to "objective negritude"—"patterns of culture" genetically or geographically correlated with the black race and now carried all over the world.[12] Leaders of the black consciousness movement in South Africa hold many of Senghor's writings in high regard. Some of the racial tensions that originally provoked subjective negritude in Europe have surfaced anew in the events leading up to the current military confrontation along the Senegal-Mauritania border between white North Africans, or Moors, and black Africans.

But negritude has been plagued with ironies and contradictions. Soon after its birth, Sartre appropriated many of its advocates (including Césaire) and much of its intellectual capital for revolutionary Marxism. Today, one hardly hears any reference to negritude among ordinary people in Senegal, where it was for twenty years official government doctrine. When Senghor came to draw up policy for Senegalese schools, he modeled the curriculum so closely on the French system that his opponents accused him of forgetting Africa and favoring Europe. Almost no informed and reflective member of either race would today accept a sentence in one of Senghor's earliest writings that has come back often to haunt him: "Emotion is Negro, as reason is Hellenic."

Senghor has spent a long career promoting a negritude to which he was born again in his late twenties and from whose early racist associations he has had to keep distancing himself. His personal encounter with Nazism as a prisoner of war in World War II cured him of any taint of "racism."

WILL SENGHOR'S POETRY assure him a major place in the world of literature? In the current enthusiasm for African studies, his work will undoubtedly receive much attention among scholars. Translators are at work on his poetry in many parts of the world. A complete English version of *Oeuvre poétique* by Melvin Dixon appeared in 1991 in the enterprising CARAF (Caribbean and African literatures translated from the French) series from the University Press of Virginia. As time goes by, Senghor's poems will, we are confident, be seen increasingly as an integral part of his political and intellectual career rather than as a freestanding accomplishment demanding separate literary treatment.[13] Not that Senghor's poems are all didactic or discursive. But as he nears the end of his life, we can see them more clearly as occasional compositions in the best sense, works attached to the moods of his career and, in a few cases, creations that leap beyond the vagaries and contingencies of his life. The same might be said of Rimbaud.

6.

A century ago, the impatient Liberian voice of Edward Blyden asked in a letter "whether black men, under favorable circumstances, can manage their own affairs." They had been doing so, of course, for ages; Blyden was referring to the special situation being created in Africa by European colonization. Of the many answers to that question now presented by newly independent states, Senegal offers one of the most courageous. This small country beset by the encroaching desert and dependent on a woefully unreliable rainfall, was able to produce a founding father not intent on leaving behind a reigning dynasty or a new capital city bearing his name. In a Muslim country, Senghor saw to it that the constitution established complete

freedom of religion and that the Code de la Famille recognized both monog-
amous and polygamous marriages. For a black people, Senghor founded
republican institutions and an educational system that combine European
and African precedents. These are the true creations of *métissage,* the principle of synthesis to which Senghor subscribed with increasing fervor.

One of the great problems for Africa today, at least among the elite, lies
in the fact that each of its fifty-odd resolutely independent states wishes to
have its own founding parent and its own separate history. For a few years
between 1958 and 1960, Senghor came as close as any leader to uniting the
splintered factions of French West Africa. But the goal of federation failed
everywhere. When Senghor resigned the presidency in 1981, he left a country that had been brought close to economic coma by drought, population
increase, rising oil prices, and poor management. But he never stooped to
malfeasance for personal gain of the kind practiced by some other African
leaders. The International Monetary Fund and the World Bank had to help
the new president to undertake painful measures of economic austerity and
reform.

The true monument to Senghor will be found in no economic miracle,
in no structure of steel and stone, but in the conviction with which ordinary
Senegalese citizens affirm that their country stands for tolerance. That tolerance now faces two serious challenges. A dynamic renewal of a militant
Islam, fed by many former Marxist intellectuals, seeks to increase its political
power and to reduce the voice of secularism and nonsectarianism. And dealing with a rebellion in the southern breadbasket province of Casamance
reinforces the Jacobin, centralist tendencies of the government. But most of
the people, encouraged by Senghor's example, continue to believe in tolerance.

ALMOST ON THE last page of her summation, Vaillant tells us about a
dream Senghor described to her in a letter:

> He began as the intellectual who would understand and speak for
> his toiling black people. Then he became their ambassador to the
> assembled nations, and finally, their president. This vocation was
> synonymous with the person Senghor had become. He seemed to
> sense this, for he once wrote that he had awakened from a dream in
> panic. He had dreamed that he had become white. The panic
> derived, he wrote, from the knowledge that if he were white there
> would be no reason for his suffering. He could no longer be the
> leader of his black people. Under such circumstances, he would

have no choice but suicide. Questioned further why this dream held such terror for him, he answered more prosaically that if he were white, he would have no defense against his pride.

This is the most revealing and moving moment in a biography that elsewhere maintains a respectful distance from its subject. For the first time, the word *suffering* appears, and properly. Why did Senghor experience such intense panic over the dream? We understand that waking up white, while lifting from him the black's burden of suffering in a white-dominated world, would also deprive him of his mission as leader of his people. But the second response, if accurately recorded and translated, is more difficult to fathom: "he would have no defense against his pride."

We find these words enigmatic, even Delphic, rather than prosaic. The passage taken as a whole suggests that negritude has provided Senghor with the source of his primary pride in a mission and also, out in the white world, with an acute awareness of an inescapable condition that protects him from a more dangerous pride of individual achievement and fame. Senghor seems to have glimpsed through his dream a deeper level of Du Bois's "double consciousness, this sense of always looking at oneself through the eyes of others." As in some of his early poems, Senghor acknowledges the suffering that double consciousness brings. Here lies the tragic side of an often admirable life.

NOTES

1. Ernest Milcent and Monique Sordet, *Léopold Sédar Senghor et la naissance de l'Afrique moderne* (Paris: Seghers, 1969); Jacques Louis Hymans, *Léopold Sédar Senghor: An Intellectual Biography* (Edinburgh: Edinburgh University Press, 1971).

2. Some errors appear almost gratuitous. Senghor and de Gaulle never "stood side by side to preside over the ceremonies marking Senegal's independence" (p. 2). Vaillant correctly records Senghor's date of birth as 1906. She does not raise the question of who tampered with his birth certificate in order to allow him to enter the lycée when he was two years over age. The assassination attempt against Senghor in 1967 involved a gun, not a knife (p. 326). A number of factors lead us to believe that many chapters of Vaillant's biography were written more than a decade ago. For instance, the only mention of the shifting usage of the words *Negro* and *black* in French and English has been belatedly inserted on page 143 as the lone footnote in the body of the book itself.

3. Especially *The Image of the Black in Western Art* (Cambridge, Massachusetts: Harvard University Press, 1976–); vols. 1, 2, and 4 have appeared to date.

4. Robert W. Tucker, *The Inequality of Nations* (New York: Basic Books, 1977), p. 9.

5. Vaillant refers several times in her notes to the excellent book by Hymans (see note 1) that records this information. In too many places, Vaillant falls short of Hymans's discussions of philosophical and political questions.

6. See V.Y. Mudimbe, *The Invention of Africa* (Bloomington, Indiana: Indiana University Press, 1988), chapter 4. Blyden's works have now been reedited in various editions and collections.

7. Gide's *Travels in the Congo* (1927) and *Back from Tchad* (1928) exposed the despotism of the colonial system and in effect vindicated René Maran, a West Indian who had lost his job in the colonial administration because of his prize-winning novel *Batouala* (1920), set in Africa. Gide's confession, "I have come to feel a whole race of suffering humanity—a poor oppressed people, whose beauty, whose worth we have failed to understand," was obviously well received by black intellectuals. But these literary types bear watching. How do they really grasp the mentality and humanity of Africans? Vaillant notes the case of Rimbaud, who in "Bad Blood" wrote the cry of self-degradation, "I am a beast, a Negro," and an explosive paragraph to follow. After expressing sympathy for suffering Africans, Gide offered unfounded and troubling thoughts about their mental capacities.

As a rule the natives cannot understand the word "why?" and I even doubt whether any equivalent word exists in most of their idioms. . . . It seems as though their brains were incapable of establishing a connection between cause and effect. . . .

When the white man gets angry with the blacks' stupidity, he is usually showing up his own foolishness! Not that I think of them as incapable of any but the slightest mental development; their brains, as a rule, are dull and stagnant—but how often the white man seems to make it his business to thrust them back into the darkness. . . .

The people of these primitive races as I am more and more persuaded, have not our method of reasoning; and this is why they so often seem to us stupid. Their acts are not governed by the logic which from our earliest infancy has become essential to us . . . (*Travels to the Congo,* [London: Penguin, 1986], pp. 66, 79, 198.)

8. After his 1958 tour of French territories in Africa, de Gaulle accepted a change from "federation" to "community" in the language of the constitution referring to the colonies. Community status for the colonies would allow for eventual independence, with no time limit specified. This way, a vote for community was not a vote against independence, and many African leaders, including Senghor, declared in favor of community. Senghor has stated that the constitutional change was suggested to de Gaulle by Georges Pompidou after Pompidou received a despairing letter from Senghor. Other accounts attribute the change to the Madagascar deputy, Philibert Tsiranana.

9. Sékou Touré, who delivered the vote in Guinea for immediate independence, became a hero for many black Africans. In the early 1980s, when information was coming out about the economic disaster of his regime and the violence and torture by which it stayed in power, Touré was still popular among radical groups for his bold gesture in grasping independence.

10. The Arabic expression *Bilad as Sudan* means "in the land of the blacks." In the colonial period, the name Sudan was applied to the east-west Sahelian strip south of the Sahara. French Sudan in West Africa corresponded to present-day Mali.

11. Translations of Senghor's poetry are by Roger Shattuck.

12. Abiola Irele has written a careful survey and analysis of negritude from Senghor and Fanon to Towa and Hountondji. See his "Contemporary Thought in French-Speaking Africa," in Isaac James Mowe and Richard Bjornson, eds., *Africa and the West: The Legacies of Empire,* (Westport, CT: Greenwood Press, 1988). The same volume contains a short essay by Senghor and several valuable discussions of the intellectual climate in West Africa.

13. This opinion parallels that of Sylvia Washington Bâ expressed in her fine book *The Concept of Negritude in the Poetry of Léopold Sédar Senghor* (Princeton, New Jersey: Princeton University Press, 1973).

33

A MASTERPIECE
FROM SENEGAL

The teacher had shifted the grip of his fingernails and they were now piercing the cartilage at another place. The child's ear, already white with scarcely healed scars, was bleeding anew. Samba Diallo's whole body was trembling, and he was trying his hardest to recite his verse correctly, and to restrain the whimpering that pain was wresting from him.

Nobly born of the West African Diallobé tribe, Samba is no more than seven or eight years old. The aging Islamic teacher calls him a miserable piece of mold whose tongue should be cut out. Then the boy must repeat with perfect articulation "the glistening sentence" which, without understanding it, "he loved for its mystery and somber beauty."

Samba could well spend the rest of his youth in the Qur'anic school attaining spirituality by memorizing the Holy Word, learning humility by begging for food in the village streets. Instead, after a year or two, his family reluctantly sends him to the French colonial school in a nearby town. He does well enough in the new system to earn a fellowship to study philosophy in Paris during the 1950s. The tension between his tribal culture and Western ways becomes increasingly intense. "I have become both. No head remains clear between the horns of a dilemma." At a dinner party, he recalls

La Grande Royale, the oldest princess of his tribe, whose authority has sealed his fate.

"I have an elderly cousin," he said, "in whose mind reality never loses its just claims. She has not yet emerged from the astonishment into which the defeat and colonization of the Diallobé plunged her. They call her the Most Royal Lady. I should not have gone to the foreign school, and I should not be here this evening, if it had not been for her desire to find an explanation for our defeat. The day I went to take leave of her she said to me again, 'Go find out, among them, how one can conquer without being in the right.' "

Those instructions define his dilemma in the novel.

Samba is summoned home and finds he is expected to replace his former *maître* as spiritual leader of the Diallobé people. But he "no longer burns at the heart of things and beings" as he did in his youth. He has lost the Sacred Word and cannot become the new Islamic master for his village. Exasperated by this refusal, a half-crazed follower of the former *maître* kills Samba. The instant of his death is narrated as a lyric conversation or litany among several voices—the spirit of darkness, the angel of death, his childhood, his spirit or soul, the mortal Samba dying.

Before I went to Senegal for a year in 1984, no one spoke to me of Cheikh Hamidou Kane's *L'Aventure ambiguë,* published in Paris in 1969. It won the Grand Prix Littéraire de l'Afrique Noire. Since that time, Kane, trained by the French as an administrator, has devoted himself to the political and economic survival of his country and has published one more novel. I now rate his first book as the best West African novel, ranking high among the handful of great modern works from black Africa.

Ambiguous Adventure is as much of a roman à clef as Proust's portrait of Parisian society. The Diallobé is a real pastoral tribe living along the south bank of the Senegal River. When the historic princess, after whom La Grande Royale was modeled, died, Dakar's major newspaper, *Le Soleil,* carried a long tribute, identifying her as Kane's character. The portrait of village life, of the Qur'anic school, and of the French school document colonial life just before independence.

The narrative style hovers between archaic and modern. Kane's story jumps without transition from one momentous conversation to the next to produce a highly stylized effect. The Paris chapters offer no trace of the existentialism that reigned in those years and confine their literary allusions to Pascal, Descartes, and Rilke. Kane calls the book "a *récit*" to distinguish this

346 CANDOR and PERVERSION

concentrated tale from a full-blown novel. His deliberate prose rhythms recall Mme. de Lafayette and Benjamin Constant. It is as if Kane had set out to write the classic version of a conventional story: An alien, half-stranded and half-assimilated in a Western capital, returns home, only to be devoured by darker stresses and dilemmas among his own people.

It is the story retold most recently in a supercharged Anglo-Indian version by Salman Rushdie. *The Satanic Verses* carries so complex a freight of allusions to Islamic and Indian history and legend that few Western readers can hear its full sound. Muslim ears hear the barely mediated voice of Satan talking English with an anti-Islamic message. Rushdie set out to write an all-purpose intellectual satire of vast dimensions attacking every faith. The defiant title he chose suggests he must have hoped to hit a land mine and pay dirt at the same time. He succeeded—and far overshot the "alien in the West" story.

The well-known Senegalese novelist and filmmaker Ousmane Sembene wrote a highly autobiographical early work on the same theme, *O pays, mon beau peuple!* (1957). Like *Ambiguous Adventure,* it ends with the murder of its protagonist, who is overwhelmed by demands that exceed his capacities. Both novels register a debt to the intensely moving Haitian prose epic of peasant life, *Gouverneurs de la rosée* (1944) by Jacques Roumain. In a highly plotted narrative full of violence, Sembene remains the militant anticolonialist impatient with his unenterprising people. Kane has a more reflective mind and a chaster style in French. Sembene propels his events inexorably toward moments of conflagration and apocalypse. Kane, displaying an uncanny resemblance to Malraux, arranges his story around a series of exchanges between vividly drawn protagonists placed at the symbolic summit of existence. Late at night, the tribal chief, the Islamic *maître,* and La Grande Royale discuss Samba's future. One accepts the implication that they are talking about the future of black Africa. In another scene, Samba's father, who is the top local administrator, referred to as *le chevalier* (the knight), and Paul Lacroix, his sympathetic French boss, watch the sunset from their shared office and grope tentatively in the gathering darkness toward their profoundest thoughts. Lacroix speaks first.

> "No. And, if you please, let us keep away from metaphysics. I should like to know your world."
> "You know it already. Our world is that which believes in the end of the world: which at the same time hopes for it and fears it. Just now, I rejoiced greatly when it seemed to me that you were in anguish there in front of the window. See, I was saying to myself, he has a foreboding of the end. . . ."

"No, it was not anguish, truly. It did not go so far as that."

"Then from the bottom of my heart I wish for you to rediscover the feeling of anguish in the face of the dying sun. I ardently wish that for the West. When the sun dies, no scientific certainty should keep us from weeping for it, no rational evidence should keep us from asking that it be reborn. You are slowly dying under the weight of evidence. I wish you that anguish—like a resurrection."

"To what shall we be born?"

"To a more profound truth. Evidence is a quality of the surface. . . . The external is aggressive. If man does not conquer it, then it destroys man and makes him a victim of tragedy. A sore which is neglected does not heal but becomes infected to the point of gangrene. A child who is not educated goes backward. A society which is not governed destroys itself. The West sets up science against the invading chaos, sets it up like a barricade."

At this moment Lacroix had to fight against the strong temptation to push the electric light switch which was within reach of his hand. He would have liked to scrutinize the shadowed face of this motionless man who sat opposite him. In his voice he perceived a tonality which intrigued him and which he would have liked to relate to the expression of his face. But, no, he thought, if I turn on the light this man may stop talking. It is not to me that he is talking, it is to himself. He listened.

"Every hour that passes brings a supplement of ignition to the crucible in which the world is being fused. We have not had the same past, you and ourselves, but we shall have, strictly, the same future. The era of opposite destinies has run its course."

This is far from the final word on the fate of the two worlds. By sending his son Samba to the French school, the knight has expressed his hope for some form of ecumenical future. But the gesture fails. Samba is sacrificed. His discussions in Paris reveal his deepening inner struggle. The final conversation Samba has back in Africa, at the point of death, with several unidentified inner voices edges into mystery and poetry. "The breath of thought must pass through the blowgun of the instant. . . . At the heart of the instant, man is immortal. For the instant is infinite while it happens." The ever-present danger of overinflation in such ambitious philosophic exchanges is usually controlled by the prose.

Everything in *Ambiguous Adventure* turns on the practical, political, spiritual question of schooling: theirs or ours? The basic story moves from Qur'anic school to colonial school to Western university and then abortively

348 CANDOR and PERVERSION

back to the beginning. What gives the book its singular magnifying power arises from its insights into the thoughts and customs of the Diallobé people. Though established among them for several centuries, Islam has not formed a flawless bond with their Pular identity. The most dramatic conflict in the book, enacted through Samba's divided loyalties, is expressed by two powerful characters exerting the most intimate influences over him. The despotic and devoted *maître* of the Qur'anic school lives only for God, as revealed in the Arabic words he teaches his students to chant. He is also human enough to laugh at his own physical decline and to love Samba's nascent sensibilities to the word of God. Large, ancient, commanding, deeply distressed by the sufferings of her people under colonial rule, La Grande Royale represents a locality and a tribe, a struggle for survival of little moment to the other worldly traditions of Islam. The *maître* fears and opposes La Grande Royale because she has the pride of nobility. "And underneath any nobility you will find a basic layer of paganism." *Pagan* is a powerful, nearly forbidden word in Islamic West Africa. For the good of her people, she wants them, beginning with Samba, to attend the foreigners' school in order to find out their secret. The *maître* opposes her. Large segments of sub-Saharan Africa incorporate this deep-seated tension, in which Christianity plays no role.

Thus Samba Diallo faces not a simple division between Europe and Africa but a three-way split among the Grande Royale, or the mother's milk of his black people; the *maître*, or the mystery of spirituality in Arabic Islam, and the series of French men and women who represent the evidence of reason and science in the West. Analysis in terms of black and white, of colonized and colonizer, African and Western, fails to come to terms with a novel that gives a complex portrait of a young African on the rack of *three* ways of life. The result is a genuine philosophical and cultural intensity that cannot be reduced to themes and ideas, that lodges only uneasily in symbols. The reader must listen carefully to shifting moods. Early in the Paris chapters, Samba alone in his room exclaims lovingly, "O mon pays" ("Oh my country!"). Later, he tells a fellow student, the French girl Lucienne, that he prefers God to his Diallobé people. At the end of the story, the angelic or unconscious voice welcomes Samba to a place where there is no ambiguity. Samba recognizes "the taste of my mother's milk found again . . . exile's end." At the moment of death, he understands that he had turned away from both Islam and the West. In its understated way, Kane's story is as scandalous as Rushdie's.

I lived several months in Dakar before a number of friends induced me to buy a French paperback edition of *L'Aventure ambiguë*. The cover shows a striking Dan mask of a female face with round, vacant, yet staring holes for eyes. I devoured the book in three days while the local mosques chanted their prayer calls and the January sun left the air comfortable even at noon. The action demands close attention; notes and a map would help many readers. Katherine Woods has done a competent translation into English, available in Heinemann's African Writers Series. But the novel is not widely read even in African studies courses. Kane never gets off on ideological rants about negritude and African socialism. Rarely does one discover a work so saturated in the sounds and motifs of the Qur'an. *Ambiguous Adventure* succeeds in crossing passionate spirituality with dispassionate scrutiny of that spirituality. I find it significant that Kane chose as his most original and imposing personage a woman who will not surrender to the authority of Islam with its essentially male spirituality. The reason may be historic or fictional, probably both. The result is a book that probes the very vessels through which the mixed blood of West Africa flows. After twenty-five years, the timeliness and mastery of *Ambiguous Adventure* have grown, not faded. Having recently left the government of President Abdou Diouf, Kane may at last offer us another work. But the one is enough to assure his place in world literature.

BLANK AND WHITE:

ILLUMINATING

OCTAVIO PAZ

RINTERS DO OBVIOUS yet puzzling things. A page to be left blank in the final book is often designated in page proofs by the word *BLANK* printed large in the middle of the white space. There lies a bottomless hole for the self-reflexive mind to fathom. Not many oxymorons pass themselves off so coolly as mere redundancy. This dead-pan naming of parts spirits us away into René Magritte's wonderland, where meticulously painted pipes proclaim that they are not pipes after all. Obviously. Or is it so? Just stop and think a moment; *nothing* is obvious. In the summer of 1966, while living in India as the Mexican ambassador, Octavio Paz wrote a poem he called *BLANCO*. Printed in Mexico on a single sixteen-foot accordion-folded page, the first edition of the work presented a flow of words. That format helps the reader make what Paz calls for: "the passage from silence before speech to the silence after speech." This new edition reveals the visual dimensions of the work by animating the meanings of its title in Spanish. *BLANCO* now displays a second mysterious passage: the passage from blank to white. An empty colorless space without value gradually turns into the full whiteness of all hues vibrating together, a plenitude. Separate words and separate colors declare themselves along the way and then withdraw again into silence, into whiteness. The most significant element of this design becomes the easiest to overlook.

For Adja Yunkers had devised a subtle yet powerful instrument to project the poem by his Mexican friend. Looking deeper than striking lines in the text like "Woman buried with her eyes open" and ". . . rain of your heels on my back," Yunkers perceived that the text escapes illustration yet lends itself to a reciprocating arrangement he calls "illumination"—after medieval manuscripts, after Rimbaud's hallucinations. He set in motion within and around the printed poem a firm rhythm of massive emblems interspersed with delicate arabesques. That rhythm both follows and leads the insistent binary movement of the poem. Toward the end, stability and lightness fuse into a composition as simple and as multiple as the word *blanco.*

But Yunkers dreamed an even more stunning analogy for *BLANCO:* embossment. Uninked letters and shapes countersunk into the paper leave the page both empty and full. *Embossment* is not quite the right term. Yunkers framed the conventionally printed parts of Paz's poem and his own colored graphics in their obverse—in inkless, colorless intaglio. On those sheets, text and/or drawing are not there until you tilt your head, or the paper, or the light. Impelled by Paz's words, Yunkers discovered the secret of rendering a finely shadowed whiteness, of drawing a blank.

I find only one expression adequate to describe this work of text and textures, of words and forms. It is a Seeing Eye book.

BLANCO TAKES SHAPE around obscurities and revelations. At first, the obscurities make the deeper impression. A powerful feminine presence, *you,* and a somewhat flickering *I,* almost impersonal, move through the 250 short lines. The division into six parts and four double interludes sketches out a rise and fall of tension without giving it dramatic or narrative content. And even that order of parts can be modified or interrupted, an explicit note leaves ambiguity in the open. Paz even reinforced the prevailing ambiguity by a change he made after the first edition. *"El mundo / es tus imagines"* becomes *"El mundo / Haz de tus imagines." Haz* (sheaf; surface) suggests that "the world is your images" both as surface splendor and as essential composition. As one reads the poem, moreover, the language begins to stand alone. Words cling to sound and achieve separateness, releasing themselves from the bonding power of syntax and discursive meaning. *Flame, desert, eye, water*—the words seem to lie speechless on the page.

This atomistic reduction of language becomes the poem's ultimate revelation. Ten years after Paz harnessed the energies of Whitman and Surrealism in the tight lines of *Sun Stone,* he perfected an even terser line almost without connectives. In *BLANCO* this verbal condensation arrests the linear flow and opens the construction out into a great reconstellation of the universe, a folding in and out of parts. The astral, circular time of *Piedra del Sol* yields here to an interpenetrating time of heightened present. Past and future never blur this text. Everything is now. All verbs are in the present tense. Shot through with obscurities and stopped in its tracks by words confronted suddenly in themselves, *BLANCO* is a poem about the immediate texture of experience. "I move / . . . in thoughts I do not think." Does consciousness float upon inner substance or upon mere sheen? Watching himself watching that iridescence, the unknowable agent of this process alternates between personal and impersonal.

Paz prepares us for this pulse with his two epigraphs. Tantric passion says yes to a world of sensations and perceptions. Mallarmé's detached watching says no in the form of immaculately congealed words. This alternating current of consciousness charges the poem in its fluctuations through a sustained present.

IT TOOK A long time for writing to free itself from pictures. Even when it did, manuscripts were often illuminated in ways that kept the eye alert and informed. Printing at first had a restrictive effect on book illustration. The artist either produced clearly framed pictures or made flourishes to decorate the printed columns. In the nineteenth century, lithography opened up a new stage of collaboration between artist and poet. Yet the great book illustrations by Manet and Redon, by Bonnard and Rouault, are still *pictures,* identifiable by title and subject. Nonfigurative compositions so related to the text that the two frame and interpenetrate one another did not emerge until Arp and Kandinsky began to make woodcuts and drawings for their own poems. What they produced was neither illustration nor decoration. Following their lead, Dada artists in Switzerland, Germany, and France developed a form of nonobjective composition to complement nondiscursive poems. One of the most wholly satisfying works in this genre is Arp's *Auch das ist eine Wolke* (1920–1951).

When Yunkers says "illuminations," he is laying claim to this recent tradition, a symbiotic relation between visual shape and written text. Mallarmé's *Un coup de dés* arrays itself in the lineaments of its own thought forms. Apollinaire's *Calligrammes* make bold claims on both ideogram and painting. The collaboration between Yunkers and Paz has equally ambitious aims, closer to Mallarmé's than to Apollinaire's. In addition, colored or incised forms penetrate and punctuate the text of *BLANCO* in a sustained reinforcement of its rhythm. Across the poles of yes and no falls the long shadow of an inchoate emblem. Mere book illustration has been left far behind.

A POET WHO has travelled through many countries of the mind, Paz has had two guides in his explorations: Mallarmé and Duchamp. The gentle

French poet staked the ultimate intellectual claim of all time in a single sentence. "Everything in the world exists to end up in a book." Duchamp, equally astute and more gifted than Mallarmé as an engineer, considered a book to be "a machine for producing meanings." Haunted by these two statements, *BLANCO* remained a dark utterance, fourteen interlocking poems in search of an artist, until Yunkers created their apparatus, their white box. This reading machine, whose operation requires patience and a certain motor dexterity, is not an eternal art object for permanent collections. Use will slowly wear its materials and blur its lines. Nor is it trash art to be disposed of next season in order to make way for something else. It will last. Yet one gasps at the logistics and the economics of producing such a work. It contains both a facsimile of the original in Paz's handwriting and a fine translation by Eliot Weinberger. The liquid quality of the Spanish text and his own control allowed Eliot Weinberger to siphon the poem into English with a minimum of disturbance. The design combined hand-set type, lithography, silk screen, and facsimile, all on the highest-quality Arches paper. Typefaces were chosen that vary almost imperceptibly to match tone. Yunkers then stood over the printer at his press and insisted on the rejection of hundreds of slightly flawed sheets until the design was realized. It took him months to add collages and original paintings to every "copy"—none of which, therefore, is a copy at all. It is a unique, multiple, and illuminated work embodying an attitude toward words and forms that finally justifies its own unlikely existence. For it produces meanings that words alone, and pictures alone, do not transmit.

It is also a conjugal book. At the end of *Children of the Mire*, Paz speaks of his conception of modern poetry and makes an unadorned statement of faith: "It is not a transcendence but a convergence." Poetry does not transport us into another life or time, he insists; poetry plants us firmly in the here and now, where our world converges on and in itself. So be it. But that convergence of forces, which is our life, remains sterile, a mere passing in the night, unless there is also conjugation. In this version of *BLANCO*, Yunkers and Paz conjugate times and places, ideas and images, words and colors. And the work as a whole bears witness to the first and last conjugation subsuming and expressing all others, the conjugation of human bodies. *Blanco: white nights.*

IT IS QUITE properly a blank, or white, page—the final one—that best reveals the flow of all things into the present. The truly reflective mind circles powerfully around itself.

The spirit
Is an invention of the body
The body
Is an invention of the world
The world
Is an invention of the spirit
No   Yes

Out of such oscillations arises the steadiest of sensualities.

                 Your body
   Spilled on my body
                      Seen
   Dissolved
       Gives reality to the watching

There, facing these lines, is Yunkers' poised, free-flowing intaglio—dancer, river, celestial constellation, blank white paper barely shadowing itself to produce living forms. To its last page, this is a Seeing Eye book.

35

ARTHUR MILLER'S
ACCOUNT OF HIMSELF

RTHUR MILLER HAS done it all wrong. He grew up white and Jewish in Harlem and went to college in Michigan. He worked in a shipyard and wrote a film script with Ernie Pyle to redeem his 4-F status in World War II. *Death of a Salesman* dumped fame on him at the age of thirty-four. He has never turned his back or his wrath on the Marxists and Communists he knew as a young man. He divorced his wife of fifteen years to dedicate himself to an American Helen of Troy created by the casting studio. After a few months of marriage to Marilyn Monroe, he could no longer work with her or save her from herself. No one told him that in the introduction to his *Collected Plays* a dramatist must not declare flat-footedly that "life has meaning." Mr. Miller doesn't seem to understand that in our day an artist has to cultivate some extravagance or addiction or mania in order to make his mark. He isn't even homosexual. What is he trying to be? A Jewish-American Don Quixote?

For all his pains and his sins, Mr. Miller was the only American famous enough and courageous enough in 1966 to inject new vitality into PEN International. He presided with dignity over its congress of writers in Bled, Yugoslavia, and refused to change the rules to allow the Russians to join. Unpersuaded by the Beats, whose antics had become a commercial commodity in the United States, and resistant to the Absurd, which had devoured Europe, Mr. Miller, with his Gary Cooper physique and attentive manner, created at Bled a sense of evenhanded integrity that reaffirmed PEN as the champion of writers' freedom everywhere. Above all, he stood firm against any form of fanaticism from any quarter. Having been honored and investigated and condemned in his own country without losing his faith in it, he had unbeatable credentials and learned when to use them.

Anyone who knows Mr. Miller's work has seen this "life" coming for some time. Plays as different as *A Memory of Two Mondays* and *After the Fall* incorporate extensive autobiographical materials. Many of his essays on the theater deal with the circumstances of his professional and personal life. In spite of certain weaknesses, *Timebends* embraces and surpasses all these sources in a work of genuine literary craftsmanship and social exploration. I find Mr. Miller's lengthy autobiography neither self-serving nor self-indulgent in the way Lillian Hellman and Tennessee Williams saw fit to record their lives. Most of this self-portrait makes absorbing and entertaining reading.

MR. MILLER'S COMFORTABLE childhood in the era of rotogravure and radio was transformed by his father's ruin in the Depression and the family's forced move from their Upper West Side apartment at the edge of Harlem to Brooklyn. In passages reminiscent of Alfred Kazin's lyric memoir *A Walker in the City,* Mr. Miller describes round-robin handball games against the wall of Dozick's drugstore in the thirties. It was then that he heard murmurings of the new religion that condemned religion—Marxism—and underwent an important rite of passage while competing with other boys to sing the latest hit songs:

> After I had turned fifteen these competitions seemed childish, but I continued as one of the star comics of the gang, improvised inanities, doing imitations of the Three Stooges. . . . We always had a sandlot football team going, and one of our halfbacks, a giant with a heavy lower lip named Izzy Lenowitz . . . would clap me on my thin back and implore me, "Oh, come on, Artie, enjoy us." And with sufficient encouragement I would ad-lib a monologue that with a little luck might stay airborne for five minutes or more. Without plan or awareness of what I was doing, I had begun the process of separating myself: I was moving out of the audience to face them alone.

The detail and the diction convince me that the scene is authentic, even if telescopic. A form of self-imposed performance drew the youngster gradually out of his environment toward higher education, social causes, and the theater. That amalgam of interests carried him a long way. Yet the funny, moving, exasperating sense of the family unit in racially mixed Brooklyn never disappears from the later sections of the book.

Three hundred pages and twenty-five years later, Mr. Miller was subpoenaed to testify before the House Committee on Un-American Activities. He traveled to Washington in June 1956 while the press was hounding him because of his impending marriage to Marilyn Monroe and shortly before he needed his passport renewed for a trip to England, where both of them had professional engagements. Spyros Skouras, who held Monroe's contract at Twentieth Century–Fox, had flown from Hollywood to New York to try to persuade Mr. Miller to cooperate with the committee, name names, and condemn the Left. Mr. Miller's lawyer informed him that Francis Walter, the chairman of the committee, would call off the whole charade if Monroe would consent to a photograph of herself shaking hands with Walter. What did it all mean?

I find the muted yet intense account of the hearings oddly incomplete. Mr. Miller quotes his reply to the question, "should a Communist poet have the right to advocate overthrowing the government in his poetry?": "A man should have the right to write a poem about anything." And he goes on to explain his unequivocal opposition today to Marxism as passive before history and dismissive of human rights. He passes over his candid statement to the committee that aspects of Marxist thought "suited [his] mood" in the forties but that he was "never under Communist discipline."

What does not come out here or in Mr. Miller's 1953 play about the Salem witch trials, *The Crucible,* is that behind McCarthyism and the unscrupulous and publicity-seeking HUAC investigations lay not giggling girls and a widespread belief in witches but a genuine international conspiracy that threatened Europe at the time, even if it did not threaten the United States. Mr. Miller has never been moved to write a play comparable to the novels *Nineteen Eighty-Four* or *Darkness at Noon,* or to explore dramatically how he could have been drawn to a doctrine and a practice he later rejected. At the hearings, Mr. Miller behaved honorably, never took the Fifth Amendment, and made his legal and intellectual points with eloquence. The House went on to vote 373 to 4 to cite him for contempt of Congress. In *Timebends,* Mr. Miller could have probed deeper into this complex confrontation.

On the page following his account of the hearings, Mr. Miller describes how he and Marilyn Monroe were received in England by Laurence Olivier and an immense crowd of reporters. Of the reporters, he says, "When she smiled they did, and frowned when she frowned, and if she so much as giggled they roared with delighted laughter, and listened in churchly silence when she took a moment and actually *spoke!* with her voice so soft and soothing that grown men went limp as lichens at the living sound of it."

WHAT SECRET, WHAT dream brought together the radical intellectual and Hollywood's sex goddess? In an earlier scene that tests our credulity and Mr. Miller's writing, he describes fainting in a Nevada telephone booth when he realizes that Monroe is on the verge of suicide during the filming of *Bus Stop.* He revives, talks her back down to sanity, and goes on in his commentary to reveal the fantasy he had spun for himself of their life together: "To be one thing, sexuality and mind, appetite and justice. . . . My vision had been of each of us doing our own work side by side, drawing strength from one another." One of the book's few rancorous moments comes near the end, when Mr. Miller tells us that Monroe was proof that sexuality and seriousness cannot coexist in the American psyche. The shattering of his vision of a higher coupling represents another rite of passage. Everything here suggests that his third wife, the photographer Inge Morath, with whom he has collaborated on four books, saved him from bitterness and kept him working.

The passages I have mentioned evoke most of the major themes in *Timebends*—family, theater, politics, women. But there is more. As a child, Mr. Miller was taken by his great-grandfather to the 114th Street synagogue and observed "about fifteen old men, bent over and covered completely by their prayer shawls, all of them in white socks, *dancing!*" Later, Dostoyevsky and Melville invaded his mind at about the same time as Marxism. A 1958 essay entitled "The Shadows of the Gods" describes the deep shock of the Depression on Mr. Miller's whole attitude toward life when he realized that no one, not even a businessman, was in charge: "What the time gave me . . . was a sense of an invisible world." The motif of the spiritual, without the benefit of formal religion but never isolated from moral and social dilemmas, runs strongly through Mr. Miller's work, including *Timebends.* Several times, he quotes Ibsen's line from *An Enemy of the People*—"He is strongest who is most alone"—as if it should be the key to salvation. Later, the hero's final cry in Pound's translation of Sophocles' *Ajax*—"It all coheres!"—wins out. By the last paragraph of the book, Mr. Miller has decided to devote himself to "making myself possible." I read his last sentences as close to prayer: "The truth, the first truth, probably, is that we are all connected, watching one another. Even the trees."

TEN PAGES INTO his recollections of early childhood, Mr. Miller jumps ahead forty-five years to relate how the family dining room table was used as a prop in his play *The Price*. *Timebends* does not advance in a steady narrative line. Its eight untitled sections dig up bucketfuls of past incidents ordered almost as much by association as by chronology. When Mr. Miller speaks here of wanting to write a play that will achieve the simultaneity of lines in music, that will "cut through time like a knife through a layer cake or a road through a mountain revealing its geologic layers . . . instead of one incident in one time-frame after another," he is also describing this autobiographical book full of shuttlings and diagonals.

Its somewhat lame title refers to this laminated free-form construction as well as to a deep-sea diver's malady when he comes up too rapidly from the depths. The nearly paratactic structure successfully assimilates the diaries and notebooks from which Mr. Miller must have worked, and it allows him to alternate dramatized scenes, superb descriptions of people and places, and commentary from the present. As "a life," *Timebends* is closer to the sweep and shift of *The Autobiography of Malcolm X* than to the careful analyses of *The Education of Henry Adams*. (Mr. Miller could not possibly have got away with what Adams did; Adams simply omitted his fourteen-year marriage and his wife's suicide.) In its construction, its soliloquizing voice, and its sense of time, *Timebends* resembles André Malraux's *Antimemoirs*, but it is without Malraux's grandiloquent tone of living perpetually at the summit of history.

Many characters emerge vividly: Mr. Miller's illiterate yet baronial father; Manny Newman, a Brooklyn salesman and family man who shares many of Willy Loman's fantasies; Mitch Berenson and Vincent Longhi, union mavericks who tried to buck Joe Ryan, the longshoremen's union boss, and the Mafia on the docks; Marilyn Monroe; and the director Elia Kazan (although Mr. Miller has never forgiven Mr. Kazan for his testimony to HUAC, he remains loyal to him as a man of the theater). The Monroe portrait is above all loyal, not altogether tidied up, composed by a man almost wistfully resigned to fate. It is evident that Mr. Miller himself wrote the captions for the thirty-two pages of photographs in *Timebends*. Giving no identifications, he laconically labels the center spread of pictures showing him with Monroe and others in glowing poses "The best of times." Presumably, the reader can complete the opening sentence of *A Tale of Two Cities*. Mr. Miller's mother and his first wife remain shadowy figures. Ernie Pyle, Laurence Olivier, Clark Gable, Lee and Paula Strasberg make convincing appearances in working situations that bring out Mr. Miller's shrewdness as a judge of character. Only the Strasbergs earn his contempt as self-absorbed mountebanks.

The writing varies a great deal in *Timebends*. The opening pages, woven loosely around a child's "view from the floor," reach an almost Proustian note: "It's simply that the view from the floor, filled though it is with misunderstandings, is also the purest." The account of the rehearsals and ultimate success of *Death of a Salesman* effectively mixes public fact and personal feelings without distortion. Mr. Miller describes smells with particular passion. The most apposite and amusing dialogue occurs in the plane carrying him back to New York after the shooting of *The Misfits* and his breakup with Monroe. Seeing a man about to recognize him, Mr. Miller lies: "I'm not him. I look like him, but I'm not." But the stranger thinks Mr. Miller is not Mr. Miller, but the owner of a hardware store in Poughkeepsie. After great fame, anonymity returns.

In discussing one of our most substantial authors, I cannot refrain from pointing out a troubling drift toward inept usage in this book. "Societal," "depart" as a transitive verb, "researching," "different than"—does Arthur Miller want to be quoted in future dictionaries as licensing these forms? Referring to the 1930s, he writes: "If there was a national pastime I suppose it was hanging out." He has been listening too long to his children. In the Depression years, we hung "around" or went to a "hangout."

THERE ARE TWO flaws that cut deeper than style. In analyzing presences as different as Marilyn Monroe and Robert Oppenheimer, Mr. Miller falls back repeatedly on the word *power*. He fails to distinguish the fame-glamour-stardom cluster from strength-authority-position. They are not the same, even though they overlap in notions like privilege and charisma. *Power* used alone to cover all these items belongs to a mode of fuzzy thinking Mr. Miller usually deplores. At other moments he writes true, apropos of Clark Gable for instance: "A great star implies he is his own person and can be mean and even dangerous, like a great leader."

The second flaw takes the form of a double standard of divulgence and indulgence. We learn a great deal about Mr. Miller's professional dealings and public life. Yves Montand, however, with whom Marilyn Monroe had an affair, is never mentioned in connection with her. Mr. Miller's long marriage to Mary Slattery appears only obliquely and through lenses. One can respect his discretion, but there is evidently more to say. Late in the book, he issues some ramrod-straight judgments of the self-destructiveness of drugs and liberated sex in the sixties. He refers convincingly to a "moral center." But one remembers earlier pages about Lucky Luciano and organized crime, which suggest a tolerance, even a comic sympathy for them, that I find disturbing and out of character.

In his plays, Mr. Miller has never quite resolved or fully exploited the double attraction of his talent—to collective drama, in which society itself is the protagonist, and to monodrama, which takes place inside one person's head. He is the closest we come to Bertolt Brecht. This "life," appearing when Mr. Miller was seventy-two years old and still writing, represents more than his claim to a place in twentieth-century literature. *Timebends* is really a book of falls. The central pages portray "a perpetual night of confusion" that descended on Mr. Miller in the early fifties. The original fall of the Depression was followed by the crumbling of his marriage and his disenchantment with Marxism at the moment when McCarthy's know-nothingism was sweeping the country. After the triumph of *Death of a Salesman,* his writing had reached an apparent standstill. His first trip to Hollywood was a failure. All these disasters seem to be ironically focused in Mr. Miller's searing encounter in Hollywood with a lonely Marilyn Monroe. He survived these falls and more. A book that passes through moments of numbing despair ends up close to rhapsodic.

36

NAIPAUL ON THE
AMERICAN SOUTH

I.

All day, mechanics and construction workers across North America keep a radio twanging next to the socket wrenches or hooked on to bare studs.* All night, the ghost army of workers and cleaners who service the offices and classroom buildings in our towns fill the corridors with the same music from their portable sets. To travel in this land today, you need not only wheels but also a radio tuned to Country—to one of the thousands of radio stations across the continent that now play country-and-western music day and night. Our samizdat is wide open, electronic, and commercially successful. Its wailing or driving rhythms ride on slide guitars and nasal voices. Behind the broken loves and honky-tonk lives celebrated in the lyrics, it doesn't take long to find bedrock. John Denver's bid for a new national anthem is entitled "Thank God I'm a Country Boy." It contains the essential code word.

What's going on? What does "country" mean? Country-and-western music appeals to a thick social stratum in the North and South and may

---

*Henry Glassie, folklorist, David James, sociologist, and Paul Gaston, historian, discussed with me some of the ideas and materials treated here. I wish to acknowledge their help with gratitude and to exonerate them from responsibility for the final form of the review.

even define it. Folklorists tell us that an economically and politically deprived segment of the citizenry in any country will soon find an outlet for its feelings in a folk art, often in music. With at least a sixty-year history, C&W music may well be telling us something about the inadequacy of political parties in their present form to represent the people.[1] In its several intermingled styles—hillbilly, gospel, bluegrass, cowboy—this music incorporates a strongly felt tradition of populism and protest. We should not misread today's signals: "country" protest comes from the Right.

"Country" means redneck. The second word crops up fairly frequently in today's songs as a brag. It mediates between the old slur "white trash" and the new, cleaned-up model, "country," an adjective that can enhance anything from pork to chintz. As soon as you try to define *redneck,* you turn the word into a caricature. Poor, white, undereducated, manual or farm or wage labor, disreputable, patriotic—useless half-truths. Catching the category accurately should concern us less than its expansion and its extent. Rednecks used to exist only in the South. Today, there is no state in the union, no province in Canada without a redneck culture. A diversified corporation in southern Indiana runs a highly successful year-round Country festival and calls itself Little Nashville. WBOS in Boston plays "ten Country numbers back to back" around the clock. Rednecks punish their pickup trucks and consume their six-packs in Oregon, in Vermont, in Saskatchewan as ritually as they do in Mississippi and Tennessee. The cowboy has not disappeared; he has been taken over. His ten-gallon hat has yielded to the baseball or feed-grain cap. His boots go on.

The reddening of America has already caught the full attention of the music and clothing industries. A few sociologists have given it their attention. The "greening" and later the "blueing" of America had their day in journalism and did not stay the course to become history. I put forward the "reddening of America" with my tongue only slightly in cheek. It is V. S. Naipaul's book *A Turn in the South* that has nudged me into taking the leap. He assembles striking yet still unassimilated evidence that the phenomenon has advanced a long way in the South. I extrapolate the rest.

But how far can we believe the evidence of a travel book, the product of a few months in seven southern states and little systematic "research"? Is it sociology or chicanery? The writer comes from another country, another culture, another religion. What we share is a language and something called "humanity." Is that enough? We let him travel unimpeded around the country—a self-employed spy, crank tourist, uncarded journalist, world witness. We take him into our houses and feed him. We pour out our hearts to him—maybe court him a little, tell him a few tall tales. He listens well and seems to get it all down in his notebook. A New York publisher released his book, and the critics went to work with the respect due an intelligent foreigner and distinguished novelist. We always want a fresh view, a new understanding. Maybe he sees first what we see last. This doubly displaced Trinidadian with a sphinxlike face must be the invisible man. He can go anywhere. People notice him, but they don't mind. Well, if not invisible, at least ubiquitous.

2.

In *A Turn in the South,* Naipaul writes as if a modern oracle had chosen to speak through him. The individual sentences and paragraphs read easily enough. The mysterious oracular quality comes from Naipaul's willingness to follow random leads and his disinclination to pull everything together into a set of conclusions. The absorbing case histories and conversations he records with the skill of a novelist-journalist point urgently toward a significance that the reader himself must construe. The author of superb earlier books on Trinidad, India, Africa, and worldwide Islam decided suddenly at the 1984 Republican convention in Dallas to write "my last travel book" (he was all of fifty-seven) on the old slave states. He would take a turn in the South, conduct a search without preset plan or itinerary. "The timing was pure chance," he writes on the first page, and opens in medias res. Naipaul is a seasoned-enough stylist to dispense with an introduction as briskly as with a conclusion. Then on page 164, we reach one of the several embedded introductory passages; he justifies his discontinuous montage form, which combines travel account, interviews (50 percent of the book lies between quotation marks), and personal memoir.

> And travel of the sort I was doing, travel on a theme, depends on accidents: the books read on a journey, the people met. To travel in the way I was doing was like painting in acrylic or fresco; things set quickly. The whole shape of a section of the narrative can be determined by some chance meeting, some phrase heard or devised.

The passage is preparing us for things to come. The working hypothesis behind *A Turn in the South,* developed out of *Among the Believers* (1981), has a studied naïveté; if you can just find the right circumstances, talk with people not paralyzed by their station, the culture will speak for itself. Ordinary people reveal as much about their collective lives as leaders. Like the earlier books, *Turn* is a tissue of brilliantly recorded hearsay, of intense listening by a man with a remarkable ear and unencumbered by a tape recorder. Every so often, he pauses to interview himself, primarily about comparisons with the interracial society of Trinidad, where he grew up as an Indian. Now in the American South, he travels as a professional intermediary and exotic, unthreatening, catlike in his movements, a canny Candide in his requests for explanations of the commonplace.

After an initiatory Easter trip with two friends to a small black community in North Carolina, Naipaul finds his way a bit shakily into the black politics of Atlanta. Of the four important and very different elected officials he talks to, Robert Waymer of the Atlanta School Board seems to impress him most. Having produced the Socratic caution "You got to know that you don't know anything about blacks," Waymer says quietly that "the civil-rights movement was great for everybody" but that the end of segregation led to a breakdown of black communities and institutions. This ironic consequence of success turns out to be one of the leitmotifs of the book.

In Charleston, Naipaul finds a fading city readjusting to its famous past and to a new tourist economy. A black parole board commissioner in Tallahassee develops another powerful theme. "The church is my salvation. The church keeps me sane." The following chapter carries Naipaul to Tuskegee University. He stays in the guest house and finds reason to sympathize with Booker T. Washington's vocational emphasis in the early days of the institute, a policy attacked by W.E.B. Du Bois.[2] Naipaul depicts a Tuskegee "in decay." The end of segregation removed its essential justification.

Jackson, Mississippi, Naipaul's next stop, reveals the second meaning of the "turn" in his title. He shifts perspectives.

> It was my wish, in Mississippi, to consider things from the white point of view, as far as that was possible for me. Someone in New York had told me that it wouldn't be easy. In Mississippi, though, I found that people were defensive about their reputation.[3] This seemed to give me a start. But then I wasn't sure.

Naipaul interviews a series of older white women and includes a brief talk with Eudora Welty. A catfish farm and processing plant in the Delta shows him the commercial enterprise of the New South. Suddenly on page 204, the turn becomes a veer. (By now, one hears an intellectual rhyme with his earlier title *A Bend in the River.*) Earlier mentions of crackers, poor whites, hillbillies, and rednecks have left Naipaul puzzled. He decides to ask a loquacious real estate man, "What do you understand by the word 'redneck'?" He receives in answer a character portrait close to Theophrastus and La Bruyère in its accuracy and detail. Naipaul is hooked. The remaining third of the book is essentially monopolized by the subject of rednecks.

Instead of a planned Faulknerian pilgrimage to Oxford, Naipaul makes the pilgrimage to Elvis Presley's house in Tupelo, Mississippi.

The long and searching Nashville chapter deals with the country-music industry, Church of Christ members, and the message of the widely respected churchless Baptist preacher Will Campbell. Campbell is also the author of the moving autobiography *Brother to a Dragonfly* (1980). After some pages on the new factory complexes of General Motors and Nissan outside Nashville, the last chapter on Chapel Hill closes the circle with a tour through the tobacco culture under the gentle guidance of a poet, James Applewhite. *A Turn in the South* closes with four lines of his poetry, in which "poor-white powder" rhymes with "a brownface river." The oracular touches stay with us to the end.

DESPITE ITS BRILLIANT moments, Naipaul has not worked this book up to his highest standard. Some fleeting details add only puzzlement. A turbaned student in the hotel driveway reads aloud and chants in Arabic. Jesse Jackson's limousine is parked in front of a restaurant with its hood up and without its occupant. An undertaker's name is Breeland. Paula, a waitress who believes Satan is trying to tempt her, is given an almost sibylline voice in her plight. None of these moments becomes consequential. And there are too many vocal males named Campbell in the book. Occasionally, a sentence jars by its odd usage.

The highway looked like highways everywhere else in the United States: boards for motels and restaurants and gas stations.

[Spoken by an uneducated, oddball black.] "But you must know that I truly respect my past, be it segregated, be it filled with racism, be it whatever."

I had the vaguest idea of what a redneck was.

At the opening of the Nashville chapter, Naipaul splices into the narrative two pages on his "writing anxieties" and his concern "to define a theme." The pages strike me as writer's talk, out of place.

Naipaul never tips his hat to Tocqueville, never tries his hand at the Frenchman's masterful marshalling of observation into general statements about a foreign society. Nor does Dickens's *American Notes* provide a comparison. Dickens traveled everywhere as Boz, a celebrity with a cause (international copyright) and a method (visit prisons, orphanages, insane asylums). Naipaul moves less decisively across the landscape, listening rather than talking. His prose follows rather than leads his quest. What he finds emerges slowly and unemphatically.

3.

"In one lifetime, then, it seemed that she had moved from frontier culture, or the relics of a frontier culture, to late twentieth-century Jackson and the United States."

Here is the third "turn" of Naipaul's title. Approaching the question of the New South versus the Old South that confronts every historian of the region, Naipaul seems to feel that his observations have proved the case for discontinuity: Conditions have changed markedly, especially since the 1954 Supreme Court desegregation decision and the civil rights marches. I doubt that Naipaul's modestly urged hypothesis will change the mind of anyone who has looked carefully at the question. What he contributes is anecdotes, case histories, without any irritable reaching after statistics and overall patterns. The word *identity* surfaces very early, contrasted not with a stereotypical "alienation" but with a different state Naipaul has observed in his earlier travels. "I always knew how important it was not to fall into nonentity." At the end of the chapter on Tallahassee, he reiterates "the final cruelty" that desegregation may be depriving blacks of the supports of faith and community that gave them identity. "It is hard to enter into their vacancy." The horror of that flat sentence can be measured when one sets it alongside the opening of Naipaul's powerful novel of Africa, *A Bend in the River.* "The world is what it is; men who are nothing, who allow themselves to become nothing, have no place in it." His sympathy is unsparing.

A Turn in the South does not shrink from the desperation of southern blacks in an ostensibly improved condition. Their attitude toward the past, examined throughout the book, settles into an awkward ambivalence shared by whites: "separation, and kinship." Aware of how in India the past can paralyze, can kill, Naipaul keeps looking for the new. He finds it in the rehabilitation of one of the oldest of human activities, religion. On page after page, the skeptical ex-Hindu notes with amazement and considerable admiration the deep significance of both religious faith and the community of churches to blacks and whites from Church of Christ to Presbyterian. When the Baptist preacher Will Campbell describes his intellectual round-trip from fundamentalism to liberalism and back, he produces a sentence as political as it is religious: "Jesus asked us to be mindful of the one near at hand." Then Campbell takes his guitar and sings a parable to explain that line.

No, we don't fit in with that white-collar crowd.
We're a little too rowdy and a little too loud.
But there's no place that I'd rather be than right here,
With my red neck, white socks, and Blue Ribbon beer.

The lesson Naipaul draws from his travels is not only the expected sympathy he felt for the despair of blacks but also an unexpected feeling for whites who have fallen among thieves (and their own vices) and need a Samaritan's help.

Rednecks become both the central characters and the chorus of the crucial Jackson and Nashville chapters. The portrait sketched for us derives more from Daumier than from Walker Evans. In Jackson, the words that pour out of the real estate salesman named Campbell like a prose ode deflect Naipaul's enterprise in a new direction.

"A redneck is a lower blue-collar construction worker who definitely doesn't like blacks. He likes to drink beer. He's going to wear cowboy boots; he is not necessarily going to have a cowboy hat. He is going to live in a trailer someplace out in Rankin County, and he's going to smoke about two and a half packs of cigarettes a day and drink about ten cans of beer at night, and he's going to be mad as hell if he doesn't have some cornbread and peas and fried okra and some fried pork chops to eat—I've never seen one of those bitches yet who doesn't like fried pork chops. And he'll be late on his trailer payment.

"He's been raised that way. His father was just like him. And the son of a bitch loves country music. They love to hunt and fish. . . .

"You know, I like those rednecks. They're so laid back. They don't give a shit. They don't give a shit.

". . . The rednecks have the pioneer attitude, all right. They don't want to go to the damn country club and play golf. They ain't got fifteen damn cents, and they're just tickled to death.

". . . Old Mama, she's gonna wear designer jeans and they're gonna go to Shoney's to eat once every three weeks. . . .At Shoney's you'll get the gravy all over it. . . .

"The rednecks are about sixty to sixty-five percent of the white population. I'm running the good old rednecks and the upscale red-

necks and a whole bunch of lower-middle-class rednecks. . . .
Daddy is home a little more often. But they're tickled pink that they
ain't got nothing. You wouldn't believe."

Naipaul runs four pages of this rhapsody. Only a gifted writer would have
heard those cadences and caught them in his notebook, with added articles
and choral repetitions. Both parties command a certain solfège, a dressage of
language. The collaboration brings us the only laughs in the book and a
miniature masterpiece.

A few pages later, Naipaul designates his newfound friends as a "threatened species" with shrinking hunting grounds, like the Indians. All those
statements need revision. Way back in Charleston, someone gave Naipaul
an idea he could quickly register. "The crackers, like the blacks, had their
own place in the local caste system." When Naipaul goes dutifully and
uncomprehendingly to the Grand Ole Opry, "It was like a tribal rite . . . the
expression of a community." I sense that he turns his attention and his sympathy to the rednecks because he feels they sometimes project a stronger
identity than blacks. By sheer orneriness and vainglory, they refuse to fall
into nonentity. Not the finest ideal.[4]

In the delicate matter of cultural interpretation, Naipaul might have
paid more attention to the music. (No radio traveled in his baggage.) Late in
the game, he tries to catch up. An interview with a country music producer
in Nashville informs him about Elvis Presley representing "secular and
gospel, white and black" and directs him to Bob McDill, who works full-
time writing successful country music lyrics. But country and western
music remains as incomprehensible to Naipaul as rhythm and blues. One of
McDill's lyrics quoted in the book describes a Daddy "with gin on his breath
and a Bible in his hand" kissing his son good night. The son sings the
refrain.

> *I guess we're all gonna be what we're gonna be.*
> *So what do you do with good ole boys like me?*

The lines might have told Naipaul that the rednecks have by no means overcome nonentity to attain freedom and identity. And a little music history
would have cast light on his reconciliation thesis.

For quietly and obliquely, Naipaul implies that black and red might discover common ground against white. He could easily deny ever having said
such a thing. But the asides sometimes speak more directly than the central

argument. Andrew, a young Mississippi politician, referring to blacks and rednecks, concludes, "If we can't get together we are lost." Real estate man Campbell has his own version. "We got to change that redneck society and that black society, or the wealth is going to be just in the few hands that it's always been in." Will Campbell sees rednecks as "sharing an ancestry of servitude."

Could there ever be a joining of causes between blacks and rednecks based on deprivation, political ostracism, strong sense of the past, and religious sentiment? Country music offers a parable in answer to that question. In the forties, Bill Monroe and his entourage drew on both black music and hillbilly music to mount a driving synthesis he called "bluegrass." Monroe described it beautifully as "jazz in overdrive." In the fifties, Elvis Presley, saturated in rhythm and blues and gospel, produced the stunningly successful hybrid we know as rock and roll. It can hardly be said that Bob Dylan synthesized all the folk, protest, and black elements that contributed to his art. But he kept faith with them all. We thought he had chosen country with *Nashville Skyline*. Then *Self-Portrait* decomposed any synthesis into a sampler and let all the different styles hang out. Only one black musician, the great Charley Pride, has succeeded in achieving full recognition as a country-music star. After fifty years of cross-fertilization and mutual admiration among professionals, country-and-western music remains essentially all white, and occasionally coded "racist." Can politics and society accomplish what has not happened in the privileged domains of music? Redneck culture and C&W music may travel across the rest of the continent more easily than they can come to terms with their immediate black neighbors. Still, we can hope the reconciliation thesis is right for a longer run.

Naipaul gets an astonishing number of things right during his turn in the South watching the South turn. Unfortunately, he omits TV evangelists from his account and underplays the KKK and other forms of organized prejudice. The genre of a series of interviews held during a few months prevents the book from having an adequate sense of time and the endurance of things. No scene begins to match the subtle comic sense Naipaul showed in his earliest novels of Trinidad. Is he too close? Too rushed? When he remarks after talking to a white politician, "Optimism in the foreground; irrationality in the background," we know this line will lead to pathos, not comedy.

Unlike Gandhi, whom he dared to criticize, Naipaul has no program. There is nothing of the guru in him. He probably knows that there can be no program. Gandhi's, he angrily argues in *India: A Wounded Civilization* (1977), transformed his fellow citizens from colonial subjects into a state of independent, atavistic passiveness. When he seeks out the American South and writes without long experience and without anger, I found myself wondering if dispassionate observation of the present moment of a culture is possible. Out of his wrath in *India*, Naipaul answers that question with a fine authority. "When men cannot observe, they don't have ideas; they have obsessions."

NOTES

1. David Duke, in his successful run for the Louisiana legislature in 1989, ex–Ku Klux Klan Grand Wizard and president of his own National Association for the Advancement of White People, deployed no singers and fiddlers in his campaign. He may be too upscale. But we should not forget that Jimmie Davis, composer and performer of "You Are My Sunshine," was elected governor of Louisiana and beat the Huey Long machine in 1944 and 1960. One of the greatest Grand Ole Opry stars, Roy Acuff, ran for the same office in Tennessee. Country music has also played a singular role in Texas politics. President Bush's trainer, Lee Atwater, former chairman of the Republican party, has a mean stage presence as a rhythm-and-blues guitarist. The politics of music runs very deep.

2. Naipaul has read *The Souls of Black Folk* (1903) and observes that it "seems lyrical for the sake of lyricism." I am surprised he does not remark on how much Du Bois's elevated, sometimes Emersonian, rhetoric contributed to that of Martin Luther King, Jr., and, occasionally, Jesse Jackson.

3. Addressing "racial problems" near the end of the first volume of *Democracy in America,* Tocqueville wrote: "In the southern states, people don't talk. They will not speak about the future to strangers; they avoid discussions with friends; each person hides the subject from himself." (RS)

4. In his elegantly tendentious classic, *The Mind of the South* (1941), W. J. Cash almost shows Naipaul the way. Cash's recurring discussion of poor whites (he never mentions the term *redneck*) circles around "the savage ideal," which combines shiftlessness and energy, yeoman stock and degeneracy, hedonism and paternalism.

37

A POET'S STORIES:
W. S. MERWIN

A *NUMBER OF* modern poets have tended to explore aspects of their sensibility and of their surroundings more boldly in prose than in poetry. Baudelaire excelled at the critical essay; his prose poems and intimate journals complement *Les Fleurs du mal* in subtle ways we are still discovering. Hofmannsthal made a major poetic statement in *The Letter of Lord Chandos* (1902). Rilke speaks to many of us through the intense scenes of *The Notebooks of Malte Laurids Brigge*. I could make a strong case for Rimbaud and even for Mallarmé as poets sometimes at their best in prose. Dylan Thomas came down to earth in his ripely sensuous stories. A related rule of thumb tells us that poets have been the best critics of poetry.

The fine command of prose by a poet gives to *The Lost Upland: Stories of Southwest France* a strong appeal in a genre that alternates between description and narrative. In the first two stories, "Foie Gras" and "Shepherds," W. S. Merwin finds his range and his voice for depicting the rhythms of life in one of the oldest rural regions of France. "Blackbird's Summer" is a 150-page novella whose appeal lies in its discovery of listenings and revelations among the most ordinary moments of unfamiliar lives. I shall try to explain why I find *The Lost Upland* Merwin's most impressive book as well as a rare achievement.

The translations Merwin has published from his earliest years have disciplined his language and his mind. They now add up to fifteen volumes, ranging from *Poem of the Cid* to Jean Follain's poetry. Translating for a living has helped Merwin avoid the confinements and hypocrisies of creative-writing programs. Two visits to Ezra Pound at St. Elizabeth's Hospital when Merwin was eighteen steered him in the healthy direction of a career as an independent writer.

Through twelve or so collections, Merwin's poetry has followed a fairly common trajectory. His early formalist writing sometimes seemed to hover in midair between the attractions of Pound and of Stevens. With his fourth book, *The Drunk in the Furnace* (1960), he found a diction of his own. The cultural and political gales of the sixties drove many young American poets toward a freer line and engaged subjects. While he was living primarily in France, Merwin's poetry not only adopted a loose line; for a time, he eliminated all punctuation, as Apollinaire had done. In 1971, Merwin announced he was giving his Pulitzer Prize money to Draft Resistance (after appearing at first to refuse the award). Yet his poems alternated primarily between family motifs from the Lackawanna region in Pennsylvania and French goat sheds. In the early eighties, he began reeling in his verse structures, and he tried out a clumsy typographical experiment emphasizing the caesura by means of a channel down the center of the page dividing all lines in two.

Looking again at Merwin's substantial published poetry, I have the impression of one underlying theme. He returns over and over again to the basic act of noticing, of paying attention. Around that fragile encounter of subject and object, everything else becomes embellishment, the necessary ritual that frames and protects the fleeting moment of revelation. This remark applies also to the highly miscellaneous collection, *House and Travelers* (1977), which includes several successful prose poems.

THE STORIES THAT make up *The Lost Upland* are linked by their association with a single region in southwest France where Merwin bought a house and lived for several years. His previous prose collections have tried out earlier versions of portions of these stories. Since the names of all but major and distant towns have been changed, I cannot pinpoint the area. It apparently lies east of Bordeaux and south of Limoges, near the Lot River. The three stories also form a sequence of statement, variation, and full elaboration corresponding to their lengths (50, 100, and 150 pages, respectively). "Foie Gras" appeared in *The New Yorker*, "Shepherds" in *The Paris Review*. "Blackbird's Summer" is published for the first time. It could easily stand alone, but the overlap and contrast of the three pieces achieve a cumulative effect, like collage, like sampling different vintages of wine.

Monsieur le Comte, the central character in the first story, attempts with declining success to survive on his minor aristocratic lineage, his stories, and his knowledge of the countryside and its history. In order to support his family and a decaying château, he is reduced to taking in paying guests from foreign countries and to dealing in antiques. Obese from an addiction to foie gras, the colorful and contemptuous count gradually becomes a run-down scrounger and petty thief. His neighbors both despise him and laugh at him. At the end, after being caught stealing cans of foie gras from the new supermarket, he tries to die in state in his Renaissance room. The burial is a fiasco because of his oversize coffin. The tale has become a cartoon of a lost nobleman, whose attempt to keep up appearances turns him into a grotesque imposter—Don Quixote in reverse.

In "Shepherds," Merwin puts aside the quiet ventriloquism by which we hear the count's gossip and endless prevarications After the third-person narrative of "Foie Gras," the second story opens in a distant key. "For a few years I had a garden in a ruined village." While the narrator cultivates his vegetables and flowers, the two sheep-raising neighboring families (they do not speak to each other) gradually accept him and exchange visits and favors. One shepherd named Michel, considered totally backward by the other family, has refused to install electricity and clings to a small flock, traditional practices, and bare survival. Michel is not above using the almost invisible stone shelters built by the Gauls to protect themselves from wind and rain. Merwin's imagination responds carefully and beautifully to a man-made symbol that conforms to the contours of nature.

Each of the shelters was sited to watch over a wide expanse of grazing land. Each of their arched doorways framed a place that was like nowhere else. Sockets. Michel would never have admitted to sitting in one. Never. Not as a child, when they were regarded with awe. Children did not play in them. The huts were the abodes of figures of the past, and were spoken of as though they were haunted, though it was never said, and there were no stories. In the present age there was a certain shame attached to the notion of actually entering one and sitting there, taking shelter in so rude and small a place, the kind of protection that humans had been making for themselves in that region, out of the stones lying there, for thousands of years. Nobody wanted to be thought of as backward. Almost no one in the region had sat in the huts for a long time.

Roots came through the roofs. Trees grew up through them. Every year the reclamation project devoured a few more, along with the walls into which they had been built. But Michel sat in them, unseen, and looked out on pastures that were his own and on others that were not. He emerged from them cautiously, and looked up at the open air overhead, while his sheep flowed around him.

Monsieur Vert, the other neighbor, keeps a prosperous and progressive farm with a large extended family and constant building projects. In a final moving sequence, forty of M. Vert's sheep break through a fence and are killed or maimed by an express train. When they have to be burned in an enormous pyre, the narrator and even Michel turn out to help. A cautious neighborliness has flowed back into the abandoned village. When the narrator leaves for a trip, Michel murmurs to him what has not been lost on anyone: "You weren't born here. But you're from here." In this low-key story that moves like the seasons, the words veer close to sentimentality. But the ending maintains an undemonstrative dignity.

In the third story Merwin removes himself and centers the action on "Blackbird," a successful widowed wine merchant and owner of a hotel-restaurant run by his daughter and son-in-law. Like the count, Blackbird travels around the countryside—in his case, to make deliveries, take orders, and visit his customers. Driving his small truck, this poised reflective traveler holds the entire region in his mind—its inhabitants, its customs, its topography, its buildings. He works out of the redolent fastness of his ancient stone cellars.

But Blackbird has no son. In this late summer of his life, his concerns turn increasingly to how he will leave that life. He decides to have a mason wall up a dozen bottles of his finest wines, all hand-labeled "To the Demolishers of this Building." Since neither his daughter nor his son-in-law drinks wine, his principal worry is the succession of the wine business. We are a party to his investigations into who would have the requisite taste, tact, and devotion to tradition to replace him. Impetuously, he offers his business to two devoted foreign customers, one after the other, without success. Everything (except the name Blackbird) folds back into place when he confers the business on his nephew Pierre. They shake hands solemnly in a café and look forward to traveling out together on cold autumn mornings to sample the summer's wine.

Especially if you have some familiarity with this kind of countryside and the struggle of the inhabitants to reconcile tradition and progress, you will be drawn to these quiet narratives. Merwin's prose, which varies between the succulent and the lean, responds readily to the sensuous ("Blackbird's Summer" opens in the dark), to fragile moods, and to language itself. In "Shepherds," Michel and his brother Robert have just shorn the flock with hand clippers and are watching the animals, which looked "as though they had been made by a wood carver who had left them covered with the marks of the adze." The brothers begin to speak of the virtues of the wool from their rocky plateaus *(causses).*

"It's the only thing," Robert the roofer said. *"Causse* wool."
"Nothing like it," Michel said. "For the health. But it has to be raw wool."
"Winter," Robert said. "It's the only thing. It keeps the feet warm."
"Best thing to sleep on," Robert said. "Wool mattress."
"We don't sleep on anything else," Michel said.
"Sweaters," Robert said.
"You put it against your back," Michel said, pushing his hand up inside his red sleeveless jersey, "like that. Pure wool. For rheumatism. For the kidneys. It draws it out. My mother puts it there. My father put it there."
"It warms you," Robert said.
"It absorbs," Michel said.
"It absorbs everything," Robert confirmed, with a gesture of his hand like a magician's about to draw a handkerchief out of the air. "Primordial."
"Even wet," Michel said. "It's good in the rain. Impermeable. The old shepherds' cloaks."
They both nodded.
"To the ground," Michel said. "My grandfather wore one. That was all they needed. You could live in it."

The passage is not a Hemingway pastiche but a stylized attempt to move close to a conversation. One of Merwin's devices or conventions is to handle the French language through virtual transliteration. He goes astray in carrying the word *snobbism* into English. "To modernize the old building at pleasure" sounds quaint rather than vernacular. But the passage just quoted records simultaneously a rhythm of speech, an extended moment of time, and a way of life. Merwin successfully enlarges the English usage of *one* to include the generalized French meanings of *we, everyone, they, people.* Most readers will be puzzled by the passage in which Blackbird "rolled the unspoken sound of his name with a slow curiosity." Merwin could easily have told us that the French word for blackbird is *merle,* a sound one can roll and ponder, particularly if one's own name shares the first syllable.

Except in "Shepherds," Merwin uses a spacious third-person narrative that sometimes attaches itself so closely to the principal character that we are carried into Flaubert's *style indirect libre* without quotation marks. Other times, the narrative becomes so autonomous that it seems to volunteer its own observations. The prose itself informs us of a curious family trait, a tendency to look up expectantly, and adds: "none of them seemed to have noticed it." Many passages approach the timeless, detached feeling of Balzac's openings (for example, *Eugénie Grandet, Le Père Goriot*) before he introduces the pull of the plot. Merwin wants to convey something simple: This is how life is lived here. Clean edges and *mots justes* document the way people and place adjust to one another by acts of wearing and building and yielding.

On the jacket, Peter Davison suggests that Merwin's sensibility can be compared to that of Jean Giono or Maurice Pagnol. I am also reminded of Eleanor Clark's *The Oysters of Locmariaquer,* which chronicles daily life in a Breton community, and of Pierre-Jakez Hélios's *The Horse of Pride,* also about Brittany. Some will think of Lawrence Wylie's *Village in the Vaucluse,* a reliable and sympathetic study that surpasses its sociological categories. But Merwin creates his own particular ethos of moods and tones. The scenes in which Blackbird leads the priest at night to the local sulfur spring to relieve his eczema form a secret, comic, and fully credible idyll in both their lives. The darkness seems to concentrate their existence there in the woods next to the spring.

DURING WORLD WAR II, a short book of intimate journals appeared in England, *The Unquiet Grave,* richly praised on the jacket by Elizabeth Bowen and V. S. Pritchett and signed simply "Palinurus." In the opening pages, after a rant against Group Man, meaning socialism, we come upon a one-page entry entitled "A Charm against Group Man THE MAGIC CIRCLE." Underneath appears a circular map whose circumference passes near Toulouse, Rodez, and Bergerac and encompasses the Dordogne, Lot, Aveyron, and Tarn rivers. The motto *Quod petis hic est* ("Here is what I seek") is lettered in around the circle. In the caption, we read that the author's "peace aims" include "a yellow manor farm inside this magic circle" and "a helicopter to take me to an office in London or Paris." Merwin has spent a long time surveying the topography and tasting the wines of the countryside that suggested magic to Cyril Connolly. Merwin wants no helicopter.

As in the *causse* pastures, we don't have to dig far in Merwin's stories to find bedrock. It is the same buried ledge that I find in his poetry. At long intervals, what stops the movements of ordinary living is the mental act of noticing that you are noticing something. The moment occurs with fleeting intensity—nothing spiritual, closer to a physically registered loss of psychological equilibrium, followed by recovery.

> Blackbird realized that he had not seen M. and Mme. Bright for months, not since the early autumn. People always looked different after a winter, as though they had been covered with dust and then wiped off. But how strange they looked to him, standing there like a picture of people singing. How far away it all looked. The next moment he swung forward to greet them, just as Françoise appeared at the open French door of the kitchen and shrieked to welcome them.
>
> . . .
>
> Blackbird was not listening. He felt, as he put it to himself, much older than he really was, standing there in the middle of the room. He had not always been so polite, he thought. Once he had been known for other things, and that was not so long ago either. As Mme. Riordan set down the plate of *crème caramel* in front of him he stared quite openly into the low-cut of her dress and the deep fold displayed before him, and was seized with an impulse to reach out and thrust his fingers, indeed his whole hand, down between her breasts. Then he looked up and caught her eye, and the presence of the Bad Blackbird whom many remembered withered in a rush of heat like that of the day outside, as the door opened and M. Riordan came in, and he heard the sound of yet another bottle being opened, and became aware that his face was caught in an uncomfortable smile. He heard that nobody was saying anything.

These stories patiently explore a sensuous solitude—everyone's.

QUANTUM TALES:
RENATA ADLER

Stories happen only to people who can tell them.

(ATTRIBUTED TO THUCYDIDES)

NATURE ABHORS A vacuum—at least in the little nook of the universe we inhabit. According to continuities and correspondences we cannot easily explain, the descriptive power of that statement appears to extend to some areas of art. When during the first decades of the century Kandinsky began to empty his paintings of the representation of external reality, a surrounding pressure of motifs awaited the opportunity to enter the vacated space. Theosophy, Besant's and Leadbetter's thought forms, and the geometry of the spiritual filled his nonobjective works as fragmented trees and figures had filled his earlier visionary landscapes.

A comparable development has affected some advanced areas of literature. For a number of years, I have kept a list of devices and terms proposed from many sides to replace unity as the central organizing principle, particularly in the novel: digression, parody, marginal discourse, reflexivity, fragment, miscellany, theme and variations, *écriture*, palimpsest, and many more. The peculiar quality of Renata Adler's latest book, like the earlier *Speedboat*, is that, while adopting several of these devices, it insists on describing the vacuum itself. *Pitch Dark* injects into the seemingly vacant life of the author's surrogate narrator-protagonist enough dye to give the emptiness shape and visibility. The dye is compounded of short anecdotes, comic asides, deadpan refrains, and dissertations on far-fetched topics. It

shows up the vacant space without filling it, and the resultant style veers
rapidly between liveliness and diagnosis.

> What's new? the biography of the opera star says she used to ask in
> every phone call, and What else? I'm not sure the biographer under-
> stood another thing about the opera star, but I do believe that
> What's new. What else. They may be the first questions of the story,
> of the morning, of consciousness. What's new. What else. What
> next. What's happened here, says the inspector, or the family man
> looking at the rubble of his house. What's it to you, says the street
> tough or the bystander. What's it *worth* to you, says the paid
> informer or the extortionist. What is it now, says the executive or
> the husband, disturbed by the fifteenth knock at the door, or phone
> call, or sigh in the small hours of the night. What does it mean, says
> the cryptographer. What does it all mean, says the student or the
> philosopher on his barstool. What do I care. What's the use. What's
> the matter. Where's the action. What kind of fun is that. Let me say
> that everyone's story in the end is the old whore's, or the Ancient
> Mariner's: I was not always as you see me now. And the sentient
> man, the sentient person says in his heart, from time to time, What
> have I done.

Pitch Dark is a Book of Questions, often without the usual punctuation,
suggesting they seek no answer. Speculation is called for here more than
interrogation or detection. A few lines after the above passage, an "anti-
claque"—the voice of a persecuting conscience—murmurs to the narrator-
protagonist, ". . . you remember everything, out of context, and then you
brood."

These questions and these brooding, intermittent memories create the
effect of a constant hovering. Everything Adler writes in her "novels" hovers
among genres, among generations, among far-flung places, and among available moral attitudes. We would have to go at least as far back as Constant's
Adolphe to find a beginning for this tendency toward psychological inconclu-
siveness. Unamuno carried it to exasperating extremes in his coy masterpiece
of 1914, *Niebla.* It flows powerfully about us now in the work of Cynthia
Ozick, of Milan Kundera, and of Nathalie Sarraute, about whom Adler has
written a perceptive essay. Within this strain of hovering and inconclusive-
ness, Adler has succeeded in establishing a magpie niche of her own.

SYMMETRICAL AS A triptych, *Pitch Dark* offers three loosely interlocking
stories of approximately fifty pages each. Using half-page chunks—false

starts, vignettes, insistent echoes—"Orcas Island" describes the never-quite-realized breakup of an affair between Kate Ennis, the narrator, and Jake, an older married man. He is vaguely understanding, preoccupied, and always offstage. The most sustained passage works up a five-page parable about a sick raccoon who takes shelter beside Kate's stove and will not leave. Not very subtly, the parable suggests that Kate is caught between her desire to go away for just a week with Jake to New Orleans and her need to take refuge alone on an island. The ruminations in this first section end characteristically with a question: "Did I throw the most important thing perhaps, by accident, away?" By now, the reader understands that "the most important thing" can be stated in this frequently repeated form: "You are, you know, you were, the nearest thing to a real story to happen in my life."

The second section, which gives its title to the book, relates with relatively few interruptions what I read as a diversionary and cautionary tale told from the middle outward. On the way to a friend's loaned estate in Ireland in search of quiet and rest, Kate has a minor car accident whose consequences infect her with a sense of disgust and guilt. She refers to herself as a "tortfeasor." These pages, whose mood of self-isolation may be taken to connect with the first section, held me more by the occasional clarity of detail than by any power in the events. There are two exceptions. Driving late at night, she reverts out of habit to the right lane in a left-handed country and just misses a head-on collision with an Irish priest. (In *Speedboat,* a head-on collision is successfully consummated in a Buñuel-like apotheosis of bodies tossed into telephone wires. Then they all sit down together undismayed. Later, we learn that there are convergent and divergent plots.) The other incident coyly reveals the book's umbilical cord to the outer world. Half-convinced at the airport that she should take a false name in order to escape undetected from Ireland, Kate Ennis writes, "I should make the name as like my own as possible to account for the mistake. Alder, I thought." Kate gets out of Ireland in a confusion of names; on a similar basis, Adler or Alder remains very much inside *Pitch Dark.* Cervantes would have shaken his head over these clumsy maneuvers.

In "Home," the last section, the prolonged breakup with Jake is brought back into the foreground and compressed into an insistent telephone obbligato. Every third or fourth page, one encounters a shred of despairing conversation overheard in London, where Kate is working as a journalist. The rest of the time, she is either shaping a fragile life in a small house with pond in a New England town within commuting distance of New York or seeking refuge and solitude on Orcas Island off Seattle. Constant interruptions block any continuity that might be called a story line. The interruptions themselves, on the other hand, rough in a motif that concerns the betrayal of reality by inaccurate reporting. We follow an argument about alleged collaboration between the Nazis and the early Zionists, an outburst about the disastrous effects of anonymous sources and the advent of the byline on newspaper stories, and an essay on the abuse of the legal system.

MEANWHILE, JAKE HAS a cautious reaction to reading "Orcas Island," the first part of this book you hold in your hand. Gradually, it all circles back on itself in an accelerating swirl so that the last ten pages push nineteen distinct items of flotsam in front of the patient or distraught reader. Someone who cannot let go is drowning.

> In the repetitions and formulas, the courts sometimes rise from their droning with a phrase so pure, deep, and mighty that it stays. It remains forever just the way to say that thing. More probably than not. Utterly without fault. Not my act. Beyond a reasonable doubt. Last intervening wrongdoer. Cloud on title. An ordinary man. A prudent man. A reasonable man. A man of ordinary intelligence and understanding. Wait, wait. Whose voice is this? Not mine. Not mine. Not mine. Res ipsa loquitur. A man must act somehow.
> Do you sometimes wish it was me?
> Always.
> Pause.
> It is you.

By dint of repetition, variations in phrasing and speech patterns, and frequent interventions, Adler has created in *Pitch Dark* a sense of form that could be called "Cubist." The three sections do not develop a careful self-portrait of the central character. Yet the impulse behind the book is autobiographical, even confessional, rather than novelistic—that is, genuinely concerned with other people's lives. The reader has to assemble Kate as the sum of her scattered parts—shy-bold, cosmopolitan, idealist, nostalgic, farouche. It does not spin a tale in spite of one underlined reference to the Penelope story. Rather, it depicts a mode of vision, a process of gathering odds and ends into a "piece" in both the fictional and the journalistic sense. Two hundred years ago, Laurence Sterne had already mastered the art of self-interruption and elaborate detour. In reading Adler, I began jotting in the margins "aecp" to designate the occasional voice of an alter ego-critic-professor bringing things to a halt, shaking her finger, and breaking any illusion of narrative momentum.

Do I need to stylize it, then, or can I tell it as it was?

So there is this pressure now, on every sentence, not just to say what it has to say, but to justify its claim upon our time.

And this matter of the commas. And this matter of the paragraphs.

Are we speaking of the anti-claque? No, not at all, of an actual person.

The frequent gaps in the prose imply both a fainthearted hope of connection and the kind of total breakdown and fresh start that Sartre detected between every successive sentence of Camus's *The Stranger.* In this inwardly impassioned work by a writer who lived as student and journalist through the fifties, sixties, and seventies, there seems to be no moral center beyond the end of an affair. *Sputnik,* the sit-ins, the assassinations, the moon shot, Vietnam, Watergate do not even ruffle the surface. How are we to take hold of this antinovel and its predecessor, *Speedboat,* to which it seems to be a close sequel?

I BELIEVE THESE astutely shuffled works take shape and have an effect in two related ways. Despite the lack of reference to major social and political events, the books convey the sense of an era that cohabits uncomfortably with its past. The antepenultimate sentence of *Speedboat* holds out a small key. "I think there's something to be said for assuring the next that the water's fine—quite warm, actually—once you get into it." Next *generation,* she means. Even though both novels describe, primarily through fractured form and terse diction, a version of trauma, an ego detached like a retina, still the neurosis is bearable and has its small rewards. I am reminded of how Henri Murger half-unwittingly caricatured his milieu in a little book of sketches called *Scènes de la Vie de Bohème* (1845–1849). In an era of revolutions and social upheaval, he helped to create the myth of young provincial idealists surviving on love and art in their attic rooms in Paris.

We still haven't rejected that myth. Adler's reverse parable concerns an intelligent woman who has reached the top professionally and socially and finds herself unhappy in her accomplishments, forlorn among many importunings. She yearns for an attic, for an island. Her episodic musings will hardly make a successful leap to stage and opera the way Murger's sketches did. Film? Who knows? The book is saturated with nostalgia—for the fifties, when the system still seemed to work; for *la boue,* which Kate contemplates and shies away from. The oblique portrait of an era also creates a mood of persevering, of not surrendering to despair.

The second accomplishment is a completely embedded contradiction. On the one hand, every aspect of *Pitch Dark,* formal, stylistic, and thematic, affirms what I shall call the "innarratability principle." You cannot tell your essential story straight out; Adler-Ennis quotes Emily Dickinson on telling it "slant." As the Symbolist poets hesitated to name anything for fear of destroying the fragile essence of the object so rudely named, Adler fears to narrate. She proceeds by indirection, gives us only glancing views of the breakup with Jake, of the major events of three decades. Since the narrative is always beside the point, one expects the repeated questions about what the point is. At this juncture, my apocryphal epigraph becomes pertinent and obliges us to consider the innarratability principle—advanced writer's block. Nothing has really happened until you have told it, and if you tell it, you've transformed it, distorted it, ruined it. The only possible approach to an event operates through an awkward Medusa process with mirrors and utterly discreet reports. If I am not wrong, here lies the significance of the most common and puzzling refrain in the book. "Quanta," says an unidentified Amy, on a train, in a blizzard, over and over again. It's all bits and pieces. A book should confine itself to discrete small units of experience and not try to arrange them on levels and in sequence. It's an art of juxtaposing quanta. To go further means to blow one's cover.

On the other hand, our fate, our very life, depends on stories. The first literary figure really invoked in *Pitch Dark* saved her skin by recounting fully worked-out tales of high adventure. "For a woman, it is always, don't you see, Scheherazade." The closing pages make a more elaborate and contemporary case for the story cure. "Under the American Constitution, in fact, everything is required to be, at heart, a story . . . and the only ones permitted to bring the story to the courts' attention, the only storytellers, are the ones to whom the story happened, whom the facts befell." Legal doctrine, the journalist's dilemma, and the paradoxes of literature all flow together in this impasse: To tell or not to tell? More accurately: How to tell? This narrative dilemma over divulgence represents one of the principal characteristics of the intellectual world Adler is sketching.

FACED BY THE innarratability principle, how does the writer proceed who still believes in the saving virtue of stories? For many years, there were two surgical procedures for treating a herniated spinal disk: fusion and removal. In fusion, the disk is removed and the two adjacent vertebrae are united into a single rigid unit. In removal, the disk is simply taken out and the surrounding areas are allowed to secrete substitute tissue to cushion and lubricate the link. Adler, like many of her contemporaries, abjures fusion, practices simple removal. The resulting minimalist genre should properly not be called a novel, for it answers radically different expectations, brings other rewards. Personal memoir-essay? Future-perfect archaeological report on contemporary culture? Eisenstein's "montage of attractions"? Enhanced realism of the schizoid? All apply. But the best term is Unamuno's *nivola,* his genial inside-out permutation in *Niebla* of *novela.*

A prior question probes deeper: In terms of what, in the name of what tentative hope, do we grope for the connective tissue among these fragments, these shards? Beyond his uneasy laughter, Kundera looks us straight in the eye and tells us to remember the perilous history of freedom. García Márquez constructs so firm a sense of place and such strong ties by blood and marriage that he can permit himself virtually any extravagance of event and character, including miracles. All his cock-and-bull stories finally turn homeward.

But what will guide us through Adler's labyrinth? Is anything at stake according to which we can begin to assemble the scattered pieces? No lasting sense of place, certainly, in this periplus, nor any stubborn faith in history holds it all together. Nor is there a single recognizable voice that encompasses the extremes. Adler practices a shrewd ventriloquism in the midst of her brooding solitude, and one of the languages she takes refuge in is that of the law.

> . . . the great doctrines of finality and *Stare Decisis,* that somewhere a story must end and may not be reopened, and that this story is dispositive for all stories that cannot be proven to be unlike it, mean that no stories, no stories at all, can be of more immediate, and sometimes eternal, interest than these. But stories they are. And their own eloquence grows up around them.

A Book of Common Law, then, rather than a Book of Questions? Finally not, for what we find here are stories at their most atomized—quanta. *Pitch Dark,* and even more effectively and entertainingly *Speedboat,* can properly be called exemplary of our sprawling secular culture—exemplary in both senses, serving as model, serving as deterrent.

39

SCANDAL AND
STEREOTYPES ON
BROADWAY: THE NEW
PURITANISM

I have two epigraphs for this discussion of an alleged New Puritanism. The first one is my own—that is, I'm quoting myself:

> *Democracy in America is a form of government that*
> *systematically enacts the extremes before it discovers*
> *the mean.*

The second is from Graham Greene's letters, which I have used before.

> *We exaggerate the sexual appetite in ourselves to*
> *take the place of the love we inadequately feel.*

In order to avoid received ideas and prejudgments, I want to talk about a contemporary work without at the start giving its title and author. For my purposes, and at least with some degree of accuracy, I shall call this work a "thesis novel." Let's talk first about it as a novel and then as a thesis. As is not uncommon, the work shows the strong influence of movies and television. It maintains a fast, almost relentless pace through montage techniques and jump cuts. If the scenes were staged, the repartee would just keep on sparking without pause. Nowhere does the action or the dialogue open into a silence, pregnant or vacant, yet it is just such moments of aching silence that gave Chekhov and Conrad their most human dimension.

The New York characters in the work I'm discussing strike me as a set of stereotypes. A nice Christian Scientist, a fey WASP, a demonically powerful mafioso, a not-so-nice Jewish boy, and one victimized wife. The Jewish humor soon becomes compulsive and heavy-handed entertainment, as if the author is playing for adaptation on Broadway. Very early, you see that the two parallel story lines will converge—and they do. But the mechanical plotting and conventional characters are not what trouble me most about this *roman a thèse*. It's the thesis itself. First of all, the moralizing—or perhaps antimoralizing—thesis is utterly confused. Despite their unstoppable talk, the four male characters do not enlighten us. They are all homosexual. The young Christian Scientist expresses, woodenly but movingly, genuine anguish about his impulses and responsibilities. He holds on to a certain moral integrity. He even tries to pray. The Jewish boy does not have enough love or loyalty in him to stay with either his sick grandmother or his sick lover. He hides behind a smoke screen of bitter, funny social commentary and intellectual self-analysis. Such sympathy as we are encouraged to feel for his pathetic case does not extend to the predatory mafioso. His extreme of manipulative obscenity carries him beyond the stereotype. He is HIV-positive yet he cannot face any aspect of his homosexuality. Only the WASP who is dying of AIDS displays a skittish resolve to be what he is.

The wickedly witty writing of the scenes demonstrates that if three out of four cannot be honest and brave about their condition, at least they can be stunningly funny about it. The comedy holds down the maudlin aspects of the story and encourages us to accept the attitude that male homosexuality deserves recognition as a normal way of life. We also observe that the parading and maneuvering among these four lead to several tawdry adventures and to no lasting love.

If this were all the story had to offer, one might well yawn and walk away. But the thesis does not stop here. Despite the threat of AIDS and the lurking violence, cruising is still presented as acceptable behavior. One crucial scene describes explicit, consensual sidewalk sodomy between the Jewish boy, who has just abandoned his dying lover, and a masked stranger. The act is so sudden and violent that the condom breaks. Nothing suggests that we should be much shocked by this sequence or pass judgment on it. It's just part of the passing scene. Yet it also contributes to building a sense of apocalypse that the tightening action among these four men seems to welcome. Redemption from their mounting troubles can arrive only in the form of the destruction of everything. Many religious motifs begin to appear as the plot unfolds: visions, Job-like despair, prophecies, and visits from the departed.

By the end, a monstrous corruption has overtaken all the characters except possibly the dying and hallucinating WASP. The logic of the action calls out for cataclysm, and finally the heavens do open in a great theatrical display of fire and brimstone. The immense figure that comes forth, however, is not the Horseman of the Apocalypse or the Grim Reaper with his scythe; rather, it is a white-robed and winged Botticellian angel with a Mona Lisa smile that floats out over the stage of the Walter Kerr Theater. For as some of you may have recognized, I am describing a slightly altered version of Tony Kushner's *Angels in America, Part One.*

In the play, the character I have called the mafioso is Roy Cohn, in whom unscrupulous will to political power is continuous with his macho closet homosexuality. The incoherence of the play lies in the way the horrifying behavior of its principal characters leads not to any repentance or reform but to heavenly approval poured out over them in their defiantly unregenerate condition. "History is about to crack wide open," declares one of the minor characters. Indeed it does, and the apocalypse brings down a Christian deus ex machina. What does the arrival of this angel signify? I conclude that the angel blesses the savage depravity of the play's most realistic episodes. Sodom is restored as a blessed city on a hill for the eyes of all good people to see. This biting play about greed and egoism among homosexuals suddenly changes registers at the end and recasts its three acts retroactively into an errand into the wilderness by a band of New Puritans. For here are the blessed saints of a new covenant. I find that the play leaves scant alternative to this religious reading. I finally understood why Kushner surrounds his title with two subtitles: *A gay fantasy on American Themes* and *Millennium Approaches*. Whether Kushner saw it or not, one of his American themes is an upstart New Puritanism. And at the end, the millennium does arrive, transvaluing all values and implying a new moral dimension that I cannot welcome.

Have I lost my head, or have I kept it? Both the play and the thesis struck me as very badly made. Yet no one walked out, nor did I. I attribute that fact to the ticket prices, to the immense power of intellectual fashion, and to the melodramatic confusions behind which the play veils its gay fantasy. For I doubt if many of the audience understood that beneath its antic and sometimes amusing dialogue the play advocates the extinction of moral restraints. By blessing Roy Cohn along with the others, Kushner lifts those moral restraints not only from all homosexual acts but also from all forms of dishonesty, viciousness, cruelty, exploitation, and hate. And the symbolism of the angel at the end transforms Cohn and the others into a new elect, a band of saints rather than sinners, another set of New Puritans.

My wife and I saw this play at the recommendation of our closest friend in New York, who is homosexual. In the next few days, the play dovetailed in my mind with three other trains of thought. One was the fact that some years ago at very short notice I had to teach a course at the University of Dakar in Senegal on Puritanism. I tried to distinguish for my students between Puritanism with a capital *P*, meaning the historical phenomenon, and puritanism with a lowercase *p*, which is this neopuritanism, the misguided concept that comes down from Bourne and Mencken. I learned then that the most common word in a number of writers like Jonathan Edwards is one we don't usually associate with Puritanism, namely the adjective *sweet.* Also *joy.* The second strain of thought involved Dostoevsky's *Crime and Punishment* and, in particular, its epilogue, with the final dream of the devastating plague overtaking Europe, a plague people think comes from the middle of Asia but of course is really the plague of European nihilism and intellectualism that overtakes Russia. It's not so much a physical plague as a spiritual plague that affects the morals of an entire continent. The third strand was this panel on a New Puritanism, for which I had to produce some remarks.

These four strands came together and obliged me to see that *Angels in America* represents Puritanism inverted. Its self-righteous moralizing defends *im*morality. Its religious self-congratulation in the form of an angel ex machina travesties any impulse toward the sacred. And the vengefully comic accounts of suffering by the major characters do not transcend the bitter fact that their situation is elected and defended, not fateful and resisted. Reviewers responded to this play like applause machines. It drew crowds on Broadway and in experimental theaters.

I am ashamed of myself for not having walked out when the compliant angel came forth from the flies to bless all this wisecracking intellectually fashionable evil. Our friend was both right and wrong to recommend the play. He remains our closest friend in New York.

CREDITS

The essays have appeared, sometimes in a different version or under another title, in the following publications:

"Nineteen Theses on Litriniinni"; *The ALSC Newsletter,* Spring 1995.
"Perplexing Lessons: Is There a Core Tradition in the Humanities?"; American Council of Learned Societies, Occasional Paper, No. 2, 1987.
"American Education Against Itself": *The Chronicle of Higher Education,* July 18, 1997.
"Education: Higher and Lower": *Salmagundi,* Fall–Winter 1997.
"How to Read a Book": *Philosophy and Literature* 20 (1996).
"Art at First Sight": *Salmagundi,* Fall–Winter 1990–1991.
"The Spiritual in Art": *Salmagundi,* Spring–Summer 1988.
"How We Think at the Movies": "The Moving Image," *Daedalus,* Fall 1985.
"Life Before Language: Nathalie Saurraute": *The New York Times Book Review,* April 1, 1991.
"Second Thoughts on a Wooden Horse: Michel Foucault": *Salmagundi,* Spring–Summer 1995.
"Radical Skepticism and How We Got Here": *Salmagundi,* Spring–Summer 1992.
"From *The Swiss Family Robinson* to *Narratus Interruptus*": *Boston Review,* Summer 1992.
"Teaching the Unteachable: Kipling, Proust, Nietzsche & Co.": *Salmagundi,* Fall 1995.

"The Alibi of Art": The Irving Howe Lecture, Center for the Humanities, CUNY. *The Los Angeles Times Book Review,* April 26, 1998.
"The Social Institutions of Modern Art": *The New York Review of Books,* December 18, 1986.
"Manet, the Missing Link": *The New Republic,* February 3, 1997.
"Unlikely Pen Pals: George Sand and Gustave Flaubert": *The New York Times Book Review,* February 21, 1993.
"Sarah Bernhardt, the Sacred Monster": *The New Republic,* October 14, 1991.
"Yuppies Along the Seine: The Impressionists": *The New Republic,* February 20, 1989.
"Living by Words: Mallarmé": *The New Republic,* November 14, 1994.
"The Present Place of Futurism": *The New Republic,* July 27, 1987.
"Early Picasso: Mailer's Version": *The New York Review of Books,* January 11, 1996.
"Captions or Illustrations?: Braque's Handbook": *Salmagundi,* Winter 1989.
"The Story of Hans/Jean/Kaspar Arp": *Poetry East,* Spring–Summer 1984.
"Cocteau, Native Son of Paris": In Arthur King Peters, ed., *Jean Cocteau and the French Scene,* (New York: Abbeville, 1984).
"Confidence Man: Marcel Duchamp": *The New York Review of Books,* March 27, 1997.
"*The Last Cause* (An Experimental Play)": In *Modern Art and Popular Culture: Readings in High and Low* (New York: Museum of Modern Art and Harry Abrams, 1990).
"From Aestheticism to Fascism": *Salmagundi,* Fall 1989).
"An American Roman-Fleuve: *The Beulah Quintet,*" as "Introduction": In Mary Lee Settle, *The Beulah Quintet,* 5 vols. (New York: Ballantine Books, 1981).
" 'The Great American Thing': O'Keeffe and Stieglitz": In Alexandra Arrowsmith and Thomas West, ed., *Two Lives* (New York: HarperCollins/Callaway Editions, 1992).
"Candor and Perversion: Man Ray": In Merry Foresta, ed., *Perpetual Motif: The Art of Man Ray* (New York: Abbeville, 1988).
"Born-Again African: Léopold Senghor": *The New York Review of Books,* December 20, 1990.
"A Masterpiece from Senegal": *Bostonia,* November–December 1989.
"Blank and White: Illuminating Octavio Paz": In Octavio Paz, *Blanco,* tr. Eliot Weinberger, illuminations by Adja Yunkers (New York: A. Golish, 1974).
"Arthur Miller's Account of Himself": *The New York Times Book Review,* November 8, 1987.
"Naipaul on the American South": *The New York Review of Books,* March 30, 1989.
"A Poet's Stories: W. S. Merwin": *The New York Review of Books,* August 13, 1992.
"Quantum Tales: Renata Adler": *The New York Review of Books,* March 15, 1984.
"Scandal and Stereotypes on Broadway: The New Puritanism": *Salmagundi,* Spring–Summer 1995.

CREDITS FOR

ILLUSTRATIONS

John La Farge, *Autumn: October, Hillside, Noonday, Glen Cove, Long Island*, 1860, oil on panel, 12 1/2 × 9 1/2 in. Museum of Fine Arts, Boston, Bequest of Mrs. Henry Lee Higginson, Sr. With permission of the Museum of Fine Arts.

Georges Braque, twelve pages from *Cahier de Georges Braque*, 1917–1947, 12 1/8 × 8 7/8 in., Maeght, éditeur, Paris.

Hans (Jean) Arp, *Gnome (Kaspar)*, 1930, bronze, 30 × 28 × 19 in. Palm Springs Desert Museum, Palm Springs, California. With permission of Artists Rights Society, New York.

Georgia O'Keeffe, *White Abstraction (Madison Avenue)*, 1926, oil on canvas, 35 1/2 × 12 in. Museum of Fine Arts, St. Petersburg, Florida, Gift of Charles C. and Margaret Stevenson Henderson in memory of Hunt Henderson. With permission of the Museum of Fine Arts.

Alfred Stieglitz, *Spiritual America*, 1923, gelatin silver print, 4 1/2 × 3 1/2 in. The J. Paul Getty Museum, Los Angeles. With permission of the J. Paul Getty Museum.

Man Ray, *Ingres' Violin (Le Violon d'Ingres)*, 1924, silver print, 9 13/16 × 7 5/8 in. The J. Paul Getty Museum, Los Angeles. With permission of the J. Paul Getty Museum.

INDEX

Page numbers in *italics* refer to illustrations.

Dada, 137, 140, 181, 207, 236–37, 240,
247, 269, 271, 308–10, 312, 317, 319,
337, 352
European vs. American, 255
photography and, 312
Dada and Surrealist Art (Rubin), 245
Dalí, Salvador, 266
Damas, Léon, 326, 328, 334, 338
Dame aux camélias, La, 168, 171
dandy, 140, 141, 147, 277
Dangerous Minds, 31
D'Annunzio, Gabriele, 195
Daǹte Alighieri, 49*n*
Danto, Arthur, 256
Darkness at Noon (Koestler), 357
Darragon, Eric, 149
Darwin, Charles, 37–38, 328
Daudet, Alphonse, 160, 162
Daumier, Honoré, 117, 368
David, Jacques-Louis, 154
Davidson, Abraham A., 255
Davidson, Basil, 327
Davis, Jimmie, 371*n*
Davison, Peter, 377
Death of a Salesman (Miller), 355, 359, 361
"Death of Ivan Ilyich, The" (Tolstoy), 14
Debussy, Claude, 189, 199
Decadence, 124, 140, 180, 182, 190, 254,
277–78
fascism and, 278, 281–82
deconstructionism, 188, 260*n*
Definitively Unfinished Marcel Duchamp, The
(Duchamp), 255
DeForest, Phyllis, 262–75
Degas, Edgar, 155, 173–74, 175, 176, 189
de Gaulle, Charles, 332, 343*n*
Déjeuner sur l'herbe, Le (Manet), 156
Delacroix, Eugène, 173, 230, 317
Delafosse, Maurice, 329
De l'Allemagne (de Staël), 47
Delany, Martin, 327
Delaunay, Robert, 206, 236, 237, 263, 300
Delaunay, Sonia, 192, 237, 300
Delavignette, Robert, 329
*Deliquéscences, poèmes décadents d'Adoré
Floupette,* 181, 254
democracy, 32
culture and, 3
education and, 35
public schools and, 25

Demoiselles d'Avignon, Les (Picasso), 203–4,
205, 207
Demuth, Charles, 298, 299
Denis, Maurice, 228
Denver, John, 362
Depression, Great, 358, 361
De Quincey, Thomas, 125–27, 128
Derain, André, 138, 198
dérèglement, 78
Derrida, Jacques, 6, 151, 260*n*
Descartes, René, 94, 345
Deudon, Eric, 117
Dewey, John, 25
de Zayas, Marius, 299
Dia, Mamadou, 332–33
Diaghilev, Sergey, 136, 141, 163, 240, 280,
281
Diallobé people, 344–45, 348
Dickens, Charles, 7, 366–67
Dickinson, Emily, 15, 68, 384
Diderot, Denis, 151, 152, 153, 167
Diebenkorn, Richard, 44–45, 46
Difficulté d'être, La (The Difficulty of Being)
(Cocteau), 241
Dijkstra, Bram, 195
Diop, Alioune, 328
Diouf, Abdou, 333, 349
discourse, 74–75, 79
Discourses (Reynolds), 230
disinterestedness, 122–23
Divine Sarah, The (Gold and Fitzdale),
163–66, 168–69, 170
Dix-Neuf Poèmes Elastiques (Cendrars), 192
Dixon, Melvin, 339
Dodgson, Charles Lutwidge, 156
"Donkey's Tail, The," 254, 263
Doré, Gustave, 165
Dostoevsky, Fyodor, 3, 70, 90, 277, 358,
389
Douglass, Frederick, 4
*D'où venons-nous? Que sommes-nous? Où
allons-nous?* (Gauguin), 201
Dove, Arthur Garfield, 83, 298, 299, 303
Dow, Arthur Wesley, 303
Dreams of a Spiritseer (Kant), 52
Dreier, Katherine, 244, 246
Dreiser, Theodore, 62
Dreyfus Affair, 137, 141, 198, 239
"Drunken Boat, The" (Rimbaud), 180
Drunk in the Furnace, The (Merwin), 373

ABOUT THE AUTHOR

BORN IN NEW YORK CITY in 1923, Roger Shattuck was educated at St. Paul's School and Yale College. During World War II, he served in the Pacific theater as pilot in a combat cargo squadron. After working in the film section of UNESCO in Paris, he held various jobs in journalism and publishing in New York before being named a Junior Fellow of the Society of Fellows at Harvard University.

Roger Shattuck has taught French and the humanities at Harvard, the University of Texas at Austin, the University of Virginia, and Boston University.

In 1987, the American Academy and Institute of Arts and Letters gave Roger Shattuck a special award for his writings. In 1990, the Université d'Orléans conferred on him a Doctorat Honoris Causa, and the American Academy of Arts and Sciences elected him a Fellow. He helped found the Association of Literary Scholars and Critics, which elected him its president in 1995.

A list of his books appears at the front of this volume.